THE NATURE OF NORMATIVITY

The Nature of Normativity presents a complete theory about the nature of normative thought - that is, the sort of thought that is concerned with what ought to be the case, or what we ought to do or think. Ralph Wedgwood defends a kind of realism about the normative, according to which normative truths or facts are genuinely part of reality.

Anti-realists often complain that realism gives rise to demands for explanation that it cannot adequately meet. What is the nature of these normative facts? How could we ever know them or even refer to them in language or thought? Wedgwood accepts that any adequate version of realism must answer these explanatory demands. However, he seeks to show that these demands can be met—in large part by relying on a version of the idea, which has been much discussed in recent work in the philosophy of mind, that the intentional is normative—that is, that there is no way of explaining the nature of the various sorts of mental states that have intentional or representational content (such as beliefs, judgments, desires, decisions, and so on), without stating normative facts. On the basis of this idea, Wedgwood provides a detailed systematic theory that deals with the following three areas: the meaning of statements about what ought to be; the nature of the facts stated by these statements; and what justifies us in holding beliefs about what ought to be.

Ralph Wedgwood is Professor of Philosophy at the University of Oxford and a Fellow of Merton College, Oxford

The Nature of Normativity

RALPH WEDGWOOD

CLARENDON PRESS · OXFORD

OXFORD

UNIVERSITY PRESS

Great Clarendon Street, Oxford OX2 6DP

Oxford University Press is a department of the University of Oxford.
It furthers the University's objective of excellence in research, scholarship,
and education by publishing worldwide in

Oxford New York

Auckland Cape Town Dar es Salaam Hong Kong Karachi
Kuala Lumpur Madrid Melbourne Mexico City Nairobi
New Delhi Shanghai Taipei Toronto

With offices in

Argentina Austria Brazil Chile Czech Republic France Greece
Guatemala Hungary Italy Japan Poland Portugal Singapore
South Korea Switzerland Thailand Turkey Ukraine Vietnam

Oxford is a registered trade mark of Oxford University Press
in the UK and in certain other countries

Published in the United States
by Oxford University Press Inc., New York

First published 2007
First published in paperback 2009

British Library Cataloguing in Publication Data

Data available

Library of Congress Cataloging in Publication Data

Data available

Typeset by Laserwords Private Limited, Chennai, India
Printed in Great Britain
on acid-free paper by
MPG Books Group, Bodmin and King's Lynn

ISBN 978–0–19–925131–5 (Hbk.)
978–0–19–956819–2 (Pbk.)

1 3 5 7 9 10 8 6 4 2

Contents

Preface

I have been a metanormative realist—that is, a realist about what people *ought* to think or to do, or about what *ought* to be the case—for as long as I can remember having thoughts about such questions at all. I was certainly a metanormative realist long before I started any formal studies in philosophy. Unlike some other metanormative realists, however, I have also long believed that the whole domain of the normative gives rise to many deep and difficult philosophical problems, which should not be dismissed as mere "pseudo-problems". My goal in this book is to try to solve these problems, by articulating a substantive version of metanormative realism which will provide the philosophical explanations that these problems seem to demand.

According to one of the book's central arguments, the best solution to many of these problems involves appealing to a version of an idea that has become familiar in recent work in the philosophy of mind, under the slogan "the intentional is normative". In this sense, as I put it in the Introduction, the normativity of the intentional is "the key to metaethics". I first became convinced of this point a long time ago, on reading Susan Hurley (1989) while I was a graduate student in 1991. As things turned out, I have ended up defending a theory that is very different from Hurley's; but in this crucial way, I was influenced by her work.

As this appeal to ideas from the philosophy of mind suggests, I believe that the goals of this book require drawing on ideas from many different branches of philosophy—especially from metaphysics and epistemology, and from the philosophy of language and the philosophy of mind, as well as from ethics itself. At a couple of points, I even draw on some ideas from philosophical logic (especially deontic logic, and the logic of the metaphysical concepts of essence and necessity). In this way, although this book is barely interdisciplinary, it is aggressively *intersubdisciplinary*, since it aims to combine ideas from all these different subdisciplines of philosophy into a single unified theory.

As it turned out, it has taken me a long time to work out a unified intersubdisciplinary theory of this sort. Indeed, I have been working on these ideas, off and on, for the last twelve years or so. Most of these ideas have already been presented, in earlier versions, in a series of published articles. So this book reflects work that I have done in many places. A few passages reflect some of the work that I carried out while I was teaching at UCLA and Stirling immediately after finishing my PhD at Cornell. A larger part of the book reflects some of the work that I did while I was at MIT, including the year (1998–9) when I was on leave from MIT at the National Humanities Center in Research Triangle Park, North Carolina; and even more of the book reflects the work that I have done since arriving at Oxford in 2002. Although the book restates the main arguments of several articles that I published over this period, I found it necessary in the end to rewrite my earlier statements of these arguments quite extensively. Most of this rewriting was carried out while I was a Visiting Fellow in the Philosophy Department at Princeton University, with sabbatical leave from my employers, the University of Oxford and Merton College, Oxford, and an additional research leave award from the UK Arts and Humanities Research Council. So I should thank all those institutions for their generous support.

Over the course of the last twelve years, the ideas and arguments that have made their way into this book have been presented as talks at the following places: the University of St Andrews (on no less than three different occasions), Dartmouth College, the University of North Carolina at Chapel Hill, East Carolina University, North Carolina State University, the University of Cambridge, the University of Oxford, the University of Glasgow, the University of Leeds, University College London, the University of York, the University of Reading, the University of Bristol, the University of Oslo, and the Aristotelian Society. Some of these ideas were also presented at the following conferences and workshops: the 1998 conference of the British Society for Ethical Theory at the University of Kent; the 1999 Pacific Division meeting of the American Philosophical Association in Berkeley, California; a conference on normativity at Brown University in 1999; a conference on metaphysics and epistemology at the Croatian Inter-University Centre in Dubrovnik in 2003; a workshop on moral epistemology at the University of Edinburgh in 2004; the first annual Metaethics Workshop at the University of Wisconsin, Madison, in 2004; a workshop on the metaphysics of value at the Centre for Metaphysics and Mind at the University of Leeds in 2005; a conference on truth and realism at the Central European University in Budapest in 2005; a conference on metaphysics and epistemology at the Croatian Inter-University Centre in Dubrovnik in 2005; a conference on the philosophy of Kit Fine at the University of Geneva in 2005; a conference on moral motivation at the University of Siena in 2005; a conference on normativity and truth at University College Cork in 2006; and a conference on moral contextualism at the University of Aberdeen in 2006.

I have learnt an immense amount from the comments that I received from the members of these audiences. Like many other philosophers, I am absolutely addicted to philosophical discussion and debate. For me, philosophical discussion is not just highly instructive: it provides intellectual excitement of the most thrilling kind. For this reason, I owe an enormous debt to all the philosophers whom I have had discussions with. I hope that the extent to which they have enjoyed discussing philosophy with me does not fall too far short of the extent to which I have enjoyed my discussions with them.

As I explained above, this book draws together some ideas that have been presented in a number of articles that I have published over the last twelve years. So this book inherits all the debts that I incurred while writing those earlier articles. First, I should like to thank the editors and anonymous referees who helped me to improve articles of mine that have appeared in the following refereed journals: the *European Journal of Philosophy*, *Philosophical Studies*, the *European Review of Philosophy*, *Noûs*, and the *Philosophical Review*. Secondly, in addition to the members of all the various audiences that I have already mentioned, I have also received enormously useful comments from a number of philosophers who have read drafts of these earlier articles, or who have commented on these drafts in informal discussion groups. The philosophers who have commented on these drafts in this way include at least the following: Robert Adams, Anita Avramides, Timothy Bayne, George Bealer, Alexander Bird, Simon Blackburn, Sylvain Bromberger, John Broome, Krister Bykvist, Alex Byrne, Nancy Cartwright, David Charles, Joshua Cohen, Roger Crisp, Jonathan Dancy, Alice Drewery, Michael Dummett, Dorothy Edgington, David Enoch, Philippa Foot, Michael Glanzberg, Ned Hall, Sally Haslanger, John Hawthorne, Brad Hooker, Terence Irwin, Daniel Isaacson, Frank Jackson, Mark Johnston, Karen Jones, Leonard Katz, Bill Lycan, Murray MacBeath, Alan Millar, Adrian Moore, Michael Otsuka, Derek Parfit, Philip Pettit, Oliver Pooley, James Pryor, Georges Rey, Gideon Rosen, Seana Shiffrin, Susanna Siegel, John Skorupski, Michael Smith, Robert Stalnaker, Nicholas Sturgeon, Judith Thomson, Charles Travis, David Wiggins, Timothy Williamson, Crispin Wright, Stephen Yablo, and Ümit Yalçin. Finally, I am also grateful to an anonymous reader for Oxford University Press, and to David Bostock, for useful comments on the penultimate draft of the book itself. Unfortunately, it is quite likely that I have omitted some philosophers from this list of those whom I ought to thank; I owe those philosophers an apology for the omission and my thanks for their help. I should also like to thank my editors at Oxford University Press, Peter Momtchiloff and Jenni Craig, my copy-editor, Jess Smith, and my research assistant, Amber Riaz, for their assistance with preparing the book for publication.

I owe a different sort of debt to my family, and to many friends, on both sides of the Atlantic, with whom I have had so much fun, and who have provided indispensable support through what have occasionally been discouraging times. Above all, I should like to thank my mother and father, Martin and Sandra Wedgwood. This book is dedicated to them, in gratitude and love.

Not all of the ideas and arguments that I have tried to develop over the last twelve years have made their way into this book. My plan is that some of these other ideas will be presented in a sequel to this book, tentatively entitled *The Rules of Rationality*, which will give a unified account of rational belief and rational decision, based on a unified account of reasoning (including both practical and theoretical reasoning), and of what it is for a process of reasoning to count as rational or irrational. Looking yet further ahead, I hope that I will eventually be able to draw on these ideas to pursue research into some foundational issues in first-order moral theory. I have had some great adventures in philosophy already; but I am looking forward to many more such adventures in future.

As I have already mentioned, earlier versions of most of the ideas in this book have been presented before in a number of published articles. In the end, I found it necessary to rewrite much more than I had originally envisaged. Nonetheless, some sentences or paragraphs here and there have made their way out of these articles into the book. The relationship between this book and those earlier articles is as follows.

The introduction is new, as are Sections 1.1, 1.2, and 1.4 of Chapter 1. Section 1.3 and a couple of paragraphs in Section 1.5 are based on the first section of "The Metaethicists' Mistake", *Philosophical Perspectives*, 18 (2004). Chapter 2 is an almost completely new restatement of the same general sort of argument that I gave in "Non-Cognitivism, Truth and Logic", *Philosophical Studies*, 86 (1997). Chapter 3 is again almost completely new, although a few paragraphs in Section 3.2 are based on some material from "Theories of Content and Theories of Motivation", *European Journal of Philosophy*, 3 (1995). In Chapter 4, Section 4.1 is new, while Section 4.2 is based on part of "Conceptual Role Semantics for Moral Terms", *Philosophical Review*, 110 (2001). The rest of Chapter 4 is based on the first half of "The Meaning of 'Ought' ", *Oxford Studies in Metaethics*, 1 (2006), with the correction of a couple of serious mistakes that I made in that paper. In Chapter 5, Sections 5.1 and 5.2 are based on the second half of "The Meaning of 'Ought' ", while Section 5.3 is new.

In Chapter 6, Section 6.1 is new, while Sections 6.2 and 6.3 are based on parts of "The Essence of Response-Dependence", *European Review of Philosophy*, 3 (1998). Sections 6.4 and 6.5 are loosely based on parts of "The Price of Non-Reductive Moral Realism", *Ethical Theory and Moral Practice*, 2 (1999). In Chapter 7, Sections 7.1 and 7.2 are new, while the rest of the chapter is based on "The Normativity of the Intentional", *Oxford Handbook of the Philosophy of Mind*, edited by Brian McLaughlin (forthcoming *a*). In Chapter 8, Sections 8.1– 8.3 are new, while Sections 8.4 and 8.5 are based on parts of "The Normative Force of Reasoning", *Noûs*, 40 (2006). Chapter 9 is based on "The Price of Non-Reductive Physicalism", *Noûs*, 34 (2000), with the correction of some mistakes.

Chapter 10 is an expanded and amended version of "How We Know What Ought to Be", *Proceedings of the Aristotelian Society*, 106 (2005). Chapters 11 and 12 are new.

Material from the articles that originally appeared in *Philosophical Studies* and in *Ethical Theory and Moral Practice* is reprinted here with the kind permission of Springer Science and Business Media. Material that originally appeared in the *Proceedings of the Aristotelian Society* is reprinted by courtesy of the Editor of the Aristotelian Society, © 2005. In general, I thank all the editors and publishers concerned for their kind permission to reuse this material.

Introduction

1 THE KEY TO METAETHICS

What are we doing when we talk or think, not about what *is* the case, but about what *ought* to be the case, or about what people *ought* to think or do? What are we doing when we come to grips, either in dialogue with others or in our own solitary thoughts, with such questions about what *ought* to be? This is the central topic that I shall try to deal with in this book.

As I shall use the term, these questions about what *ought* to be the case are "normative" questions—indeed they are the paradigmatic examples of normative questions. More precisely then, the goal of this book is to attempt to give an account of the following three issues.

1. First, I shall give an account of what such normative questions *mean*. That is, I shall give an account of the *semantics* of normative discourse and of the *content* of normative thought. This will be the theme of Part I of the book.

2. Secondly, since my account of the meaning of such normative questions involves the idea that some answers to these questions are right, while other answers to these questions are wrong, I shall then offer an account of what would *make* something the right answer to such a normative question. That is, I shall offer an account of the *metaphysics* of normative truths. This will be the theme of Part II of the book.

3. Finally, I shall try to give an account of how we could ever *know*, or have a rational or justified belief about, the right answer to such a normative question. That is, I shall offer an account of the *epistemology* of normative belief. This will be the theme of Part III of the book.

The overall account that I shall develop will be a staunchly *realist* account. What exactly is realism? Following Kit Fine (2001), I shall suppose that a realist about the normative is a theorist who says that there are normative facts or truths—such as the fact that certain things ought to be the case, or that it is not the case that certain things ought to be the case—and that at least some of these normative facts are part of reality itself.

The notion of *reality* invoked here is a notion that has its home within a certain sort of metaphysical project—namely, the project of giving a metaphysical account or explanation of everything that is the case in terms of what is real. In effect, then, reality is what provides this metaphysical account or explanation of what is the case. So, if certain normative facts are part of reality, then these facts cannot be explained or accounted for in terms of anything else (that is, they cannot be accounted for without mentioning normative facts or truths or properties or relations), and these normative facts, properties, or relations may also form part of the fundamental account or explanation of certain other things that are the case.

It is just this sort of position that I shall argue for in this book. Thus, I shall argue that there are normative facts or truths, and that these normative facts must be mentioned in any adequate account of our thought and discourse. Moreover, these normative facts are metaphysically irreducible, and so cannot themselves be explained or accounted for without mentioning normative facts, properties, or relations.

As many opponents of such realism about the normative insist, this sort of realism about the normative faces several *prima facie* problems. In general, these problems take the form of demands for explanation. These demands for explanation arise in each of the three main areas that I shall be considering in this book. Fortunately, as I shall argue, my theory has the resources to meet these demands.

One crucial element in meeting these explanatory demands is the idea behind the slogan, which has often been repeated in recent work in the philosophy of mind, that *the intentional is normative*—that is, that there is no way of explaining the nature of the various sorts of mental states that have intentional or representational content (such as beliefs, judgments, desires, decisions, and so on), without using normative terms.

In short, if the point of the book could be summed up in one sentence, that sentence would be: *the normativity of the intentional is the key to metaethics.* Specifically, the specific version of the normativity of the intentional that I defend is, in effect, a simultaneous account *both* of the nature of these mental states that have intentional content *and* of the various normative properties and relations—that is, of the properties and relations that are referred to by terms like 'ought', 'right', 'wrong', and the like. Moreover, this version of the normativity of the intentional forms a crucial premise in my argument for the conclusion that these normative properties and relations are metaphysically irreducible and causally efficacious. In this way, the normativity of the intentional forms the core of my metaphysical account of the nature of normative truths, properties, and relations.

At the same time, the idea that the intentional is normative also helps to solve the problems that are often alleged to beset this sort of realism about the normative. In particular, it enables us to give a credible *semantic* story, about how our normative terms succeed in *referring* to these irreducible normative properties and relations; and it also enables us to give a credible *epistemological* story, about how we can *know* anything, or even have any *justified or rational beliefs*, about the ways in which these irreducible normative properties and relations are instantiated. We are not left with nothing more than the quietist story according to which we just know such things, as if by magic, in a way of which no further explanation of any kind can be given.

In a way, the position that I am trying to defend can be regarded as a form of Platonism about the normative. Indeed, the doctrine that the intentional is normative can be viewed as a way of cashing out Plato's metaphor that the Form of the Good is to the understanding what the sun is to vision (*Republic*, 507b –509a). We count as sighted because we are appropriately sensitive to light, the ultimate source of which is the sun; in a similar way, we count as thinkers because we are appropriately sensitive to normative requirements, the source of which is a coherent system of eternal and necessary truths about what we ought to think or do or feel.

Almost since its inception, Platonism has repeatedly been accused of being no more than an extravagant metaphysical mythology. More specifically, the charges against Platonism are the following. First, it is alleged that Platonism is a theory that there is obviously no good reason to believe; secondly, that it is obviously incompatible with a plausible naturalistic conception of the world; and thirdly, that it raises a series of pressing demands for explanation, to which it can offer nothing more than mystical pseudo-explanations in response.

I hope to show here that all these charges are unjust. As I shall argue, the broadly Platonist theory that I shall outline offers the best explanation of the most uncontroversial intuitive data—the basic data that all theories in this area must explain. Secondly, it is perfectly compatible with the more modest and plausible forms of *metaphysical naturalism* (according to which absolutely all contingent facts are realized in facts of the sort that are studied by natural sciences such as physics). And finally, as I have already noted, I shall argue that my Platonist theory can also give a satisfactory response to all the additional demands for explanation to which the theory itself gives rise.

2 A MAP OF THE METAETHICAL DEBATES

The theory that I shall defend here occupies a distinctive position within the con-temporary metaethical debates. In the last ten years, the most prominent recent contributions to the debate about the nature of normative thought have been: (i) the expressivist and non-cognitivist theories of Simon Blackburn and Allan Gibbard; (ii) various "constructivist" theories, such as that of Christine Korsgaard; (iii) the theories built around a "conceptual analysis" of normative concepts, such as those of Frank Jackson, Philip Pettit, and Michael Smith; (iv) "Cor-nell" moral realism, of the sort that has been advocated by Nicholas Sturgeon, David Brink, and Richard Boyd; and (v) "quietist" realist approaches, such as that of John McDowell, or the approach that is currently being developed by Derek Parfit.

My approach will be importantly different from all of these. Like the "quietist" realists, I reject expressivism and non-cognitivism, constructivism, and the quest for "conceptual analysis" as traditionally understood; but unlike them, I accept, and aim to meet, the demand for a substantive philosophical explanation of normative thought and normative truth. It may be helpful to explain in more detail exactly how my theory will differ from those more familiar approaches.

One of the most important semantical issues concerning normative discourse is the debate between expressivists, such as Simon Blackburn (1993 and 1998) and Allan Gibbard (1990, 2002, and 2003), and their opponents. According to expressivists, the fundamental explanation of the meaning of normative statements is to be given in purely psychologistic terms—that is, in terms of the kind of mental state that those normative statements express—and not in terms of those normative statements' having as their contents normative propositions which give those statements' truth conditions. (Of course, the expressivist may say that eventually we "earn the right" to speak of normative statements' expressing propositions and of their being true or false; but according to the expressivists, such notions do not belong in the most fundamental explanation of the meaning of normative statements.)

Expressivists must also give us an account of the nature of normative judgments—that is, of the distinctive sort of mental states that normative statements express. Most expressivists aim to give an account of the nature of these mental states in wholly non-normative naturalistic terms. This is what enables their theory to be a sort of anti-realism about the normative. According to this sort of expressivism, such normative facts do not themselves appear in the fundamental explanation of the nature of our normative thought or discourse—nor, presumably, in the fundamental metaphysical explanation of anything else. In that sense, these expressivists would not accept that normative facts are part of reality, as I am understanding it.

It is particularly common for expressivists to claim that the mental states that are expressed by normative statements are not strictly *cognitive* states. The paradigmatic example of a cognitive state is a *belief*—that is, a state that under favourable conditions can count as a piece of *knowledge* about how things are. The paradigmatic example of a non-cognitive state is a *desire* or an *emotion*. According to non-cognitivists about the normative, then, the mental states that are expressed by normative statements are in some crucial way more like desires or emotions than like beliefs.

The theory that I shall defend emphatically rejects both expressivism and non-cognitivism. According to expressivists, even if there is a way in which it is correct to claim that normative statements express propositions, and that these propositions give the conditions under which those statement are "true", this claim plays no role in the *fundamental* explanation of the meaning of normative statements; instead, this fundamental explanation takes the form of a purely psychologistic semantics for normative statements, not a truth-conditional semantics. I argue that this expressivist view is false. The correct semantics for normative statements is truth-conditional: any adequate account of the meaning of normative statements must, even at the most fundamental explanatory level, involve the idea that normative statements express propositions that give those statements' truth conditions. Indeed, I believe (for reasons that have little to do with metaethics) that once we accept that there are normative propositions of this sort, there is no reason not to admit a larger class of normative entities, such as normative facts, properties, and relations as well. For this reason, my truth-conditional approach to the semantics of normative statements could also be called a *"factualist"* approach. Moreover, I also insist that the mental states normally expressed by normative statements are quite simply beliefs. In that way, they are cognitive states, not non-cognitive states like desires or emotions.

Another approach to the task of giving an account of the meaning of normative terms that I shall reject is the approach that tries to assimilate the semantics of normative terms to that of *natural kind terms*. (Since the most prominent proponents of this approach include Richard Boyd (1988) and Nicholas Sturgeon (1985), this approach has come to be known as "Cornell" moral realism.) Proponents of this approach typically assume that the meaning of a natural kind term consists in the way in which the term refers to that natural kind (if any) that causally regulates our use of the term in some appropriate way. That is, this approach advocates a causal theory of reference for normative terms.

As I shall argue, this approach cannot give an adequate account of the meaning of normative terms. There are powerful reasons in favour of what has come to be known as *"internalism"* with respect to normative judgments—that is, in favour of the view that there is an essential or "internal" connection between normative judgments and practical reasoning or motivation for action. Moreover, it is a constraint on any adequate account of the meaning of normative terms that it should provide an explanation for this sort of internalism. But the approach that tries to assimilate normative terms to natural kind terms cannot provide any explanation for this sort of internalism. So, as I shall argue, this approach must be rejected.

The Cornell approach to the semantics of normative terms often goes along with a strong form of *metaphysical naturalism*, according to which the property or relation that the normative term stands for is actually *identical* to a "natural" property or relation—that is, roughly, a property that can also be picked out in wholly non-normative terms.

I also reject this strong form of metaphysical naturalism. The claim that normative properties and relations are identical to natural properties and relations is not absurd; but as I shall argue, it is false. Normative facts, properties, and relations are *metaphysically irreducible*, and so cannot be in any way identified with or reduced to natural facts, properties, or relations. However, even though I reject this strong form of naturalism, I do accept a *weaker* form of naturalism. According to this weaker sort of naturalism, even if normative facts are not *identical* to natural facts, at least all contingent normative facts are *realized* in natural facts. Moreover, I shall also accept one of the main metaphysical theses of proponents of this naturalistic approach to metaethics—namely, the thesis that normative facts and properties are *causally efficacious*, and play an essential role in causal explanations of certain contingent facts.

A final rival approach to the semantics of normative statements is the approach based on an attempt at a "conceptual analysis" of those statements. (In view of its most recent proponents, Frank Jackson and Philip Pettit (1995), and Michael Smith (1994), this could be called the "Australian" approach to the semantics of normative terms.) A "conceptual analysis" typically takes the form of a biconditional, with the sentence that can be used to make a certain normative statement on the left-hand side, so that the whole biconditional amounts to a specification of a condition that is both necessary and sufficient for the truth of that normative statement. Crucially, the proponents of this approach must claim that this biconditional is not just true, but is in some sense a *conceptual* truth: its truth is guaranteed by the nature of the concepts that are expressed by the terms involved. In addition, many (though not all) of the proponents of this approach insist that the conceptual analysis should be *non-circular*. That is, no normative terms may appear on the right-hand side of the biconditional; the analysis must specify a condition that is both necessary and sufficient for the truth of the normative statement in wholly non-normative terms.

I reject this approach as well. I deny that any non-circular biconditional of this sort is a conceptual truth. If we allow ourselves to include biconditionals that are "circular" in the relevant sense, then I accept that there are some such circular biconditionals that are conceptual truths. However, I deny that the claim that such a biconditional is a conceptual truth could possibly amount to an adequate account of the meaning of the normative statement. An adequate account would have to take an altogether different form. Specifically, as I argue, it must take the form of a certain sort of *conceptual role semantics* for normative terms.

Another distinguished recent contribution to metaethics is the "constructivist" approach of neo-Kantian theorists such as Christine Korsgaard (1996*a* and 2003). There has been some controversy about how best to interpret this constructivist approach. But at all events, it seems quite clear that this approach is incompatible with the realist—indeed, Platonist—approach that I shall be defending here. In particular, the constructivist is committed to denying at least some of the following claims that form part of my realist approach. First, I claim that there are normative entities, such as normative facts, properties, and relations. Secondly, I claim that these normative facts can be known through the exercise of our capacities for theoretical reason. Finally, I claim that when a procedure for answering a normative question reaches the right answer, that is not because of the intrinsic character of the procedure in question (indeed, in my view all such procedures are fallible), but simply because the answer corresponds to an appropriate normative truth or fact. Since at least some if not all of these claims would be rejected by constructivists, it seems clear that my approach is incompatible with constuctivism.

There is one other approach that contrasts with mine in a crucial way. This is the "quietist" realist approach, such as that of John McDowell (1998), or the approach that is currently being developed by Derek Parfit (in work in progress). According to this quietist realist approach, all forms of anti-realism are mistaken; but it is also a mistake to attempt to offer any substantive or illuminating explanation in this area of philosophy. The only task for such a quietist form of realism is to diagnose the errors that lead philosophers into the mistake of anti-realism. In that sense, this sort of realism is a purely negative or critical theory: in this domain, there is simply no positive theory to be given.

Thus, according to this quietist form of realism, there is no substantive or illuminating explanation of what it is for our *normative terms* to have the meaning that they have: all that can be said about this are such things as that the sentence 'You ought not to lie about your age' means that the person addressed ought not to lie about his age. There is no substantive explanation of what it is for a *belief* to be the belief that one ought not to lie about one's age; it just is that belief—there is nothing more to be said about what it is for this to be the case. There is no substantive explanation of what it is for it to *be the case* that one ought not to lie about one's age: it is just for it to be the case that one ought not to lie about one's age—there is nothing more to be said about that. There is not even any substantive explanation of how we can *know*, or have *justified or rational beliefs* in, normative propositions. We just do know such things, by exercising our capacities for rational reflection. That is all that can be said, and all that needs to be said; no further explanation is necessary.

My approach is completely different from this quietist approach. Unlike the quietists, I am convinced that these phenomena all cry out for explanation. To say that a certain sequence of words in our language just means that a certain thing ought to be the case, but that nothing more can be said about why these words have this particular meaning, seems to me tantamount to saying that these words have this meaning by something like *magic*. It seems to me even more incredible to claim that we can just know such things as that a certain thing ought to be the case, by means of exercising a certain faculty for rational reflection, but that nothing more can be said about how this faculty actually operates. This claim seems to make this capacity into something utterly mysterious, which it is far from clear that we have any reason to believe in. So this quietist approach to the semantical and epistemological issues in metaethics seems to me indefensible.

One of the main reasons why philosophers are drawn to this quietist approach is because they believe that it is the only alternative to an anti-realist or reductionist conception. This belief is mistaken. As I shall try to make clear, it is quite possible to give substantive explanations of these questions without embracing an anti-realist or reductionist conception. To think otherwise is to have an unnecessarily blinkered view of the theoretical options that are available.

With respect to the epistemological issues surrounding normative questions, I follow most ethicists in thinking that a pure coherentist epistemology must be rejected, and something must play a role analogous to the role that observation plays in our empirical knowledge of the external world. In normative thinking, what plays this role is not empirical observation itself, but something that deserves to be called "normative intuition". To that extent, my epistemological account is a form of *intuitionism*. However, I offer an account of what these normative intuitions are, and of where they come from, that is quite unlike the approach that is taken by all other proponents of intuitionism. These intuitions are different in kind from our mathematical or logical intuitions, and from our intuitions of conceptual truths. In a sense, they are *a priori*, but they are a special case of the *a priori*. This aspect of my theory also explains why it differs from some other approaches to the epistemology of normative beliefs in yet another way: unlike those other approaches, it does not deny the possibility of rationally irresoluble disagreements about normative questions. Underlying this account of normative intuitions is the key idea that unifies my whole theory of the nature of the normative—the idea that is expressed by the slogan "the intentional is normative".

Let me sum up what I have said in this section. The theory that I shall defend will accept *internalism* about the connection between normative judgments and practical reasoning or motivation for action. Semantically, my theory will reject expressivism and non-cognitivism, and embrace a *factualist* semantics and a *cognitivist* conception of normative judgments; and it will reject both the approach that relies solely on a causal theory of reference to give an account of the meaning of normative terms, and the attempt to give a conceptual analysis for such terms, in favour of a form of *conceptual role semantics* for such terms. Metaphysically, my theory will be a form of *realism* about the normative; it will claim that normative facts, properties and relations exist and are both *metaphysically irreducible* and *causally efficacious*; it will be incompatible with the strong form of naturalism according to which normative facts and properties are identical with natural facts and properties, but compatible with the *moderate naturalist* view that all contingent normative facts are realized in such natural facts. Epistemologically, my theory will reject purely coherentist and empiricist accounts of what it is for our normative beliefs to be justified or rational. Instead, it will be a version of *intuitionism*—albeit a special kind of intuitionism that permits the existence of rationally irresoluble disagreements about normative issues. The whole account is unified around one central idea—the idea that is expressed by the slogan "the intentional itself is normative".

3 THE PLAN OF THE BOOK

As I mentioned above, this book will have three parts. Part I of the book is devoted to broadly *semantical* issues. How are we to conceive of the *meaning* of normative statements, and of the nature of the mental states ("normative judgments") that are expressed by such statements? As I explain in Chapter 1, this problem is particularly pressing because an adequate account of normative judgments must somehow explain the fact that these judgments at least appear to have an essential or "internal" connection to motivation and practical reasoning.

Many philosophers think that this fact supports a non-cognitivist account of normative judgments, according to which these judgments do not count as genuine beliefs or cognitive states, but rather as non-cognitive states of some kind. Such non-cognitivist accounts of normative judgments naturally go along with an expressivist approach to the semantics of normative statements. As I argue in Chapter 2, however, such expressivist accounts face insuperable problems; hence both expressivism and non-cognitivism should be rejected.

In Chapter 3, I consider two other rival accounts of normative statements. First, I consider the account that is based on applying the causal theory of reference to normative terms. Secondly, I consider accounts that are based on the attempt to give a "conceptual analysis" of normative statements. Both of these approaches also fail, I argue, largely because they cannot accommodate the sort of "internalism" that was argued for in Chapter 1.

In Chapter 4, I give my account of the semantics of normative terms. This account is a version of *conceptual role semantics* for normative concepts. Such an account can explain the connection between normative judgments and motivation. It can also give a satisfactory account of the truth conditions of normative propositions (it entails a version of the "fitting attitude analysis": for example, very roughly, x is better than y if and only if it is correct to prefer x over y).

In Chapter 5, I examine some of the detailed implications of my semantics. As I explain, it can give a good account of *deontic logic* (the *logic* of 'ought'); it can explain the way in which terms like 'ought' are systematically context-sensitive, and express different concepts in different contexts of utterance; and it can explain the logical relations between the normative concepts that are expressed by 'ought' and those that are expressed by such evaluative terms as 'better' or 'best'.

Part II of the book is devoted to *metaphysical* issues. Given certain plausible assumptions, the semantic theory that I advocated in Part I entails the existence of *normative truths* or *facts*, and of *normative properties* and *relations*. So, what is the place of these normative facts and properties in the world? How are they related to natural facts (facts of the kind that are investigated by natural science)?

In Chapter 6, I explain the metaphysical framework that I will be working within in more detail. Then, in Chapter 7, I explore the metaphysical implications of the semantical account developed in Part I of the book. Under natural assumptions, it seems to amount to a version of the idea that is expressed by the slogan "the intentional is normative". I explain exactly which version of this idea I have in mind, and then I argue in defence of this version of the idea. In this sense, as I shall argue, the intentional is indeed normative.

In Chapter 8, I argue for two crucial corollaries of this metaphysical conception. First, normative facts, properties, and relations are irreducible and *sui generis*: they cannot be reduced to natural facts, properties, or relations. Secondly, contrary to what many philosophers hold, they are causally efficacious: they enter into causal explanations of contingent facts about what happens in the world.

In Chapter 9, I attempt to answer the central objection that many philosophers will have to this metaphysical conception. According to a plausible *naturalistic* conception of the world, there is a sense in which the natural facts determine the fundamental nature of the world. But how can we unite my conception of normative facts, properties, and relations as irreducible and causally efficacious with such a naturalistic conception of the world? The solution, I argue, is to interpret naturalism as the view that all contingent facts whatsoever are *realized* in (and so also *supervene* on) natural facts. This view can be reconciled with the thesis that there are irreducible and causally efficacious normative facts and properties (although the reconciliation requires some far-reaching reflections on fundamental metaphysical concepts like 'realization', 'reduction', 'essence', and 'metaphysical necessity').

Part III of the book is devoted to *epistemological* issues. If there are objective normative truths, then how could we ever know them? How could we even have any rational or justified beliefs in normative propositions? In Chapter 10, I argue that the idea that the intentional is normative supports a new solution to these epistemological problems; it allows us to give a new account of where a thinker's so-called "normative intuitions" come from, and why (and under what conditions) it is rational for the thinker to trust them. This account, I argue, is preferable both to the rival versions of intuitionism about normative beliefs, and to those epistemological accounts that are incompatible with intuitionism.

In Chapter 11, I trace out some of the implications of this epistemological account. First, I explain how the account developed in Chapter 10 implies that under favourable conditions, normative truths are knowable *a priori*; but they are a special case of the *a priori*, differing in important ways from other forms of *a priori* truths. This enables this account to solve the following dilemma: on the one hand, it seems that if normative truths can be known at all, some normative truths must be *a priori*; on the other hand, normative truths seem radically different from the classic cases of *a priori* truths, such as logical or mathematical truths—so how can they be *a priori*?

The remainder of Chapter 11 is devoted to a further problem about the epistemology of normative beliefs: the existence of widespread and persistent disagreement about normative questions. I argue that it can be rational to persist in one's normative belief despite the fact that others who are equally intelligent, thoughtful, and well informed about non-normative matters disagree with one's belief. As I argue, this view is quite compatible with the realist conception of the normative that this book is designed to defend.

Finally in a concluding chapter, Chapter 12, I try to give an overview of the whole theory that I have outlined in the previous chapters, by outlining the theory's implications for various other branches of philosophy. Specifically, I outline the theory's implications for the following four branches of philosophy: (i) the philosophy of mind and language, (ii) the theory of rational belief and rational decision, (iii) first-order normative ethical theory, and (iv) the philosophy of religion.

4 SOME METHODOLOGICAL REMARKS

It should be clear by now that I am planning to argue for a bold, large-scale philosophical picture. This is bound to raise doubts about whether the project that I am pursuing is feasible at all. Even in a book of this size, how could I possibly prove that such a big, bold philosophical picture is correct?

I am under no illusions here: it is clear that the arguments that I shall offer in this book do not amount to a *proof* that my philosophical picture is correct. My arguments will exemplify the standard form for constructive theorizing in analytic philosophy. First, I shall canvas a number of intuitions that seem compelling to philosophers regardless of their controversial theoretical commitments, and I shall set out some of the philosophical problems to which these intuitions give rise. Then I will try to articulate a theory as precisely as possible, and argue that this theory provides a better solution to those problems than the best-known alternative theories. Finally, I will try to show that this theory has the resources to respond to the obvious objections and criticisms that might be directed against it.

Inevitably, however, I will not be able to survey all of the pros and cons of this philosophical theory; still less will I be able to compare it with every other position on all the relevant issues. So I will not be able to demonstrate that this philosophical theory really does provide the best explanation of everything that requires explanation in this area. At best, these arguments succeed in showing that this philosophical theory has certain advantages over some of its rivals, and can answer some of the obvious objections and criticisms. Even though the upshot of my arguments will be limited in this way, it should still be of some interest to philosophers to consider my new formulation of a broadly Platonist theory and to see that when reformulated in this way, such a theory has a number of hitherto unnoticed advantages.

I very much doubt whether anyone alive today is entitled to any great degree of confidence in the correctness of any theory that attempts to answer any of the larger questions of philosophy. Since the theory that I am advocating here is a theory that attempts to answer some of these larger questions, I doubt that I am entitled to much confidence in the correctness of this theory. At times, however, I know that enthusiasm gets the better of me, and I express myself as though I regarded myself as entitled to much greater confidence than I really am. I could have tried to rewrite the whole book in a more tentative style; but the main result would just have been to make the arguments more verbose and harder to follow. So the style of the book may at several points make my claims sound stronger and more confident than they really are. I hope that readers will not be misled by this, and will not begrudge me the pinch of salt with which many of my claims will need to be taken.

5 THE "NATURE" OF NORMATIVITY?

As I conceive of it, then, the only method for answering the larger questions of philosophy is by means of a sort of inference to the best explanation. The kind of explanation that is in question here is not causal explanation. Causal explanation seems typically to consist in an explanation of a contingent fact about one region of space-time by appeal to some other contingent fact about some other (earlier, nearby) region of space-time. The sort of explanation sought by philosophical theories, I believe, is an explanation of a necessary fact by appeal to some more fundamental necessary fact; and ultimately, I believe, this more fundamental necessary fact will be a fact about the *essence* or *nature* of things. (I attempt to elucidate and defend this conception of philosophical explanations in Chapter 6 of this book.) Thus, as I conceive of it, the theory that I will be advocating in this book is ultimately a theory about the *nature* of normative thought and discourse, of normative facts, properties, and relations, and of rationality in normative reasoning. This is why I have called this book *The Nature of Normativity*.

At the same time, there is another meaning of the word 'nature', which features in one of the main objections that may be raised against my broadly Platonist conception of the normative. This is the objection that my conception cannot be reconciled with a plausibly *naturalistic* view of the world—where a naturalistic view of the world is one according to which facts of the sort that are studied by the natural sciences have a uniquely fundamental role in the world as a whole. According to the theory that I am advocating here, the essence of normativity (that is, the "nature" of normativity in the first sense of that term) consists above all in the principle that is expressed by the slogan "the intentional itself is normative". It is this that explains how it can be that in a world whose fundamental character is given by the facts that are investigated by the natural sciences, it is nonetheless part of reality that there are normative thoughts, statements, facts, properties, and relations. In this way, it is the nature of normativity that allows us to reconcile normativity with nature.

PART I

THE SEMANTICS OF NORMATIVE THOUGHT AND DISCOURSE

1

Thinking About What Ought To Be

1.1 THE THEORETICAL PROJECT: THOUGHT AND TALK

We often think, not just about what *is* the case, but about what *ought to be* the case. I shall call this sort of thinking "*normative* thinking". But what are we *doing* when we engage in normative thinking? What sort of thinking is this? How exactly does this normative thinking differ from thinking of other kinds?

The first part of this book is largely devoted to this question. But I shall treat this question in parallel with the corresponding question about normative *talk* or *discourse*. That is, I shall also focus on the question of what we are doing when we *talk* about what ought to be. What sort of discourse is this? What exactly do the statements and terms that are characteristic of this sort of discourse mean?

My reason for focusing on talk as well as on thought is not that I believe that the nature of every branch of thought must be explained in terms of the nature of the corresponding branch of discourse; it is not even that I believe that it is impossible to explain the nature of *normative* thought—thinking about what ought to be—except by means of an account of the nature of normative discourse. Indeed, in the end I shall do the opposite: I shall offer an account of the meaning of normative language in terms of the distinctive type of mental states that are expressed by normative statements.[1]

My reason for focusing so much on normative discourse and normative language, as well as on normative thought, has to do with the dialectical position of my arguments, not with the content of the theory that my arguments are ultimately designed to support. There are fierce controversies about almost every aspect of our normative thought. In particular, there is a long-standing controversy about whether normative thought ever involves the so-called *cognitive* attitudes of belief, judgment, knowledge, and so on, or whether it consists exclusively of *non-cognitive* attitudes instead (such as a special attitude of "normative judgment"

---

[1] That is, I shall in the end reject the approach of such philosophers as Michael Dummett (1993*a*) and Robert Brandom (1994); instead, I shall side with such philosophers as Gareth Evans (1982) and Christopher Peacocke (1986), by offering an account of language in terms of thought, rather than an account of thought in terms of language.

perhaps).[2] Normative language is at least to some extent less controversial: it is obvious, and agreed on all sides, that we make normative statements, and the logical structure of the sentences that we utter in making these statements (unlike the inner structure of our thoughts) is more or less open to view.

Of course, there are many fierce controversies in the philosophy of language as well. But at least in the philosophy of language there is a body of data that we can appeal to in order to evaluate our theoretical claims that is largely independent of these disputed theoretical questions—specifically, the structure of the sentences that we use in making our normative statements and utterances, and our intuitions about which of these utterances are intelligible, acceptable, or felicitous in various contexts.

Thus, even though my fundamental account of normative language will ultimately be given in terms of normative thought, a lot of the primary evidence on which my account will be based is the evidence of normative language. Taking account of this evidence will require investigating normative language as well as the normative thoughts that our normative utterances express.

1.2 WHAT SORT OF ACCOUNT IS CALLED FOR, ANYWAY?

I have said several times now that the goal of my theoretical project is an "account" of normative thought or discourse. But what exactly would such an "account" be if it exists? And what reason is there for thinking that it makes sense to look for such an "account"?

There are two dominant approaches to this metaphilosophical question. First, some philosophers will insist on a *reductively naturalistic* account of normative thought and discourse. An account of this sort would give a *non-circular analysis* of what it is to have such normative thought, or to make such a normative statement, in purely naturalistic terms; that is, it would give necessary and sufficient conditions for having such a thought, or for making such a statement, without using any non-naturalistic terms. Secondly, some other philosophers will take a doggedly *quietist* approach, according to which no substantive, non-trivial "account" of normative thought or discourse is possible. According to this quietist approach, nothing more can be said about the meaning of statements of the form '*A* ought to φ' except things of the following forms: that this statement means *that A ought to φ*, that it can be used to state that *A* ought to φ, and to express the belief that *A* ought to φ, and so on.[3]

---

[2] This issue will be discussed in Chapter 2. For some of the most important contributions to this debate, see Blackburn (1998), Gibbard (2003), Kalderon (2005*a*), and Horgan and Timmons (2000*a*).

[3] For statements of this quietist approach, see Derek Parfit (in preparation), Ronald Dworkin (1996), and John McDowell (1987).

I shall not follow either of these two approaches here. My most principled reasons for rejecting the quietist approach will not emerge until much later on, but even at this stage, it should be clear that it is hardly obviously true. Indeed, it would seem to me incredible that it could be an absolutely unanalysable feature of a particular thought or statement that it is about one thing rather than another. For example, it surely cannot be an absolutely unanalysable, primitive feature of a certain statement or thought that it is *about George W. Bush*, say (rather than being *about Tony Blair* or *about Vladimir Putin*). Surely, this feature of the thought or statement must be explained on the basis of some facts about that thought or statement that can be described in some other way (perhaps including some causal relation between that thought or statement and George W. Bush himself). If this point applies to thoughts and statements about Bush and Blair, why doesn't it also apply to thoughts about what ought to be the case?

It is hardly idiosyncratic of me to think this. Compare the way in which Saul Kripke (1980: 68) demands that an account of the reference of a particular term "must not be circular". The example that Kripke gives of a theory that is circular is William Kneale's (1962) suggestion that the name 'Socrates' just means "The individual called 'Socrates' ". Kripke (1980: 70) objects to this theory of reference as follows:

Someone uses the name 'Socrates'. How are we supposed to know to whom he refers? By using the description that gives the sense of it. According to Kneale, that description is 'the man called "Socrates" '. And here, … it tells us nothing at all. Taking it in this way it seems to be no theory of reference at all. We ask, 'To whom does he refer by "Socrates"?' And then the answer is given, 'Well, he refers to the man to whom he refers.' If this were all there was to the meaning of a proper name, then no reference would get off the ground at all.

What Kripke is objecting to here is an account of the meaning of the proper name 'Socrates' that simply *presupposes* what it is for someone to be the person called 'Socrates'—whereas it is precisely the task of an account of the reference of this name to *explain* what it is for someone to be the person referred to by 'Socrates'. Hence, for an account of the reference of the name 'Socrates' to be acceptable, it must not use the notion of "being called 'Socrates' " or "being referred to by the name 'Socrates' ", on pain of simply presupposing what is to be accounted for.

Here Kripke only objects to accounts of the reference of a *name* that use the notion of the reference of that very name. But would it be much more satisfactory to give an account of the name 'Socrates' just by saying: "The meaning of the name consists in the fact that it is standardly used to express thoughts about Socrates"? The notion of a thought's being "about" Socrates is just the analogue, at the level of thought, of the notion of a name's "referring to" Socrates, at the level of language. It is obviously incredible to suppose that the name 'Socrates' refers to a particular individual purely by *magic*, as it were.

It seems only marginally less incredible to me to suppose that a thought can be about Socrates even though nothing illuminating can be said about what makes it a thought *about Socrates* (rather than, say, a thought about Charmides or Thrasymachus instead).

For this reason, I shall aim to give an account of what it is for a thought or a statement to be about what ought to be the case, without making any use of the notion of what I am trying to give an account of—namely, the notion of a thought's or a statement's being about what ought to be the case. I shall seek to give an account that is in this way *non-circular*.

I shall assume here that any notion of a thought's or statement's being thought or statement *that* this or that ought to be the case (or a thought or statement *that* this or that person ought to do such-and-such or to have such-and-such mental states or attitudes) in effect also involves the notion that I am seeking to avoid—the notion of a thought's or a statement's being *about* what ought to be. So in giving my account of what it is for a thought or utterance to be about what ought to be, I shall aim to avoid using the term 'ought' within the scope of 'that ... '-clauses (or 'about ... '-phrases) that would express some complex notion that involves the very notion that I am seeking to explain.[4]

Thus, I shall reject the quietist approach, and aim instead to find an account of what it is to think or talk about what ought to be that is non-circular in this way. But it is important to see that this does not commit me to the reductively naturalistic approach. In Kripke's example, what we are trying to account for is a term's *referring to Socrates*. We are not trying to give a general account of what it is for a term to be a meaningful singular term at all, as opposed to a meaningless symbol or piece of gibberish; that would be a different project within the philosophy of language altogether. So in giving our account of the reference of 'Socrates' it is fine for us to *assume* that we are dealing with a meaningful term; and it is equally fine for us to use *general* semantic notions like 'truth', 'reference', 'meaning', and so on. What we must avoid is using *specific* semantic terms like 'refers to Socrates' or 'about Socrates' and the like. So in embracing this non-circularity constraint, we are not committed to the general project of explaining the semantic in non-semantic terms.

Just as it is permissible for our account to use general semantic notions (like 'truth', 'reference', and 'meaning'), so too it is quite permissible for it to use the terms of intentional folk psychology. We may quite happily use the notions of reasoning and inference, the notions of forming or revising our beliefs or intentions for a reason, deliberating and decision making, and so on. Thus in aiming to give an account that is non-circular in this way, we are not committed to the general project of "explaining the intentional in naturalistic terms", as Robert Stalnaker (1984: 24–5) once put it. I shall indeed make some claims about the nature of these general types of intentional mental state in Part II of

---

[4] Compare Peacocke (1992: ch. 1).

this book; but here in Part I, my concern is just with the nature of normative thought and discourse—with what it is for a thought or statement to be about what ought to be the case—so here I shall simply take these general intentional notions for granted.

Equally, in giving an account of what it is for a thought or statement to be *about* what ought to be the case, I am *not* giving an account of what it is for a thing to *be* something that ought to be the case. My concern in this part of the book is with our *thought* and *talk* about what ought to be the case, not directly with what ought to be the case itself. Similarly, philosophers of language like Kripke can give accounts of what it is for a term to *refer* to a person like Socrates without giving any account of the metaphysics of persons—that is, of what it is for something to *be* a person. They can give an account of what it is for a term to refer to water without giving any account of what it is for something to be a sample of water—indeed, the latter question, about the nature of water, appears to be a question for chemistry rather than for any branch of philosophy (let alone for the philosophy of language or the philosophy of thought).

Thus, in giving an account of what it is for a term to refer to Socrates, or to cows, it is perfectly permissible to talk about Socrates, or about cows. For example, it would be perfectly permissible to say that the meaning of the term 'Socrates' partially consists in the fact that the term stands in some relation to Socrates himself, or that the meaning of 'cow' partially consists in the fact that the term stands in some relation to actual cows. That is, there need not be any objection to using the term 'Socrates' or 'cow' in the metalanguage in which we are giving our account of these terms. We must only avoid using these terms in the scope of 'that ... '-clauses or 'about...'-phrases—since that would be simply presupposing what we should be giving an account of.

In exactly the same way, I shall allow myself to use normative terms in the metalanguage in which I am giving my account, subject to this non-circularity constraint that I have described above. This does not trivialize the account, or make it viciously circular—no more than it is viciously circular to use logical constants (like 'not', 'if', 'and', and so on) in giving an account of the meaning of these very logical constants, or to use semantic terms (like 'truth', 'meaning', 'reference', and so on) in giving an account of the meaning of such semantic terms.

Curiously, a great many philosophers seem to overlook this point when it comes to giving an account of normative terms like 'ought'. These philosophers appear convinced that either we must embrace quietism or else we must give some account of what 'ought' means in wholly non-normative terms. But this, as we have seen, is a mistake. It is an unreasonable demand to impose on accounts of 'ought' that they should not use normative terms anywhere in the metalanguage in which the account is given, just as it would be an unreasonable demand to impose on accounts of the logical constants that they should not use logical constants in the metalanguage in which the account is given.

There seem to be at least three reasons why some philosophers are tempted to make this mistake. First, some of them assume that the task of giving an account of the meaning of the term involves giving a *definition*—where a definition is supposed to be something that could enable someone who did not understand the term to come to acquire a mastery of it. But this is not my purpose here at all. I assume that you and I both understand these normative terms perfectly well. My task is to give a theoretical account of what this everyday understanding consists in.[5] We are speaking as theorists, about the ordinary citizen's understanding of those terms: it is perfectly permissible to avail ourselves of our own ordinary understanding in giving our theoretical account.

Secondly, some philosophers will insist that normative terms are in some way *metaphysically problematic*. J. L. Mackie famously thought normative properties metaphysically "queer"; and Simon Blackburn objects to "unexplained appeals" to the normative as metaphysical mystification.[6] It might seem that the only way to domesticate the metaphysically wild character of normative terms is to give an account of their meaning in wholly non-normative terms. I shall try to argue later on that the allegedly troubling metaphysical character of normative terms is entirely illusory. I shall address this issue mainly in Part II, which is directly devoted to the metaphysical issues surrounding the normative.

In addition, however, the other parts of this book should also help to dispel the sense of metaphysical mystification that clings to normative terms. Part I will show that we do not have to rest content with the mystifying and unilluminating quietistic picture, according to which the human mind simply has an utterly primitive power of referring to or thinking about normative states of affairs: we can give a substantive and genuinely explanatory account of what it is for a thought or a statement to be about what ought to be. Similarly, Part III will show that we do not have to rest content with blank appeals to a mysterious faculty of *intuition* in explaining how we know or have justified beliefs about what ought to be; we can provide a substantive and genuinely explanatory account of this. In short, the suspicion of a metaphysical mystery is often encouraged by suspicion of semantic and epistemological mysteries; but the latter suspicion can be dispelled without imposing a ban on normative terms in the metalanguage.

Thirdly, it may seem that normative terms are just desperately *unclear*, so that using normative terms in our metalanguage will preclude any precise or perspicuous account. We may compare this point with Wittgenstein's criticism of A. C. Ewing's definition of 'good', as recorded by O. K. Bouwsma (1986: 41–2):

Towards the end of our discussion..., [Wittgenstein] spoke of A. C. Ewing's definition— ... "Good is what it is right to admire". Then he shook his head over it. The

---

[5] Compare the point that P. F. Strawson (1992: ch. 1) illustrates by citing Queen Isabella's puzzlement about what use there could be in a grammar of the Spanish language.
[6] See Mackie (1977: ch. 1) and Blackburn (1993: essay 6).

definition throws no light. There are three concepts, all of them vague. Imagine three solid pieces of stone. You pick them up, fit them together and you get now a ball. What you've now got tells you something about the three shapes. Now consider you have three balls of or lumps of soft mud or putty—formless. Now you put the three together and mould out of them a ball. Ewing makes a soft ball out of three pieces of mud.

The account of normative terms that I shall give will provide some support to Wittgenstein's criticism. According to my account, terms like 'good', 'right', and 'ought' are profoundly *context-sensitive*, so that they express different concepts in different contexts. This does not create too many problems in everyday life, where the context in which these terms are used is usually sufficiently rich to determine which of these many concepts the term expresses in the context. But in philosophy, the context may be too impoverished to determine this. In this sense, "language goes on holiday". In short, the problem with Ewing's definition is not that it has no meaning. On the contrary, there are far too many different things that it might possibly mean; and Ewing has not done enough to help us to see which of these many different things it is that he is actually asserting.

This is a danger that will arise when we give an account of the meaning of normative terms and allow ourselves to use normative terms in the metalanguage; we may fail to make it sufficiently clear exactly what concept is being expressed by those metalanguage terms in the context. But it should be possible to avoid this danger by being sufficiently self-conscious about the terminology that is being used, and by trying to elucidate the normative terms that appear in the metalanguage as best we can.

For all these reasons then, there seem to be no insurmountable objections to using normative terms in the metalanguage in which we are giving our account of the meaning of normative terms. Thus, I shall seek a genuinely substantive, non-circular, and explanatory account of the meaning of these terms, without being in any way committed to any sort of reduction of the normative to the naturalistic, let alone any reduction of the intentional and semantic to the naturalistic.

1.3 THE INTERNALIST CHARACTER OF NORMATIVE JUDGMENT

In this section, I shall argue for a version of the claim that is known as "normative judgment internalism" (NJI)—that is, the claim that there is an essential or "internal" connection between normative judgments and practical reasoning or motivation for action.

The word 'judgment' is often contrasted with 'belief': when the terms are used in this way, a "belief" is an enduring mental state, while a "judgment" is a mental event in which we consciously form a belief. I am not using the terms in this way here. Since many non-cognitivists deny that the sincere utterance of an indicative normative sentence expresses a belief at all, I am just using the term 'judgment' as a neutral term for the mental state (whatever exactly it may be) that is expressed by the sincere utterance of such a sentence.

As I am using the term here, "normative judgments" are not the same as *moral* judgments. Moral judgments are judgments that are based on considerations such as fairness and kindness, rights, duties, and so on. But not every normative judgment is a judgment of this kind. For example, if I judge that I ought to buy a new pair of shoes, this need not be a moral judgment. I need not be violating anyone's rights, or neglecting any of my duties or obligations, or failing to show due consideration for the needs and interests of others, if I didn't buy a new pair of shoes. Perhaps no one else would be entitled to blame me if I didn't. But it can still be true that I ought to buy a new pair of shoes.

Some philosophers have claimed that the word 'ought' has at least two different senses—a moral sense, and a prudential (or "instrumental") sense.[7] Even if this claim is true, it seems that there must be a further sense of 'ought' that is neither narrowly moral nor narrowly prudential. Consider a case where you know that you are morally required to do X and prudentially required to do Y, but it is impossible to do both. In this case, it seems quite intelligible for you to ask yourself, "Ought I to do what I am morally required to do, X? Or ought I to do what I am prudentially required to do, Y?"[8] Neither of these questions seems equivalent to the trivial question, "Ought I to do what I ought to do?" But if that is true, then the term 'ought' cannot occur here in a narrowly moral sense, or a narrowly prudential sense. It must occur here in a more general normative sense.[9] When understood in this way, a statement of the form 'A ought to φ' seems equivalent to a certain interpretation of the corresponding statement 'There is a conclusive reason for A to φ'. This statement does not just mean that A is morally required to φ, or that it would best serve A's interests or purposes for A to φ; it means that A ought to φ *all things considered*—that is, given *all* relevant considerations (which might include both moral and prudential considerations), A ought to φ.

The version of normative judgment internalism (NJI) that I shall argue for here is exclusively concerned with normative judgments that can be expressed by statements of the form 'A ought to φ', when the term 'ought' is used in this

---

[7] For this claim, see for example Prichard (2002: 126). In fact, the evidence typically offered in defence of this claim is hardly compelling. For an argument against the claim that 'ought' is ambiguous in this way, see Thomson (2000: 44–7).

[8] Some philosophers deny that this question is intelligible; see for example Richard Price, reprinted in Raphael (1969: §714). But intuition surely tells against denying this.

[9] For this point, see Cullity and Gaut (1997: 1). Note that even Sidgwick (1907: 508) seems to believe in such a sense of 'ought' (it is just that he believes that in "cases of a recognised conflict between self-interest and duty" practical reason is "divided against itself", inconsistently telling us *both* that we ought to do what we are morally required to do, X, *and* that we ought to do what best serves our self-interest, Y).

more general normative sense. More specifically, it is concerned with *first-person* normative judgments, of the form 'I ought to φ'—where φ-ing is, as I shall put it, "something of the appropriate sort". (I shall explain later what exactly I mean by describing φ-ing as "something of the appropriate sort".)

Now, suppose that you ask yourself a first-person question involving this sense of 'ought', "What ought I to do?" Although this question is overtly about what you *ought* to do, it is natural to hear it as a *deliberative* question—that is, as a question that is simply about *what to do*. But why should there be this connection, between asking yourself what you ought to do and asking yourself what to do? Why isn't asking yourself what you ought to do an entirely different business from asking yourself what to do?

I propose the following explanation: we hear your question "What ought I to do?" as a deliberative question about what to do, because in interpreting you, we typically assume that you are *rational*, and if you are rational, your question "What ought I to do?" *is* a deliberative question about what to do.[10] For example, if you are rational, and your answer to the question 'What ought I to do?' is that you ought to go to bed (and going to bed is something "of the appropriate sort"), then you will not just judge that you ought to go to bed; you will also *intend* to go to bed.

This is hardly a surprising conclusion. It is widely accepted by philosophers that *akrasia* is a kind of irrationality; and *akrasia* consists in willingly failing to do something that one judges that one ought to do. For reasons that I shall explain in the next section, so long as φ-ing is something of the appropriate sort, if you do not intend to φ, you will count as willingly failing to φ. So, at least as long as φ-ing is something of the appropriate sort, if you judge that you ought to φ, and yet do not intend to φ, you are being *akratic*—and so irrational.

These points support the claim that all instances of the following schema are true:

(1) Necessarily, if one is rational, then, if one judges 'I ought to φ', one also intends to φ.

But this claim is already in effect a version of NJI, close to the versions of NJI that have been defended by Michael Smith (1994: 61) and Christine Korsgaard (1996b: 321).[11] According to this claim, there is a necessary connection between

---

[10] I am not claiming that if you are rational, the deliberative question about what to do can *always* be expressed as a question about what you *ought* to do. You might know that you are in a "Buridan's ass" situation, so that none of the relevant options is something that you *ought* to do. I claim only that if you are rational, the question 'What ought I to do?' is one sort of deliberative question about what to do.

[11] I say that this formulation is "close" to those of Smith and Korsgaard, not "equivalent" to those formulations. My formulation differs from Korsgaard's because it focuses on 'ought'-judgments rather than on "rational considerations" more generally. It differs from Smith's formulation because it allows that the irrationality involved in simultaneously failing to intend to φ and judging that one ought to φ may not always be "practical irrationality". If the judgment 'I ought to φ' is itself

first-person normative judgments and intentions to act, at least in all rational agents. It is admittedly a weaker version of NJI than the strong version that postulates a necessary connection between first-person normative judgments and motivation in all agents whatsoever (whether those agents are rational or not).[12] Many philosophers have objected to this strong version of NJI, on the grounds that it seems to make *akrasia* impossible, even though such *akrasia* seems intuitively possible (as in cases involving agents who suffer from drug addiction or depression).[13] This weaker version of NJI is immune to those objections: it does not entail that *akrasia* is impossible—only that it is irrational.

Even though this version of NJI is much weaker and less controversial than the stronger version that rules out *akrasia* as impossible, a number of simple criticisms have been raised against it. First, this version of NJI may seem simply *unclear*, because there are many different things that could be meant by the term 'rational'.[14] Secondly, as Jean Hampton (1998: 73) objects, it may seem that when the term 'rational' is interpreted so that this formulation of NJI comes out true, this formulation simply becomes *trivial*—as it plainly would be if all that the term 'rational' meant here were "intending to do whatever one judges that one ought to do".

The first criticism is clearly right to claim that there are many different things that could be meant by the term 'rational'. For example, in one very weak sense, any action that is done for a reason—even a very bad reason—counts as "rational". In this sense, *akrasia* is not usually irrational, since the akratic agent usually has some reason (even if it is a bad reason) for his akratic action. But it is not this sense of 'rational' that I am using here.

Rather, the relevant sense of 'rational' is the one that is most prominent in discussions of rational choice and rational belief. When the term is used in this way, there are two main kinds of requirements of rationality. First, there are *synchronic* requirements: to be rational, one should avoid certain incoherent combinations of beliefs and intentions—that is, combinations of beliefs and intentions that intuitively conflict with each other. Secondly, there are *diachronic* requirements: to be rational, one should follow the proper rules or procedures in one's reasoning (that is, in the process of forming and revising one's beliefs and intentions). (1), the version of NJI that I have formulated above, is a statement

---

irrational, it may be possible that one's failure to intend to φ is itself perfectly rational, and the only irrationality present is one's irrational *belief*. On this point, see Arpaly (2000), and Broome (1999).

[12] For such stronger versions of internalism, see for example Hare (1952: 124–6), McDowell (1998), and Gibbard (2002).

[13] For this objection to the strong version of internalism, see Smith (1994: 119–25) and Stocker (1979).

[14] As Blackburn (1998: 65) puts it: "Doing what you know to be bad is bad. We might describe it as irrational, and since Plato many philosophers have done so. But that is not, as it stands, a very interesting thing to say, for it is not at all obvious what further or different specific charge it makes."

of a synchronic requirement of rationality.[15] As I am using the term here, to assess a thought or action as "rational" or "irrational" is to assess it on the basis of its relations to the thinker's other mental states, not on the basis of its relations to the external world. In that sense, irrationality always consists in some sort of *internal incoherence*.

Intuitively, *akrasia*—simultaneously judging 'I ought to φ' and yet failing to intend to φ—does involve an incoherent combination of mental states: one's judgments and one's will are in conflict with each other; one's will refuses to pursue the course of action that one judges that one ought to pursue. So, even in a fairly clear, narrow sense of the term, *akrasia* of this kind seems irrational. Thus, this formulation of NJI seems to be true. Moreover, once it is clear that this is the sense of 'rational' that we are using here, it seems clear that this formulation of NJI is not simply trivial (in the strict sense of being definitionally equivalent to a truth of logic).

In addition, given certain widely held assumptions, this version of NJI (1) entails another version of NJI that is not restricted to rational agents in this way. When 'rationality' is understood in this way, it may be that rationality is in a certain sense constitutive of mentality itself. For a variety of reasons, many philosophers have held that it is necessary that everyone who has any beliefs and desires at all has some *disposition* to conform to the basic requirements of rationality that apply to them. One reason why some philosophers have held this is that they believed that *interpretation* must be constrained by a principle of charity: we must attribute mental states to people in such a way that our attributions make them as rational as possible.[16] On this view, for example, it is necessary that all thinkers who have any beliefs of the form '*not-p*' at all have some disposition to avoid simultaneously holding beliefs of the form '*p*' and '*not-p*'. If they had no such disposition, it would not be correct to interpret the beliefs in question as being of the form '*not-p*' at all.

According to this view, then, it is necessary that all thinkers have a disposition to conform to the basic requirements of rationality that apply to them. I shall give my own reasons for thinking that this view is correct later on, in Chapter 7. At this point let us just assume, for the sake of argument, that this view is correct, in order to see what the implications of this view will be.

There has been much discussion among philosophers about the nature of dispositions.[17] To fix ideas, let us suppose that a disposition can be defined by means of a function from *stimulus* conditions to *response* conditions. Fragility, for example, can be defined by means of a function that maps the stimulus

---

[15] A corresponding *diachronic* requirement might be this: it is always a proper procedure for forming intentions about what to do, if one forms an intention to φ directly on the basis of a rational judgment of the form 'I ought to φ'. Unfortunately, I shall not have space to discuss the requirements of diachronic rationality here.

[16] Compare, among others, Davidson (2001: essays 9–10), and McDowell (1986).

[17] See for example Bird (1998) and Fara (2005).

condition *being struck at time t* onto the response condition *breaking shortly after t*. Something has this disposition if and only if it has some intrinsic feature in virtue of which, in any normal case in which it is in one of these stimulus conditions, it also goes into the response condition onto which the relevant function maps that stimulus condition.[18]

It is plausible that this version of NJI (1) expresses a *basic* requirement of rationality that applies to all agents who judge anything of the form 'I ought to φ': that is, NJI is a necessary truth about rationality that cannot be derived from any deeper truth about rationality. So, if it is necessary that all thinkers have at least some disposition to conform to the basic requirements of rationality that apply to them, it must also be necessary that all thinkers who judge anything of the form 'I ought to φ' have a disposition to conform to the requirement that is expressed by NJI. A thinker has this disposition if and only if she has some intrinsic feature in virtue of which, in any normal case in which she judges something of the form 'I ought to φ' (where φ-ing is something of the appropriate sort), she also has the corresponding intention to φ. I shall say that such agents have a "general disposition to intend to do whatever they judge that they ought to do". If an agent had absolutely no such disposition, it would not be correct to interpret any of her judgments as being of the form 'I ought to φ' at all.

So, given these suppositions, our first version of NJI (1) entails the following:

(2) Necessarily, if one judges anything of the form 'I ought to φ', then one also has a general disposition to intend to do whatever one judges that one ought to do.

This claim (2) is also quite compatible with the existence of cases in which people (such as drug addicts or people suffering from depression) judge something of the form 'I ought to φ' but do not intend to φ. One may still have a general disposition of this sort even if, in certain cases, the manifestation of this disposition is inhibited or blocked by some interfering factor (such as drug addiction or depression). The person suffering from depression may still have this general disposition: she has some intrinsic feature in virtue of which, in any *normal* case in which she judges something of the form 'I ought to φ', she has the corresponding intention to φ. But on account of her depression, the case that she is currently in is not a "normal" case in the relevant sense. So she could still have this general disposition, even if (say) she judges 'I ought to clean my home' but has absolutely no inclination to form an intention to clean her home.[19]

---

[18] It is hard to specify exactly which cases are "normal" (it may be that the context in which the disposition is ascribed makes a difference to which cases may truly be described as "normal"). Unfortunately, I cannot go into this issue here.

[19] In an "abnormal" case of this kind, it could be that this depressed agent has the *general* disposition to intend to do whatever she judges that she ought to do, and also judges 'I ought to clean my home', but does not have any *specific* disposition to intend to clean her home. In such abnormal cases, the general disposition does not entail the corresponding specific disposition.

1.4 OBJECTIONS TO NORMATIVE JUDGMENT INTERNALISM

There are some further objections to NJI that need to be considered. These objections all take the form of alleged counterexamples—that is, cases in which allegedly it might be quite rational for someone simultaneously to judge 'I ought to φ' and yet not have any intention to φ. To respond to these counterexamples, I shall have to be more explicit about the conditions under which φ-ing is, as I put it above, something "of the appropriate sort".

First, one might wonder about judgments that concern the fairly remote future. Suppose that in March 2006, I judge that I ought to file my tax return for the following year (2006–7) before the deadline of 30 September 2007. Would I really be being irrational if at the time of making this judgment, I do not yet have any intention to file next year's tax return before this deadline? After all, I still haven't filed *this* year's tax return! Does rationality really require me to form intentions about *next* year's taxes as well?

I think this objection may seem more impressive than it really is if one confuses simply *having* an intention with *taking some active steps* to execute that intention. It is relatively easy to have intentions about what to do in the remote future, since having the intention does not yet require taking any active steps. Having an intention only requires that the question of what to do on the relevant occasion is settled in one's mind. If one does not have the intention (to do something of the appropriate sort), then the question of what to do at that point has not yet been settled in one's mind; in that sense, one is still leaving it an open question what to do at that point. It seems to me that one *would* be being irrational in a way if one simultaneously judged that one ought to file next year's tax return on time while still leaving it an open question whether or not to file next year's tax return on time. So it seems to me that even where the judgment 'I ought to φ' concerns the relatively remote future, it would still be irrational for one simultaneously to make this judgment and yet not to have the intention to φ. Thus, this first objection to NJI does not seem persuasive to me.

The second objection that we need to consider can be illustrated by the following example. Surely I could judge that I ought not to kidnap and torture the US Vice President Dick Cheney. But suppose that I do make this judgment. Surely there need not be anything irrational about me if I just simply do not have any definite intention not to torture Cheney?[20]

I agree that in this case, it need not be irrational for me simply not to have any intention not to torture Cheney. But the reason for this, it seems to me,

---

[20] I owe this example to Joseph Raz, who put this objection to me especially clearly.

is that even if I did have this intention, it would hardly make any difference to my chances of not torturing Cheney. It is to all intents and purposes completely certain that I will not torture Cheney. (If I set out to torture him, my chances of success would be basically zero.) This is why there is nothing irrational about my lacking the intention not to torture him. Suppose that I rationally believe that there is a significant chance that I may end up torturing Cheney, and that my forming an intention not to do so would to some degree lessen the chance of my torturing him. (For example, suppose that I rationally believe that I have supernatural powers, and am at least slightly tempted to torture him.) Then it seems to me that it *would* be irrational for me to judge that I ought not to torture Cheney without simultaneously having the intention not to torture him.

Many other examples seem to illustrate the same point. For example, it need not be irrational to judge that one ought to continue breathing for the next five minutes without forming any intention to continue breathing for the next five minutes. The reason for this is that one will continue to breathe for the next five minutes whether or not one has any intention to do so. But under unusual circumstances, in which one rationally believes that there is a chance that one will not continue breathing for the next five minutes, and one's intending to continue breathing will raise the chances of one's continuing breathing, then it would be irrational simultaneously to judge that one ought to continue breathing and yet not to have any intention to continue breathing.

As I remarked in the previous section, NJI is only true of judgments of the form 'I ought to φ', where φ-ing is something "of the appropriate sort". The objection to NJI that we have just considered shows that *not torturing Dick Cheney* and *continuing to breathe for the next five minutes* are not of the appropriate sort. The obvious explanation for this is that for φ-ing to be of the appropriate sort, it must be the case that one knows that one's having the intention to φ will make a significant difference to the chances of one's actually φ-ing. Let us say that in fact, for φ-ing to be of the appropriate sort, something stronger must the case: one must know that one will φ if and only if one intends to. Let us say that in this case, φ-ing is a course of action that is "manifestly dependent on intention". So, if φ-ing is manifestly dependent on intention in this way, and you do not intend to φ, you will not φ. Moreover, it seems plausible that this would count as *willingly* failing to φ. This is why you are being *akratic*, and so irrational, if you judge that you ought to φ (where φ-ing is of the appropriate sort), but you do not have any intention to φ.

The third objection to NJI is the most challenging.[21] One is not always in a position to *know* what one ought to do: cases can arise in which one simply

---

[21] I am indebted to John Broome for forcing me to confront this objection. My failure to confront it was a serious flaw in some of my earlier work (Wedgwood 2004 and 2006a).

does not know what one ought to do. If we denied this, we would be committed to claiming that the truth about what one ought to do is somehow necessarily transparent or luminous; and such a strong transparency claim is surely highly implausible, to say the least.[22]

So consider a case in which one does know that one ought to do *either A* or *B*, but one doesn't know which. In some such cases, it might be that one also knows that if in fact it is *A* that one ought to do, then *B* will be utterly disastrous, whereas if in fact it is *B* that one ought to do, then *A* will be utterly disastrous. In some cases of this kind, it might be quite rational for one to form the intention to go for a second-best option, *C*, instead of either *A* or *B*—even though one knows that one ought really to do either *A* or *B*, and not *C*.

Some philosophers may be tempted to say that such cases are impossible. These philosophers will start by emphasizing the platitude that one's knowledge of one's circumstances is always itself part of the circumstances that affect what one ought to do. More specifically, then, these philosophers may suggest that the precise way in which one's knowledge of one's circumstances affects what one ought to do will always guarantee that in a case of this kind, if one does not know which of *A* or *B* will be better, and which of the two will be disastrous, then what one really ought to do is in fact *C*, rather than either *A* or *B*. But to insist that one's knowledge of one's circumstances *must always* have this consequence is precisely to insist that the truth about what one ought to do is necessarily transparent or luminous; and this transparency claim seems to me simply too implausible to serve as a basis for defending NJI.

To defend NJI, it is more plausible to put a further restriction on the concept that takes the place of 'φ' in the sort of normative judgment of the form 'I ought to φ' that NJI is concerned with—in other words, on what it is for the referent of this concept 'φ-ing' to be of the appropriate sort. In particular, we should require that the situation in which one might φ or not φ should be a situation *with no relevant uncertainty*. That is, it must be the case that for every course of action that one could possibly intend to pursue in that situation, one is not in any way uncertain or unsure about whether or not one ought to pursue that course of action. In the example that I have just given, the situation in which one either *does A or B* or does not *do A or B* is not a situation "with no relevant uncertainty", because there are some courses of action that one could possibly intend to pursue in this situation—such as *doing A*—such that one is uncertain about whether or not one ought to pursue that course of action. If we restrict NJI to normative judgments about situations "with no relevant uncertainty" of this kind, as well as to judgments about courses of action that are "manifestly dependent on intention", then NJI seems to be immune to objections of this third sort as well.

---

[22] For a general argument against any non-trivial luminosity claims of this sort, see Williamson (2000: ch. 4).

1.5 NORMATIVE JUDGMENTS AND MOTIVATION

With the two qualifications that we found to be necessary in the previous section (Section 1.4), the argument of Section 1.3 appears to have the resources to counter all the objections that we have considered. So (given the assumption that φ-ing is something of the appropriate sort) it is plausible that both of these versions of NJI are correct:

(1) Necessarily, if one is rational, then, if one judges 'I ought to φ', one also intends to φ.

(2) Necessarily, if one judges anything of the form 'I ought to φ', then one also has a general disposition to intend to do whatever one judges that one ought to do.

If either of these versions of NJI is correct, then this seems to show that normative judgments are judgments of a distinctly special kind. NJI is a strong claim, about all possible agents and all possible actions, a claim that would be completely devoid of plausibility with respect to most other sorts of judgments. For example, it does not seem that all instances of the following schema are true:

(3) Necessarily, if one is rational, then, if one judges 'My φ-ing would please the President of the College', one also intends to φ.

It does not seem *necessary* that all rational agents will intend to do whatever they judge to please the College President. The same point holds for countless other schemas similar to (3), concerning judgments about the causal effects of actions, or about their non-evaluative intrinsic features. But the only difference between (1) and (3) is the type of judgment involved. So, if all instances of the schema (1) are true, while most instances of (3) are not true, then this can only be explained by something special and distinctive about the judgments involved in (1)—that is, judgments of the form 'I ought to φ'. In this way, NJI imposes a constraint on any account of normative judgments of this sort. Any account of these judgments must explain why these judgments have this special feature that so few other judgments have.

In order to achieve a better understanding of this special feature that NJI ascribes to normative judgments, it may be helpful to investigate the implications of NJI for the theory of *motivation*.

What exactly is "motivation"? Suppose that a person A does something intentionally—for example, φ-ing. Then A's motivation for φ-ing consists of the set of A's mental states that motivated A to φ. To say that a set of mental states "motivated" A to φ is to say that one can give a certain sort of *correct explanation* of A's intentionally φ-ing, by saying that A intentionally φ-ed precisely *because* A was in those mental states. More specifically, if those mental states were A's motivation for φ-ing, then, given that A was in those mental states, it is entirely intelligible and unsurprising that A intentionally φ-ed.

We can also raise exactly the same sort of question about what "motivated" an intention. To say that a set of mental states "motivated" A's having a certain intention is to say that one can give this sort of correct explanation of A's having that intention, by saying that A has that intention precisely because A was in those mental states. Now it is plausible that whenever some antecedent mental states make it intelligible or unsurprising that an agent has a certain intention, this is because there is a suitably *intelligible disposition*, which the agent was manifesting in responding to those antecedent mental states by having that intention.

If the second version of NJI (2) is true, then anyone who makes normative judgments of the form 'I ought to φ' must have a general disposition to intend to do whatever she judges that she ought to do. Moreover, it seems that this disposition is also an eminently *intelligible* disposition to have. First, it is, we are assuming, a disposition that must be possessed by anyone who is capable of making judgments of the form 'I ought to φ' at all. Secondly, it is in a sense a *conditionally rational* disposition: so long as one's judgment of the form 'I ought to φ' is itself rational, then it is plausible that it will also be rational for one to manifest this disposition by having the corresponding intention to φ. Such conditionally rational dispositions are intelligible if any mental dispositions are. So this disposition seems to be in the relevant sense an intelligible disposition.

Suppose that you have this disposition, and that you come to make the judgment that you would express by saying something of the form 'I ought to φ'. Then it must also be possible for this judgment to activate this disposition, with the result that you have the intention to φ. If that happened, we could give a *correct explanation* of your having the intention to φ, by saying that you have this intention precisely because you judged that you ought to φ.[23] Obviously, we could also say more to explain why you made this judgment; but otherwise, this would be a perfectly adequate explanation of your having this intention. As I have argued, this disposition, to respond to such a judgment by having the corresponding intention, is an entirely intelligible disposition to have. So, given your normative judgment that you ought to φ, it is entirely intelligible and unsurprising that you have the intention to φ. That is, this judgment was your *motivation* for having the intention to φ.

Moreover, there is a clear sense in which this judgment is *sufficient all by itself* to constitute your motivation for your intention to φ. In explaining why you have this intention, we do not need to add anything over and above the fact that you made the judgment that you ought to φ. In particular, we do *not* have to add that you have this disposition, since according to (2), it is metaphysically impossible for anyone to make this judgment without also having

---

[23] Essentially the same account of how normative beliefs can explain action is given by Broome (1997: 141–2).

this disposition. In general, whenever we ascribe to someone a judgment of the form 'I ought to φ', we do not need to *add* that she has this disposition, since anyone who makes such judgments must also have this disposition. There is also no need to add that you have a general *desire* to do what you ought to do: such a general desire is either simply identical to this disposition (in which case its presence is already implied by the presence of the normative judgment in question) or else it is distinct from this disposition (in which case there is no need for any such desire to be present at all).

In that sense, then, the two versions of NJI that I have defended here, (1) and (2), together lead to the conclusion that a normative judgment, of the form 'I ought to φ', may, under normal conditions, be sufficient all by itself to motivate the agent to have the corresponding intention. I have not argued for the strong conclusion that there is any sort of judgment that *necessarily* motivates the agent to have the corresponding intention. On the contrary, it is always possible that some interfering factor (like depression or drug addiction) will intervene, with the result that the normative judgment does not trigger this disposition, and so does not motivate the corresponding intention. However, I have argued for the weaker conclusion that normative judgments of this sort are *capable* (under normal conditions) of motivating all by themselves. In the next chapter, I shall argue that these normative judgments are in fact just ordinary beliefs. So I am committed to the conclusion that there are some beliefs that are capable of being sufficient all by themselves to motivate the corresponding intention to act.

Some philosophers regard this conclusion as incredible: according to these philosophers, no belief by itself can ever be sufficient to motivate the agent to have the corresponding intention; in their view, such motivation is impossible except in the presence of a desire, and the presence of a desire can never be entailed by the presence of any belief.[24] Unfortunately, the arguments that these philosophers offer in favour of their view are in some respects rather obscure; so it would take too long for me to explain why these arguments seem mistaken to me. The purpose of this section has just been to emphasize how special normative judgments are. In addition to the features that are expressed by these two versions of NJI itself, (1) and (2), these judgments are capable of motivating the agent to have the corresponding intention. This clearly sets them apart from almost all other judgments that we are capable of making. The problem for an account of normative judgments is to explain *why* they have this special feature.

[24] For defences of such "Humean" theories of motivation, see especially Smith (1994: ch. 4) and Lewis (1988 and 1996*b*).

2

Expressivism

In this chapter and the next, I shall consider a number of familiar approaches to the task of explaining the meaning of normative statements—that is, of statements about what ought to be the case, or about what people ought to do or to think. (As I am using the term, a "statement" is just the speech act that is performed by the sincere utterance of a declarative sentence. So a "normative statement" is just the speech act, whatever exactly it may be, that is performed by the sincere utterance of a declarative sentence involving a normative term like 'ought'. As I explained in the previous chapter, I shall use the term 'judgment' to refer to the type of mental state that is expressed by a statement; so a "normative judgment" is just the type of mental state, whatever exactly it may be, that is expressed by a normative statement.)

In this chapter, I shall consider a certain well-known approach to the task of giving an account of the meaning of normative statements. This is the approach that is based on an *expressivist* account of normative statements—the approach whose most distinguished exponents in recent years have been Simon Blackburn and Allan Gibbard.[1] In this chapter, I shall argue against the expressivist approach, and in favour of the rival *truth-conditional* or *factualist* approach.

2.1 EXPRESSIVISM AND NON-COGNITIVISM

According to an expressivist account of normative statements, the fundamental explanation of the meaning of normative statements, and of the sentences that are used to make those statements, is given in terms of the type of *mental state* that the statements made by uttering those sentences *express*. That is, the fundamental explanation of the meaning of these statements and sentences is given by a *psychologistic semantics*.[2] According to a plausible version of the principle of *compositionality*, the meaning of a sentence is determined by the meaning of the terms that it is composed out of, together with the compositional structure of the sentence (perhaps together with certain features of the context in which that sentence is used). So assuming this version of the compositionality principle, this

---

[1] See especially Gibbard (1990 and 2003), and Blackburn (1993 and 1998).
[2] I borrow this term from Rosen (1998: 387).

expressivist approach will also give an account of the particular terms involved in these sentences in terms of the contribution that these terms make to determining what type of mental state is expressed by sentences involving them.

I shall suppose that all such expressivist accounts aim to conform to the non-circularity constraint that I outlined in the previous chapter (Section 1.2). Thus, according to these expressivist accounts, the fundamental explanation of the meaning of normative statements, such as statements of the form 'I ought to φ', must not identify the mental state that is expressed by this statement simply as *the belief that one ought to φ* (or the feeling or the sentiment that one ought to φ), or anything of that sort. This mental state must be identified without using any normative terms like 'ought' within the scope of propositional attitude ascriptions of any kind. Otherwise, we would be presupposing what we are seeking to give an account of—namely, what it is for a thinker to have such normative attitudes.

In fact, many expressivist accounts conform to a yet stronger constraint: they seek to give their fundamental explanation of the meaning of normative statements *in wholly non-normative terms*. So they not only avoid using normative terms in any way that would effectively amount to presupposing what it is for a statement to be a normative statement, or what it is for a judgment to be a normative judgment: they insist on banishing all normative terms from the metalanguage altogether. The main reason for this is that the proponents of expressivist semantics usually aspire to give an account of normative statements that is wholly compatible with a strong form of *naturalism*, according to which all of our thought and discourse can ultimately be satisfactorily explained purely in the terms that are characteristic of natural science.[3]

The main rival to the expressivist approach is a broadly *truth-conditional* or *factualist* approach. According to the truth-conditional or factualist approach, the fundamental explanation of the meaning of the term in question must essentially involve the idea that if a declarative sentence involving the term has any content at all in a given context, then that content involves[4] a *proposition*, where it is an essential feature of any proposition that it is *truth-apt*—that is, apt to be either *true* or *false*. In this way, then, this proposition gives the *truth conditions* of the sentence in the context in question: the sentence is true in that context if, and only if, the corresponding proposition is true.[5] It is often assumed that there is a close link—perhaps identity, or at least one-to-one

---

[3] The importance of these two constraints for expressivists is rightly stressed by Rosen (1998: 388).

[4] I say that according to the truth-conditional or factualist approach, the content of the sentence "involves" a proposition to allow for accounts according to which the content of the sentence also involves *other* elements —such as a Fregean Thought (if that is not to be identified with the proposition itself), or the aspects of meaning that Dummett (1981: 1–7, and 1993b: 38–41) called "tone" and "force".

[5] I do not mean to imply that the truth-conditional approach must deny the possibility of "truth value gaps"—that is, propositions that are neither true nor false. It may be possible for a

correspondence—between *true propositions* and *facts*; this is why I shall also describe the truth-conditional approach to the semantics of normative terms as a "factualist" approach.

In saying that the expressivist approach is a "rival" of the truth-conditional approach, I do not mean to say that expressivists must *deny* that the content of any of the sentences involving the term in question involves a proposition that is apt to be true or false. The point is just that according to the expressivist, the *fundamental* explanation of the term's meaning need say nothing about such propositions' being involved in the contents of the sentences in which this term appears: instead, this fundamental account should be given in strictly psychologistic terms, without mentioning these sentences' having truth conditions or propositions as part of their content.

Typically, expressivism has tended to go along with a *non-cognitivist* account of the normative judgments that are expressed by normative statements: until recently, all non-cognitivists have been expressivists, and all expressivists have been non-cognitivists. Nonetheless, these two views should in principle be distinguished. *Non-cognitivism* is a view about the nature of normative judgments. Specifically, it is the view that these normative judgments are not "cognitive" mental states, like ordinary beliefs (of the sort that under favourable conditions could constitute knowledge), but "non-cognitive" mental states of some kind, like desires, preferences, emotions, intentions, or the like.

The reason why the two views tend to go together seems to be this. First, suppose that expressivism is false. Then, it is widely assumed, the correct explanation of the meaning of normative statements will be some sort of truth-conditional or factualist account. In that case, the sentence that is used to make any normative statement has a proposition as at least part of its content; and reference to this proposition can play a significant role in an explanatory account of the nature of normative discourse. But then it is hard to see what could make it impossible for this propositional content to be the object of the full range of propositional attitudes—including not only the non-cognitive attitudes (like intention, hope, desire, and the various types of emotion), but also the cognitive attitudes (such as the type of attitude that is involved in ordinary beliefs). If it is possible to have such a cognitive attitude towards such a propositional content, then it is also hard to see why it should be impossible to express that attitude by means of making the corresponding normative statement.

Admittedly, this truth-conditional or factualist account does not imply that the mental state that is *actually normally* expressed by normative statements is a cognitive state.[6] But it does at least make it plausible that the burden of proof

---

proposition to be "apt" to have a truth value (that is, the proposition might have truth conditions), even if in some circumstances it lacks any definite truth value.

[6] Recently, Mark Kalderon (2005*a*) has investigated the possibilities of a *fictionalist* approach, according to which normative sentences do indeed have essentially truth-apt propositions as

should be on someone who claims that the mental state normally expressed by the sincere utterance of a declarative sentence is something other than belief in the propositional content of that sentence. Moreover, I shall show later on in the book that some of the best-known arguments for non-cognitivism (that is, for the view that normative judgments cannot be cognitive states) are unsound. So if, as I shall argue in this chapter, expressivism is false, and as I shall argue later in this book, there are no sound arguments for thinking that these normative judgments are anything other than ordinary beliefs, we have good reasons for concluding that non-cognitivism is false as well.

Conversely, suppose that cognitivism is true. Then there is no sense in which normative judgments are any less "cognitive" than ordinary beliefs. There are strong reasons for thinking that such ordinary beliefs or cognitive states have propositions as at least part of their contents, where reference to such propositional contents is capable of playing a genuinely explanatory role in accounting for various features of the beliefs in question. But if the contents of normative judgments involve such propositions, it will surely seem irresistible to explain the meaning of normative statements at least partly in terms of these propositions. Thus, if non-cognitivism is false, it seems overwhelmingly plausible that expressivism will also be false.[7] For these reasons then, it is reasonable to assume that expressivism and non-cognitivism stand or fall together. For the rest of this chapter, however, my arguments will focus entirely on expressivism, not non-cognitivism.

At the beginning of this chapter, I said that the most distinguished recent exponents of expressivism—the view that I am planning to attack here—are Simon Blackburn and Allan Gibbard. But any attribution of views to Blackburn and Gibbard has to proceed carefully, on the grounds that both of these philosophers have recently adopted a "quasi-realist" program, seeking to show that they can accept practically all of the theses that were formerly thought to be definitive of "moral realism". In the remainder of this section, I shall briefly defend my claim that the sort of expressivism propounded by Blackburn and Gibbard is indeed a rival of the truth-conditional or factualist approach that I have characterized here.

These philosophers' quasi-realist program has two main elements. First, there is an element that has largely been developed by Blackburn, which involves arguing that expressivists need not deny such things as that normative statements can be *true* or *false*, or that normative terms stand for normative *properties*, or that

---

their contents, but the sincere acceptance of such a sentence does not normally consist in our *believing* the content of that sentence, but rather in having some *non-cognitive* attitude instead. In this way, Kalderon aims to exploit the fact that a factualist semantics for normative statements is at least logically consistent with non-cognitivism about the nature of normative judgments.

[7] However, see Horgan and Timmons (2000*a*) for a cognitivist form of expressivism (or as they prefer to call it, "nondescriptivism").

true normative statements correspond to normative *facts*, or that ordinary people *believe* many normative *propositions*. The principal way in which Blackburn seeks to argue for this is by insisting on a relatively *minimalist* interpretation of such notions as 'truth', 'properties', 'facts', 'belief', and 'propositions'.[8] For example, according to this minimalist interpretation, to claim that it is "true" that genocide is wrong is just to claim that genocide is wrong—or at least it follows immediately from the very definition of 'true' that these two claims are equivalent. Similarly, to say that genocide has the "property" of being wrong is also just to say that genocide is wrong; to say that there is such a fact as the fact that genocide is wrong is, once again, just to say that genocide is wrong. The claim 'There is such a proposition as the proposition that genocide is wrong' is guaranteed to be true by the mere fact that the embedded sentence 'genocide is wrong' is a complete meaningful sentence; and the claim, made about a thinker *S*, '*S* believes that genocide is wrong' is true if and only if *S* has an attitude of the very same kind that one would normally express by making a sincere statement of the form 'Genocide is wrong'.

Even though Blackburn makes all of these claims, however, he still holds that the notions of normative propositions, normative facts or truths, and normative properties play no real *explanatory role* within the fundamental account of the meaning of normative statements. The fundamental account is still purely psychologistic: that is, it is couched entirely in terms of the special mental states ("normative judgments" or "normative attitudes") that those statements express. Moreover, these notions of normative propositions, facts, and properties also play no real explanatory role within the expressivist's account of the nature of these special mental states: that account is given in other terms (for example, most contemporary expressivists choose to account for the nature of these mental states in broadly functionalist terms). So Blackburn's minimalist quasi-realism does not prevent him from being an expressivist, or from rejecting the rival truth-conditional approach.

The second element in these philosophers' quasi-realist program has mainly been developed by Allan Gibbard. This is Gibbard's "natural constitution claim". There is a separate version of this claim involving each normative concept. For example, consider the concept that Gibbard expresses by means of the phrase 'the thing to do' (which in many contexts will be equivalent to such phrases as 'the right thing to do' or 'the thing that one ought to do'). The version of

[8] See especially Blackburn (1998: 317–19 and 1993: 3–6). As is well known, a minimalist theory of truth needs to be very carefully stated to avoid the Liar Paradox; see e.g. Halbach (2001). In fact, the same is true of minimalist theories of properties: we have to avoid being committed to the existence of the property of *being a property that does not instantiate itself*, and to the general claim that something instantiates the property of being F if and only if it is F—since taken together, these two commitments entail that this property of *being a property that does not instantiate itself* instantiates itself if and only if it does not instantiate itself. On this point, see Bealer (1982: ch. 4, esp. § 26).

this "natural constitution claim" involving this concept would be the claim that there is some natural property N such that, necessarily, something is the thing to do just in case it has property N. As Gibbard argues, this claim follows, at least in the most widely accepted modal logic,[9] from two plausible assumptions: (i) the assumption that the normative *strongly supervenes* on the natural—that is, necessarily, if something is "the thing to do", then it is impossible for there to be anything that is exactly like that first thing in all natural respects without also being exactly like that first thing in normative respects as well (and so itself being "the thing to do" as well); (ii) a relaxed conception of properties according to which there is a huge plethora of properties, with at least one property for every way of mapping each possible world w onto a subset of the entities that exist at w.[10] If, as Gibbard argues, every competent user of normative terms is committed to these two assumptions, then every competent user of these terms is also committed to accepting the "natural constitution claim", and in that sense accepting that there is a naturalistic property that the normative term "signifies".

In this way, it seems to be a crucial part of Gibbard's account that the fundamental explanation of the meaning of normative statements *quantifies* over naturalistic properties, and includes the thesis that every competent speaker is committed to the "natural constitution claim" that *there is* a natural property such that something is "the thing to do" if and only if it has that property. However, it still seems that this fundamental explanation does not actually need to *refer* to any *particular* property as the property that the normative term signifies. In that sense Gibbard's semantics is not really a referential semantics for these normative terms. Every competent speaker is committed to claiming that the term 'the thing to do' "signifies" a particular natural property N, but as Gibbard (2003: 115–16) puts it, such claims "are not purely matters of linguistic fact, or of linguistic and psychological fact combined". In other words, Gibbard does not accept that there is any particular property determined purely by the *meaning* of the relevant normative term (such as 'ought' or 'the thing to do') as the property that that term stands for.

Thus, according to Gibbard, the meaning of the normative term can be explained without referring to any particular property as the property that the term signifies. In this sense, then, Gibbard's semantics remains crucially different from a truth-conditional semantics, according to which the fundamental explanation of the meaning of normative statements must refer to a particular property or relation in giving the truth conditions for these normative statements. His account must still be distinguished from a truth-conditional account.

---

[9] The claim does not in fact follow from these assumptions in any alethic normal modal logic weaker than S5. I explore the significance of this point in Chapter 9 of the book.

[10] See especially Gibbard (2002, and 2003: ch. 5).

2.2 THE ARGUMENTS FOR EXPRESSIVISM

Most of this chapter will be devoted to developing an argument against expressivist theories and in favour of the rival factualist or truth-conditional approach. But before developing that argument, I shall briefly consider the various arguments that have been offered in favour of expressivism.

Some philosophers argue for expressivism simply on the basis of the failure of other attempts to explain the meaning of normative terms.[11] In Chapter 4, I shall try to outline a new account of the semantics of normative terms. If, as I believe, this new account is a successful alternative to expressivism, then obviously this argument for expressivism fails.

Another and better-known argument for expressivism starts out in the first instance by arguing for non-cognitivism, on the grounds that non-cognitivism is the best explanation of the thesis of normative judgment internalism (NJI), which we considered in the previous chapter (Section 1.3). Then these philosophers go on to argue from non-cognitivism to expressivism along the lines that I sketched in the previous section. I shall show that these arguments fail in Chapter 4, by giving a cognitivist interpretation of normative judgments that will provide a satisfactory explanation of NJI.

A slightly different version of this argument starts out from a strong assumption to the effect that beliefs cannot have any essential connection to motivation (this assumption is sometimes referred to as the "Humean Theory of Motivation"), and then argues on the basis of this assumption about belief that NJI actually *entails* non-cognitivism.[12] I shall not pause to analyse this argument in detail (in fact, every version of this argument that I have encountered seems to assume a subtly but importantly different version of the "Humean Theory of Motivation"); but I take it that the fact that my account in Chapter 4 has no difficulty in explaining how some beliefs can be essentially connected to motivation will undermine the strong assumption, on which this argument is based, that no belief can be essentially connected to motivation in this way.

A third sort of argument that is sometimes offered in support of expressivism starts from the allegedly weird and unacceptable metaphysical and epistemological consequences of a truth-conditional semantics for normative statements.[13] It is supposed that these allegedly weird metaphysical and epistemological consequences can all be avoided if expressivism is correct. Indeed, it is often supposed that because expressivism does not accept that there are any "normative facts" or "normative properties" or "normative relations" in any non-minimal sense, there

---

[11] This is the argument that is stressed by Allan Gibbard (1990: ch. 1).

[12] This argument is in effect one way of taking what Michael Smith (1994) calls the "moral problem".

[13] This theme is prominent in Blackburn (1998: ch. 4).

cannot be any difficult metaphysical issue for the expressivist to confront about the nature of these facts, properties, or relations, and what place if any they have in the world. Equally, it is often also supposed that there are significant epistemological problems in explaining how we could ever know such normative facts, which do not arise if expressivism is true.

However, it is not at all clear to me that expressivism does have such pronounced advantages over the truth-conditional approach in this respect. The reason for this is just that it appears, at least *prima facie*, that the metaphysical and epistemological issues can all be raised without explicitly using any non-minimal sense of ontological terms like 'fact', 'property', or 'relation', or of semantical terms like 'truth' or 'proposition'. Indeed it seems that such terms are only used in metaphysical and epistemological questions in order to achieve generality. It is quite clear that we can ask the epistemological questions just by using normative terms, in the material mode, along with certain epistemological terms like 'knowledge' and 'justified belief'. Thus, for example, we can ask: 'How can we ever know that something is wrong, or that something ought to be the case?' Similarly, we can ask the metaphysical questions just by using the normative terms together with certain distinctively metaphysical terms such as 'essence', 'necessity', 'causation', and so on. So, for example, we can ask such questions as the following: 'What is *essentially involved* in something's being wrong?', 'If *x* is wrong, is it *metaphysically impossible* for there to be anything exactly like *x* in all non-moral respects that is not also wrong?', 'Does anything ever happen *because* something is wrong?', and so on. Indeed, recent expressivists have not dismissed these questions, but have explicitly grappled with them.[14]

At all events, I do not need to investigate what the metaphysical and epistemological consequences of expressivism would be. Any arguments for expressivism that are based on the allegedly unacceptable metaphysical or epistemological consequences of the rival truth-conditional approach will be answered in Parts II and III of this book, where I develop a plausible account of the metaphysics and epistemology of normative discourse based on the truth-conditional semantics that I defend in Part I. This, then, is how I propose to respond to the arguments that have been offered in favour of expressivism.

2.3 GEACH'S FREGEAN PROBLEM

In arguing against expressivism, I will build on the objections that other philosophers have made against expressivism. One of the main objections that I will build on here is the broadly Fregean argument that P. T. Geach used against an earlier generation of expressivists.

---

[14] e.g., on supervenience see Blackburn (1993: essay 7) and Gibbard (2003: ch. 5); and on whether ethical facts can be causes, see Blackburn (1993: essay 11) and Gibbard (2003: ch. 10).

A memorable statement of the views of these earlier expressivists was given by A. J. Ayer (1946: ch. 6). Ethical concepts, in Ayer's view, "are mere pseudo-concepts". The role of ethical symbols in language is not to add anything to the "factual content" of statements in which they appear, but simply to show that the utterance of the sentence "is attended by certain feelings in the speaker" (1946: 107). The function of an ethical word is purely "emotive". "It is used to express feeling about certain objects, but not to make any assertion about them" (108). 'Stealing is wrong' simply expresses a feeling of moral disapproval towards stealing; it does not offer a description of stealing, or ascribe any property to it. This is why normative statements lack truth conditions, and cannot be described as true or false.

This relatively crude form of expressivism was decisively refuted by Geach (1972: 250–69), in an argument that was inspired by a famous point that Frege (1977: 45–8) made about negation. Some normative statements are effected by the utterance of sentences in which normative terms have largest scope; and it may be plausible to regard these statements as expressions of emotion or some other non-cognitive attitude. But sentences containing normative terms can also be *embedded* within the scope of sentential operators of all kinds.

For example, sentences containing normative terms like 'ought' and 'wrong' occur in the antecedents of conditionals, or as disjuncts in disjunctions, or as the objects of propositional attitude ascriptions. Normative terms also occur in non-declarative sentences, the utterance of which does not count as a statement but as a speech act of some other kind, such as a question. In many of these contexts, these occurrences of normative terms simply cannot be seen as expressing the speaker's feelings in the way that Ayer describes. If I say 'Rape is wrong', I may well be expressing moral disapproval of rape. But if I say 'Helen believes that abortion is wrong', or 'If gambling is wrong, then encouraging people to gamble is also wrong', or if I ask 'Is the death penalty really always wrong?', I am not expressing moral disapproval of abortion or gambling or the death penalty. Yet the word 'wrong' is plainly used in the same sense throughout. It would be unbearably *ad hoc* to claim that normative terms are systematically ambiguous, depending on whether or not they have largest scope in the sentences in which they occur. So Ayer's account of the meaning of normative terms is unacceptable as it stands. An adequate account of the meaning of normative terms must explain how they can figure, without a shift of meaning, both in statements in which they have largest scope, and embedded in subsentences of complex utterances in which they do not have largest scope.

Moreover, it seems to me, we should not only require that normative terms can occur, without a shift of meaning, both in embedded contexts and elsewhere; we should also require a uniform interpretation of the sentential operators within whose scope they are embedded. It would seem to me even more intolerably *ad hoc* to claim that the logical operators are systematically ambiguous, depending on whether or not the sentences embedded within their scope contain normative language. 'If' may be tricky, but surely it isn't quite as tricky as that! To adapt a point of Elizabeth Anscombe's (1963: 58), if we are willing to tolerate a special "normative conditional", then why not tolerate a special "mince pie conditional" (whose meaning has to be explained by appealing to special facts about sentences concerning mince pies)? We should respect the intuition that, in the statement 'If gambling is wrong, encouraging others to gamble is also wrong', 'if' is used in a perfectly ordinary sense.

Since they can be embedded within the logical operators, normative terms can also occur in logical inferences of all the customary kinds. An account of the meaning of a logical operator must supply an account of the validity of the customary forms of inference in which it appears; so if we insist on a uniform account of the meaning of 'if', we must also insist on a uniform account of the validity of all these forms of inference. In the case of 'if', the central example is *modus ponens*. Take any inference of the form: 'If A then B; but A: hence B.' This inference is valid in exactly the same way regardless of whether or not 'A' or 'B' contains normative language. Expressivists must not only explain how normative terms can occur, without shifts of meaning, both in embedded contexts and elsewhere; they must also explain how the meaning of normative terms and of the logical operators allows all the customary forms of inference to be valid, in exactly the same way as they usually are, regardless of whether or not they contain normative language.[15]

This is a strong requirement to impose. But we should not assume straight off that it can only be met by adopting a truth-conditional semantics for normative statements. Indeed, it seems to me that the problem, at least in the form in which it has been stated so far, is adequately solved by Gibbard's recent version of expressivist semantics.

2.4 GIBBARD'S SOLUTION TO GEACH'S FREGEAN PROBLEM

Ayer maintained that the meaning of a normative statement consisted in the type of emotion that it expressed. In an essentially similar way, Gibbard maintains that the meaning of a normative statement consists in its expressing a special type of mental state that he calls a "normative judgment". Ayer did not offer any analysis of emotions. By contrast, Gibbard offers an elaborate account of

---

[15] Oddly enough, many philosophers who have written about Geach's Fregean problem seem open to the postulation of a special "normative conditional", and of special forms of inference involving this special conditional. Dummett's (1981: 327–54) attempt to solve the problem is of this kind, as is Simon Blackburn's first (1984: 189–95) attempt at the problem. Some acute critics of Blackburn, such as Bob Hale (1993), are willing to consider such attempts in great detail. My complaint about these attempts to circumvent Geach's problem is essentially the same as Susan Hurley's (1989: 180–5) objections to Dummett and Blackburn.

the nature of normative judgments—an account that is explicitly designed to provide a solution to Geach's Fregean problem.

In his earlier work, Gibbard offered a broadly *functionalist* account of normative judgments.[16] In his most recent work (2003: ch. 3), he does not reject this sort of functionalism, but he no longer explicitly relies on it. Instead, his idea is to give an account of the nature of normative judgments by using two basic psychological notions. The first is the idea of having a *plan*, where this plan may be a *contingency plan*—a plan about what to do in some circumstance when one regards it as possible but not certain that one will at some time be in that circumstance—or even a purely *hypothetical plan*—that is, a plan about what to do in a circumstance that one knows full well one will never be in. Thus, according to Gibbard (2003: 53), I could have a hypothetical plan about what to do in the circumstance of being Julius Caesar on the brink of the Rubicon in 49 BC. The second psychological notion that he relies on is the notion of the mental state of *disagreeing with* (or as he also puts it, *rejecting* or *ruling out*) an action or a mental state.

According to Gibbard, the content of a normative judgment is determined by the actions and other mental states that it disagrees with—and especially by the *plans* and *attitudes of disagreement* that it disagrees with. The type of normative judgment that Gibbard analyses in most detail consists of judgments about what courses of action are, and which courses of action are not, "the thing to do". According to his analysis, what is essential to the judgment that in circumstances C_1, φ-ing is the thing to do is that this judgment consists in an attitude of *disagreeing* with any course of action that involves not φ-ing in circumstances C_1. Now, the judgment that φ-ing is "the thing to do" in certain circumstances could also be expressed by the statement that φ-ing is "*required*" in those circumstances. In this way, this judgment contrasts with the judgment that φ-ing is *permissible* (but perhaps not required) in certain circumstances. According to Gibbard, what is essential to the judgment that it is permissible to φ in certain circumstances C_2 is that this judgment consists in an attitude of *disagreeing with the attitude of disagreeing with* (as Gibbard puts it, an attitude of "permitting") the action of φ-ing in circumstances C_2.

In order to state this view more precisely, Gibbard introduces the idea of a *hyperdecided* overall mental state (a "hyperstate", as I shall call it for short).[17] Such a hyperstate would include the following two elements. First, it would include a complete consistent set of *beliefs* about ordinary factual matters. Secondly, it would include a *hyperplan*—roughly, a complete and consistent plan about what to do and what to think for every conceivable circumstance.

To make the notion of a hyperplan more precise, we will first need to identify a certain category of mental states. According to Gibbard (1990: 57 and 72–6),

---

[16] For this earlier account, see Gibbard (1990: 101–2, and 1992).
[17] I am grateful to Gibbard for helping me to understand his views.

this category of mental states consists of those states that are susceptible to "normative governance"—that is, the states that one can have as a direct result of planning to have those states. According to Gibbard, these mental states include beliefs and plans; they also include the attitude of *disagreeing with* a course of action, and, for every mental state that they include, they include the attitude of disagreeing with (or rejecting or ruling out) that mental state.

We can now explain the sense in which these hyperplans must be *complete*: every one of these hyperplans must contain, for every possible circumstance, a plan to do one of the alternative actions that are available in that circumstance, and for every mental state in the relevant category that is available in that circumstance, either a plan to have or a plan not to have that mental state. Moreover, for every possible circumstance, and every course of action and every mental state in the relevant category, the hyperplan must include a plan either to have the attitude of *disagreeing with* that course of action or that mental state in that circumstance, or else to have the attitude of *permitting* (that is, *disagreeing with disagreeing with*) that course of action or mental state in that circumstance.

We can also explain the sense in which this hyperstate must be *consistent*: first, all the beliefs that it contains must be logically consistent with each other; secondly, for every possible circumstance, it must be logically possible to realize everything that the hyperplan prescribes for that circumstance; and thirdly, if the hyperstate contains a given mental state, or a plan to have a given mental state or to do a given action in a given circumstance, it will never also contain a plan to *disagree with* having that mental state or doing that action in that circumstance.

Now we can continue to identify an atomic *normative* judgment either with an attitude of disagreeing with an action or mental state, or with an attitude of permitting (that is, disagreeing with disagreeing with) an action or mental state, in the way that I explained above. We can say that an atomic normative judgment disagrees with a hyperstate if and only if the hyperstate contains a plan to disagree with this attitude. If a judgment does not disagree with a hyperstate, we can say that the judgment "allows" that hyperstate. For example, consider the judgment that the thing to do now is to turn to the Left. We can identify this judgment with the attitude of disagreeing with the action of *not* turning Left. So this judgment allows all and only those hyperstates that do *not* include a plan to permit (that is, disagree with disagreeing with) the action of not turning Left.

We can now explain the content of logically complex judgments in the following way. Let us interpret the disjuncts of a disjunctive judgment as themselves judgments—namely, the judgments that one would be expressing by uttering the disjuncts of the disjunctive sentence that can be used to express the disjunctive judgment in question; and similarly for the other logical operators. Then we can say that a disjunctive judgment allows a hyperstate if and only if at least one of its disjuncts allows that hyperstate; a negation allows a hyperstate if and only if the judgment of which it is the negation does not allow that hyperstate; and so on.

Moreover, we can also give a quite straightforward account of the notions of logical consequence and logical consistency: a conclusion logically follows from a set of premises if and only if every hyperstate that is allowed by all the premises of the inference is also allowed by the conclusion of the inference; and a set of judgments is logically inconsistent if and only if there is no hyperstate that is allowed by all members of that set.

The crucial feature of this account is that it offers an absolutely *uniform* account of the logical operators, and of the validity of the customary forms of inference—an account that applies both to cases in which the premises of the inference are normative judgments and to cases in which they are ordinary factual judgments. In the case of purely factual non-normative judgments, the only relevant part of the hyperstate is the set of beliefs; since this set of beliefs is complete, it in effect mimics a possible world. So in the case of purely factual non-normative judgments, Gibbard's semantics coincides with a familiar sort of possible-worlds semantics. It is only when normative statements are involved that we need take account of the fact that these hyperstates involve plans as well as beliefs.

In this way, then, Gibbard appears to have produced interlocking accounts of the meaning of normative statements and of the logical operators, and of the validity of the customary rules of inference, that meet all the constraints that we have at least so far seen to be imposed by Geach's Fregean puzzle.

2.5 A FURTHER CONSTRAINT ON ACCOUNTS OF NORMATIVE STATEMENTS

There is a further element of the meaning of normative statements that we have not yet discussed. As Crispin Wright (1992: 74) would put it, normative discourse is a thoroughly *disciplined* discourse: in making normative statements, speakers aim to comply with, and are assessed or evaluated according to, certain standards of justification or warrantedness.

As Dummett (1993*b*: 57 and 72–6) has emphasized, an utterance may be assessed or criticized in many ways—for example, as impolite, as in poor taste, or as a breach of confidence. What will be especially relevant for our purposes are the special sorts of criticism that apply to statements precisely *because* they are statements, and not because these statements belong to some wider category of communicative action, or because they are statements of some special kind. Thus, for example, even though statements may be criticized when they are impolite, this is not especially because they are statements. All communicative actions (including questions, requests, and gestures, as well as statements) may be criticized if they are impolite. So even though statements may be criticized when they are impolite, this is not because they are statements, but because they belong to the wider category of communicative actions. On the other hand, some statements are made in special institutional contexts in which they are open to rather special criticisms. For example, when testifying in court, a statement that is made on the basis of hearsay may be criticized, whereas outside this special institutional context, there may be no objection at all to making statements on the basis of reliable hearsay evidence. Thus, the reason why courtroom testimony based on hearsay may be criticized is not simply that such testimony consists of statements, but rather that it consists of statements of this special kind.

What we are concerned with here is the special kind of assessment or evaluation that applies to statements precisely *because* they are statements. One striking feature of this special kind of assessment is that whenever a statement is open to an assessment of this kind, a precisely analogous assessment also applies to the inner mental event of judgment, which the statement expresses—that is, the judgment that the speaker could self-ascribe by using the very same sentence that he used to make the statement in question, embedded inside a phrase like 'I judge that ... '. If according to this special kind of assessment it is unwarranted or unjustified for one to make a certain statement, then in some closely analogous way it is also unwarranted or unjustified for one to make the judgment that that statement expresses. Similarly, if a statement is justified or warranted, then in a closely analogous way the judgment that that statement expresses is also justified or warranted.

Another distinctive feature of this special kind of assessment that statements are subject to is the connection between this sort of assessment and *logic*. Of course, logic is relevant to other sorts of speech acts as well. For example, one can certainly criticize someone if he issues a set of commands that are jointly inconsistent, just as one can criticize someone if he makes an inconsistent set of statements. But the relationship between logic and statements is nonetheless importantly different from the relationship between logic and commands. Part of the difference is that while it is a fundamental criticism of a set of commands that they are mutually inconsistent, there are plenty of situations in which there is some proposition p such that one would be justified in commanding p, and one would also be justified in commanding *not-p*. In such situations, one cannot sensibly make both commands, but one would be equally justified in making either. It seems that this situation can never arise with statements. If one is justified or warranted in stating p, then one is not justified or warranted in stating *not-p*, and vice versa.[18]

Moreover, there is a further connection between the status of statements as justified or warranted and *logically valid arguments*. If a given statement is justified or warranted, and one competently infers a further statement from the

---

[18] James Lenman (2003) argues that, given that inconsistency is clearly a serious failing in any set of commands, it should be possible to develop a logic for commands, which could then be used as the logic of normative statements. I believe that this approach is vitiated by the profound differences, which I have highlighted here, between the sorts of "discipline" that commands and statements are subject to.

first statement by means of a logically valid argument, and the first statement remains justified or warranted even after one has inferred that further statement, then the further statement is also justified or warranted as well. A further connection between logically valid arguments and the standards of assessment, evaluation, and criticism that apply to statements emerges with respect to *suppositional reasoning*. In addition to straightforwardly *making* a statement, one can use the sentence that would be involved in making the statement to express a *supposition*—where to "suppose" that *p* is true is not straightforwardly to state *p*, but simply to hypothesize *p* for the sake of argument. Now one can infer a conclusion, not just from a sentence that one is using to make a statement, but also from a sentence that one is using merely to express a supposition—where to "infer" this conclusion means, roughly, that one accepts this conclusion *conditionally*, given the supposition that is expressed by the first sentence. Whenever one competently infers a conclusion from a supposition by means of a logically valid argument, then one is warranted or justified in inferring that conclusion from that supposition—that is, one is justified in accepting the conclusion conditionally, given the supposition in question.[19]

Finally, we should note that the conditions under which statements and inferences count as warranted or justified seem to supervene on the *meaning* of the statements or sentences involved. If there are two statements or inferences that do not differ at all with respect to the meaning of the statements or sentences involved, then it seems that they also cannot differ with respect to the conditions under which they count as warranted or justified in the relevant sense.

All of these points should be accepted by expressivists as applying to normative statements, just as much as to paradigmatically factual assertions. The standards or conditions of justification or warrantedness that apply to normative statements supervene on the meaning of the statements involved; they are intimately connected, in the ways that we have examined, with the notions of logical consistency and validity, which the expressivists also regard as notions that the fundamental account of the meaning of normative statements must explain; and the standards or conditions of justification or warrantedness that apply to a normative statement are precisely analogous to those that apply to the corresponding normative judgment, which is what the expressivist appeals to in order to explain the meaning of the normative statement. Taken together, all these points make the following conclusion highly plausible: the fundamental

---

[19] This formulation of this connection between logically valid arguments and the standards of warrantedness and justification that apply to statements involves the notion of inferring *competently*. I cannot give a full discussion here of what such competence involves. But here is a quick suggestion. Suppose that one has a *disposition* in virtue of which one tends to respond to one's considering a logically valid inference by making that inference. (Of course, one's disposition will be imperfect: one will be liable to fail to respond to some of the logically valid inferences that one considers; but this does not prevent one from having a disposition of this sort.) Then, if one manifests this disposition by making a valid inference, this manifestation of the disposition will count as a case of "inferring competently" in the relevant sense.

explanation of the meaning of a normative statement must provide some account of these conditions or standards of justification and warrantedness.

Many expressivists seem quite happy to embrace this conclusion. In particular, Gibbard spent a large part of his earlier (1990) book characterizing the standards of justification and warrantedness to which normative judgments are subject. According to Gibbard, these standards consist chiefly in the consistency of one's normative judgments both among themselves, and with one's higher-order norms (or "epistemic stories") about the best way to go about forming such normative judgments (1990: 193). He also argues that one must accord a certain "fundamental authority" to the normative statements of other speakers (180), especially of other speakers in one's own community (203): we must try to avoid paying the "price" of regarding others as bad judges and excluding them from discussion (197). In effect, in Gibbard's view, warranted normative judgments arise from a process of striving for ever greater consistency, both among one's own judgments, and within the community at large.

However, it is not clear that it is enough for an account of the meaning of normative statements simply to *enumerate* the standards of justification and warrantedness that these statements are subject to. Consider an agent who is agonizing about a normative question. For example, suppose that she is agonizing over the question of whether she ought to inform the police about a friend's criminal activities. In agonizing about the question, she is striving to reach an answer to this question that is justified and warranted. But why should she bother agonizing about this? What is the point of going to so much trouble? What would be so bad about reaching an answer to the question that is not justified or warranted?

Suppose that Gibbard's account of these standards of justification and warrantedness is basically correct. Why should the agent strive so hard to achieve the sort of intrapersonal and interpersonal consistency that is such a crucial element of meeting these standards of justification and warrantedness? It surely cannot just be that we simply have a bizarre *fetish* for logical consistency, thinking that it makes for a *prettier overall pattern* in our statements or mental states than inconsistency does.

Several philosophers, including both Simon Blackburn (1992: 951) and Walter Sinnott-Armstrong (1993: 301–2), have inquired how exactly Gibbard can explain what is *bad* about making an inconsistent set of judgments according to his theory.[20] Gibbard's most recent response to this inquiry is as follows (2003: 59):

A set of judgments is *consistent* if there is a hyperstate that every judgment in that set allows. It is *inconsistent* otherwise: it is inconsistent if every possible hyperstate is ruled out by one or another of the judgments in the set. If, then, my judgments are inconsistent,

---

[20] Rosen (1998: 391–2) asks the same question of Blackburn's account of the logic of normative statements.

there is no way I could become fully opinionated factually and fully decided on a plan for living—no way that I haven't, with my judgments, already ruled out.

But suppose that my judgments, taken together, rule out every possible hyperstate (so that there is no way that I haven't already "ruled out" in which "I could become fully opinionated factually and fully decided on a plan for living"). What is so bad about that? After all, as Gibbard (2003: 54) concedes, none of us will ever be in such a "hyperstate", and indeed "trying to approach this ideal would be a waste". At some points, Gibbard seems to suggest that the importance of consistency in one's plans is connected with the need for one's plans to offer one guidance about what to do. But suppose that I have inconsistent plans about what to do in the position of being Julius Caesar on the brink of the Rubicon in 49 BC. These plans will then be incapable of providing me with any guidance on what to do in that situation. But so what? I know full well that I will never be in that situation. What is so bad about having inconsistent fantasy plans about what to do in that situation?

In the next section, I shall argue that any acceptable solution to this problem will in effect be incompatible with expressivism. In this way, it turns out, expressivism is incapable of providing a satisfactory account of normative discourse.

2.6 EXPRESSIVISM DEFEATED

Even without giving an account of the point or purpose of conforming to the standards of justification or warrantedness that apply to normative statements, we can identify certain features that this point or purpose must have. Let us return to the example of the agent who is agonizing about whether or not she ought to inform the police about her friend's criminal actions. It seems reasonable to assume that there must be some *desirable property*, which a judgment could have, such that in agonizing about this question, our agent is striving to reach a judgment about this question that has this desirable property. (I shall consider an objection to this assumption at the end of this section.) Similarly, in agonizing about whether or not to accept the statement that she ought to inform the police about her friend, she is striving to ensure that she accepts that statement only if that statement has a certain analogous desirable property.

To give this desirable property a label, let us say that a statement that has this desirable property is a "winning" statement, and a judgment that has the analogous desirable property is a "winning" judgment. Let us also say that if the statement that would be made by uttering a given sentence (in a given context) is a winning statement, then the sentence in question is a "winning" sentence (in that context). The point or purpose of conforming to these standards of warrantedness or justification is to ensure that one makes only "winning" statements and "winning" judgments. This does not mean that conforming to these standards *guarantees* that one makes only winning statements and judgments. It may be possible, if one is unlucky, for a judgment to be justified even if it is not in fact a winning judgment. The point is rather (to put it roughly) that conforming to these standards of justification is the *means* that one uses in order to achieve the goal of making only winning statements and judgments.

As I have already argued, the fundamental explanation of the meaning of a normative statement must give some account of the specific standards of justification or warrantedness that the statement is subject to. But as we have seen, the very point and purpose of these standards is to ensure that one makes only winning statements. So it also seems plausible that this fundamental explanation of the meaning of the statement must also give some account what it would be for this statement to be a winning statement.

Whatever exactly this desirable property of being a "winning" statement may be, the goal of making only winning statements must be served by conforming to these standards of justification and warrantedness—and in particular it must be served by conforming to standards that have the precise connection to logic that I have described.

One of the connections between logic and these standards of justification and warrantedness is the principle that if one is justified or warranted in making a given statement, then one is not justified or warranted in making any statement that is logically inconsistent with the first statement. So it seems that this desirable property of being a winning statement must have an analogous connection to logical inconsistency. That is, no statement that is logically inconsistent with a winning statement can itself be a winning statement.

Moreover, the attitude of *inferring* the conclusion of an argument (that is, accepting the conclusion of the argument *conditionally*, given the supposition of the argument's premises) can presumably also be a winning attitude. The obvious suggestion to make here is the following. If one infers a conclusion from certain premises, and this attitude of inferring that conclusion from those premises is a winning attitude, then *if* each of the premises is a winning sentence, the conclusion of the argument is also a winning sentence. That is, if the attitude of inferring the conclusion from the premises is a winning attitude, then the property of being a winning sentence is *preserved* from the premises to the conclusion. Since a relevantly competent reasoner is always warranted in accepting a logically valid inference, it seems that the property of being a winning sentence is always preserved from the premises to the conclusion of any logically valid argument.

If this is true, then we can derive numerous further features of this desirable property of being a winning sentence: a disjunctive sentence has this property if and only if at least one of its disjuncts has this property; a sentence in which negation is the dominant operator has this property just in case the sentence embedded inside the negation operator does not have this property; and so on.

Moreover, there is in fact an extremely easy way of supplementing Gibbard's semantics for normative statements so that it can explain all these features of the property of being a winning statement. Let us just say that some of the "hyperstates" that Gibbard invokes are *designated* states, while the other such hyperstates are not designated. Then we could say that an atomic judgment is a winning judgment just in case it allows all of the designated hyperstates.[21] We could give the semantics of the logical operators in the following simple way: the negation of a judgment counts as a winning judgment if and only if the judgment of which it is the negation does not count as a winning judgment; a disjunctive judgment counts as a winning judgment if and only if at least one of its disjuncts is a winning judgment; and so on.

There is one final feature of this property of being a winning sentence that I should like to highlight. Suppose that one makes a statement; then it seems that one is thereby committed to accepting that the statement that one has made is a winning statement—that is, not merely that the statement is justified or warranted, but that the statement has achieved the point or purpose of conforming to the relevant standards of justification or warrantedness—and so the sentence that one utters in making that statement is itself a winning sentence. Conversely, suppose that one accepts that a particular sentence is a winning sentence; then it seems clear that one is thereby committed to accepting the statement that one could make by uttering that sentence. In short, the sentences *s* and '*s* is a winning sentence' are equivalent, in the sense that the statement made by uttering one of these sentences commits one to the statement that one could make by uttering the other.

The identity of this property of being a "winning" sentence should by now be clear. We have established that this property has the following features: an account of the meaning of a sentence must include some account of the condition that has to be met if the sentence is to have this property; if a sentence has this property, then the statement that is made by uttering this sentence will achieve the point or purpose of conforming to the distinctive standards of justification or warrantedness that apply to statements; if a sentence *s* has this property, then no sentence logically inconsistent with *s* has this property; this property is preserved in all logically valid inferences (so that a disjunctive sentence has this property if and only if at least one of its disjuncts has this property; a negative sentence has this property if and only if the negated sentence does not have this property; and so on); and accepting that a sentence *s* has this property commits one to accepting the statement that one could make by uttering that very sentence.

---

[21] I am allowing that *several* hyperstates may count as "designated" to accommodate "Buridan's ass" situations, where all the designated hyperstates contain an attitude of *permitting both* going Left *and* going Right, and so some designated hyperstates will include a plan to go Left, while the other designated hyperstates include a plan to go Right.

It is surely highly plausible that the only property of sentences that has all these features is *truth*.[22] To be a "winning" sentence is just to be a *true* sentence; and to be a "winning" statement is just to be a *correct* statement, in the sense in which it is plausible to say that a statement is correct if and only if the sentence that one uttered in making that statement is true.

To say that truth is the only property of sentences that has all these features is not to embrace any sort of minimalist or deflationist conception of truth.[23] First, since these features include the feature of being the point or purpose of conforming to the distinctive standards of justification or warrantedness that apply to statements, they already go beyond the "platitudes" usually appealed to by such minimalist or deflationist accounts of truth. Indeed, my suggestion that it is one of the distinguishing marks of truth that truth is the "point" or "purpose" of conforming to the distinctive standards of justification or warrantedness that apply to statements has much more in common with Dummett's (1993*b*: 42–52) idea that the "root of our concept of truth" is our grasp of what it is for a belief or an assertion to be correct, or with Wiggins's (1989: 147) idea that "truth is the primary dimension of assessment for beliefs", than with any ideas in the minimalist or deflationist tradition. Secondly, to say that truth is the only property that has these features is not to say that these features exhaust the nature or essence of truth; it may well be that truth has some deeper nature—such as the nature that is articulated by some version of the correspondence theory of truth[24]—even if it is also the only property that has the features that I have identified.

I have already argued that, even at the most fundamental explanatory level, an adequate explanation of the meaning of a normative sentence must give some account of the conditions that must be met for the sentence to have this desirable property. Since this desirable property is in fact truth, any adequate account of the meaning of a normative sentence must somehow explain the sentence's truth conditions. That is, the semantics of normative terms is truth-conditional, contrary to what the expresssivist claims.

One serious objection to the argument that I have given in this section ought to be considered at this point. At the beginning of the argument, I assumed that if there was some further point or purpose in conforming to the

---

[22] Suppose that the "equivalence" of the sentences *s* and '*s* is a winning sentence' warrants all of the Tarski-style biconditionals (such as " 'Snow is white' is a winning sentence if and only if snow is white", and the like). Then if there were any two properties that have all these features, these properties would be exemplified by exactly the same sentences—which surely makes it seem more plausible that they are not in fact two distinct properties after all.

[23] For minimalist or deflationary conceptions, see Horwich (1998*a*), and especially Field (1986 and 1994). My first attempt at developing this sort of argument against expressivism (Wedgwood 1997) appears to have been interpreted as committed to a form of minimalism by some readers (see Lenman 2003: *n*. 47). I wish to emphasize here that this interpretation is mistaken.

[24] I am in fact sympathetic to the version of the correspondence theory of truth that is advocated by Bealer (1982: 199–204). But I obviously cannot defend this theory here.

standards of justification and warrantedness that apply to normative statements and judgments, then there must be some "desirable property" such that the point or purpose of conforming to these standards of justification and warrantedness is to ensure that each of one's normative statements has this property. But perhaps there is no such desirable property that *individual* statements can have, but only a desirable property that whole *sets* of normative statements can have? Perhaps the point or purpose of conforming to these standards of justification and warrantedness is to ensure that the whole *set* of statements that one accepts has this desirable property? What justifies my assumption that there is a desirable property of *individual* statements such that the point or purpose of conforming to these standards of justification and warrantedness is to ensure that each of one's statements has this property?

Suppose that there is a property P_1 such that the ultimate point or purpose of conforming to these standards is just to ensure that the whole set of normative statements that one accepts has property P_1. Then of course we can just *define* a property P_2 that individual statements can have—namely, the property of being a statement that belongs to a set that has this desirable property P_1. Now, one might still object that even if there is a set of statements each of which has this property P_2, it does not follow that the whole set will have the desirable property P_1. However, once we take into account some of the features that this desirable property P_1 must have, we will see that this last objection is just false: any set of statements each member of which has P_2 will itself be a set of statements that has P_1.

First, as I have argued, these standards of justification and warrantedness imply that if one is justified or warranted in accepting a statement, then one is *not* justified or warranted in accepting the negation of that statement, and vice versa. So it seems that if a set that has this desirable property P_1 contains a statement *s*, then *no* set that contains the negation of *s* can have this desirable property P_1. Secondly, it seems that there will be a *maximal* set that has this desirable property P_1—specifically, a set that, for every statement for which one might possibly have any justification at all, contains either that statement or its negation. Taking these two points together, it follows that there will be a *unique maximal* set of statements that has this desirable property P_1, such that every set of statements that has P_1 is itself a subset of this unique maximal set. Finally, one is justified in accepting a set of statements if and only if one is also justified in accepting each subset of that set of statements; so it seems that a set of statements can have this desirable property P_1 if and only if each of its subsets also has this property P_1. Thus, if a statement belongs to *any* set that has this desirable property P_1 (that is, if the statement has desirable property P_2), it will belong to this unique maximal set that has property P_1; and any set of such statements will be a subset of this unique maximal set, and so will itself also have property P_1. So in fact, any set of statements each member of which belongs to some set that has this desirable property P_1 (that is, any set each member of which has property P_2)

will itself be a set that has the desirable property P_1. Hence, the aim of accepting only sets of statements that have this desirable property P_1 does not differ in any way from the aim of accepting only statements that have property P_2: nothing could possibly promote one of these aims without also promoting the other. For this reason then, it was reasonable for me to assume that there is some desirable property, which *individual* statements can have, such that the purpose or point of conforming to the standards of justification and warrantedness that apply to normative statements is to ensure that each and every one of the statements that one accepts has this desirable property.

It seems then that my argument is sound: the meaning of normative statements is truth-conditional. By itself, this conclusion does not imply metaphysical realism with respect to normative truths—at least not if we understand metaphysical realism along the lines that have been suggested by Kit Fine (2001), which I outlined in the Introduction to this book. In particular, the conclusion of this chapter is quite compatible with the claim that normative truths are wholly reducible to naturalistic truths. Nor does the conclusion of this chapter establish the sort of semantic realism that Dummett (1993b) has famously tried to raise problems for. For all that I have argued so far, the notion of truth applicable to normative statements might just be the notion that is favoured by intuitionistic logicians, according to which for a statement to be true is for there to be an effective procedure that will yield a proof of it.[25] All that I have argued here is that expressivism fails, and that even at the most fundamental explanatory level, any adequate account of the meaning of normative statements must ascribe truth conditions to these statements.

2.7 GIBBARD'S SEMANTICS TRANSFORMED

I remarked above that there is an easy way of revising Gibbard's semantics so that it can accommodate the idea of "winning" sentences or statements—by adding the idea that some of the hyperstates are, as I put it, "*designated*", while others are not. Then Gibbard could say that an atomic normative sentence or statement counts as "winning" if and only if it allows all these designated hyperstates.

Now that we have seen that the property of being a winning sentence is simply *truth*, and the property of being a winning statement is the property of being *correct*, we can reformulate this revision of Gibbard's semantics. These "designated" hyperstates are simply the *correct* hyperstates. That is, all the beliefs and plans contained in these hyperstates are correct: each of these beliefs is a belief in a truth; and each of the "hyperplans" contained in these hyperstates involves planning on doing everything that one really ought to be doing, and nothing that

---

[25] For this conception of truth, see Dummett (1978: 313–15), and Tennant (1987: 128–33).

one ought not to be doing. When supplemented in this way, Gibbard's theory will imply that an atomic normative sentence, of the form 'One ought to φ in C', is true if and only if the attitude of disagreeing with the plan of not φ-ing in C is allowed by all the correct hyperstates—that is, no correct hyperstate permits the plan of not φ-ing in C. (Then we can explain the truth conditions of logically complex sentences in the standard truth-conditional way: a disjunctive sentence is true if and only if at least one of its disjuncts is true; a negative sentence is true if and only if the negated sentence is not true; and so on.)

This is, more or less, the sort of account of the truth conditions of normative sentences that I shall develop in Chapters 4 and 5. My account, like Gibbard's, will give a prominent role to the notion of a *plan*, and even to the notion of a maximally detailed plan or "hyperplan". The crucial difference is that I shall also be employing the notion of a plan's being *correct*. This is why my theory will be an overtly truth-conditional theory, and will have no problem with explaining the features of normative discourse that are, as we have seen, beyond the power of any expressivist theory to explain.

3

Causal Theories and Conceptual Analyses

3.1 TRUTH-CONDITIONAL SEMANTICS

In the previous chapter, I argued against expressivism, and in favour of the rival truth-conditional approach to the semantics of normative terms. There are of course many different versions of truth-conditional semantics. But the disagreements between them are general problems in the philosophy of mind and language, and have little to do with the special problems about normative statements and normative judgments that I am focusing on. So I shall simply assume a particular version of truth-conditional semantics here. This is solely for the purpose of making the discussion more definite and easier to follow. Everything that I will say should be capable of being translated into the framework of other versions of truth-conditional semantics without materially affecting my arguments.

According to the version of truth-conditional semantics that I shall assume here, statements have truth conditions, which are given by *propositions*—where propositions are what are referred to by 'that ... '-clauses (such as 'that 2 + 2 = 4' or 'that Julius Caesar was assassinated', etc.). Philosophers have articulated many different conceptions of propositions. According to one such conception, propositions are composed, by means of operations analogous to predication, negation, conjunction, existential quantification, and the like, out of ordinary entities like individuals, properties, and relations. I shall assume that propositions of this sort give the truth conditions of statements and judgments, and so form at least part of the content of those statements and judgments. We may assume that *facts* either are, or at least correspond very closely to, true propositions of this sort; this is the reason for labelling this approach to the semantics of normative statements a kind of factualist semantics.

Assuming that any acceptable semantics is *compositional*, a factualist semantics for normative statements will have to assign certain properties or relations to the relevant occurrences of the normative terms, as the properties or relations that feature in the truth conditions of the statements that involve those occurrences of those terms. In that sense, these occurrences of the normative terms *refer to* these normative properties and relations; in other words, these normative properties or relations are the *semantic values* of those occurrences of those terms.

There is also a second conception of propositions that we seem to need to invoke in our semantic theory. According to this second conception, propositions are entities that are built up (by means of operations that are analogous to predication, conjunction, negation, and so on) out of *concepts*. Concepts are related to propositions of this second sort in roughly the same way as individual words are related to the sentences that are built up out of them: the relevant occurrence of the whole sentence expresses a proposition; and each occurrence of the constituent terms of the sentence expresses one of the concepts that the proposition is built out of. We may assume that this concept is the *sense* of the occurrence of the term that expresses it; and *understanding* this occurrence of the term requires recognizing this occurrence of the term as expressing that concept.

I shall also assume that it is propositions of this second sort —the propositions that are built up out of concepts, rather than the propositions that are built up out of ordinary entities like individuals, properties, and relations—that are the primary objects of the propositional attitudes like belief, hope, fear, and the like. I shall assume that these concepts in some way *represent* ordinary entities like individuals, properties, and relations. Thus, we can say that these concepts also have semantic values, in much the same way as the terms that express these concepts have. Hence a concept can be regarded as a "way" in which its semantic value may be "presented" in thought; in effect, it is what Frege (1986a) called a "mode of presentation" of its semantic value.[1] This approach allows for the possibility that concepts may be more finely individuated than their semantic values: that is, this approach allows for the possibility that the same object, property, or relation may be presented in thought in more than one way. For example, the very same property could be presented both by means of the concept *made of water* and by means of the distinct concept *made of H_2O*.

When it is necessary to distinguish between these two kinds of propositions, I shall refer to the propositions that are built up out of concepts as *thoughts*, and to the propositions that are built up out of ordinary entities like individuals, properties, and relations as *conditions*. I shall assume that the content of an occurrence of a sentence (and of a judgment) consists of propositions of both of these two kinds—both a thought (built up out of concepts) and a condition (built up out of the semantic values of those concepts). On this approach, then, explaining the meaning that the occurrence of a term has in a particular context will have two main components: first, one must explain

---

[1] Although I shall be assuming a couple of Fregean theses about concepts (or senses or "modes of presentation"), I shall not be assuming all of Frege's doctrines about senses; in particular, I shall not assume Frege's (1986a) interpretation of propositional attitude ascriptions as contexts in which terms actually refer to what are ordinarily their senses. I intend to remain quite neutral about the correct semantics for propositional attitude ascriptions here.

what *concept* this occurrence of the term expresses (or in other words, what the *sense* of the term is, or what an *understanding* of the term consists in); and secondly, one must explain what the *reference* or *semantic value* of that concept is.

In Chapter 1, I argued against the quietist or minimalist approach, according to which it is a mistake to ask for any sort of substantive explanation of the meaning of normative terms. So I shall suppose that any adequate account of the semantics of normative terms must give a substantive explanation of what it is for these terms to have the meaning that they have. In the context of this version of the truth-conditional approach, an adequate account of the meaning of a particular occurrence of a normative term would have to give a substantive explanation of the following two things: first, what is the essential nature of the concept that that occurrence of the term expresses—what makes that concept the normative concept that it is; and secondly, why it is that that concept has the semantic value that it has.

In the current philosophical literature, there are two well-known approaches to the semantics of normative terms that aim to offer such an explanatory account of the nature of normative concepts and of why they have the reference or semantic value that they have.

The first is the approach that is sometimes called "Cornell moral realism", according to which the semantics of normative terms is fundamentally similar to that of "natural kind terms", such as terms like 'water', 'tiger', and so on.[2] According to this view, the world contains certain properties that count as "natural kinds": these are the properties that play a particularly important role in the causal laws and regularities that are investigated by natural science. What is essential to the meaning of natural kind terms is the way in which their use is causally regulated by such natural kinds; the reference or semantic value of such a term is that natural kind that in some way plays the dominant role in causally regulating the use of the term. I shall call this approach the "causal theory of reference" for normative terms.

The other well-known approach to the semantics of normative terms —which in contemporary philosophy could perhaps be called the "Australian" theory—is the approach that seeks to give a *conceptual analysis* of normative statements.[3] A conceptual analysis of a sentence typically aims to give non-trivial necessary and sufficient conditions for that sentence's being true; so, such conceptual analyses traditionally take the form of a biconditional, with the sentence that is being analysed on the left-hand side of the biconditional, and a different analysing sentence on the right-hand side. Typically, the proponents of such conceptual analyses claim that to understand the sentence that is being analysed, one

---

[2] For this view, see especially Boyd (1988). This conception of natural kind terms is largely due to Putnam (1975).

[3] See Jackson and Pettit (1995), Smith (1994), and Lewis (1989).

must have various "inferential and judgmental dispositions" that taken together amount to a sort of "implicit" or "practical" belief in the biconditional.[4]

As I shall argue here, neither of these approaches can give an adequate account of the meaning of normative terms. The reason for their failure is the same in both cases: neither approach can give an adequate explanation of normative judgment internalism (NJI)—the essential connection between normative judgments, on the one hand, and motivation and practical reasoning, on the other.

It is not surprising that the causal theory of reference cannot explain NJI, since most proponents of the causal theory have been outspoken opponents of NJI, and their account of the meaning of normative terms was never designed to explain NJI. It is more surprising that no conceptual analysis of normative sentences can explain NJI, since at least in recent years, the proponents of each of these conceptual analyses have claimed that it is one of the great advantages of their analysis that it can explain NJI. Nonetheless, they are mistaken: NJI cannot be explained on their approach.

3.2 THE CAUSAL THEORY

As I argued in the Chapter 1, an account of the meaning of normative statements must provide some explanation of NJI, the essential connection that seems to hold between normative judgments, on the one hand, and motivation and practical reasoning, on the other. If a causal theory of the meaning of normative statements is to explain NJI, then this must be because this causal theory of normative statements goes along with a parallel causal theory of normative *judgments*. Such a causal theory would in effect be the application to the special case of normative judgments of what has by now become a familiar idea—the idea of a causal or informational theory of mental content.[5]

Here is a sketch of such a causal or informational theory of mental content. According to this causal or informational theory of content, for a judgment to involve the concept F is for it to involve a concept which, in the relevantly central types of case, would be used in a judgment to describe an object in the thinker's environment if and only if (and because) the object in question really had the property of being F. Such a theory might maintain, for example, that for a judgment to involve the concept *cow* is for it to involve a concept which, in the relevant central cases, would be used in a judgment to describe an object in the thinker's environment if and only if (and because) the object in question really was a cow. If this is the case, it may be said that, in the central type of

[4] The phrase 'inferential and judgmental dispositions' is due to Smith (1994: 30); the reference to "practical" belief is due to Jackson and Pettit (1995).

[5] For such causal or informational theories of mental content, see Stampe (1979), Dretske (1981), Stalnaker (1984: 12–19), and Fodor (1987: ch. 4, and 1990: ch. 4).

case, judgments involving this concept tend to "indicate", or "co-vary" with, the presence of a cow. Crudely, a belief is a cow-belief because it is a belief which tends to be caused—in the right sort of circumstances—by cows.

There are many different versions of this type of theory: several different interpretations of the central relation of "covariance" or "indication" are possible. The theory sketched here is only an illustration. Equally, there are many different accounts of what makes a case of forming a belief a "central" case in the relevant sense: for example, Dretske holds that the central cases are those that occur during an initial learning period in which the concept is originally acquired (1981: 194–5), while Fodor holds that the central type of case is that type on which all other uses of the concept in a certain sense asymmetrically depend (1990: 90–2). What matters for our purposes is just that something like the following is true of all these causal or informational theories: these theories imply that the content of an attitude is simply a matter of the object or property that each of its constituent concepts refers to, and this is just the object or property that causes or explains the formation of certain central beliefs involving the concept.

Here, we are concerned with causal or informational accounts of normative judgments. Now there may be many different sorts of normative judgments. In this chapter, however, we shall focus on the sort of normative judgment of which the version of NJI that I defended in Chapter 1 is true—that is, the sort of judgment of the form 'I ought to φ' that necessarily disposes any rational agent to have the corresponding intention to φ. Let us suppose that the concept corresponding to the term 'ought' in this judgment refers to a *relation* between the relevant agent A and the proposition that A φ-s.[6] I shall call this relation the "ought-relation".

A causal or informational account of such judgments would account for what it is for a judgment to involve the concept expressed by 'ought' by appealing to cases in which such judgments are caused by the ought-relation itself. According to this sort of account, for a judgment to be a normative judgment is for it to involve a concept that, in central cases, would be used in a judgment, to characterize the relation between an agent and a proposition that are within the thinker's ken, if and only if (and because) the agent and the proposition are related by the ought-relation. Roughly, it is a normative judgment simply because it is a type of belief that is reliably caused by the ought-relation.

Some philosophers will object to this account because it requires that the ought-relation can enter into causal relations, and somehow causally regulate our judgments and beliefs.[7] For the purposes of evaluating this account, however, I propose to concede that the ought-relation can enter into causal explanations. The problem that I wish to focus on is the inability of this account to provide an

---

[6] I defend this interpretation of 'ought' as a propositional operator in Chapter 4 (Section 4.3).

[7] For this objection, see especially Harman (1977: ch. 1), and the reply to this objection by Sturgeon (1985).

explanation of NJI, the fact that it is an essential feature of normative judgments that they are disposed to play a certain distinctive role in motivation and practical reasoning.[8]

The proponent of the causal or informational account might try to claim that NJI is explained simply by the fact that these normative judgments are, at least in the central or canonical cases, responses to the ought-relation itself. But how can the mere fact that judgments involving a given concept are responses to the ought-relation be enough to explain why anyone who possesses this concept must be disposed to be motivated to act by their first-person judgments involving this concept? Clearly, a causal or informational theorist would have to claim that it is a necessary truth that everyone tends to be motivated to realize any proposition *p* whenever they make a judgment that characterizes the way in which they are related to *p* by means of a concept which, in central cases, is caused to appear in such judgments by the presence of the ought-relation itself. (Perhaps they will also claim that this is just a basic constitutive fact about this relation and about motivation.)

Such claims however would be clearly false. Their falsity is perhaps best illustrated by means of a science-fiction example. Suppose that some extraterrestrial scientists build an android for the purpose of giving them advice about what they ought to do. This android, let us suppose, is in fact highly reliable as a source of information about what the agent that it is observing ought to do. By some mischance, the android is marooned on a planet far from home. The inhabitants of this faraway planet succeed in deciphering most of the android's language except for the android's word for 'ought', and so they introduce a concept by means of the reference-fixing description 'whatever relation is causally responsible for the android's use of that term'. Through monitoring the android's statements, the inhabitants of the planet form a number of reliable hypotheses about this relation. Over time, their hypotheses about this relation become ever more refined, so that in theorizing about this relation they even achieve a large degree of independence from the android's statements. In this way, the inhabitants of the faraway planet would then have a concept whose presence in their judgments is reliably caused by (and reliably co-varies with) the presence of this relation. Nonetheless, it is quite possible that their judgments involving this concept might have absolutely no tendency to motivate them to act accordingly (for example, this might be because the views that they would express by means of their ordinary word for 'ought' are radically different from the android's).

---

[8] Another objection that philosophers have raised against the idea of a causal theory of reference for normative terms is the objection of Horgan and Timmons (1992*a*), according to which there could be a "Moral Twin Earth" where it is a different property that causally regulates the use of the relevant moral term, but intuitively the inhabitants of Moral Twin Earth mean exactly the same by their term as we do by ours. My objection will be the converse of theirs: I claim that there could be cases where the very *same* relation causally regulates the use of the term, but intuitively the term does not express the concept 'ought'.

One fairly straightforward response to this example would be to deny that the judgments that the inhabitants of the faraway planet make using the concept that they introduced by this reference-fixing description are genuine normative judgments at all. They are not really judging that they *ought* to φ. They are like the thinkers whom some philosophers have described as using normative terms like 'ought' in an "inverted commas sense" (Smith 1994: 67–9). However, this response is not available to proponents of the causal or informational theory of content. The inhabitants of the faraway planet make judgments that involve a concept whose presence in their judgments is reliably sensitive to the ought-relation: and that it is all it is for a judgment to be a normative judgment, according to the causal theory, and so their judgments are genuine normative judgments.

Someone might object that there is another way for the causal theory to provide an explanation of NJI. According to the causal theory, all that it is for a judgment to be a normative judgment is that it should involve a concept whose presence in judgments is reliably caused by the ought-relation *in certain central or canonical cases*. Perhaps the judgments of the planet's inhabitants are not central or canonical cases of beliefs that are caused by this relation; and perhaps in the relevant central or canonical cases, normative judgments will be disposed to motivate the thinker to act in the way that NJI requires.

This objection rests on a misunderstanding of the argument.[9] The faraway planet's inhabitants are a counterexample to NJI just in case they make genuine normative judgments but have no disposition to be motivated by them. Even if their judgments are not "canonical cases" of normative judgments, this does nothing to show that they are not genuine normative judgments; and, assuming the causal theory of content, it is easy to show that the judgments of the planet's inhabitants are in fact genuine normative judgments.

According to the causal theory, the content of a judgment is entirely determined by the object or property that each of the relevant concepts refers to, and this is just the object or property that, in central or canonical cases, causes judgments involving the concept. All we need then is the assumption that the planet's inhabitants' judgments involve some concept—whatever concept it is that they introduced by their reference-fixing description 'the relation that is causally responsible for the android's statements of this kind'. Then there will be some judgments that count as central cases of judgments involving this concept (we do not need to worry about what makes them "central" cases in the relevant sense).

---

[9] This objection also seems to rest on a misunderstanding of the role that central cases play in the causal theory of content. The causal theorist appeals to these central cases simply in order to rule out cases in which a belief involving a given concept is not caused by the property that causes the central cases of beliefs involving that concept—cases in which a cow-belief is caused by a horse or a hallucination, for example. (Central cases do not encapsulate any further features of the beliefs' functional role, for example.)

Ex hypothesi, these central cases of judgments involving this concept are reliably caused by the ought-relation. So according to the causal theory, these judgments are also normative judgments.

The underlying point is that it seems always possible for any property or relation to cause judgments in a number of different ways; and, according to the causal theory, the exact way in which the property or relation causes the judgments makes no difference to the content of those judgments. This is a point that proponents of the causal theory of content frequently stress. As Fodor (1990: 91) puts it: "'cow' tokens get caused in *all sorts* of ways, and they all mean *cow* for all that." According to the causal theory, 'cow' tokens still mean *cow*, even though they get caused in all sorts of ways, because that is all it is for a judgment to be a cow-judgment—its being of a type that is reliably caused by cows. In our story, the planet's inhabitants' concept means *ought* for exactly the same reason: central cases of judgments involving this concept are reliably caused by the ought-relation. The fact that these judgments are caused in a radically different way from our normative judgments makes no difference to their content, even though it does prevent them from having any disposition to motivate action.

We cannot get round this problem by holding that the ought-relation resembles a secondary quality, in being definable in terms of the kinds of sensory or motivational responses to which it typically gives rise. Even a secondary quality, like greenness, can cause beliefs in numerous different ways; so we can tell an analogous story about greenness to the story that we told about the ought-relation. Suppose a community of intelligent blind creatures on another faraway planet find a spectrometer in the wreck of a human spacecraft. They then come to use the spectrometer to detect whether or not objects have a certain property, and introduce a concept by means of a reference-fixing description 'the property of objects that this instrument is detecting'. According to the causal theory of content, these creatures are forming judgments involving the concept 'green'; this is so even though these judgments have no disposition whatsoever to be accompanied by visual experiences with the phenomenal character that we get from seeing green things, and it will be so even if a statement of the "real essence" of greenness would have to mention visual experiences of that type. Similarly, no matter how anthropocentric or response-dependent the ought-relation may be, if it can cause judgments at all, then it is presumably possible for it to cause judgments in a multitude of different ways, including some ways that will prevent the judgments formed in those ways from having any disposition to motivate action.

In short, the causal or informational theory of content seems unable to accommodate NJI. This theory cannot allow that it is *essential* to any type of belief that it is disposed to motivate action. In view of the fact that NJI seems to be so plausible, it seems that we should reject the idea of offering any causal or informational theory of normative judgments.

3.3 VARIETIES OF CONCEPTUAL ANALYSIS

Prototypically, a conceptual analysis takes the form of a universally quantified biconditional, such as the following:

(1) For all x, x is an uncle if and only if x is the brother of a parent

—where this universally quantified biconditional is usually understood to be not merely contingent but necessary.

If this universally quantified biconditional proposition is indeed necessary, then it is plausible that it does explain what the semantic value of the term 'uncle' is, at least in all ordinary contexts. This conceptual analysis can be taken as giving a specification of the extension of the term 'uncle', not just with respect to the actual world, but with respect to every possible world: in particular, according to this analysis, for every possible world w, the extension of 'uncle' with respect to w is the set of individuals in the domain of w who are brothers of parents in w. In this way, this analysis explains the contribution that the term 'uncle' makes (at least in ordinary contexts) to the truth conditions of sentences in which it appears.

Of course, one objection that is often raised against such conceptual analyses is that the universally quantified biconditional that forms the core of the analysis is not in fact necessarily true. But even if it is necessarily true, there is a further problem that this approach must face. This further problem does not concern the way in which the conceptual analysis explains the term's semantic value. It concerns the way in which it performs the other central task of an account of the term's meaning—the task of explaining what *concept* the term expresses, or in other words, what the *sense* of the term is, or what an *understanding* of the term consists in. The fact that this universally quantified biconditional is necessarily true does not by itself give any explanation of what concept the term in question expresses, or of what understanding the term consists in.

Typically, the proponents of such conceptual analyses answer this further question by saying that understanding the term consists in some sort of *implicit* knowledge of the universally quantified biconditional that forms the core of their analysis.[10] The different proponents of such conceptual analyses have different conceptions of what it is to have implicit knowledge of a proposition. Thus, Michael Smith (1994: 30) suggests that an understanding of the term consists in a set of "judgmental and inferential dispositions", which are in some way summarized by the universally quantified biconditional in question. In at least some of his work, Frank Jackson (1998) appeals to what he calls "platitudes" or "commonplaces"—obvious truths that anyone who understands the term must

---

[10] See especially Peacocke (2004: 220–6).

have some implicit knowledge of—and then suggests that the correct universally quantified biconditional analysis would in effect be a complete specification of these platitudes, along with the claim that these platitudes are what determine the reference of the term.[11]

I shall not examine these different conceptions of what it is to have "implicit knowledge" of a proposition. I shall just rely on the following assumption about the notion of "implicit knowledge" of a proposition: if a phenomenon cannot be explained by the fact that someone *explicitly* knows a proposition, then *a fortiori* the phenomenon cannot be explained by the fact that they "implicitly know" that proposition. The reason for this assumption is that implicit knowledge is supposed to be closely akin to explicit knowledge, but in some way weaker—lacking some of the special features of explicit knowledge that make it explicit. Implicit knowledge of a proposition p is not supposed to be a radically different sort of state from explicit knowledge of p: if it were a radically different state, then it would be highly misleading to characterize it as implicit knowledge of p, as though it were just like explicit knowledge of p, and differed only in being implicit rather than explicit.

However exactly the notion of implicit knowledge is interpreted, there is another important distinction between two different kinds of conceptual analyses. Some conceptual analyses are supposed to be *non-circular*: that is, the right-hand side of the universally quantified biconditional that forms the core of the analysis does not contain the term in question, nor any trivial variants of that term. Other conceptual analyses are *not* supposed to be non-circular: the right-hand side is allowed to contain the very term in question, or trivial variants of the term. Some circular analyses may simply be *trivial*, if by substituting terms with their trivial variants, they can be transformed into logical truths, such as logical truths of the form 'For all x, x is F if and only if x is F'. But clearly not all such circular analyses are trivial: for example, a circular conceptual analysis might have the obviously non-trivial form 'For all x, x is F if and only if x is both F and G'.

Circular conceptual analysis may be useful for many purposes, but it is far from clear how they can really answer the question of what it is for someone to understand the term (or to possess the concept that the term expresses). For example, consider the following analysis:

(2) For all x, x is an uncle if and only if x is an uncle and x is male.

Clearly, this is non-trivial (it entails that all uncles are male, which is not a mere logical truth). But equally clearly, it is circular. Now suppose that a theorist claims that understanding the term 'uncle' (or possessing the concept 'uncle') consists in an implicit knowledge of this analysis. This claim seems simply to presuppose what is to be accounted for—namely, what it is for a thinker to

---

[11] See also Jackson and Pettit (1995).

possess the concept 'uncle'. This claim does not give any illuminating account of any feature of our understanding of the term 'uncle' that differentiates it from our understanding of terms like 'bachelor', since of course the following universally quantified biconditional is equally true and equally implicitly known by everyone who understands the term 'bachelor':

(3) For all x, x is a bachelor if and only if x is a bachelor and x is male.

For this reason it is unclear whether circular conceptual analyses can succeed in giving any adequate answer to our question about what it is to understand the term.

By contrast, a non-circular analysis certainly can answer this question. Consider once again our prototypical analysis:

(1) For all x, x is an uncle if and only if x is the brother of a parent.

If it really is essential to understanding the term 'uncle', and to possessing the concept that this term expresses, that one has some implicit knowledge of this proposition (1), then that clearly would give an illuminating specification of a feature of our understanding of the term 'uncle' which differentiates it from our understanding of other terms—since it is obviously *not* essential to understanding the term 'bachelor' that one have some implicit knowledge of the proposition that something is a bachelor if and only if it is the brother of a parent.

So, it is doubtful whether a circular analysis can really provide what we need. Moreover, it is not just analyses that use the very term that is being analysed on the right-hand side of the analysing biconditional, or trivial variants of that term, that face this problem. Intuitively, the same problem is faced by any analysis that uses a term that is clearly very closely related in meaning. Even if such an analysis gives a correct account of the term that is being analysed, it immediately raises the problem of how to explain the meaning of the closely related term that is used on the right-hand side. I shall assume here that *evaluative* terms like 'good', 'desirable', and 'valuable' are so closely related to normative terms like 'ought' that a genuinely non-circular analysis would have to eschew all normative and evaluative terms on the right-hand side of its core biconditional.

3.4 NON-CIRCULAR ANALYSES

One classic objection that is often levelled against non-circular conceptual analyses is G. E. Moore's "open question" argument.[12] This argument has two main premises. The first premise is as follows. If there is a correct conceptual

---

[12] See Moore (1903: ch. 1); for contemporary philosophers who endorse a version of this argument as an objection to these conceptual analyses, see especially Gibbard (1990: ch.1) and Wedgwood (2001).

analysis, of the form 'For all x, x is F if and only if x is G' then in a certain sense it should not be an "open question" whether or not something that is G is also F. That is, it should be a *basic rational requirement* on anyone who understands the term 'F' that they should accept that anything G is also F; any such speaker should have at least some *disposition* to accept that anything G is also F—if someone had no such disposition, then we would have to conclude that they do not mean the same thing as we do by their term 'F'. The second premise of the open question argument is that for every attempted non-circular analysis of a normative or evaluative notion, the relevant question *is* an open question. Hence the argument concludes that no such non-circular analysis is correct.

For example, consider the claim that the following schematic biconditional gives the correct analysis of the term 'ought':

(4) For all agents x, x ought to φ if, and only if, (i) x has the capacity to φ, and (ii) x will be happier if x φ-s than if x does not φ.

To wield the open question argument against this analysis, we would have to claim first that there might be agents who know perfectly well that they will be happier if they φ than if they do not, but for whom it is still an open question whether they ought to φ. (For example, perhaps these agents are wondering whether they are in a situation in which they ought to sacrifice their own happiness for some greater good.) These would be agents who lack the general disposition to accept that whenever they have the capacity to φ, and would be happier if they φ than if they do not, they ought to φ. Then the second premise of this application of the open question argument would be that these agents need not be violating any basic rational requirement, and need not be understanding the term 'ought' in any unusual or non-standard sense.

The objection that I wish to press against these conceptual analyses is closely related to the classic open question argument. According to NJI, once one has judged that one ought to φ, the *practical* question of whether or not to φ has been settled. This is because it is a basic requirement of rationality that if one judges that one ought to φ, one must also intend to φ (at least so long as φ-ing is "of the appropriate sort"—that is, a course of action that is manifestly dependent on intention, in a situation with no relevant uncertainty). Accordingly, any agents who are capable of making judgments about what they ought to do must have the general disposition to intend to do whatever they judge that they ought to do.

Now, suppose that someone proposes an analysis of the concept that is expressed by 'ought', of the following form:

(5) For all agents x, x ought to φ if and only if x stands in relation R to the proposition that x φ-s.

If this is a correct analysis, then the claim that everyone who understands the term 'ought' has some implicit knowledge of (5) must somehow explain why

NJI is true. But how could it explain this? As I mentioned above, I will assume here that this appeal to implicit knowledge of (5) cannot possibly provide the necessary explanation unless an appeal to *explicit* knowledge could provide this explanation. But even if everyone had explicit knowledge of (5), how could that explain why NJI is true?

If everyone had explicit knowledge of (5), then it might seem plausible that everyone who judged something of the form 'I ought to φ' would also make the corresponding judgment of the form 'I stand in relation R to the proposition that I φ'. But that would only help to explain NJI if the judgment 'I stand in relation R to the proposition that I φ' had the very same "internalist" connection to motivation and practical reasoning that NJI attributes to judgments with the content 'I ought to φ'.

The claim that judgments of the form 'I stand in relation R to the proposition that I φ' have this sort of internalist connection to motivation and practical reasoning will be refuted if there could be rational agents who had absolutely no disposition to respond to the judgment 'I stand in relation R to the proposition that I φ' by intending to φ. If there could be such agents, then when these agents judge 'I stand in relation R to the proposition that I φ', it would still be an open practical question for them whether or not to φ; and judgments with the content 'I stand in relation R to the proposition that I φ' would not have the same internalist connection to motivation and practical reasoning as judgments of the form 'I ought to φ'. So if there could be such agents, this analysis would fail to provide any explanation of NJI.

It seems that we can deploy exactly this sort of argument against the sample analysis that I proposed above (4). It seems that there could be an agent who is strongly attracted towards an ideal of sacrificing his own happiness for the greater good. This agent might surely be quite rational, even if he has no disposition at all to respond to his judgment 'I have the capacity to φ, and I will be happier if I φ than if I do not φ' by intending to φ. So this judgment does *not* have any essential or "internal" connection to motivation or practical reasoning. So the claim that everyone who understands 'ought' has implicit (or even explicit) knowledge of (4) cannot explain why NJI is true.

In effect, this objection is closely akin to what Mark Johnston (1989: 157–8) called the 'So what?' objection. If a conceptual analysis of 'ought' consists in a biconditional, then there will be some relational concept R that corresponds to 'ought' on the right-hand side of the biconditional. According to Johnston, if this analysis is correct, it must be impossible for a completely rational agent to respond with complete indifference to the judgment that she stands in relation R to the proposition that she φ-s (given that φ-ing is a course of action of the appropriate sort). That is, it must be irrational to respond to this judgment with the reaction, 'Yes, but so what?' The main difference between my objection and Johnston's 'So what?' objection is that my objection is not based on the claim that it is possible for a rational agent to respond to this judgment with *complete indifference*, but only that it is possible for a perfectly rational agent *not* to respond to this judgment by having the *corresponding intention to act*.

In fact, it is not just this particular analysis (4) that falls prey to this objection. There is a compelling reason to think that *any* strictly non-circular analysis will fall prey to this objection as well. NJI, the necessary connection that normative judgments have to motivation and practical reasoning, is a *special* feature of normative and evaluative judgments. It is a feature that is *absent* from all judgments that are wholly non-normative and non-evaluative in content. Indeed, this seems to be precisely one of the features that distinguishes normative and evaluative judgments from judgments of all other kinds. For every possible non-normative content, it *is* possible for there to be a perfectly rational agent who judges that content but is not motivated to form the corresponding intention to act. This is precisely what makes the content in question a non-normative content in the first place. So, it seems, no non-circular conceptual analysis can possibly explain why NJI is true.

We can illustrate this point with the conceptual analysis of the concept of value that was proposed by David Lewis (1989). (Lewis's analysis is an analysis of the concept of "value", not of the concept expressed by 'ought', but *mutatis mutandis* essentially the same points apply.) According to Lewis, something is a value if and only if under ideal conditions we would be disposed to value it. Moreover, he also analyses the notions of "ideal conditions" and of "valuing something" in wholly non-normative, non-evaluative terms: according to his analysis, "ideal conditions" for valuing x are just conditions in which one imagines x as fully and vividly as possible, and to "value" something is just to desire to desire it.

As Johnston (1989: 157–8) convincingly argues, it seems possible for there to be an agent who is not in any way motivated by the information that if she imagined x as fully and vividly as possible, she would desire to desire x. For example, consider someone who suspects that her psychological tendencies to desire to desire things under such peculiar conditions may well be unreliable (perhaps she has some evidence that seems to show that imagining things too fully and vividly leads to various psychological illusions or pathologies). Moreover, it seems that this person need not be violating any basic requirement of rationality by failing to be motivated by this information; this person could still possess the concept of "what she would desire to desire under ideal conditions" even if she lacked any disposition to be motivated accordingly. Thus, Lewis's analysis seems incapable of explaining any sort of "value-judgment internalism" (VJI): that is, his analysis cannot explain why there is an "internalist" connection between judgments about value and motivation.

It might seem unfair to claim that an account like Lewis's cannot explain such value-judgment internalism. After all, his account was explicitly designed to guarantee the existence of a necessary connection between value and motivation. However, what Lewis's account guarantees is a connection between the *facts* about value and motivation. VJI, on the other hand, is not a doctrine about the nature of facts about value: it is a doctrine about the nature of value *judgments*. It applies just as much to judgments that are *false* (where there is no question of there being any corresponding fact) as to judgments that are true. So for this reason, Lewis's account seems to be looking in the wrong place for an explanation of VJI.

The situation is slightly more complex with respect to the analysis of Jackson and Pettit (1995). Their proposal is that the "platitudes" or "commonplaces" involving normative terms—the intuitively obvious propositions that anyone who understands those terms must have some implicit knowledge of—collectively serve as a big implicit definition of those terms (rather as functionalists in the philosophy of mind hold that "folk psychology" serves as a big implicit definition of the psychological terms). Before considering the way in which Jackson and Pettit themselves attempt to explain NJI, I shall first examine a number of other ways in which this "implicit definition" approach might be thought to provide an explanation of NJI. My conclusion will be, once again, that this approach cannot offer any explanation of NJI.

One striking feature of Jackson and Pettit's (1995: 23) account is that among the "commonplaces" that they regard as giving an implicit definition of normative terms are "commonplaces about motivation", such as the commonplace that anyone who believes that an option is right and desirable will typically desire and choose such an option. That is, in effect, one of these commonplaces is NJI itself.[13]

By itself, however, this point—that NJI is one of the commonplaces an implicit knowledge of which is required for understanding the normative terms—is certainly not enough to explain NJI. Even if NJI is a "commonplace" in this sense, that does not explain why it is *true*. The fact that you *believe* that some judgment has an internalist connection to motivation is not enough to ensure that when you make that judgment, it will have any such internalist connection to motivation.

However, Jackson and Pettit's claim that these commonplaces collectively serve as a big implicit definition of the normative terms entails that if normative terms refer at all—or in other words (given that the semantics of these terms is truth-conditional), if any atomic sentences involving normative terms are true—the commonplaces must themselves all be true. If normative terms have any reference at all, their reference must make all these commonplaces true. So

---

13 In fact, the only version of NJI that Jackson and Pettit focus on here is the second version that I introduced in Chapter 1 (according to which every thinker who is capable of making ought-judgments at all must have a general *disposition* to do whatever they judge that they ought to do). They do not focus on the first version, according to which it is a *basic requirement of rationality* that if one judges that one ought to φ, one must also intend to φ. Approaches that focus only on the second version seem to me to face an analogue of the 'So what?' objection. It seems to me quite possible that someone might, without violating any basic requirement of rationality, say to herself, 'I know that a disposition to choose anything that I judge to be *F* is essential to possessing the concept *F*, but why shouldn't I *resist* this disposition whenever I can?'

if NJI is one of the commonplaces, and normative terms are not afflicted by massive reference failure, NJI will have to be true. Can the implicit definition approach explain NJI in this way?

In fact, however, it is not quite clear what is involved in including NJI in the set of commonplaces that has to serve as a big implicit definition of the normative terms. In treating these commonplaces as such an implicit definition, we are in effect quantifying over properties and relations, and claiming that if the normative terms refer at all, then there is a unique sequence of properties and relations that, when assigned as the references of those normative terms, makes all those commonplaces come out true. But in NJI, the normative term 'ought' occurs only within the scope of the phrase 'judges that … '; and on most views of the matter, there are several different *ways* in which one and the same property or relation can be presented in a judgment. (These ways in which something can be presented in thought are what I am here calling "concepts". So another way of putting the point is that there may be several different concepts that can figure in our thoughts, which all refer to the very same property or relation.)

So, in including NJI as part of our big implicit definition, we could be claiming either of the following two things: (i) if there is any relation R referred to by 'ought', then for any thinker x, if x is rational, and makes *any* judgment that predicates relation R of x and the proposition that x φ-s, *no matter how relation R is presented in that judgment*, x will be motivated to φ; or alternatively (ii) if there is any relation R referred to by 'ought', then there is *some* way in which R can be presented in judgments such that judgments in which it is presented in *that* way have the appropriate connection to motivation. Whichever way the proponents of this sort of conceptual analysis choose to go here, this attempted explanation of NJI will fail.

First, suppose that they take the first path. The problem here is that there does not seem to be any relation R such that *any* judgment that predicates this relation of the thinker and the proposition that the thinker φ-s will have the required internalist connection to motivation and practical reasoning. It is always possible for this relation R to be presented in thought in the wrong sort of way. We saw this earlier in Section 3.2, with the example of the judgments that the inhabitants of the faraway planet express with the term that they introduced by the reference-fixing description 'whatever relation the android is referring to by its use of that term'. The content of these judgments involves a concept that refers to what is in fact the ought-relation—in that sense, they are judgments in which the ought-relation is presented in thought—but clearly in these judgments the ought-relation is presented in the wrong way to have any essential connection to motivation and practical reasoning.

To give another example, suppose that there is a true theory of the following form: 'For all agents x, x ought to φ if, and only if, x is related to the proposition that x φ-s by relation R'. For instance, this theory might be our earlier example (4): 'For all agents x, x ought to φ if, and only if, (i) x has the capacity to φ and (ii)

x will be happier if x φ-s than if x does not φ'. If this theory gives the *nature* of the ought-relation, then surely the ought-relation just *is* relation R. (Compare the point that, if the theory 'Something is made of water if and only if it is made of H_2O' gives the nature of the property of being made of water, then the property of being made of water just *is* the property of being made of H_2O.) If I believe that I have the capacity to φ, and will be happier if I φ than if I do not, it might be true to say of me that I believe that I am related to the proposition that I φ by relation R, but if I do not accept this theory about the nature of the ought-relation, there is no reason at all to think that *this* belief must motivate me to form the intention to φ, even if I am perfectly rational. So this too seems to be an example of a judgment that involves a concept that refers to the ought-relation even though this judgment has no essential internalist connection to motivation.

For these reasons then, it seems that there is no relation R such that *all* judgments predicating this relation have an essential connection to motivation, irrespective of the way in which this relation is presented in thought. So if the proponents of the implicit definition approach take the first path, then they will be committed to the unattractive conclusions that their favoured interpretation of NJI is false, and that in consequence normative terms suffer from massive failure of reference (and so all atomic sentences involving normative terms are false).

Suppose then that the proponents of the "implicit definition" approach take the second path. That is, they claim only that if 'ought' refers at all, there is *some* way in which the ought-relation can be presented in thought such that judgments in which it is presented in *that* way have an essential or "internal" connection to motivation or practical reasoning. But then, even though their account will guarantee that if normative terms refer at all, there is *some* sort of judgment that has an essential or "internal" connection to motivation and practical reasoning, their account does not explain why *normative* judgments have this essential connection to motivation. That is, it does not explain NJI. Suppose that there is a concept that we possess in virtue of our implicit knowledge of these "commonplaces". Call this concept C_1. If C_1 refers at all, then there are some judgments in which the relation that C_1 refers to is presented in a certain way, by means of some concept or other, such that *those* judgments have such an internalist connection to motivation or practical reasoning. But this does not entail that judgments *involving* C_1 have any such internalist connection to motivation or practical reasoning. On the contrary, this account leaves it completely open that it is judgments involving some *other* concept C_2 that have this internalist connection to motivation or practical reasoning, and not C_1 (the concept that we possess in virtue of our implicit knowledge of these commonplaces).

Although this is certainly not how they put it, it seems to me that in the end the explanation that Jackson and Pettit actually give of NJI is precisely of this kind. That is, they in fact end up giving a sketch of a *different concept C_2*—quite different from the concept C_1 that we possess in virtue of our implicit knowledge of these commonplaces—and argue that judgments involving C_2 will have the relevant sort of essential connection to motivation and practical reasoning.

As Jackson and Pettit put it (1995: 32–8), it is possible to believe the "content" that one ought to φ in both an "intellectual" way and a "non-intellectual" way. The "intellectual" way of believing this content involves deploying a capacity that depends on one's implicit knowledge of all these platitudes or commonplaces. By contrast, the "non-intellectual" way of believing this content does not necessarily require any knowledge of these platitudes or commonplaces; instead, when thinkers believe this content in a non-intellectual way, their capacity for having attitudes towards this content depends on their engaging in certain unreflective *habits* and *practices* of reasoning (34). For example, these reasoning dispositions include a tendency to "move from the identification of something as fair to its identification as right and desirable", and a tendency "to desire and choose such an option, at least when they explicitly identify it as right and desirable" (36).

It is, however, extremely unclear that this is just a different way of believing a content that is built out of the very same concepts. This seems to be an account of the nature of normative concepts in terms of their distinctive *conceptual role in reasoning*—where the forms of reasoning in question do not just amount to having implicit knowledge of a set of platitudes or commonplaces. Jackson and Pettit give no arguments for thinking that anyone who possesses a concept in virtue of having these sorts of unreflective habits of reasoning is committed to the sorts of platitudes or commonplaces that they enumerate, or that the best way of accounting for the reference or semantic value of such a concept is by appeal to the idea that these platitudes collectively constitute a big implicit definition of the concept. For this reason, it is not even clear that the concept that we possess in virtue of these unreflective habits of reasoning is *a priori* necessarily coextensive with the concept that we possess in virtue of having implicit knowledge of these platitudes.

Moreover, even if they could establish that the concept that we possess in virtue of these unreflective habits of reasoning *is* necessarily coextensive with the concept that we possess in virtue of our implicit knowledge of these platitudes, we should still reject the claim that they are the same concept. Two concepts can be *a priori* coextensive but still be distinct concepts (this seems to be the case with pairs of logical concepts like '*p or q*' and '*Not both: not-p and not-q*'). The mental states that Jackson and Pettit call "intellectual" and "non-intellectual" belief clearly have profoundly different functional roles; and one can easily imagine that it would be informative for someone to realize that the contents of an intellectual belief and of a non-intellectual belief are coextensive. Thus, it seems overwhelmingly plausible that they should be recognized as distinct concepts.

The approach that appeals to the distinctive conceptual role of normative concepts seems to have a much better chance of explaining NJI than the approach that appeals to the idea of implicit knowledge of such a set of platitudes. It is a matter for further investigation whether the best way of accounting for the reference of these normative concepts will invoke the idea of an implicit definition in this way. In the following chapter, I shall argue that it will not: there is an alternative, and better, way to develop the idea of such conceptual role semantics for normative terms.

3.5 SMITH'S "NON-REDUCTIVE ANALYSIS"

In the previous section, I focused on *non-circular* conceptual analyses of normative concepts—where the core of such a conceptual analysis is a universally quantified biconditional the right-hand side of which can be formulated without any use of normative terms. In fact, some of the objections that I raised also apply to certain conceptual analyses that do not aspire to be non-circular. In particular, some of these objections also apply to Michael Smith's "non-reductive analysis" of normative reasons.

According to Smith's (1994: 181) analysis, "to say that we have a normative reason to φ in circumstances C is to say that, if we were fully rational, we would want that we φ in C." As he puts it, "the idea of being fully rational is ... a summary idea" (162)—that is, "the role of this idea in the analysis is ... to capture, in summary style, a whole host of more specific platitudes about practical rationality" (156). More specifically, to be "fully rational", one "must have no false beliefs"; one "must have all relevant true beliefs"; and one "must deliberate correctly". The idea of deliberating correctly is also a "summary idea"; according to Smith, correct deliberation consists largely of adjusting one's mental states in such a way that they can all be "integrated into a more coherent and unified desiderative profile and evaluative outlook" (159); in effect, this involves the attempt to find what John Rawls (1971) called a state of "reflective equilibrium" among our evaluative beliefs.

It is only because of this last element in Smith's analysis that the analysis counts as non-reductive.[14] As Smith (1994: 162) puts it:

in spelling out our idea of what it is to be fully rational we have had to use normative concepts. This was evident in our description of systematic reasoning; for in giving that description we said that we aim to find a more "unified" desiderative profile, and this is itself, of course, a normative notion.

Since Smith's analysis is non-reductive in this sense, but still takes the form of a traditional conceptual analysis, it seems that it cannot provide a non-circular

---

[14] In saying that to be fully rational, one must have all relevant true beliefs, Smith does not mean to include true beliefs about what normative reasons one has, as Smith has confirmed to me in conversation. (Including such true beliefs would obviously run a serious risk of completely trivializing the analysis.)

account of the meaning of normative terms or of the nature of normative concepts. The question that we are faced with is: What is it for a statement to *mean that* it is desirable for x to φ in circumstances C? Or, what is it for someone to *think that* it is desirable for x to φ in circumstances C? Smith's answer is: It is to mean that (or to think that) if x were fully rational, x would desire that she φ in C. But 'rational' is itself a normative term. So the idea of what it is for a statement to have a normative meaning, or of what it is for a thinker to possess a normative concept, is simply presupposed rather than explained.

In consequence, it is doubtful whether this non-reductive analysis can really offer an *explanation* of NJI. This is what Smith (1994: 177) says about how his analysis explains NJI:

According to the analysis, the belief that we have a normative reason to φ, or that it is desirable that we φ, can be represented as the belief that we would desire to φ if we were fully rational. But now, suppose that we believe that we would desire to φ if we were fully rational and yet fail to desire to φ. Are we irrational? We most certainly are. And by our own lights. For we fail to have a desire that we believe it is rational for us to have. In other words, if we believe that we would desire to φ if we were fully rational then we rationally should desire to φ. And that is just [NJI].

What Smith says here may seem plausible, at least on first inspection. But really all that he is doing here is just *asserting* that any rational thinker who believes that she would desire to φ if she were fully rational must also desire to φ. But this is just to assert an instance of the very phenomenon that calls for explanation—namely, that certain beliefs with normative contents rationally require the believer to have some corresponding motivation to act. It does not explain how it is *possible* for there to be such beliefs, or what it is about these beliefs that explains why they have this special feature that no other beliefs have.

Moreover, even though the assertion that Smith makes here may seem plausible on first inspection, on further inspection it appears not to be *necessarily* true (as it would have to be to provide an adequate explanation of NJI, which is a claim about the necessary or essential features of normative beliefs of the form 'I ought to φ' and the like). This is because in fact, Smith is using the term 'rational' in a highly specialized way. To be "fully rational" in his sense is to have no false (non-normative) beliefs, to have all relevant true (non-normative) beliefs, and to have a suitably coherent and unified overall set of mental states.

This notion of a coherent or unified set of mental states is a normative notion in the sense that it is an analytic or conceptual truth that, roughly, there is some reason in favour of such coherent or unified overall sets of mental states; that is, it is in some sense a *virtue* of an overall mental state if it is coherent or unified in this way. However, it is a rather special virtue of one's overall mental state: whether or not one's set of mental states is coherent or unified in this sense is supposed to be determined purely by one's mental states alone; it does not depend on how things are in the world independently of one's mental states. Moreover, Smith's view does not give any deeper explanation about what exactly is good about such coherent or unified sets of mental states. It is just supposed to be a basic platitude, for which no further explanation is required, that such coherence or unification is a good or valuable feature of one's mental states. In effect then, it is supposed somehow to be just *intrinsically* good or valuable for one's mental states to be unified and coherent in this way—perhaps because such coherence or unification makes for a particularly pretty pattern among one's mental states.

It now seems clear that Smith's analysis is vulnerable to the 'So what?' objection. Why should this pretty pattern among one's mental states be the supreme virtue, so that what one desires when one's mental states form this sort of pretty pattern is authoritative over what to do? Consider a rational agent who acknowledges that if she had no false beliefs and all relevant true beliefs about non-normative questions, and her mental states formed a pretty coherent unified pattern of the relevant kind, she would desire that she φ in C. This agent could surely still wonder whether or not to φ in C, because she could wonder whether the desires that she would have in these rather specific conditions correspond infallibly to the reasons that she has.

For these reasons, then, it seems to me that even though Smith's analysis forgoes the crucial advantage of non-circular analyses—such as those of Lewis (1989) and Jackson and Pettit (1995)—it still succumbs in the end to the same problem. Even though the analysis is designed precisely for the purpose of providing an explanation of NJI, it cannot provide the required explanation.

3.6 CONCLUSION

There are various lessons to be learnt from the failure of the attempts to give a causal theory of reference for normative terms, and to give these terms a traditional conceptual analysis.

The causal theory was vitiated in the end because it does not pay enough attention to the distinctive *role* that the normative concepts play in *thought*. Instead, it just focused on the existence of causal relations of some kind or other between our use of the term and the normative properties or relations that those terms refer to. But the sense of normative terms, and the nature of normative concepts, must involve more than just their reference or semantic value; it must somehow also involve their *conceptual role* in our thinking and reasoning.

In a way, the attempt to give an account of the meaning of a term, or of the nature of a concept, by means of a "conceptual analysis" does invoke the concept's role in our thinking. Specifically, it invokes the role that the concept plays in certain pieces of implicit knowledge or belief. But this is only one very special sort of role that a concept can play in thinking and reasoning. It seems likely that the correct account of normative concepts will invoke a very different sort of role that these concepts play in thinking and reasoning.

The main problem with conceptual analyses, however, was that they all tried to force their account into a universally quantified biconditional, couched entirely in the *object language* (or in the "material mode", as Carnap would put it). As we have seen, in the end this approach turns out to be a Procrustean straitjacket. The correct account of normative terms, it seems, will have to be couched in a *metalanguage* (or in the "formal mode" in Carnap's phrase). There need be no objection to using normative terms in the metalanguage, so long as they are not used in actually specifying the content of thoughts or the meaning of terms or utterances.

In this respect, the correct account will resemble the causal theory, which is explicitly given in a metalanguage, and allows itself to use the very term in question in the metalanguage. (For example, the causal theorist will say that a term like 'cow' refers to cows if and only if its use is appropriately causally regulated by cows themselves.) It is only in this way that we can give a substantive non-circular account of the meaning of normative statements and the content of normative thoughts, without pursuing the quixotic project of attempting to give an explanation of the nature of normative concepts in wholly non-normative terms.

This then is the sort of account that I will try to develop in the next two chapters: it will be a conceptual role account, in which the essential role of normative concepts in reasoning and thinking is not just their role in certain pieces of implicit knowledge or belief; and I will allow myself to make use of normative terms in the metalanguage, so long as such normative terms are not used in directly specifying the content of thoughts or the meaning of terms or utterances.

4

Conceptual Role Semantics

4.1 THE CONCEPTUAL ROLE OF NORMATIVE CONCEPTS

In the previous chapter, we saw that none of the best-known truth-conditional accounts of normative concepts can give an adequate explanation of normative judgment internalism (NJI)—that is, of the fact that normative judgments have an essential or internal connection to practical reasoning or motivation for action.

In this chapter, I shall begin to develop an account of normative concepts that can explain NJI. This explanation is based on the following two ideas. First, quite generally, the nature of a concept consists in its essential *conceptual role* in thought and reasoning. Secondly, the essential conceptual role of normative concepts consists of a certain *regulative* role that these concepts play in *reasoning*—including *practical* reasoning. In that sense, normative judgments about what actions one ought to perform are essentially connected to motivation and practical reasoning because they involve a concept whose essential conceptual role is its role in practical reasoning. In effect, these normative judgments involve a concept that amounts to an *essentially practical mode of presentation* of the ought-relation.

It is a common view about concepts (or modes of presentation) that they are individuated by their essential "inferential role" in thought. According to this view, the essential features of each concept are given by a certain inferential role that that concept plays.[1] But if many concepts are individuated by their inferential role, why shouldn't there be some concepts that are individuated by their role in *practical reasoning*? After all, inference and practical reasoning are both species of a common genus—namely, reasoning.

In fact, it seems quite possible that there should be a concept expressed by the term 'ought' that is individuated at least in part by the fact that NJI is true of this concept. That is, we could partially characterize the essential role of this concept as follows: any judgment of the form 'I ought to φ', involving this concept, *rationally commits* the thinker to intending to φ. (As I noted in Chapter 1, for this claim to be plausible, φ-ing must be, as I put it, something "of the appropriate

---

[1] See, for example, Harman (1999), Field (1977), and Block (1987).

sort": that is, φ-ing must be a course of action that is "manifestly dependent on intention", in a situation "with no relevant uncertainty".) To say that a judgment "rationally commits" the thinker to having a corresponding intention is to say that if this judgment is rational, then that makes it irrational for the thinker not to have the corresponding intention. If this really is an essential feature of this concept, then this can explain the first version of NJI that I formulated in the first chapter—the version according to which it is a basic requirement of rationality that if one makes a first-person judgment of the form 'I ought to φ', one must also intend to φ.

Moreover, suppose that it is true that all thinkers must have at least some disposition to comply with the basic requirements of rationality that apply to them. (I shall present some arguments in favour of this claim in Chapter 7.) Then this account of the essential conceptual role of the concept 'ought' also supports the second version of NJI that I formulated in Chapter 1—the version according to which all thinkers who make judgments of the form 'I ought to φ' at all must have at least some general disposition to intend to do whatever they judge that they ought to do.

Some philosophers may object to this explanation of NJI, on the grounds that it will seem doubtful to them whether it can be essential to any concept that it plays this role in practical reasoning. After all, the notion of a concept (or a "mode of presentation") is not just a catch-all. What is essential to concepts is just that they play a *representational* role: the nature of a concept consists purely in the contribution that it makes to the nature of the thoughts in which it appears; and such thoughts are nothing more than ways of representing some possible state of affairs. So how can it be an essential feature of a concept that it has a connection of this sort to practical reasoning or motivation?

I shall assume that when this objection speaks of "possible states of affairs", these possible states of affairs are nothing other than *conditions*—that is, propositions of the sort that are composed (by means of operations analogous to predication, negation, conjunction, existential quantification, and so on) out of ordinary entities like individuals, properties, and relations. A thought is a "way of representing" a condition of this kind because this condition is determined by the semantic values of the concepts that feature in the thought, together with the way in which those concepts are put together, in such a way that it is an essential feature of the thought that it is true if and only if this condition obtains. So, to say that all that is essential to a concept is its representational role is just to say that the essential features of a concept must all be relevant to determining the concept's reference or semantic value.

So, to defend my proposed explanation of NJI, I will have to explain how the conceptual role that this concept plays in practical reasoning can be what determines its semantic value. That is, this conceptual role must be what determines that it is the relevant ought-relation (rather than any other relation) that this concept refers to or has as its semantic value. Ultimately, the semantic value of a term or a concept must be capable of explaining the *logical behaviour* of the term or concept. Thus, a full defence of my account of the concept that is expressed by an occurrence of the term 'ought' will have to involve an account of the basic logical principles that govern this concept; that is, it will have to involve an account of the basic principles of *deontic logic*.

In the next section, I shall first explain in more detail how I think the most plausible version of conceptual role semantics will work, by looking at the example of how it applies to certain *logical concepts*—the concepts expressed by logical operators like the truth-functional connectives and the quantifiers.[2] Then in the remainder of this chapter, I shall give a sketch of how this approach could be applied to the concepts that are expressed by terms like 'ought'. In the next chapter, I shall develop this approach in greater detail. In this more detailed account, I shall argue that the word 'ought' in English is in fact systematically *context-sensitive*, and expresses different concepts in different contexts. I shall also offer an account of the basic principles of deontic logic—that is, of the logical principles that apply to all of these different concepts that the term 'ought' can express.

4.2 AN EXAMPLE OF CONCEPTUAL ROLE SEMANTICS: THE LOGICAL CONSTANTS

There are many different versions of conceptual role semantics.[3] According to the version of conceptual role semantics that I wish to develop, the nature of a concept is given by the *basic rules of rationality* governing its use. That is, what individuates the concept—what makes it different from all the other concepts—are certain rules that specify ways in which it would be rational or irrational to use the concept. As I shall try to show, the basic rules of rationality governing the use of a concept can explain both what it is for someone to possess that concept, and why the concept has the distinctive reference or semantic value that it has.

Moreover, once we have an account of the nature of a concept, we can also give an account of the meaning of the *linguistic expressions* that express that concept, on the assumption that our understanding of a term or expression consists of

---

[2] This account of the logical constants owes much to Christopher Peacocke (1987). One of the main goals of Peacocke's work on the logical constants is to show how the insights of conceptual role semanticists like Gilbert Harman (1986), and intuitionists like Dag Prawitz (1979), can be combined with a realist truth-conditional semantics. I have noted the main points where I diverge from Peacocke in *nn.* 10 and 11 below.

[3] For example, Gilbert Harman (1999) regards conceptual role semantics as a *rival* to truth-conditional semantics. Hartry Field (1977), on the other hand, has advocated a "two-factor view" according to which a term's meaning involves both its conceptual role and its contribution to truth conditions as two mutually independent elements. In contrast to these approaches, I shall propose that it is precisely the conceptual role of normative concepts that fixes the reference or semantic value of those concepts; compare Ned Block (1987).

our ability to use the term to express that concept, and the semantic value of the concept also explains the semantic value of the corresponding term.

First, however, we should remind ourselves of some of the key features of the project that we are engaged in. We are aiming to give an account of the nature of a concept—that is, of a certain type of thought, a type of thought in which a certain property or relation is presented in a certain way; our goal is to explain what makes this concept different from all other concepts. We are not aiming to give a general account of concepts as such, or to pursue the reductive project of explaining the intentional in wholly naturalistic terms. For this reason, there is no objection to our simply assuming that there are concepts, and that these concepts combine to form thoughts, which are the objects of attitudes like belief, intention, and the like.

We are also not aiming to produce an account of logical concepts (such as the concepts expressed by 'not', 'if', and so on) that could enable someone who has not yet acquired these concepts to come to possess them. We are working as *theorists*, trying to understand what it is for a thought to be of a certain type (what is it for a thought to be of the form '$p \mathbin{\&} q$', for example)—where this is a type of thought that is common among ordinary thinkers who have no theoretical ambitions of this kind at all. Since it seems clear that every thought of this type involves the thinker's exercising an *ability* to have thoughts of this type, we are in effect trying to explain the nature of this ordinary, everyday ability. Hence there is no objection to our simultaneously *using* these very abilities in giving an account of the nature of these abilities. That is, there is no objection to our using terms that express logical concepts (like 'if', 'not', and so on) in the metalanguage of the theory in which we are explaining the nature of these very concepts. What we must avoid is using these terms inside the scope of propositional attitude ascriptions, or in some other phrase that specifies the content of a thought or sentence; that would be presupposing what we are aiming to give an account of—what it is for a thought to be a thought involving the concept in question.

Let us start with disjunction, the concept expressed by the English word 'or'. What would it be for a concept A to be disjunction? First, A must be a binary operator on thoughts: given any pair of thoughts, p and q, there must be a third thought built up out of p, q, and A, in which A has largest scope.[4] Let us give this third thought the name 'Apq'. (Since we are assuming that A is a genuine concept, we may assume that there is a further thought Apq, even though we may not make any assumptions at this stage about *which* thought it is.)

Secondly, the basic rules governing thoughts involving A are the following:

Rule 1
Acceptance of p commits one to accepting Apq

---

[4] This has the consequence that there are infinitely many thoughts, including thoughts of arbitrary length and complexity. As I am understanding them, however, thoughts are universal types of mental state, not particular mental events; and so this consequence seems to me quite harmless.

Rule 2
    Acceptance of q commits one to accepting Apq

(Strictly speaking, these rules should be reformulated so that they also cover the case of purely *suppositional* reasoning, in which one merely *supposes p* or *supposes q*—"purely for the sake of argument"—and then infers Apq from that supposition.)

As I explained in the previous section, to say that one's acceptance of p "commits" one to accepting Apq is to say that if one's acceptance of p is not irrational, then that makes it irrational for one not to accept Apq as well (at least if the question of whether or not to accept Apq arises). So, to conform to these rules, one must meet the following condition: if one either accepts p or accepts q, and this acceptance is not irrational (and the question of whether or not to accept Apq arises), then one must also accept Apq. (When one merely supposes p or supposes q purely "for the sake of argument"—then conforming to these rules requires accepting the conclusion Apq *conditionally* on the supposition of the premise p, or on the supposition of the premise q.) At all events, conforming to these rules requires that if one rationally either accepts p or accepts q, then one must not take the *opposite* attitude towards Apq, by *rejecting Apq* instead of accepting it.[5]

There is a fundamental difference between rules about how one mental state *commits* one to having another mental state, and rules about how one mental state counts as a *ground* or *basis* for another mental state. In some cases, simply *having* a mental state is enough to make it rational for one to have a certain further mental state, regardless of whether or not that first mental state is rational. For example, simply being in pain is enough to make it rational for one to believe that one is in pain; it is not required that one's pain should be "rational" in any sense. In these cases, the first mental state does not in my sense "commit" one to that further mental state; instead it merely constitutes a rational ground or basis for that further mental state.

Given how I am understanding what it is for one mental state to "commit" a thinker to another mental state, these rules about how both acceptance of p and acceptance of q commit one to accepting Apq may be called "rules of rationality": they specify conditions in which it is rational to accept Apq, and conditions in which it is irrational to reject Apq. If these are indeed the *basic* rules governing A, then these requirements about how it is rational to use the concept A in thought must be fundamental truths about rationality, which cannot be explained on the basis of any more basic principles about how it is rational to use the concept A in thought.

---

    [5] To "reject" a thought or a proposition is to *disbelieve* that thought—that is, to be in the state that would be expressed by *denying* the thought in question. More importantly, for our purposes, it is correct to reject a thought if and only if the thought is not true. Thus, acceptance and rejection are *opposites*, in the sense that it cannot be correct simultaneously to accept and reject any thought.

Why should we insist that it is the "*basic*" rules governing a concept, rather than *all* such rules, that determine the nature of the concept?[6] If the nature of a concept were determined by all the rules that governed its use, then there could be no difference between logically equivalent thoughts. Consider, for example, the thoughts '*p* or *q*' and 'Not both not-*p* and not-*q*'.[7] Since these two thoughts are logically equivalent, it seems that exactly the same rules of inference govern them both. But intuitively these two thoughts are different: someone might believe one without believing the other. It is plausible however that the rules of disjunction-introduction are *basic* rules for '*p* or *q*', but not basic rules for 'Not both not-*p* and not-*q*'; and according to the version of conceptual role semantics that I am working with, this explains why these two thoughts are different from each other.[8]

We can distinguish between merely *conforming to* these rules and actually *following* these rules. One might conform to these rules purely by accident, without exercising any ability or competence for reasoning in accordance with these rules. To follow these rules, on the other hand, one need not be explicitly thinking about these rules, or even representing these rules to oneself in any way; but one must not be conforming to these rules purely by accident—one must be exercising an ability or competence for reasoning in accordance with the rules. We can appeal to this notion of following a rule to explain what it is for a thinker to possess the concept *A*. To possess the concept, one must have a general disposition to follow these rules. (As we saw earlier, in Chapter 1, one can have a general disposition even if one does not manifest that disposition on every occasion; indeed, it is even possible for one to have a disposition that one never manifests.) If someone did not have a general disposition to follow these rules, then it would not be correct to interpret them as having thoughts involving the concept.[9] More specifically, to possess the concept one's disposition to follow

---

[6] This focus on the *basic* rules governing the use of a term parallels Harman's idea that a concept's essential conceptual role is determined by what the concept "*immediately* implies" or "*immediately* excludes" (1986: 130–2), and Peacocke's idea that possession of a concept requires finding certain patterns of reasoning "*primitively* compelling" (1987: 154–6).

[7] I should note that I am being rather free and easy with the use of single quotation marks, which form expressions that refer sometimes to linguistic types, and sometimes to propositions or thoughts, and sometimes function as Quinean corner-quotes. I doubt that any serious confusions will result from this.

[8] Of course, another way of explaining why these two thoughts differ from each other is by claiming that 'Not both not-*p* and not-*q*' has a *more complex compositional structure* than '*p* or *q*'. But suppose that there were a compositionally simple concept *V* such that *Vpq* is primitively or immediately obviously equivalent to 'Not both not-*p* and not-*q*'. Then it would be arguable that *Vpq* is still a different thought from '*p* or *q*', even though the two thoughts are logically equivalent and have the same compositional structure. So the fact that the basic rules for the two thoughts are different seems a better explanation of what makes them different from each other.

[9] Some philosophers believe that it is *impossible* for anyone not to follow the rules of disjunction-introduction without failing (at least on that occasion) to possess the concept 'or'. But this is a very bold claim indeed. Frege's (1964: 14) claim, that flouting these rules would be a "hitherto unknown type of madness", seems the most that it is plausible to claim here.

these rules must be *non-derivative*—that is, one's disposition to follow these rules must not be due merely to one's having some independent justification for these rules.[10]

To give an adequate account of the concept *A*, however, these rules must not only explain what it is to possess the concept; they must also explain the concept's semantic value, its contribution to the truth conditions of thoughts in which it appears. But how can these basic rules for *A* determine the concept's semantic value?

As I explained at the beginning of the previous chapter, we are assuming the background of a general semantic theory. Above all, this background semantic theory is "compositional": it determines what sort of semantic value is appropriate for sentences, and it requires that the semantic value of a sentence must be a function of the semantic values of its constituent terms. I shall assume that the way in which this semantic theory applies to the level of concepts is exactly parallel to the way in which it applies to the level of linguistic expressions. So this semantic theory determines what sort of semantic value is appropriate for thoughts, and requires that the semantic value of a thought is a function of the semantic values of its constituent concepts.

Since the concept *A* is a binary operator on thoughts, its semantic value must be a binary function on the semantic values of thoughts. As I explained in the previous chapter, I am assuming that the semantic value of a thought is a *condition* (that is, a proposition of the sort that is composed, by means of operations analogous to predication, negation, and so on, out of ordinary entities like individuals, properties, and relations). Then the semantic value of *A* must be a function from pairs of conditions to conditions—that is, a binary operation on conditions.

Once this background semantic theory has determined what sort of semantic value *A* must have, it is not hard to see how these basic rules for *A* can determine what its semantic value is. Specifically, the semantic value of *A* must make all instances of these rules of inference *valid*. An inference is valid, let us suppose, if and only if it is necessarily truth-preserving. In general, to follow a rule of inference, one must accept and not reject the conclusion of an inference of the relevant form (at least if the relevant question arises) whenever one accepts the premises of that inference. Now, if a thought is true, it is correct to accept that thought, whereas it is incorrect to reject that thought. As we might say, it is "uniquely correct" to accept that thought: acceptance is the *only* correct attitude of this sort than one can have towards that thought. So, every valid inference

---

[10] As I shall argue in Chapters 7–8, we cannot explain what it is to "follow" a rule except in partly *normative* terms. For this reason, I do not accept Peacocke's claim that the possession conditions for concepts should be "non-normative" (1992: 139); on this point, I agree with Millar (1994). Robert Brandom (1994) offers an explicitly normative version of conceptual role semantics. However, my approach is not committed to Brandom's claim that normative notions are prior to intentional notions (nor to his claim that the notion of inference is prior to the notion of representation, nor to his radical holism about concepts).

has the following feature: necessarily, if one's acceptance of the premises of the inference is correct, then it is uniquely correct to accept the conclusion—that is, accepting the conclusion is correct, while rejecting the conclusion is incorrect.

This suggests a way in which we can generalize this notion, of a rule's instances' being "valid", to apply to other rules, besides rules of inference. Take any rule, according to which a certain mental state S_1 (for example, the state of accepting a certain thought) commits one to having a certain other mental state S_2 (for example, the state of accepting a certain other thought), and so also to *not* having the opposite mental state S_3 (such as the state of *rejecting* that other thought instead of accepting it). This instance of the rule is "valid" just in case it is necessary that if the "input" state S_1 is correct, the "output" state S_2 is uniquely correct—that is, it is correct to be in the output state S_2, while it is incorrect to be in the state S_3 that is the opposite of that output state.

Suppose then that these basic rules for A are valid in all instances. This is still not sufficient to fix the semantic value of A, since all instances of these rules would also be valid if the truth conditions of Apq were the same as those of the intuitively weaker thought 'p or q or r'. To fix the semantic value of A, we should require that this semantic value must also make this set of rules in a certain sense "*complete*". The claim that these rules for A are valid in all instances in effect specifies certain conditions in which it would be mistaken or incorrect to reject Apq. Specifically, it implies that rejecting Apq would be incorrect if p is true, and would also be incorrect if q is true. But if the truth conditions of Apq were the same as those of 'p or q or r', this set of rules would be *incomplete*; it would fail to capture the fact that rejecting Apq would also be incorrect if r is true. This set of rules is, in the relevant sense, complete just in case it captures *every possible condition* in which rejecting Apq would be such a mistake. In general, the claim that certain rules for a given concept are valid in all instances in effect specifies certain conditions in which it would be mistaken or incorrect to accept (or reject) a thought in which that concept has largest scope. This set of rules is complete just in case these are the *only* conditions in which acceptance (or rejection) of that thought would be mistaken or incorrect in this way.[11]

In this way, these rules can fix the semantic value of A. To make all instances of these rules valid, the semantic value of A must make it necessary that Apq is true if p is true, and also if q is true. But to make this set of rules complete, the semantic value must make it impossible for Apq to be true except when either p or q is true. So, this semantic value must be the operation on conditions that maps any pair of conditions $<x, y>$ onto a third condition z such that, necessarily, z is a condition that obtains if and only if either x or y obtains.[12]

---

[11] This idea simplifies and generalizes some of the points that Peacocke (1987: 160–2) makes about the existential quantifier.

[12] This semantic value can then justify all the other rules of inference (such as the elimination rules) that apply to the use of the concept. Since the concept's semantic value is determined by the

A similar account could be given for the other logical concepts. For example, suppose that for a concept N to be the concept '*not*' is for the basic rule for N to be the following rule of incompatibility:

> Acceptance of Np commits one to rejecting p; and acceptance of p commits one to rejecting Np.

To follow this rule, let us suppose, one must reject p whenever one accepts Np; and at all events, one must never simultaneously accept both p and Np. To possess the concept N one must have a non-derivative disposition to follow this rule.[13]

Given the account of validity that I proposed above, an instance of this rule will be valid just in case it is necessary that, if it is correct to accept Np, then it is also correct to reject p, while it would be incorrect to accept p. In effect, an instance of this rule for N is valid if and only if it is necessary that if Np is true then p is false. One way in which all instances of this rule might be valid is if Np had the same truth conditions as the intuitively stronger thought 'Not-p and q'. But then the set of rules would be incomplete: the claim that all instances of this rule are valid would not capture every possible case in which it would be incorrect to accept Np. To make this a complete set of rules, as well as making all instances of the rule valid, the semantic value of N must not only make it necessary that p is not true whenever Np is true; it must also make it necessary that Np is true whenever p is not true.

Clearly, this account, of what it is for a concept to be the concept *not*, itself makes use of negative terms like 'incompatible', 'never', and so on. But as I explained earlier, there is nothing objectionably circular about this. The purpose of this account is to give a theoretical explanation of what it is to possess the concept '*not*', not to convey that concept to someone who lacks it. According to this account, possessing the concept '*not*' consists in a disposition to follow this rule of incompatibility; it need not involve any knowledge (not even implicit knowledge) of this account of the concept. This account of the concept '*not*' is not viciously circular, since it specifies the basic rule for the concept N, and explains how this rule determines the concept's semantic value, without at any point using the term 'not' in characterizing the contents of anyone's propositional attitudes, or assuming that any object-language term means *not*. The word 'not' is used only in the *metalanguage*.

---

basic rules that apply to it, it is plausible that *all* the other rules applying to the use of A are justified, at least in part, on the basis of these basic rules.

[13] This idea, that the nature of negation is given by a rule of incompatibility, is due to Harman (1986) and has been developed by Peacocke (1987) and more recently by Rumfitt (2000). Rumfitt's account of negation in effect adds the converse rule: rejection of p commits one to accepting Np, and rejection of Np commits one to accepting p. I do not need to appeal to this additional rule, because within my framework, the semantic value of N must be the *weakest* possible value that will make all instances of the primary rule valid.

4.3 THE LOGICAL FORM OF 'OUGHT'

This is the approach that I wish to adapt in giving an account of normative concepts, the concepts that can be expressed by terms like 'ought' and its cognates. Unfortunately, however, as we shall see, 'ought' gives rise to certain controversies that do not arise in the case of the logical constants, which we explored in the last section.

First, it is quite uncontroversial that the logical concept expressed by 'or' is a binary operator on thoughts (just as the term 'or' itself is a binary sentential operator), so that its semantic value will be a binary function on the semantic values of thoughts; and that the concept expressed by 'not' is a unary operator on thoughts, so that its semantic value is a unary operator on the semantic values of thoughts. By contrast, it is controversial what is the fundamental logical form of the thoughts that are expressed by sentences involving 'ought'.

In view of this controversy, it will be easier at this point to try to address this question by turning to normative *terms*. This is for the methodological reasons that were mentioned in Chapter 1: the data regarding terms or linguistic expressions are at least somewhat less slippery than the data regarding thoughts and concepts.

Many philosophers understand the term 'ought' as a *propositional operator*—that is, as a term whose semantic value is a function from an embedded proposition (which is somehow indicated in the sentence in which 'ought' occurs) to a further proposition. But other philosophers—most notably P. T. Geach (1991) and Gilbert Harman (1973)—hold that it is a mistake to assume that 'ought' is always a propositional operator; according to these philosophers, at least sometimes, 'ought' must be understood as a *relational predicate* applying to triples consisting of an agent, a possible course of action, and a time.

There are admittedly some contexts in which it may seem plausible to interpret 'ought' or its close relative 'should' as a relational predicate that applies to an agent, a course of action, and a time. For example, suppose that a non-philosopher on the appointment committee for the Professorship of Metaphysics at a British university says in the course of the committee's deliberations:

(1) We ought to hire that man David Lewis.

It is tempting to interpret this sentence as asserting that a certain relation holds between an agent (in this case, a collective agent, referred to by the term 'we'), a course of action (specifically, hiring David Lewis), and a time (specifically, a time in the relatively immediate future after the utterance in question). In these cases, it generally seems to be required for the truth of the sentence that the course of action in question be one that it is possible for the relevant agent to perform at the time in question. This is why it seems to be a decisive objection to this utterance (1) to point out, "It's not possible for us to hire Lewis: he's dead!"

By contrast, there seem to be other sorts of 'ought' or 'should' that it is overwhelmingly plausible to interpret as propositional operators. For example, consider the opening lines of Wordsworth's poem *England 1802*:

(2) Milton! Thou shouldst be living at this hour.
England hath need of thee ...

No particular course of action is explicitly mentioned in this sentence; and even though a certain agent (Milton) and a certain time (1802) are mentioned, it is obvious that the truth of this sentence does not require that it should be possible for that agent to do anything at all at that time. (It hardly seems that it would be a good objection to this utterance to reply to Wordsworth, back in 1802, "It's impossible for Milton to be alive now: he died in 1674, which was 128 years ago!")

It might be suggested that (2) does contain an *implicit* reference to an agent (such as God, perhaps), a time, and a possible course of action—namely, the course of action of *bringing it about that Milton is alive in 1802*. But this interpretation of (2) seems to me too *ad hoc* to be credible. The proponent of this interpretation would have to say that in some sentences involving 'ought' or 'should', in order to find an implicit reference to a possible course of action, we have to import the concept 'bringing it about that ... '. But in other sentences involving 'ought', it seems that we should not import the concept 'bringing it about that ... '. For example, in saying 'You ought to proportion your belief to the evidence', I need not be saying that you ought to *perform the action of bringing it about that* you proportion your belief to the evidence; I am simply saying that you ought to proportion your belief to the evidence. Similarly, in saying 'You ought to run away right now', it seems that the relevant possible course of action is just *running away right now* (an action that I can only perform right now), and not the quite different action of *bringing it about that I run away right now* (which is an action that I could have performed some time earlier—say, by paying someone to hypnotize me so that I run away at this time).

It seems then that it is not plausible to treat the occurrence of 'should' in (2) as expressing a relation between an agent, a course of action, and a time. The most plausible way to construe 'should' in (2) seems to be as a propositional operator. Grammatically, 'ought' and 'should' in English are auxiliary verbs, like the modal auxiliaries 'can' and 'must'. When an occurrence of 'ought' or 'should' modifies the main verb of a sentence, it can be taken as a propositional operator applying to the proposition that would be expressed by the unmodified form of that sentence. Thus, in (2), 'should' is a propositional operator applying to the proposition that would be expressed by the sentence 'Milton is living at this hour'.

We have seen then that there at least two kinds of 'ought'—the two kinds illustrated by our examples (1) and (2) respectively. It is one central mark of the first sort of 'ought' that for any statement in which this sort of 'ought' has largest scope, there is a *particular agent* and a *particular time* such that the statement is true if and only if that person is able at that time to realize whatever the statement says that he ought to realize. Thus, for an utterance of the sentence (1) to be true, the particular university committee that is referred to by 'we' must have the ability to hire David Lewis in the near future after the time of the utterance. In this way, this sort of 'ought' is always *indexed* to an agent and a time.

It is clear that the time to which an occurrence of this sort of 'ought' is indexed is often only implicit, and not explicitly mentioned in the sentence. But in fact, the same is true of the agent to whom the 'ought' is indexed, who also need not always be explicitly mentioned in the sentence in question. Thus suppose that a mafia family's consigliere is advising the mafia boss about how long they should allow Alfredo to live, and says:

(3) Alfredo should stay alive for at least the next 24 hours.

Here the truth of the statement does not depend on whether *Alfredo* has the ability to ensure that he stays alive for the next 24 hours: it depends on whether the *mafia family* has that ability. So, again, it would be a decisive objection to this statement to say: "We can't keep Alfredo alive for another 24 hours: he was killed last night!" Thus, the agent to whom this occurrence of 'ought' is indexed is not Alfredo but the mafia family—which is not explicitly mentioned in this sentence.

This first sort of 'ought', which is always indexed to an agent and a time, is often used to express either advice, or a conclusion of deliberation or practical reasoning about what to do. This is why Williams (1981*a*: 119–20) called it "the practical or deliberative *ought*". This label might be misleading if it suggests that this sort of 'ought' can *only* be used to express conclusions of deliberation (in first-person contexts), or advice (in second-person contexts). There is no reason to think that this sort of 'ought' cannot occur in third-person or past-tensed contexts (as in 'Napoleon ought not to have invaded Russia') where there is no question of the speaker's giving advice or deliberating about what to do. The point is just that this sort of 'ought' is particularly appropriate for expressing advice or deliberation.

By contrast, the sort of 'ought' that occurs in Wordsworth's line (2) appears not to be indexed to any particular agent and time. There is no particular agent such that Wordsworth's point is that *that* agent ought to ensure that Milton is alive in 1802. Wordsworth's point is just that in the possible states of affairs that are—in some respect that is salient in the context—*most desirable*, Milton would be alive in 1802. We could call this the 'ought' of general desirability.[14] Since these two sorts of 'ought' have different logical implications, they must have different references or semantic values. I shall use the term 'concept' in

---

[14] Sidgwick (1907: 33) calls this the "political *ought*", and he illustrates it by means of the following example: "when I judge that the laws and constitution of my country 'ought to be' other than they are, I do not of course imply that my own or any other individual's single volition can directly bring about the change."

such a way that the concept that a term expresses determines its semantic value. It follows that these two sorts of 'ought' express different concepts. In this way then, the term 'ought' is context-sensitive in some way: it expresses different concepts in different contexts.

Geach insists that the difference between these two sorts of 'ought' is a difference in logical form: the second sort of 'ought'—the 'ought' of general desirability—is indeed a propositional operator; but the first sort of 'ought'—the practical or deliberative 'ought'—is a predicate standing for a relation that holds between an agent, a course of action, and a time. But it seems more plausible to me to treat *both* sorts of 'ought' as propositional operators wherever they occur.

First, I have argued that we must treat 'ought' and 'should' as sometimes functioning as propositional operators. So we would clearly achieve a more unified account if we suppose that they *always* function as such operators. We would also be able to unify our account of the auxiliary verbs 'ought' and 'should' with that of the modal auxiliaries 'can' and 'must', which practically all philosophers and semanticists would interpret as always functioning as propositional operators.[15]

Secondly, there is an argument, which in outline is due to Williams (1981*a*), that seems to show that even the practical 'ought' always functions as a propositional operator. Suppose that a group of people are involved in a joint deliberation, as a result of which a speaker concludes:

(4) Someone ought to go and inform the manager.

Even if one keeps constant the interpretation of 'ought' as having its practical or deliberative sense here, this sentence is clearly ambiguous. The ambiguity is most naturally interpreted as involving a scope ambiguity: on one reading, (4) means the same as 'It ought to be that: someone goes and informs the manager'; on the other reading, it means the same as 'Someone is such that: *he* ought to go and inform the manager'.

Philosophers like Geach, who hold that the practical or deliberative 'ought' is a relational predicate, would interpret the second reading of (4) as asserting that someone stands in the ought-relation towards the course of action of *going and informing the manager*. However, the only way of construing the first reading of (4) as involving a predicate that stands for the ought-relation would be to take it as asserting that "we" (the group involved in the joint deliberation, viewed as a collective agent) stand in this ought-relation to the possible course of action of *bringing it about that someone goes and informs the manager*. But this possible course of action is not explicitly mentioned in the sentence. So, just as in our

---

[15] In many languages, the closest equivalent to 'ought' is an impersonal verb followed by a noun clause, which is a construction that it is particularly tempting to interpret as representing a proposition embedded inside a propositional operator: *il faut* in French, *dei* and *chrê* in ancient Greek, *prepei* in modern Greek, *rhaid* in Welsh, *opportet* in Latin, and so on.

example of the 'ought' of general desirability (2), this construal seems simply too *ad hoc* to be credible. (How can the first reading of (4) require importing the concept 'bringing it about that …' if the second reading does not?) Thus, it seems preferable to read 'ought' in this first reading of (4) as a propositional operator; and as Williams (1981*a*: 116) argues, "it is hard to see what requires it, or even allows it, to turn into something else" in the second reading.

For this reason, even the practical or deliberative 'ought' seems to function as a propositional operator. As we have seen, the practical 'ought' is always indexed, at least implicitly, to an agent and a time; and in this way it does indeed differ from the 'ought' of general desirability.[16] But just like the 'ought' of general desirability, the practical 'ought' is an operator that attaches to a proposition. Thus, the two readings of (4) differ in the following way. In the first reading, the 'ought' is indexed to "us" (the collective agent that is involved in the deliberation); and the proposition to which the operator is attached is the proposition that would be expressed by the sentence 'Someone goes and tells the manager'. In the second reading, it is the quantifier 'Someone' that has largest scope; the occurrence of 'ought' is indexed to the variable (which might be represented by 'x') that is bound by this quantifier; and the proposition to which the operator is attached is the "open proposition" that would be expressed by the *open* sentence 'x goes and tells the manager'.

For the rest of this chapter, I shall focus on the practical or deliberative 'ought'. (In the next chapter, I shall explore how my account can be generalized to deal with other kinds of 'ought' as well.) I shall represent the practical 'ought'-operator that is indexed to the agent A and time t by the symbol '$O_{<A,\ t>}$'.[17]

I shall assume a principle of unrestricted compositionality here. So, if there is a propositional operator '$O_{<A,\ t>}$', then this operator can be attached to *any* proposition p, to yield a further proposition '$O_{<A,\ t>}(p)$'. Moreover, given bivalence, this further proposition will have a definite truth value, either true or false. But we should note that it will often be hard to find a sentence of standard English (or any other natural language that I know) that has the complex proposition '$O_{<A,\ t>}(p)$' as its content.

In English, one common way to convey that an occurrence of 'ought' has its practical or deliberative sense, and is indexed to a particular agent A, is to make A the grammatical subject of 'ought'. (Making an agent the grammatical

---

[16] Some philosophers believe that we must distinguish between "the time of the act" and "the time of the 'ought'". I think this is wrong. In my view, there is no "time of the 'ought'"; at most, the fact that makes the 'ought'-statement true may be a fact about some particular time, such as the fact that one made a certain promise at a certain time. It is true, however, that the proposition embedded inside the time-indexed 'ought'-operator may itself concern a different time from that to which the operator is indexed. For example, an adviser might say to you, 'Your nephew ought to inherit your property after you die'; in this case, 'ought' is indexed to you and the time at which you have the ability to draw up your will, not to the time after you die when your nephew will inherit.

[17] To avoid certain complications, let us suppose that this symbol has no content unless 'A' refers to someone who is an agent at the time referred to by 't'.

subject of 'ought' does not always indicate that this occurrence of 'ought' is indexed to that agent, as we saw with our example of the mafioso's advice (3) 'Alfredo ought to stay alive for at least the next 24 hours'. If this is the practical 'ought', it is indexed not to Alfredo—the grammatical subject of the verb 'ought'—but rather to the advisee.) However, in English, the proposition to which the 'ought'-operator is attached is indicated by an *infinitive*—where the grammatical subject of the infinitive must be the same as the subject of the auxiliary verb 'ought'. So there is simply no way in grammatical English to affix the phrase 'You ought ... ' to an expression that indicates a proposition that does not somehow involve the person referred to as 'you'. For this reason, when the practical 'ought'-operator '$O_{<A,\ t>}$' is conveyed in English by the phrase 'At t, A ought ... ', there is a *grammatical* barrier to attaching this 'ought'-operator to any propositions that do not in some way involve A. Nonetheless, according to my assumptions, there is no *logical* barrier to attaching the operator '$O_{<A,\ t>}$' to propositions that have nothing to do with A.[18]

Another way of conveying the operator '$O_{<A,\ t>}$' (more common in other languages than in English) is to use an impersonal construction like 'It ought to be the case that ... ', and leave it *implicit* in the context that this occurrence of 'ought' is indexed to a particular agent A and time t. Even if one uses a personal construction, so that the relevant agent is the grammatical subject of the auxiliary verb 'ought', it is still merely implicit in the context that this occurrence of 'ought' is the practical or deliberative 'ought' (as opposed to the 'ought' of general desirability, or some other kind of 'ought'). Because the practical 'ought' is especially connected with deliberation and advice, the easiest way to indicate that it is the practical 'ought' that is in play is if the context somehow makes it clear that the statement is made from the standpoint of the relevant agent's deliberations about what to do at the relevant time (or of someone advising the agent about what to do at that time).

It will be very hard to convey that a statement is made from this standpoint if the proposition embedded inside in the 'ought'-operator is causally independent of everything that the agent might do or think at that time; as Aristotle famously observed (*Nicomachean Ethics* III.3, 1112a18–30), no one deliberates about things that they cannot affect in any way. So, if nothing that the agent could do or think at that time will make any difference to whether or not p is the case, then it will be almost irresistible to hear the sentence 'It ought to be the case that p' as involving a different sort of 'ought'. For example, if someone says, 'You ought to have been born ten years earlier than you were', or 'You ought to have been

---

[18] If p is a proposition that does not in any way involve A, then we *cannot* convey '$O_{<A,\ t>}(p)$' by saying 'At t, A ought to bring it about that p'; the proposition p and the proposition 'A brings it about that p' are distinct propositions, which must not be confused with each other. Even 'At t, A ought to be such that p' does not really convey '$O_{<A,\ t>}(p)$', but rather '$O_{<A,\ t>}(A$ is such that $p)$'. 'A is such that p' is not strictly speaking the same proposition as p itself: the former entails that A exists, while the latter may not.

born at exactly the time that you were born', it will be almost impossible to hear this as involving the practical 'ought' (as opposed to some other kind of 'ought'). Still, I am assuming that in principle, *any* proposition p can be embedded inside the practical 'ought'-operator indexed to an agent A and time t, '$O_{<A,\ t>}$', to yield another more complex proposition '$O_{<A,\ t>}(p)$'.

We might try enriching natural language by introducing an explicitly indexed 'ought'-operator: 'It ought, from the standpoint of A and t, to be the case that ... '. But we have no clear intuitions about sentences like 'It ought, from the standpoint of me and now, to be the case that there are nine planets in the solar system', even though, as noted above, I shall assume here that this proposition has a truth value. In the absence of any clear intuitions about these propositions, the question of what their truth conditions are must be decided by theoretical considerations, rather than by any direct appeal to intuition.

To sum up: 'ought' is a propositional operator whenever it occurs. The practical 'ought' (unlike the 'ought' of general desirability) is implicitly indexed to a particular agent and time. It will be hard to hear the term 'ought' as having this practical or deliberative sense, and as indexed to a particular agent A and time t, if the proposition that is embedded within the 'ought'-operator is causally independent of all of A's thoughts and actions at t. But this does not make it impossible for such propositions to be embedded inside this operator. Indeed, I shall suppose that the proposition '$O_{<A,\ t>}(p)$' has a definite truth value whatever the embedded proposition p may be. It might be hard to express this proposition using 'ought' in ordinary English; but this proposition will be true or false nonetheless.

4.4 THE CONCEPTUAL ROLE OF THE PRACTICAL 'OUGHT'

In the first section of this chapter, I suggested that the essential conceptual role of the concept that is expressed by the practical 'ought' may consist precisely in the fact that NJI is true of this concept. In fact, however, there is a snag that we will have to deal with in developing this suggestion. As I formulated it in Chapter 1, NJI is restricted to normative judgments of the form 'I ought to φ', where 'φ-ing' must refer to something "of the appropriate sort" —specifically, to a course of action that is "manifestly dependent on intention" in a situation with "no relevant uncertainty". But to determine the concept's semantic value with respect to *all* propositions to which the concept can be attached, the concept's essential conceptual role will have to be its role with respect to *any* proposition that it can be attached to. The essential conceptual role of the practical 'ought' will have to *entail* NJI in the special case in which the proposition that is embedded in its scope is the proposition 'I φ' (and φ-ing is a course of action of the appropriate sort), but it will have to be a more general conceptual role that includes other ways in which we are rationally required to use this concept. Nonetheless, I propose to stick with the general idea that the nature of the concept is given by the role that this concept essentially plays in deliberation and practical reasoning.

The first problem concerns the restriction of NJI to propositions that are about courses of action that are "manifestly dependent on intention". I propose to solve this problem by shifting from using the stricter notion of an *intention* to the somewhat wider notion of a *plan*. Even if you cannot strictly be said to *intend* that your friend Daniel will be in New York tomorrow (because whether or not you intend that Daniel will be in New York tomorrow will not in any way affect the chances of his being in New York tomorrow), it may still be *part of your plan* that Daniel will be in New York tomorrow. As we might ordinarily say, you could plan on Daniel's being in New York tomorrow, even if you cannot intend that Daniel will be in New York tomorrow unless it is up to you whether or not he is in New York tomorrow. Daniel's being in New York tomorrow is part of your plan because you believe that if everything goes according to your plan, Daniel will be in New York on that day.

Your "plan about what to do at *t*", as I am understanding it, is just a proposition—roughly, a proposition that represents a way in which you might behave at *t*, and a way things might be if you did behave in that way. To "adopt" the proposition *p* as your plan about what to do at *t* is to have a set of intentions about what to do at *t* such that, if the conjunction of the contents of those intentions is *q*, you believe 'If it were the case that *q*, it would be the case that *p*'. Then we can define "making the proposition *p* a part of your plan" simply as: adopting as your plan a proposition that logically entails *p*. Clearly, it will be perfectly rational for all sorts of propositions that are causally quite independent of your intentions to be part of your plans. So shifting from intentions to plans (on this interpretation of what plans are) seems to deal with the first problem with formulating the essential conceptual role of the practical 'ought'.

The second problem has to do with the fact that one may not always know everything about what one ought to do. So long as the truth about what one ought to do is not necessarily luminous or self-intimating, situations can arise in which you know that you ought to do either *A* or *B*, but you do not know which. In some situations of this kind, the rational intention to have might be an intention to pursue a third option *C*, which you know to be second-best. In this case, it could be quite rational for you to believe 'I ought to do either *A* or *B*', and yet not to make the proposition 'I will do either *A* or *B*' part of your plans. (Indeed, since it is rational for you to make the proposition 'I will do *C*' part of your plans, and you know that if you do *C*, you will not do either *A* or *B*, it seems rational for you to make the proposition 'I will *not* do either *A* or *B*' part of your plans.)

Still, in this case, even if you do not make the proposition 'I will do either *A* or *B*' part of your *actual* plans, you may at least make that proposition part of your *ideal* plan. Your "ideal plan" about what to do at *t* is in effect the proposition that you treat as what *would* be your plan if your planning and practical reasoning were not affected by relevant ignorance and uncertainty about what to do in the situation that you face at *t*. So, in a situation that is without relevant uncertainty (as I put it in Chapter 1), your ideal plan and your actual plan will coincide. (Otherwise, if your situation is characterized by such relevant uncertainty, your actual plan may be some second-best plan, rather than your ideal plan.)

With this distinction between ideal plans and actual plans, we may be in a position to characterize the essential conceptual role of the practical 'ought':

Acceptance of the first-person proposition[19] '$O_{<me, \ t>}(p)$'—where '*t*' refers to some time in the present or near future—commits one to making *p* part of one's ideal plan about what to do at *t*.

In Chapter 2, I argued in favour of a *cognitivist* interpretation of the mental states expressed by statements involving the term 'ought'; so to "accept" the proposition '$O_{<me, \ t>}(p)$' is just to have an ordinary *belief* in that proposition. As I explained above (Section 4.2), to say that this belief "commits" one to making the proposition *p* part of one's ideal plan is to say that, if it is rational for one to hold this belief, then that makes it irrational for one not to make *p* part of one's ideal plan (at least if the question of whether or not to make *p* part of one's ideal plan arises).

This, then, is my proposal about the essential conceptual role of the practical or deliberative 'ought'. For a concept to be the practical or deliberative 'ought' is for it to be a concept for which the basic rule of rationality governing its use is the rule that I have given above. This is the essential conceptual role that makes this concept the concept that it is. If this is the concept's essential nature, then it is clear that first-person judgments involving this concept will be essentially connected to practical reasoning and the formation of plans and intentions to act. In this way, then, my proposal about the essential nature of this concept will have no difficulty explaining why NJI is true.

Some philosophers might object that being subject to this rule is not *sufficient* to make it the case that '$O_{<A, \ t>}(p)$' is the proposition 'It ought to be that *p*', involving the practical or deliberative 'ought' implicitly indexed to *A* and *t*. Suppose, for example, that what Derek Parfit (1984: part II) calls the self-interest theory of rationality is correct. According to this self-interest theory, one is always rationally required to intend to act in a way that one believes will optimally promote one's own interests. In that case, it seems, this rule would apply, not

---

[19] In the terms that I introduced in Chapter 3 (Section 3.1), this proposition is a *thought* (the sort of proposition that is composed out of concepts) rather than a *condition* (the sort of proposition that is composed out of entities like individuals, properties, and relations, which are the semantic values of those concepts). But I shall stick with the term 'proposition' from now on. The context will make it clear which sort of proposition is in question.

only to the proposition 'It ought (in relation to me and t) to be the case that p' but also to the proposition 'If I optimally promote my own interests at t, then it will be the case that p'. But at least offhand, these seem to be different propositions: it seems possible for someone to believe one of these propositions without believing the other.

Let us assume for the sake of argument that these are indeed different propositions. Then the rule prescribed by the self-interest theory—the rule that accepting 'If I optimally promote my own interests at t, it will be the case that p' commits one to incorporating p into one's ideal plans—is distinct from the rule that I am focusing on—the rule that accepting 'It ought (in relation to me and t) to be the case that p' commits one to incorporating p into one's ideal plans. If it is true that we are rationally required to follow both these rules, how are these two rules related? The two rules surely cannot just be completely independent rules of rationality. One of these rules must be somehow more *basic* than the other. But then it seems much more plausible that the self-interest rule (if it really is a rule of rationality at all) is derivative from the rule that I am focusing on, rather than the converse. If both these rules are indeed rules of rationality, then it is plausible that there is a rule of inference according to which acceptance of 'If I optimally promote my own interests, it will be the case that p' commits one to accepting 'It ought to be the case that p'. But then, given this rule of inference, the self-interest rule could be derived from the rule that I am focusing on—the rule that accepting 'It ought to be that p' commits one to incorporating p into one's ideal plans. On the other hand, it is much less plausible that the rule that I am focusing on is derived from the self-interest rule. So the rule that I am focusing on, unlike the self-interest rule, seems a genuinely *basic* rule of rationality. Thus, even if the self-interest theory is true, the fact that this is the *basic* rule for '$O_{<A,\ t>}$' is sufficient to make it the case that '$O_{<A,\ t>}(p)$' has the meaning of 'It ought to be that p', involving the practical 'ought' indexed to A and t.

Some philosophers might raise a different objection to my claim that the whole of the essential conceptual role of the practical 'ought' is given by the rule that I have proposed above. According to this objection, it is not only the belief in '$O_{<A,\ t>}(p)$' that commits one to incorporating p into one's ideal plans, but the same is also true of the belief in the proposition 'It is part of my ideal plans about what to do at t that p'. However, this objection misunderstands what I mean by speaking of what a belief "commits" one to. It is just not true that the *belief* 'It is part of my ideal plans that p' commits one to making p part of one's ideal plans. Even if this is a rational belief, it does not follow that it is rational for one to make p part of one's ideal plans: one might rationally believe that p was part of one's ideal plans even though it was decidedly *irrational* for one to have such ideal plans in the first place.

As I mentioned in Section 4.1, some philosophers think that it is impossible for a concept's essential conceptual role to be its role in practical reasoning in the way that I am proposing. Part of their reason for thinking this, as I said, is that it seems plausible that nothing can be essential to a concept unless it is involved in determining the concept's reference or semantic value. As I shall explain in the next section, however, this account of the conceptual role of the practical or deliberative 'ought' *can* determine the concept's semantic value.

4.5 THE SEMANTIC VALUE OF 'OUGHT'

According to the account that I am proposing here, the basic rule for the practical 'ought' is the rule that a belief in the first-person proposition '$O_{<me,\ t>}(p)$' rationally commits one to making the proposition p part of one's ideal plan about what to do at t.

Within the semantic framework that I am assuming here, the semantic value of the concept '$O_{<A,\ t>}$' will in effect be a certain property of propositions—presumably, a relational property that propositions have in virtue of some relation in which they stand to the agent A and the time t.

The basic rule for the concept expressed by the practical 'ought' can determine this concept's semantic value because this semantic value must do two things. First, it must guarantee that all instances of that rule are *valid*. (In speaking of "all instances" of the rule here, I mean to include not only instances that arise from substituting other concepts of the appropriate syntactic category for 'p' and 't', but also instances that arise in other possible contexts, where different agents would be referred to by the term 'me'.) Secondly, the concept's semantic value must also make this a "*complete*" set of rules for the concept, in the sense that I outlined in my discussion of the logical constants in Section 4.2. One way in which we could make all instances of this rule valid would be by making the truth conditions of '$O_{<A,\ t>}(p)$' ludicrously strong (for example, if we made it a logical falsehood, which it would be necessarily incorrect to accept, then all instances of the rule would be trivially valid); but then this would not be a complete set of rules for the concept. To make this a complete set of rules for the concept, the semantic value of '$O_{<A,\ t>}$' must be the *weakest* property of propositions that will make all instances of this rule valid.

What would it mean to say that an instance of this rule is "valid"? An instance of a rule can be regarded as having "inputs" and an "output", where these inputs and outputs are types of mental state. Where a rule is a rule about how certain input mental states *commit* one to a certain output mental state, it would not be plausible to say that for an instance of such a rule to be valid, whenever one is *in* the input state, the output state must be a correct or appropriate state to be in. That may be plausible for a rule that is merely about how one mental state counts as a *ground* or *basis* for another. What is required for the validity of a rule about how certain input mental states commit one to a certain output mental state is rather, roughly, that the *correctness* of its inputs guarantees the correctness of its output.[20]

More precisely, if the content of the rule is that the input mental states *commit* one to having the output mental state as well, then if the rule is valid, the correctness of the input mental states must guarantee that the output mental state is *uniquely* correct—that is, that the output mental state is correct, and the "opposite" mental state is incorrect.[21]

I shall suppose that the "opposite" of the state of making the proposition p part of one's ideal plan about what to do at t is the state of making the *negation* of p part of one's ideal plan about what to do at t—that is, to adopt as one's ideal plan a proposition that logically entails the negation of p. On this approach, then, the semantic value of the practical 'ought'-operator '$O_{<A,\ t>}$' will be the weakest property of a proposition p that makes it the case that it is correct for A to make the proposition p part of her ideal plan about what to do at t, and incorrect for A to make the negation of p a part of her ideal plan.

Intuitively, this seems plausible as an account of the practical 'ought'. Suppose that my judgment 'I ought to buy some new shoes this week' is true. Then it seems plausible that it would be correct for me to make it part of my ideal plan that I will buy some new shoes this week, and incorrect for me to make it part of my ideal plan that I will *not* buy any new shoes this week. Conversely, if it is correct for me to plan on buying some new shoes this week, and incorrect for me to plan on not buying any new shoes this week, then it also seems plausible that my judgment 'I ought to buy some new shoes this week' is true. Still, to evaluate this account of the semantic value of 'ought', we need to know more about what it means to say that a plan of this sort is "correct" or "incorrect".

We have in fact already encountered this notion of "correctness" before, in Chapter 2, when I argued that there must be some "point" or "purpose" to conforming to the distinctive standards of justification or warrantedness that apply to statements. We could express the idea that this point or purpose is achieved by saying that the statement in question is *correct*; I also argued that the property of a sentence that makes it correct to make a statement by uttering that sentence is *truth*. A parallel story, I believe, can also be told about belief.[22] There are certain standards of justification or rationality that distinctively apply to beliefs; indeed, as I shall argue in Chapter 7, it is an essential feature of beliefs that they tend to be regulated and guided by these standards. The point or purpose of conforming to these standards of justification or rationality is to

---

[20] This is in effect my answer to one of the main objections of Schroeter and Schroeter (2003: 200–1).

[21] We shall consider what it is for instances of other sorts of rule (that is, rules that are not about how some input mental states "commit" one to some further mental state) to count as "valid" in the next chapter.

[22] For a defence of this claim, see Wedgwood (2002c).

achieve some external goal or purpose—the goal of "getting things right" in one's beliefs. Just as with statements, it is plausible that a belief succeeds in achieving this goal or purpose if and only if the content of the belief is true. As I am using these terms here, then, the paradigmatic example of a mental state that counts as "incorrect" or "wrong" or "mistaken" is a *false belief*. Thus, an incorrect mental state need not take the form of any internally incoherent or irrational reasoning. It is some more *external* failure to achieve what may be called the "goal" or "purpose" of the type of mental state in question.

The underlying idea of a correct mental state, then, seems to be this. There are certain standards (such as standards of justification or rationality or the like) such that it is essential to mental states of the relevant type that they are guided and regulated by those standards. Conforming to these standards is not just important for its own sake, however; there is some further point or purpose in conforming to these standards. It is when a mental state achieves this further point or purpose that it counts as a correct mental state.

Clearly, our plans and intentions are subject to standards of justification or rationality. We constantly assess plans and intentions on the basis of whether or not they count as rational. But it seems that the point of conforming to these standards of rational planning and intention is not just to avoid irrational plans and intentions purely for its own sake; there is some further "goal" or "purpose" of practical reasoning. The point of avoiding irrationality in one's plans and intentions is to achieve this goal or purpose, to "get things right" in one's plans and intentions. A plan would count as correct just in case it achieves this goal or purpose. (To say that a plan is correct in this way is not necessarily to say that there is anything incorrect about adopting an incompatible plan instead. In the situation of Buridan's ass, the plan to go to the left is correct, but so too is the plan to go to the right; in this situation, neither plan is incorrect.)

What *is* the goal or purpose of practical reasoning? Here is one suggestion that seems plausible to me: the ultimate goal of practical reasoning is to have a set of intentions that one will actually execute in such a way that as a result one will act in a manner that is genuinely choiceworthy.[23] However, it does not matter for our purposes whether this suggestion is exactly right; the suggestion is given here only as an illustration.

What about the notion of an *ideal* plan's being correct or incorrect? According to the definition that I gave in the previous section, to make a proposition part of your ideal plan is to treat it as a proposition that *would* be part of your actual plan if uncertainty did not require you to adopt some second-best plan instead. It seems plausible that the propositions that it is correct to treat in this way are precisely those propositions that are logically entailed by some plan that is *genuinely* or *fully* correct—where a plan that is fully correct in this sense is

---

[23] For an attempt to develop this sort of answer in more detail, see Wedgwood (2003).

correct, not because it is a second-best plan that it is rational to adopt because of one's ignorance or uncertainty, but because of the real facts (possibly including facts that one does not know) about one's situation.

Let me sum up. I proposed above that the semantic value of the practical 'ought'-operator '$O_{<A,\ t>}$' is the weakest property of a proposition p that makes it the case that it is correct for A to make the proposition p part of her ideal plan about what to do at t, and incorrect for A to make the negation of p a part of her ideal plan. As I have just argued, it is correct to make a proposition p part of your ideal plans about what to do at t if and only if p is logically entailed by a fully correct plan about what to do at t. Thus, we may also state my account as follows: for any proposition p, '$O_{<A,\ t>}(p)$' is true just in case there are fully correct plans for A to have about what to do at t that logically entail p, and no such fully correct plan that logically entails the negation of p.

There are many further questions that can be raised about this notion of a correct mental state. In particular, how are we to understand this idea of the "point" or "purpose" of conforming to the relevant standards of justification or rationality? Should we suppose that the *thinker* actually has an aim or goal in conforming to these standards? Or is this reference to a "point" or "purpose" of conforming to these standards a metaphorical way of indicating something like the *evolutionary proper function* of our disposition to conform to these standards? Or is it a metaphorical way of articulating a principle that can be literally formulated only in *normative* terms?

I shall try to answer these questions in Part II. My answer will involve the idea that the notion of a correct mental state is in fact itself a normative concept. Some philosophers will worry that if this is a normative concept, then my account is viciously circular. But in my account the notion of a correct mental state is used only in extensional contexts in the metalanguage; it is not used in specifying the contents of anyone's mental states or utterances. Thus, the appearance of a normative term in the metalanguage of our account of the nature of a normative concept is no more viciously circular than the appearance of a logical constant (like 'not') in our account of the nature of a logical concept. Indeed, if Dummett (1993b: 42–52) is right to claim that the root of our grasp of the concept of *truth* lies in our grasp of what it is for a belief or an assertion to be correct, and if I am right that the relevant notion of correctness is itself a normative concept, then in a sense the notion of truth itself is a normative concept. So there should be no more objection to using the notion of a "correct plan" in the metalanguage in which we are giving our semantic theory than there is to using the notion of a "correct belief" or "true proposition" in our metalanguage.

Various other objections can be raised against my account of the semantic value of 'ought'. One sort of objection accepts that my account makes a definite claim about what the semantic value of 'ought' is, but tries to show that this claim is false, by producing alleged counterexamples. Another sort of objection takes the opposite line, and complains that my account is trivial and empty. I shall respond to these two objections in turn.[24]

The first objection might start from the observation that my account of the semantic value of the practical 'ought' has some affinities with the "fitting attitude analysis" of value (or "FA analysis" for short). According to the FA analysis, as Rabinowicz and Rønnow-Rasmussen (2004: 391) put it, "to be valuable is to be a fitting object of a pro-attitude". Just as the FA analysis invokes the notion of a "fitting pro-attitude", so in a broadly similar way, my analysis invokes the notion of a "correct plan" or more generally a "correct mental state".

This naturally suggests that my account may face some of the same objections as the FA analysis of value. The best-known objection to the FA analysis is a problem that has recently been extensively discussed, especially by Roger Crisp (2000), D'Arms and Jacobson (2000), and Rabinowicz and Rønnow-Rasmussen (2004). Let us take as our example the FA analysis of the property of being admirable: to be admirable is to be a fitting object of admiration. Now suppose that a demon will inflict unspeakable torments upon you unless you admire him. Then it seems true in some sense to say that you *ought* to admire the demon. So, surely, the demon is a "fitting" object of admiration. But there is surely nothing admirable about the demon. So it seems that not every fitting object of admiration is admirable.

Moreover, it seems possible to construct counterexamples to the converse principle as well. Suppose that Florence Nightingale is admirable, but the demon will destroy the world if anyone admires her. Then it seems true in some sense that we ought *not* to admire Florence Nightingale; so Florence Nightingale is not a "fitting" object of admiration. But *ex hypothesi* she is admirable. So, it seems, not everything admirable is a fitting object of admiration.

It is in fact quite easy to adapt these problems into *prima facie* objections to my account of 'ought'. To adapt the first problem into an objection to my account, we need only find a case in which it seems plausible to say that we ought to *plan* to take a course of action, but not plausible to say that we ought to *take* that course of action. A good example of this would be Gregory Kavka's (1983) "toxin puzzle". The eccentric billionaire will give you £ 1 million for *planning* to drink the toxin, but is quite indifferent to whether or not you *actually* drink the toxin; so why isn't this a case in which it is correct to plan on drinking the toxin, and incorrect to plan on not drinking the toxin, but not true that you ought to

[24] For yet another sort of objection, see Horgan and Timmons (2000*b*), who argue that every version of "naturalistic moral realism" will be vitiated by one or the other of the following two flaws. The first flaw is that the theory will fail to assign any determinate reference to moral concepts at all. The second flaw is that it will postulate some naturalistic relation *R*, and claim that moral concepts refer to whatever property or relation they bear relation *R* to—even though in fact there are possible communities who intuitively possess the same moral concepts as we do, but whose moral concepts stand in relation *R* to *different* properties and relations from ours. As I explain elsewhere (Wedgwood 2006*a*: 141–2), my account is not open to this objection, for the simple reason that it is not in Horgan and Timmons's sense a "naturalistic" account at all.

drink the toxin? (Moreover, since the apparent correctness of the plan to drink the toxin does not depend on any ignorance or uncertainty about the options that are available in this situation, it also seems plausible that this is a correct *ideal* plan, and not just a correct actual plan.)

To adapt the second problem into an objection to my account, we need to find a case in which it seems plausible to say that we ought to *take* a course of action, but not plausible to say that we ought to *plan* on taking that course of action. For example, perhaps you ought to be less anxious, or more spontaneous, but *planning* on being less anxious, or more spontaneous, will simply be counterproductive.

I propose to respond to these two objections in rather different ways. My response to the first objection is fairly straightforward. It may that in some sense you "ought" to plan on drinking the toxin, but this does not show that the plan is *correct* in the relevant sense. The point is precisely parallel to a familiar point about belief. If a billionaire will pay you £1 million for believing that the number of books in the Bodleian library at midnight tonight is odd, then even if there is some sense in which it is true to say that you "ought" to believe this, this does not show that this belief is correct. For the belief to be correct, the content of the belief would have to be true. Similarly, at least according to the suggestion that I made above about what it is for a plan to be correct, for the plan to drink the toxin at t to be a correct plan for you to have about what to do at t, it would have to be true that if you act in a genuinely *choiceworthy* way at t, then you will drink the toxin at t. But the fact that the billionaire will pay you so handsomely for having this plan does not show that the plan is correct in this way.

My response to the second objection is not quite so straightforward. In the next chapter, I will argue that if a statement of the form 'It ought to be that p' involves the practical 'ought', indexed to an agent A and time t, then the statement is true only if there is some way in which A can intentionally behave at t such that if A does behave in that way at t, then p will be the case. That is, A must have the ability to realize the proposition p by means of her intentional behaviour at t.[25] However, it does not follow that the intention that must lie behind this intentional behaviour is the intention to bring it about that p is the case. It may be some entirely different intention altogether.

According to my account, if the statement 'It ought to be that p' contains the practical 'ought', indexed to an agent A and time t, then the statement is true if and only if there are correct plans for A to have about what to do at t that *logically imply* the proposition p, and no such correct plans that logically imply the negation of p. For one to adopt a plan that implies a proposition p is, in effect, for the contents of one's beliefs and intentions, taken together, to

[25] As I am using the term, "intentional behaviour" includes intentional *omissions* as well as intentional actions.

imply *p*. So it is quite possible that it really is correct for you to adopt a plan that logically implies this proposition *p*, even though you could not realize this plan if you actually had an *intention* with a content the semantic value of which is *p*.

For example, suppose that your mental states include (i) the belief that if you take more exercise, you will sleep better and be less anxious, and (ii) the intention to take more exercise. Then, as I am understanding the terms, you have adopted a plan that logically implies that you will sleep better and be less anxious—even though you do not actually *intend* to sleep better and be less anxious.

For these reasons, then, it will not be easy to construct a case in which 'It ought to be that *p*' is intuitively true, and involves the practical or deliberative 'ought' indexed to agent *A* and time *t*, but there are no correct plans for *A* to have about what to do at *t* that logically imply the proposition that is the semantic value of the embedded thought *p*.[26] Thus, it is far from clear that my account is vulnerable to any version of the second of the objections that are inspired by these well-known objections to the FA analysis of value.

There is also a completely different sort of objection that many philosophers will be tempted to raise against my account. According to my account, the nature of the concept expressed by the practical 'ought' is entirely determined by the rule that defines the *rational practical consequences* of accepting thoughts involving this concept. Specifically, the nature of the concept is entirely determined by the rule according to which if the proposition 'It ought to be that *p*' involves the practical 'ought', indexed to the thinker and to some time *t*, acceptance of the proposition commits the thinker to incorporating *p* into her ideal plans about what to do at *t*. But it may seem that there is a powerful objection to any such account.

According to Philippa Foot (1978: xii), no such purely practical element could "explain the *whole* meaning of moral terms such as 'right' and 'wrong'." Her reason for this claim is that there are "logical limits to the considerations that could be used to back up moral judgements"; as she says, "it would not do to suppose that, for instance, someone might have a *morality* in which the

---

[26] In addition, for one to adopt a plan that logically implies a proposition *p*, it is only necessary that one's beliefs and intentions together imply *p* under *some mode of presentation or other*. I am assuming here that the objects of attitudes like beliefs and intentions are *thoughts*, which are constituted out of *concepts*—where concepts correspond to what Frege called "modes of presentation" of ordinary objects like individuals, properties, and relations. On the other hand, the semantic value of the concept that is expressed by 'ought' is a property of *conditions*, which are composed directly out of ordinary entities like individuals, properties, and relations. The truth conditions of the thought 'It ought to be that *p*' only require that there must be some correct plans that imply the *condition* that corresponds to the embedded thought *p*, not that there be correct plans that actually imply the embedded thought *p*. This explains why rigidly co-referring singular terms can be substituted *salva veritate* inside the 'ought'-operator (so, given that Hesperus = Phosphorus, if you ought to look in the direction of Hesperus, then you ought to look in the direction of Phosphorus as well).

ultimate principle was that it was wrong to run round trees right handed or to look at hedgehogs in the light of the moon."[27]

Although Foot's argument focuses on the "narrowly moral" use of the terms 'right' and 'wrong', it seems plausible that her argument can be adapted to apply to the practical or deliberative 'ought' that I am focusing on here. There also seem to be "conceptual limits" to the considerations that can support the judgment that it ought to be the case that *p*. That is, in effect, it must somehow follow from the nature of the concept that is expressed by the practical 'ought' that certain ways of forming judgments involving this concept are necessarily irrational. In general, it seems that a good account of the concept should provide an *epistemological* account of the rational ways of forming beliefs involving the concept. But since my account of the practical 'ought' focuses entirely on what beliefs involving this concept rationally *commit* one to, it may seem hard to see how it can provide an epistemological account of the basic rational *grounds* for forming such beliefs.

Fortunately, my account has the resources to respond to this objection. In Part III of this book (especially in Chapter 10), I shall identify what I take to be the rational ways of forming beliefs involving normative concepts, and I shall argue that it does indeed follow from the nature of these concepts that it is irrational to form beliefs involving these concepts in any other ways. Nonetheless, according to my account, the rationality of this way of forming normative beliefs is not *essential* to, or *constitutive* of, the nature of these normative concepts. On the contrary, the rationality of this way of forming normative beliefs is *derived* from the way in which the concepts' semantic value is determined by their essential conceptual role; and the essential conceptual role of these concepts is given, not by the rational way of *forming* beliefs involving these concepts, but rather by what these beliefs *commit* one to.

A related objection that one might raise against my account is that it seems plausible that a good account of the concept that is expressed by the term 'ought' should not only help us to resolve these epistemological issues; it should also help us to resolve the metaphysical debates about the nature of the concept's semantic value. That is, it should resolve the debates between realists and anti-realists, and between naturalists and non-naturalists. How is my account to do this? Once again, as I shall argue in Part II of this book, my account of what determines these concepts' reference or semantic value turns out to supply the resources that we need to answer these metaphysical questions. In this way, my semantics for normative concepts will lead to an illuminating account of the nature of the properties and relations that are the semantic values of those concepts.

In the next chapter, however, before turning to these metaphysical and epistemological questions, I shall add some crucial further detail to my semantic

---

[27] Foot (1978: 120) also makes a similar point about the terms 'good' and 'harm': "it is quite impossible to call anything you like good or harm".

account of the nature of normative concepts. First, I shall try to show that the semantic account developed in this chapter helps to provide an explanation of some of the basic principles of *deontic logic*. Secondly, I shall argue that in addition to the practical or deliberative 'ought', there is a range of systematically related normative concepts, and that the term 'ought' is systematically context-sensitive, expressing different normative concepts in different contexts. Finally, I shall address the contentious issue of the relationship between terms like 'ought' and terms like 'better' or 'best'.

5

Context and the Logic of 'Ought'

In the previous chapter, I proposed an account of the semantics of the practical 'ought'. According to this account, the essential conceptual role of the practical 'ought' is given by the rule that acceptance of a first-person judgment involving this sort of 'ought', of the form '$O_{<me,\ t>}(p)$', commits the thinker to making the embedded proposition p part of her ideal plans about what to do at t. As I argued, this leads to the conclusion that the semantic value of the practical 'ought', when it is indexed to an agent A and a time t, is that property of a proposition p that makes it correct for A to incorporate p into her ideal plans about what to do at t, and incorrect for A to incorporate the negation of p into any such ideal plans about what to do at t. In other words, '$O_{<A,\ t>}(p)$' is true if and only if there are plans that it is fully correct for A to have about what to do at t that logically entail p, and no such fully correct plans that logically entail the negation of p.

In this chapter, I shall extend this account of normative concepts, in three different ways. First, I shall explain how my account of the semantic value of the practical 'ought' leads to a satisfactory account of the *logic* of the concept—that is, to an account of the basic principles of *deontic logic*. Secondly, I shall try to explain how the word 'ought' in English is systematically context-sensitive, and expresses different concepts in different contexts. This is because there is in fact a large family of normative concepts, which are all systematically related to each other; and once the linguistic context in which the word 'ought' appears has fixed certain parameters, this will determine which of these normative concepts this occurrence of 'ought' expresses. Thirdly, I shall investigate the relations between the terms 'ought' and 'best'. Here I shall argue that there is a close connection between the two terms. For every concept that can be expressed by 'ought', there is a corresponding concept that can be expressed by 'best' such that what "ought" to be the case (in this sense of 'ought') is whatever is a necessary component of the "best" state of affairs (in the corresponding sense of 'best'). It is important not to misunderstand this conclusion: in particular, it does not imply a consequentialist account of what ought to be, nor does it imply that "the good is prior to the right". When correctly understood, this conclusion has the resources to answer all the objections that philosophers have raised against the idea that the truth about what "ought" to be has the sort of "optimizing" structure that underwrites this sort of connection between 'ought' and 'best'.

5.1 THE LOGIC OF THE PRACTICAL 'OUGHT'

The general idea of how my account of the practical 'ought' can provide an explanation for the principles of deontic logic is fairly straightforward. According to this account, the semantic value of this kind of 'ought' is that property of a proposition that makes it the case that there are plans that it is fully correct for the agent to have that entail that proposition, and no such fully correct plans that entail the negation of that proposition. (In what follows, I shall save words by speaking simply of "correct plans" rather than of "fully correct plans".)

According to this account of the semantic value of the practical 'ought', if there are any consistency constraints on correct plans, then there will be corresponding consistency constraints on statements involving this sort of 'ought'. These consistency constraints are in effect what deontic logic consists in—namely, principles, flowing from the very meaning of the term 'ought' itself, about which sets of 'ought'-statements are consistent and which are not. So, according to this account, the source of deontic logic lies in these consistency constraints on planning and practical reasoning.

It certainly seems plausible that there are consistency constraints on planning. Many of these consistency constraints stem from the idea that to be correct our plans must be *realizable*. It seems to be part of what plans are *for* that they should guide us to act in such a way as to realize those plans. Thus, a plan that simply cannot be realized fails in a dramatic way to achieve the result that it is the very point of the plan to achieve. Hence, I shall suppose, no such plan can be correct. (Strictly speaking, these realizability constraints on planning take two forms. First, there is a realizability constraint that is relative to the agent's *beliefs*—that is, the agent should not adopt a plan if he *believes* that it cannot be realized; this constraint is what I shall call a "constraint on *rational* planning". Secondly, there is a realizability constraint that depends on the *facts* of the agent's situation—that is, the agent should not adopt a plan that cannot *in fact* be realized; constraints of this second kind are what I shall call "constraints on *correct* planning".)

In fact, however, my specification of the semantic value of the practical 'ought' already reflects some of these consistency constraints on correct plans. For any two propositions p and q, if p is logically equivalent to q, then there are correct plans that logically entail p and no correct plans that logically entail the negation of p if and only if there are correct plans that logically entail q and no correct plans that logically entail the negation of q. So if p and q are logically equivalent, then so too are '$O_{<A,\, t>}(p)$' and '$O_{<A,\, t>}(q)$'. In this sense, the operator '$O_{<A,\, t>}$'

behaves like a *classical* modal operator: it permits the substitution of logical equivalents.[1]

Moreover, suppose that there are correct plans for A to have about what to do at t that logically entail 'p & q', and no correct plans that logically entail the negation of 'p & q' (so, given my account, '$O_{<A, t>}(p$ & $q)$' is true). Then there are correct plans that logically entail p and no correct plans that logically entail the negation of p (since any plan that entailed the negation of p would also entail the negation of 'p & q'); and similarly, there are correct plans that logically entail q and no correct plans that logically entail the negation of q. So, the operator '$O_{<A, t>}$' also behaves like a *monotonic* modal operator: that is, it *distributes over conjunction*; '$O_{<A, t>}(p$ & $q)$' entails '$O_{<A, t>}(p)$' and '$O_{<A, t>}(q)$'.[2]

To defend the other logical principles that apply to the practical 'ought'-operator, however, we need to appeal more explicitly to the idea that any correct plan for an agent A to have about what to do at a time t must be *fully realizable* by A at t. I propose that this idea should be understood in the following way.

First, let us define what it is for a proposition to be realizable by A at t. For the *practical* 'ought', what is relevant is practical realizability—that is, realizability by means of A's *intentional behaviour* at t. To say that a proposition p is practically realizable by A at t is to say that there is some way of behaving W such that there are possible worlds in which all the actual truths that are causally independent of whatever A might do or think at t hold, and A intentionally behaves in way W at t, and in all those worlds, p is true. (Thus, all the actual truths that are causally independent of whatever A might do or think at t will, in a degenerate sense, be realizable by A at t. Roughly, for a truth p to be "causally independent of whatever A might do or think at t" is for it *not* to be the case that there is some thought or way of behaving such that there are nearby possible worlds in which A has that thought or behaves in that way at t, and in all such worlds, p is not true.) It follows from this definition of realizability that if a proposition p is realizable, then any proposition q that logically follows from p must also be realizable as well.

Secondly, it is a crucial feature of plans that we can adopt a *partial* plan, and then fill in the details of the plan (by adding further conjuncts to the proposition that we have adopted as our plan) as time goes by. Let us say that a *maximally detailed plan* for an agent A and a time t is one such that for every proposition p

---

[1] For a useful account of the various sorts of modal operators (including both normal and non-normal modal operators), see Schurz (1997: 160–1).

[2] The claim that 'ought' distributes over conjunction has been disputed. E.g., Jackson (1985) has proposed analysing '$O(p)$' in counterfactual terms, as equivalent to 'If it were the case that p, things would be better than they would be if it were not the case that p'. This analysis allows for counterexamples to distributivity. Suppose that (i) the nearest possible world in which p is true is one in which q is not, and (ii) such worlds are very bad, although worlds in which both p and q are true are very good. Then given Jackson's analysis, '$O(p$ & $q)$' is true, but '$O(p)$' is false. But it seems to me that 'ought' is not well analysed in such counterfactual terms. We often say that something "ought" to be the case when it is very much only a *part* of everything that ought to be the case.

that is realizable by A at t, the plan logically entails either p or its negation. Then we can articulate the constraint on correct plans as follows: a plan is correct only if it is possible to extend the plan into a maximally detailed correct plan that is itself a realizable proposition.

Now suppose that (i) there are correct plans (for A to have about what to do at t) that entail p, and no such correct plans that entail the negation of p, and in addition (ii) there are correct plans that entail q and no such correct plans that entail the negation of q. (So, given my semantics, both '$O_{<A,\ t>}(p)$' and '$O_{<A,\ t>}(q)$' are true.) Since every correct plan is fully realizable, the propositions p and q must be realizable. So the correct plans that entail p must be capable of being extended into a maximally detailed plan that entails either q or the negation of q. But there are no correct plans that entail the negation of q. So all correct maximally detailed extensions of these plans entail q. Thus, there are correct plans that entail both p and q; hence there are correct plans that entail 'p & q'. But there cannot be any correct plans that entail the negation of 'p & q' (if there were such correct plans, there would have to be correct maximally detailed extensions of those plans that entailed either the negation of p or the negation of q; but by hypothesis there are no such correct plans). Hence, according to my semantics, the practical 'ought'-operator '$O_{<A,\ t>}$' also behaves like a *regular* modal operator: that is, it *agglomerates over conjunction*; '$O_{<A,\ t>}(p)$' and '$O_{<A,\ t>}(q)$' taken together entail '$O_{<A,\ t>}(p$ & $q)$'.

As we have seen, every proposition that is logically entailed by a correct plan must itself be a realizable proposition. Hence, given my account, if '$O_{<A,\ t>}(p)$' is true, then p must itself be realizable. Clearly it is logically impossible for any logically false proposition to be realizable. Hence, the practical 'ought'-operator '$O_{<A,\ t>}$' also conforms to the so-called "D principle": if p is logically false, then '$O_{<A,\ t>}(p)$' is also logically false.

So far, I have argued in favour of all the principles of von Wright's original (1951) deontic logic. But in fact, the account that I have given so far also supports the final principle that is needed to turn von Wright's system into standard deontic logic. This principle is the *rule of necessitation*, according to which if p is a logical truth, then so is '$O_{<A,\ t>}(p)$'. Now, the logical principles that I have already defended are enough to show that if there is *any* truth of the form '$O_{<A,\ t>}(q)$', then for every logical truth p, p follows from q, whatever q may be, and so '$O_{<A,\ t>}(p)$' is true as well. But how are we to show that it is a logical truth that there is at least one truth of the form '$O_{<A,\ t>}(q)$'? (Perhaps for some A and t, there are *no* correct plans for A to have about what to do at t?) So, this argument is not enough to show that '$O_{<A,\ t>}(p)$' is a logical truth whenever the embedded proposition p is also a logical truth.

The simplest way to argue for the rule of necessitation is probably to focus in the first instance, not on the 'ought'-operator, but on the 'may'-operator '$P_{<A,\ t>}$' (which some philosophers indicate by the term 'permissible'). Following the pattern of my account of the 'ought'-operator '$O_{<A,\ t>}$', I propose that the essential conceptual role of the 'may'-operator '$P_{<A,\ t>}$' is given by the following rule:

> Acceptance of the first-person proposition '$P_{<me,\ t>}(p)$' *permits* one to treat *p* as *allowed* by one's ideal plan about what to do at *t*.

To treat a proposition *p* as "allowed" by one's ideal plan is, in effect, to be disposed not to adopt as one's ideal plan any proposition that is *inconsistent* with *p*. To say that a belief "permits" one to treat a certain proposition as allowed by one's ideal plan is to say that it is *rational* for one simultaneously to hold that belief and treat that proposition as allowed by one's ideal plan (which is not to say that it may not *also* be perfectly rational to hold this belief while *not* treating *p* as allowed by one's ideal plan).

To accord with my earlier proposals, the semantic value of the operator '$P_{<A,\ t>}$' must be whatever property of propositions makes all instances of this rule "valid", while also making it a "complete" set of rules for the concept. (In this case, this means that it must be the *weakest* property that guarantees that all instances of the rule are valid.) Since this rule is a rule to the effect that a certain input mental state "permits" one to have a certain other mental state (rather than a rule about how the input mental state "commits" one to that other mental state), for an instance of this rule to be "valid" the correctness of the input mental state must guarantee the correctness of the output; but it need *not* guarantee that the "opposite" mental state is *incorrect*.

This proposal seems to support the conclusion that the semantic value of this operator '$P_{<A,\ t>}$' is that property of a proposition *p* that makes it the case that it is correct for *A* to treat the proposition *p* as "allowed" by her ideal plans about what to do at *t* (which is not to say that it cannot also be correct for *A* to treat the *negation* of *p* as "allowed" by her ideal plans). As I have defined it, to treat *p* as "allowed" by one's plans is to be disposed not to adopt any plan—even a maximally detailed plan—that is inconsistent with *p*. So the natural conclusion to draw is that the semantic value of this operator '$P_{<A,\ t>}$' is that property of a proposition *p* that makes it the case that there is at least one maximally detailed fully correct plan (for *A* to have about what to do at *t*) that is consistent with *p* (which is not to say that there cannot also be *other* fully correct plans that are inconsistent with *p*).[3]

Obviously, however, a logical falsehood is not consistent with anything; so, in particular, if *p* is a logical falsehood, then *p* is not consistent with any correct plans (let alone maximally detailed correct plans) for *A* to have about what to do

---

[3] Intuitively, this seems plausible as an account of the semantic value of the concept of what is "permissible". If it is permissible for me to scratch my head right now, then there is at least one maximally detailed plan that it is fully correct for me to have, as a plan about what to do now, that does not rule out that I will scratch my head right now. Conversely, if there is nothing incorrect about a maximally detailed plan that does not rule out that I will scratch my head now, then it must be permissible for me to scratch my head right now.

at t. So if p is a logical falsehood, then '$P_{<A,\ t>}(p)$' cannot be true. Since we relied on nothing but logic and the semantics of the operator '$P_{<A,\ t>}$' to establish that '$P_{<A,\ t>}(p)$' cannot be true, '$P_{<A,\ t>}(p)$' must also be a logical falsehood.

Now it is also plausible that the two operators, 'ought' and 'may', '$O_{<A,\ t>}$' and '$P_{<A,\ t>}$', are *duals* of each other.[4] That is, 'It may permissibly be the case that ... ' is equivalent to 'It is not the case that it ought not to be the case that ... ', and 'It ought to be the case that ... ' is equivalent to 'It is not the case that it may permissibly not be the case that ... '. (In symbols, '$P_{<A,\ t>}$' is equivalent to '$\neg\ O_{<A,\ t>}\neg$ ', and '$O_{<A,\ t>}$' to '$\neg\ P_{<A,\ t>}\neg$ '.) But then if p is a logical truth, '$\neg\ p$' is a logical falsehood, and so '$P_{<A,\ t>}(\neg\ p)$' must also be a logical falsehood, and '$\neg\ P_{<A,\ t>}(\neg\ p)$' must be a logical truth. So if p is a logical truth, '$O_{<A,\ t>}(p)$' must also be a logical truth. That is, the rule of necessitation is sound.

A simpler but perhaps less intuitive argument for the rule of necessitation starts from the point that as I am understanding the term, one's "plans" for what to do at t do not just consist of one's *intentions* about what to do at t. As I put it in the previous chapter (Section 4.4), to adopt the proposition p as one's plan about what to do at t is to have a certain set of intentions about what to do at t such that, if the conjunction of the contents of those intentions is the proposition q, one *believes* the proposition 'If it were the case that q, it would be the case that p'. In this way, the proposition that one adopts as one's plan incorporates not just one's intentions but also one's *beliefs about the causally independent facts*. It is especially important for one's plans to incorporate one's beliefs about the causally independent facts that will determine what the causal consequences of one's actions will be. Of course, many of the other causally independent facts will be much less practically relevant than these; and in a sense, it is quite redundant for one to incorporate these practically irrelevant facts into one's plan. But however practically irrelevant these facts may be, it is not *incorrect* to incorporate such facts into one's plan (indeed, if one's plan is "maximally detailed" in the sense that I defined above, it would have to entail all such causally independent facts). Logical truths are always among the truths that are causally independent of what one does. So it will always be correct to incorporate such logical truths into one's plans (and of course it will never be correct to incorporate the negations of such logical truths into one's plans). Thus, the rule of necessitation is guaranteed to be sound: if p is a logical truth, so too is '$O_{<A,\ t>}(p)$'.

More generally, it is correct to incorporate any causally independent truths into one's plans. So if p is such a causally independent truth, then '$O_{<A,\ t>}(p)$'

---

[4] Objection: This claim, that 'ought' and 'may' are duals of each other, conflicts with the plausible ideas that (i) deontic logic can be used to understand the logical structure of *legal* codes, and (ii) there are "gappy" legal codes, according to which certain courses of action are neither permitted nor forbidden. Reply: Even if this point shows that standard deontic logic cannot be used to understand the structure of legal codes, this does not show that there is anything wrong with standard deontic logic as an account of the logic of 'ought', since the concept of what is "legally required" is not strictly speaking a kind of 'ought'.

is true.[5] (Unless the causally independent truth p is itself a logical truth, then '$O_{<A,\,t>}(p)$' will be a truth but not a logical truth; this is because unless p is a logical truth, then logic alone cannot tell us whether or not p is a causally independent truth.)

It must be conceded that unlike the other principles of deontic logic that I have argued for, the rule of necessitation is not intuitively obvious. As I argued in the previous chapter (Section 4.3) in defending my view of the logical form of 'ought', it is hard to hear the term 'ought' as having its practical or deliberative sense and as indexed to an agent A and time t, unless the proposition embedded inside the operator is one whose truth value is causally dependent on A's thoughts or behaviour at t. So it is hard to hear the term 'ought' as having its practical or deliberative sense in sentences like 'It ought to be the case that the number 3 is not both prime and not prime', and it is all but impossible to hear this occurrence of 'ought' as indexed to a particular agent and time. As I emphasized earlier (at the end of Section 4.3), we cannot rely on a direct appeal to intuition to evaluate sentences of this kind: we must appeal to theoretical considerations instead; and as I have just argued, these theoretical considerations come down in favour of the rule of necessitation.[6]

If these logical principles involving the practical 'ought'-operator '$O_{<A,\,t>}$' are indeed correct, then there is a natural possible-worlds semantics for this operator. First, for any possible world w, there is a set of propositions that are true in w, and causally independent of all the agent A's thoughts or actions at t in w. Let us call the worlds at which all these propositions are true the worlds that are "available" to A at t in w. Then there is some selection function that picks out a subset of these "available" worlds; let us say that it picks out the "favoured" available worlds. It is a constraint on this selection function that the set of "favoured" available worlds must be a realizable proposition (in the sense defined earlier). Then we can say that for any proposition p, '$O_{<A,\,t>}(p)$' is true in w if and only if p is true at all these favoured available worlds. This possible-worlds semantics leads to standard deontic logic under the assumption that the set of favoured available worlds is never empty.

---

[5] If truths of the form '$O_{<A,\,t>}(p)$' are always themselves causally independent truths of this sort, then we should accept the S4 principle for the practical 'ought': '$O(p) \rightarrow OO(p)$'. There are several other principles that have been suggested as part of the logic of 'ought' that would also have to be considered in a fuller treatment of this topic—for example, '$O(O(p) \rightarrow p)$', '$O(p \rightarrow OP(p))$', and '$P(p) \rightarrow OP(p)$'. For a thorough list, see Åqvist (1984). Unfortunately, I will not be able to consider whether any of these principles are genuinely logical truths here.

[6] Objection: The rule of necessitation in deontic logic makes it "too easy" to answer a radical "error theorist" who believes that 'ought' is meaningful but all sentences in which 'ought' has largest scope are false. Reply: The quest for a semantics for 'ought' that is neutral on absolutely all metaethical controversies is misguided. Certainly, this radical sort of error theory is incompatible with the account that I have given of the meaning of 'ought'. But it also need not follow that if my account is correct, then this radical error theorist is irrational, or that he doesn't understand the term 'ought'. It often happens that a philosopher understands a term perfectly well but embraces a false theory about what the term means.

In effect, this possible-worlds semantics corresponds fairly closely to the account that was proposed by Fred Feldman (1986).[7] The main difference is that instead of speaking of the "favoured" available worlds, Feldman speaks of the "best" available worlds. But nothing that our discussion has covered so far justifies the claim that the "favoured" worlds are in any sense the "best" worlds. Hence I have used a more non-committal term in characterizing the relevant selection function simply as a "favouring" function. (We should also note that the relevant selection function is itself indexed to the relevant agent A and time t; so this semantics is compatible with rejecting a consequentialist moral theory in favour of a more agent-relative, deontological theory. For example, it may be that a world in which A fails to prevent two murders at t is favoured, while a world in which there are fewer murders overall but A himself commits a murder at t is not favoured in the relevant way.)

I have argued that the logic for the practical 'ought' is nothing other than standard deontic logic. Many objections have been raised against standard deontic logic over the years. I shall end this section by explaining briefly how I think these objections can be answered.

First, there is the paradox of Ross (1941: 62): in standard deontic logic, '$O_{<A,\,t>}(p)$' entails '$O_{<A,\,t>}(p \vee q)$'; so 'You ought to post this letter' entails 'You ought to: either post this letter or burn it'. But it seems to me that if we bear in mind that this entailment holds only if 'or' has its truth-functional sense, then it is clear that the statement 'You ought to post this letter or burn it' is actually true. There is an obvious Gricean explanation for why it seems an odd thing to say: it is much less informative than something else that one might say—namely, 'You ought to post this letter'. Asserting the weaker claim would tend to be a useful contribution to a conversation only if one were not in a position to assert the stronger claim—that is, only if one does not know either that you ought to post the letter, or that you ought to burn it, but only that you ought to do one or the other of these things. Thus it is easy to explain why 'You ought to either post the letter or burn it' may seem false even if it is actually true.[8]

A second alleged paradox of deontic logic focuses on the more general point that in standard deontic logic, if p entails q then '$O_{<A,\,t>}(p)$' entails '$O_{<A,\,t>}(q)$'. So for example in the Good Samaritan Paradox of Prior (1958: 144), 'You ought

---

[7] Compare also Belzer (1998), Humberstone (1983), Loewer and Belzer (1983), and Kratzer (2002).

[8] Here is an objection to my response to Ross's paradox. My response entails that if there is anything that you ought to do, then whatever you do, you will do something that, you ought to do. (If you burn the letter, you will have done something that you ought to do—viz. post the letter or burn it; similarly, if you throw the letter away, and so on.) But surely it cannot be that easy to do something that one ought to do? Reply: There are many problems with this objection (it plays very fast and loose with quantification over "things that one might do", for example). But even if my response to Ross's paradox does entail this result, the result is not obviously counterintuitive at all. On reflection, it seems clear that it *is* easy to do *something* that one ought to do: what is hard is to do *everything* that one ought to do ...

to help the traveller who was beaten and robbed' entails 'There ought to be a traveller who was beaten and robbed'. However, once we remember that we are dealing with an 'ought'-operator that is indexed to an agent and a time, it becomes clear that the conclusion 'It ought to be that the traveller was beaten and robbed' only follows if the occurrence of 'ought' in the conclusion has the *same* sense, and is indexed to the *same* agent and time, as in the premise. Presumably the premise is only true when indexed to a time *t* such that the fact that the traveller has been beaten and robbed is causally quite independent of everything that the relevant agent thinks or does at *t*.

However, as I argued in the previous chapter (Section 4.3), there is no natural way in English of expressing the proposition that results from attaching a practical 'ought'-operator that is indexed to a particular agent *A* and time *t* to an embedded proposition whose truth value is causally independent of all *A*'s thoughts and actions at *t*. We simply have no intuitions about the sentence 'From the standpoint of you now (when there is absolutely nothing that you can do that will change the fact that the traveller was beaten and robbed), it ought to be the case that the traveller was beaten and robbed'. When this sentence strikes us as false, that is because we are not hearing it as involving a practical 'ought' that is genuinely indexed to that agent and that time. Instead, we may be hearing it as equivalent to 'From the standpoint of you and some time at which there *was* something that you could do that would determine whether or not the traveller was beaten and robbed, it ought to be that the traveller was beaten and robbed' (that is, roughly, 'You ought to have seen to it that the traveller was beaten and robbed'). But my account of the logic of the agent- and time-indexed practical 'ought' certainly does not imply that *this* follows from the original premise. Thus, when the conclusion of this inference strikes us as false, that is because we are sliding between the original practical 'ought', which was indexed to a particular agent and time, and *another* 'ought', which differs either in not being a practical or deliberative 'ought', or else in not being indexed to the same agent and time. For these reasons, then, it seems to me that these objections to standard deontic logic are not compelling.[9]

---

[9] For this reason, I find it somewhat surprising that many recent deontic logicians (e.g. Hansson (1997), and Belzer (1998)) have been persuaded by these familiar "paradoxes". I suspect that part of the reason is that these deontic logicians have not considered all the evidence in favour of the hypothesis that 'ought' is systematically context-sensitive, and is implicitly indexed in different contexts of use to various different parameters; hence they have been rather uncritical in relying on their linguistic intuitions, without investigating whether these intuitions in fact involve different 'ought'-operators—that is, occurrences of 'ought' that are indexed to different parameters. Admittedly, many other "paradoxes" have been raised against standard deontic logic. But according to my account, most of these (including Castañeda's (1981) "Paradox of the Second Best Plan" and Åqvist's (1967) "Paradox of the Knower") can be solved in the same way as the Good Samaritan Paradox. The main exception is Chisholm's (1963) "Paradox of the Contrary-to-Duty Imperative". The most promising solution to this paradox is the familiar solution in terms of the *conditional* 'ought'; see Feldman (1990).

5.2 THE CONTEXT-SENSITIVITY OF 'OUGHT'

So far, I have only given an account of one kind of 'ought'—the practical or deliberative 'ought'. But there is extensive linguistic evidence that there are in fact several different kinds of 'ought': the term 'ought' expresses different concepts in different contexts of use.

I have already argued that in addition to the practical 'ought', there is also what I called the " 'ought' of general desirability" (which Sidgwick called the "political 'ought' "), which I illustrated with the example of Wordsworth's line, written in 1802, 'Milton! Thou shouldst be living at this hour'. The most striking difference between these two kinds of 'ought', as I suggested, seems to be this: the practical 'ought' is clearly indexed to a particular agent and time, and it is a constraint on what "ought" to be the case, in this sense, that it should be realizable by the agent's intentional behaviour at that time; the 'ought' of general desirability, on the other hand, is not indexed to any particular agent and time in this way.

Other philosophers have drawn attention to other examples that seem to show that there are many sorts of 'ought', which express different concepts in different contexts. For example, Bernard Williams (1981*a*) imagined that a tourist unimpressed by St Peter's Basilica in Rome might say to his travelling companion:

(1) This place ought to be a railway station.

As Williams pointed out, it does not seem a good objection to this statement to point out that it is simply not practically possible to convert St Peter's into a railway station. So this kind of 'ought' seems not to entail the same sort of 'can' as the practical 'ought' (or 'ought' of advice). This example may just be a sarcastic use of the 'ought' of general desirability. Literally, what the statement says is—roughly—that in the states of affairs that are (at least in some salient respect) most desirable, St Peter's would be a railway station; in the context, saying this can be a way of sneering sarcastically at the building's architectural quality.

Williams (2002) also pointed to such examples as the following. On some occasions, 'ought' seems to be relative to a particular *goal* or *purpose*. Thus, someone might say, pointing to someone who is fiddling with a safe:

(2) He ought to use a Phillips screwdriver to open that safe.

(Or one might even just say 'He ought to use a Phillips screwdriver'.) Intuitively, this statement is true just in case using a Phillips screwdriver is necessary for opening the safe in the best available way—even if, in many other salient senses of the term, the person ought not to be opening the safe at all. On other occasions, however, 'ought' is not relative to a particular goal or purpose in this way. Thus, in saying that the person in question ought not to be opening the safe at all, one is not simply saying that the person's refraining from opening the safe is necessary for achieving some particular goal or purpose in the best available way.

Another crucial dimension of context-sensitivity is seen in the fact that on some occasions, 'ought' seems to be relative to the information that is actually possessed by the agent who is under discussion, whereas on other occasions it is not. I shall call these the "information-relative" and the "objective" kinds of 'ought', respectively. For example, suppose that we are on the top of a tower watching someone who is making his way through a maze on the ground. Then it might be true for us to say:

(3) He has no way of knowing it, but he ought to turn left at this point.

Here what an agent "ought" to do does not depend purely on the information that is possessed by the agent at the relevant time; so this first example involves the objective 'ought', rather than the information-relative 'ought'. On the other hand, sometimes we use 'ought' in such a way that it does depend purely on the information that is available to the relevant agent at the relevant time. Thus, we might say about the man who is making his way through the maze:

(4) Given what he knows, he ought to turn right at this point.

Here what the agent "ought" to do depends only on the information that the agent actually possesses at the relevant time. So this second example involves the information-relative 'ought', not the objective 'ought'.

In general, every one of the kinds of 'ought' that I have distinguished so far seems to have both an objective and an information-relative version. Thus, there is both an objective and an information-relative version of the purpose-relative 'ought'. An information-relative version of this 'ought' might be: 'Given that he doesn't know what sort of safe it is, he ought to start with the ordinary screwdriver first'. An objective version of this sort of 'ought' might be: 'He has no way of knowing it, but he ought to use a Phillips screwdriver to open that safe'. In a similar way, there seem to be both information-relative and objective versions of all the other kinds of 'ought' that I have distinguished so far.

There are yet other examples of context-sensitivity in 'ought'. For example, there is the epistemic 'ought', as in:

(5) Tonight's performance ought to be a lot of fun.

This seems just to mean, roughly, that it is *highly probable given the evidence* that tonight's performance will be a lot of fun. But there are also yet other uses of the epistemic 'ought' that are slightly less straightforward, such as:

(6) The orbit of Pluto ought to be elliptical.

This appears to mean just that there are *some* facts that should lead one to expect the orbit of Pluto to be elliptical (not that it is highly probable given *all* one's evidence that the orbit is elliptical).

Finally, it seems quite plausible to me that in addition to the *unconditional* 'ought', there is also a *conditional* 'ought'. Consider the following conversation, between an adviser and a recalcitrant advisee:

(7) —You ought to stop shooting up heroin.

—I'm not going to stop!

—Well, if you're not going to stop, you ought at least to shoot up with clean needles.

Now, there is a well-known argument, due to the deontic logicians, such as Åqvist (1967 and 1984), who introduced a "dyadic" 'ought'-operator, that it is quite unnatural to interpret these sentences involving the conditional 'ought' by means of an unconditional monadic 'ought'-operator and an ordinary material conditional. On the one hand, if we put the 'ought' in the *consequent* of the conditional (so that the 'ought' has *narrow scope*), the result is a sentence that is intuitively *false*: even if you aren't going to stop taking heroin, it is still true that you *ought not* to shoot up heroin at all (even with clean needles). On the other hand, if we interpret the sentence as consisting of a material conditional *inside* the scope of the 'ought' (so that the 'ought' has *wide scope*), then the result is that what is said is that you ought to do one of the following two things—either (i) stopping taking heroin, or (ii) shooting up with clean needles. But that is much weaker than what the speaker presumably intends to convey by uttering this sentence, as we can see from the fact that (at least given standard deontic logic) it is equally true to say that you ought to do one of the following two things—either (i) stopping taking heroin, or (ii) killing your children. For these reasons then, it seems more plausible to take these sentences as involving a distinctive conditional 'ought'.

I shall argue that this contextual variation in the concept that the term 'ought' expresses is not mere random ambiguity (like the way in which 'bank' in current English is ambiguous between *river bank* and *money bank*). Rather, the term 'ought' is systematically context-sensitive. There are certain specific contextual parameters that are fixed by the context of a statement involving the term 'ought'; and these contextual parameters determine which of these many 'ought'-concepts the term 'ought' expresses in the context.

My account of the practical 'ought' was based on the idea that the essential conceptual role of this type of 'ought' is the *regulative* role that it plays in *practical reasoning*: a judgment that applies the relevant sort of 'ought' to a proposition commits the thinker to incorporating that proposition into his ideal plans about what to do. This approach can be generalized so that it covers other kinds of 'ought' as well. In general, the concepts expressed by 'ought' all have an essential conceptual role that is in some way a *regulative* role in *reasoning*. So the fundamental difference between all the various normative concepts must lie either (i) in the *kind of regulative role* that is the concept's essential role, or (ii) in the *kind of reasoning* in which this 'ought'-concept plays its essential regulative role.

This may help us to understand how the conversational context in which the term 'ought' is used can determine which normative concept the term expresses in that context. Suppose that this context (i) makes it clear which of the various sorts of regulative role is played by the concept that the term 'ought' expresses on this occasion, and (ii) also makes a certain kind of reasoning conversationally salient. Then in this conversational context, the term 'ought' expresses the normative concept that plays *that* sort of regulative role in *that* kind of reasoning. Moreover, as I shall also argue, if the context can determine which normative concept this occurrence of the term 'ought' expresses, then this will suffice to determine a semantic value that can be modelled by means of the same sort of possible-worlds semantics that I gave in the previous section for the practical 'ought'.

Thus, one way in which the different concepts expressed by the term 'ought' differ from each other is in the *kind of reasoning* in which they play their essential regulative role. One way in which kinds of reasoning can differ is in the kind of mental event that forms the conclusion of that reasoning. The conclusion of practical reasoning is some revision to one's *plans* about what to do; according to the account that I gave in the last chapter, the essential conceptual role of the practical 'ought' is its role in practical reasoning of this sort. In addition to practical reasoning, there is also theoretical reasoning, the conclusion of which is some revision to one's *beliefs*. The sort of 'ought' that appears in statements about what one "ought to believe" presumably has its essential conceptual role in theoretical reasoning of this kind.

Practical reasoning in the strict sense concludes with some revision to one's plans. But in addition to this kind of practical reasoning, there are other related kinds of reasoning as well. Thus, the conclusion of some kinds of reasoning might be the formation of a *preference*, among a given set of alternatives. For example, one might deliberate in order to form a preference among various different ways of reforming the British constitution. To form a preference for a proposition over the relevant alternatives is not necessarily to form a choice or intention to realize that proposition; it would at most be to form a *conditional intention*—in effect, the intention of acting in such a way that the proposition in question is true, rather than in such a way that the relevant alternative is true, *if one does either*. It may be that the 'ought' of general desirability has its essential conceptual role in preference-forming reasoning of this kind.

There are also other forms of conditional intention that might be the conclusion of certain further kinds of reasoning. Thus, one might reason about *how* to achieve some end or purpose, while completely bracketing the issue of whether or not to pursue that end at all. For example, one might reason about what means to use in order to open a certain safe, while completely bracketing the issue of whether or not to open that safe at all. This kind of reasoning might conclude with a conditional intention or *contingency plan* to use certain means in order to open the safe—if one ever sets out to achieve the end of opening the safe at all. The *purpose-relative* 'ought' may have its essential conceptual role in this kind of reasoning.

Yet another kind of reasoning would involve deliberating about what to do, under the supposition that certain options are ruled out (even if one knows full well that it is perfectly possible for one to take those options). Thus one might deliberate about what to do on the supposition that one will in fact not stop shooting up heroin, just treating the option of giving up heroin, for the purposes of this particular bit of reasoning, as if it were simply taken off the table and no longer under consideration. This is probably at least one of the kinds of reasoning in which the *conditional* 'ought' has its essential conceptual role.

Another way in which kinds of reasoning can differ is in their *subject matter*. One way of conceiving of the subject matter of a piece of reasoning is in terms of the propositions that are "held fixed" as defining the problem that the reasoning is concerned with, so that it is only propositions that are compatible with the propositions that are held fixed in this way that are the "eligible" propositions that the reasoning is concerned to assess. For example, in the case of the practical 'ought' the propositions that are "held fixed" in this way are all those actual truths that are causally independent of everything that the relevant agent might do or think at the relevant time; it is only propositions that are compatible with the propositions that are held fixed in this way that are even eligible to be incorporated into the agent's plans.

For the 'ought' of general desirability, the propositions "held fixed" will typically be a narrower class, containing just those actual truths that could not easily be otherwise—the truths that hold in all possible worlds that are "nearby" the actual world, such as the laws of nature—not all those truths that are causally independent of what a particular agent thinks or does at a particular time. It is all those propositions that are compatible with these truths that could not easily be otherwise that form the relevant domain of propositions that this sort of 'ought' is concerned to assess.

In addition to these differences between kinds of reasoning, there are also differences in the *kind of regulative role* that a normative concept may play. For example, consider the following two kinds of regulative role that normative concepts can play. When a normative concept plays the first kind of role, a judgment that applies the concept to a proposition commits the thinker to having a certain *attitude* towards that proposition. (The role that I proposed as the essential conceptual role of the practical 'ought' is of this first kind, since according to my account a suitable judgment applying this concept to a proposition commits one to incorporating that proposition into one's ideal plans about what to do.) When a normative concept plays the second kind of role, a judgment that applies the concept to a proposition directly commits the thinker to *realizing* that proposition. (An example of this would be a judgment about what one ought to believe: the judgment 'I ought to believe p' does not commit one to taking any attitude towards the embedded proposition that one believes p; it commits one directly to believing p—that is, to realizing the embedded proposition 'I believe p'.) The first of these two sorts of regulative role will normally be indicated by the fact that the proposition to which the 'ought'-operator is attached is a proposition about the *subject matter* of the contextually salient reasoning, while the second sort of regulative role will be indicated by the fact that the proposition to which the 'ought'-operator is attached is a proposition about one's having an *attitude* that forms a potential conclusion of the contextually salient reasoning.

When a normative concept's essential role is a regulative role of either of these first two kinds, its semantic value will be whatever property of a proposition it is that makes it *uniquely correct* to respond to the proposition in the relevant way (either by taking the relevant attitude to the proposition, or by directly realizing the proposition). So, for example, according to this account, the statement 'He ought to use a Phillips screwdriver to open that safe' will be true just in case the proposition that the person in question uses a Phillips screwdriver follows from some correct contingency plans for how (if at all) to open the safe, and the negation of that proposition does not follow from any such correct contingency plan.

It seems that normative concepts whose essential conceptual role is a regulative role of either of these first two kinds will be "objective" sorts of 'ought'. The essential role of the "information-relative" sorts of 'ought' is a third sort of regulative role. I shall illustrate the difference between the first and the third sort of regulative role with reference to the practical 'ought'; a similar difference will apply to the other kinds of reasoning as well. A belief involving the objective practical 'ought', of the form '$O_{<me,\ t>}(p)$', unconditionally commits the believer to incorporating the proposition p into his plans; the only way in which the believer can escape this commitment is by giving up this belief. The information-relative 'ought', on the other hand, is *relativized*, at least implicitly, to a particular body of information. The essential conceptual role of the information-relative practical 'ought' is that the canonical rational *ground* or *basis* for beliefs involving this sort of 'ought', of the form 'In relation to information I, $O_{<me,\ t>}(p)$', is the fact that one's possession of this body of information I is itself a rational state, and if that information were one's only information about the relevant question, then that information would commit one to incorporating p into one's plans about what to do at t.[10]

---

[10] In effect, my account of the information-relative 'ought' comes close to Brandom's (1994) idea that the function of normative terms like 'ought' is to "make explicit" the relations of commitment and entitlement that guide rational reasoning.

Thus, for example, the epistemic 'ought' (as in 'Tonight's performance ought to be a lot of fun') seems to be a sort of information-relative 'ought', implicitly relative to a body of information that counts in the context as *evidence*. The relevant sort of reasoning here is not practical reasoning, but theoretical reasoning. So the essential conceptual role of the epistemic 'ought' is that the canonical rational ground or basis for beliefs involving this sort of 'ought', of the form 'In relation to evidence E, it ought to be that p', is the fact that possessing evidence E is a rational mental state, and if E were all the information that one had about the relevant question, then it would commit one to at least a tentative belief in p.

I suggested in the previous chapter (Section 4.5) that when a rule is a rule about how one mental state counts as a ground or basis for another mental state (rather than a rule about how one mental state commits one to another mental state), the validity of an instance of the rule requires that merely being *in* that first mental state should guarantee the correctness of the output mental state. So, if this account of the essential conceptual role of the information-relative 'ought' is correct, then its semantic value will just be that relation between a body of information and a proposition that makes it the case that possessing that information really is a rational state, and if it were all the information that the relevant agent had on the question, it would commit the agent to responding to that proposition in the relevant way.

Thus, the semantic value of the epistemic 'ought' will be that relation between a body of information and a proposition that makes it the case that possessing that information is a rational state, and if that were all the information that one had about the relevant question, it would commit one to forming at least a tentative *belief* in that proposition. In other words (given how I am understanding the concept 'commitment'), this is the relation that makes it the case that possessing that information is itself a rational state, which rationally requires one to form at least a tentative belief in that proposition (at least if the question of whether or not to believe that proposition arises). Presumably, this is just the relation of that information's counting as genuine *evidence* that makes that proposition sufficiently *probable*. Thus, an epistemic 'ought'-statement, of the form 'In relation to evidence E, it ought to be that p' will be true if and only if p is sufficiently probable given evidence E. In most cases, E will be the relevant thinker's *total* evidence; however, there are some cases like the example that I gave above, 'The orbit of Pluto ought to be elliptical', where 'ought' is at least implicitly relativized to some body of information that is a *proper part* of one's total evidence—so that this statement is true if and only if it is sufficiently highly probable given this proper part of one's evidence that the orbit of Pluto is elliptical.

In the previous section, I argued that the logic of the practical 'ought' reflects the consistency constraints that apply to correct planning. In a broadly similar way, the logic of each of these other kinds of 'ought' reflects the consistency constraints that apply to the conclusions of the relevant other kind of reasoning.

According to the suggestions that I have made here, the conclusions of these other kinds of reasoning all involve incorporating the proposition in question into some sort of (conditional) plan—or, in the case of the epistemic 'ought', into one's system of beliefs. It seems plausible to me that essentially the same consistency constraints apply to conditional plans and to belief systems. First, for a conditional plan to be correct, the conditional plan must be logically consistent; and likewise, for a system of beliefs to be correct, the contents of the system must be logically consistent. Secondly, for a conditional plan or a system of beliefs to be correct, it must be possible to extend it into a maximally detailed plan or system of beliefs which is also itself correct. Finally, it will always be correct to incorporate a logical truth into any plan or system of beliefs, and never correct to incorporate the negation of a logical truth. Just like the practical 'ought', then, these other kinds of 'ought' are subject to all the consistency constraints of standard deontic logic. (According to the account that I have just proposed, the semantic value of the information-relative 'ought' is given in terms of when certain pieces of reasoning count as *rational*, rather than in terms of when the conclusions of those pieces of reasoning are *correct*. However, it seems plausible that the same consistency constraints apply to rational plans and to rational beliefs, as well as to correct plans and correct beliefs. So it is plausible that the information-relative 'ought' is also subject to the consistency constraints of standard deontic logic.)

We can capture these logical features of these sorts of 'ought' by means of a generalized version of the possible-worlds semantics that I sketched in the previous section for the practical 'ought'. In general, the context must determine two parameters for each occurrence of 'ought'. First, the context must determine the conceptual role of the concept that this occurrence of 'ought' expresses. Determining this will involve settling the following two issues: (i) which sort of regulative role the concept plays; and (ii) what kind of reasoning figures in this conceptual role—that is, what kind of response to a proposition is the output of this sort of reasoning (for example, this output might consist in incorporating the proposition into one's system of beliefs, or into one's contingency plans about how to open the safe, and so on). Secondly, the context must determine the relevant domain of propositions that the reasoning is concerned with; this is the domain of propositions that defines the class of propositions that are eligible for consideration in the context. This feature of the context can be represented by means of a set of propositions S, which is "held fixed" in the context, so that only those propositions that are consistent with S count as "the relevant domain of propositions" in the context. (For the objective 'ought', the set of propositions that is "held fixed" will typically be some set of truths that need not be known or believed by any of the participants in the relevant conversation, such as all the truths that are causally independent of what the relevant agent thinks or does at the relevant time. For the information-relative 'ought', the set of propositions that is "held fixed" will typically be some set of propositions that count as evidence, and so are rationally believed by the participants in the conversation.)

In general, in a context in which a set of propositions S is being "held fixed", and 'ought' expresses a concept with essential conceptual role C, 'It ought to be the case that p' is true at a world w if, and only if, p is true at all possible worlds that (i) are compatible with all members of S and (ii) belong to the "favoured" subset of those worlds (from the standpoint of w) according to the relevant selection function that is associated with C.[11] As before, this account of the semantics leads to standard deontic logic so long as the "favoured" subset of the worlds that are compatible with S is never empty.

My account of the objective practical 'ought' is an instance of this general pattern. According to my account, a proposition involving the practical 'ought', of the form '$O_{<A,\ t>}(p)$', is true if and only if p is true at all worlds that (i) are compatible with all the propositions that are true in w, and causally independent of what A thinks or does at t, and (ii) belong to the favoured subset of those worlds, when assessed in the appropriate way with respect to how A acts at t in those worlds.

Similar accounts can be given of the other kinds of 'ought', including the epistemic 'ought' (as in 'Tonight's performance ought to be a lot of fun'). A proposition involving the epistemic 'ought', of the form 'It ought to be the case that p', is true at a world w if, and only if, p is true in all worlds that (i) are compatible with what *counts as evidence in the context*, and (ii) belong to the favoured subset of those worlds when evaluated with respect to *probability on the evidence of the world's implications about p* from the standpoint of w.

Often, the set of propositions S that is "held fixed", and so determines which domain of propositions (or possible worlds) is relevant to an 'ought'-statement, is just determined implicitly by the context. In some cases, however, it may be indicated more explicitly. To take an example involving the practical 'ought', one may say: 'If you are going to keep on taking heroin intravenously, you at least ought to use clean needles'. Here the proposition 'You are going to keep on taking heroin intravenously' is explicitly added to the set of propositions S that is "held fixed", producing a set that is different from the set that would ordinarily be "held fixed" for this sort of 'ought'. In effect, this is a *conditional* 'ought' of the sort that was analysed by David Lewis (1974*b*) among others. Thus, this statement is true just in case all members of the favoured subset of the worlds in which the addressee keeps on taking heroin intravenously (and in which all the other truths that are causally independent of what the addressee does or thinks at the relevant time also continue to hold) are also worlds in which he uses clean needles. So far as I can see, there is a conditional 'ought' of

---

[11] As Kratzer (2002) puts it, 'ought'-statements involve two contextually determined parameters: (i) the "modal base" (which delimits the relevant class of worlds), and (ii) the "ordering source" (which supplies a ranking of the worlds and thereby a "favoured" subset of the relevant worlds).

this sort corresponding to every one of the various kinds of 'ought' that I have discussed above.

According to the account that I have outlined, the logical principles that apply to each 'ought'-concept stem from the consistency constraints on the kind of reasoning within which that 'ought'-concept has its essential conceptual role. The reason why the principles of standard deontic logic are correct for each of the 'ought'-concepts that I have discussed so far is that each of these concepts has its essential conceptual role within a kind of reasoning the output of which consists in incorporating some proposition into some sort of system of plans or beliefs. It seems essential to any system of plans and beliefs that to be correct, or even to be rational, its contents must all be consistent with each other. Since plans and beliefs are subject to fairly robust consistency constraints, so too are these 'ought'-concepts. At all events, as I hope to have shown in this section, my conceptual role semantics for the practical 'ought' can be seen as an instance of a more general pattern, which covers a large number of the concepts that can be expressed by words like 'ought'. Moreover, this approach also helps us to see how the context in which the word 'ought' appears can determine which of these many concepts this occurrence of the word expresses.

5.3 'OUGHT' AND 'BEST'

This account of the meaning of 'ought' naturally raises the question: What are the logical relations between an 'ought'-concept for which one set of propositions S_1 is "held fixed" and an otherwise similar 'ought'-concept for which another set of propositions S_2 is "held fixed"?

In the previous section, I introduced the idea of a *conditional* 'ought'—where the effect of this conditional 'ought' is to effect an explicit shift in the set of propositions that are "held fixed" for the relevant occurrence of 'ought'. We may formulate this conditional 'ought' by introducing a *dyadic* deontic operator, '$O\,(\psi/\varphi)$', which we can read as '*Given that φ, it ought to be that ψ*'. Where '$O_{<S,\,K>}$' is an 'ought'-operator that has a conceptual role of kind K, for which a set of propositions S is "held fixed", then if p is the conjunction of all members of S, we can write '$O_{<S,\,K>}\,(q)$' as '$O_K\,(q/p)$', or (omitting the explicit reference to the kind of conceptual role K for simplicity of exposition) '$O\,(q/p)$'. So we can now reformulate our question as follows: what are the logical relations between '$O\,(q/p_1)$' and '$O\,(q/p_2)$'?

The most important instance of this question concerns the case in which the set of propositions that is "held fixed" for one 'ought'-operator *includes* the set that is held fixed for another such 'ought'-operator. In our "dyadic" reformulation, this is the question about the logical relations between '$O\,(q/p_1)$' and '$O\,(q/p_1 \,\&\, p_2)$'.

Now it is plainly wrong to say simply that '$O\,(q/p_1)$' entails '$O\,(q/p_1 \,\&\, p_2)$', or conversely. On the contrary, it is quite possible that a pair of propositions of the form '$O\,(q/p_1)$' and '$O\,(\neg\, q/p_1\,\&\,p_2)$' might both be true. For example, given all the truths that are causally independent of whatever you might think or do, you ought to stop taking heroin and get rid of all drug-taking paraphernalia, including hypodermic needles; but given that in addition to all these causally independent truths, you're not going to stop taking heroin, you ought not to get rid of drug-taking paraphernalia—on the contrary, you ought to stock up on a large supply of clean needles instead.

Nonetheless, something a bit weaker seems acceptable. The reason why adding the proposition 'You are not going to stop taking heroin' changes things is precisely that (given all these causally independent truths) you ought to stop taking heroin. In general, if q ought to be the case given that p_1 is the case, then adding a new proposition p_2 will change things (that is, it is *not* true that q ought to be the case given that '$p_1\,\&\,p_2$' is the case) only if the conjunction of q, p_1, and p_2 is incompatible with something that *already* ought to be the case given that p_1 is the case.

If the addition of p_2 to the *total set* of propositions that ought to be the case given p_1 introduces no inconsistencies of any kind, then all the propositions that ought to be the case given p_1 will remain propositions that ought to be the case given p_1 and p_2.[12] For example, given all the truths that are causally independent of whatever you now think or do, you ought to stop taking heroin; and given that in addition to all these causally independent truths, you will soon be returning to live in England, you still ought to stop taking heroin. (It does not follow in this case that p_2 is utterly *irrelevant* to what ought to be: it may well be that certain *further* propositions ought to be the case given p_1 and p_2 that were not propositions that ought to be the case given p_1 alone; it only follows that the propositions that *already* ought to be the case given p_1 will remain ones that ought to be the case given p_1 and p_2. For example, suppose that given all these causally independent truths, you ought to stop taking heroin, but it is not the case that you ought to make sure that you are registered with a primary care physician in England. It could still be that given that in addition you will soon be returning to live in England, then it *is* the case that you ought to make sure that you are registered with a physician in England.)

At all events, if the dyadic 'ought'-operator has this logical feature, then it must be reflected in the possible-worlds semantics for this operator in the following

---

[12] On my approach, this logical feature of the dyadic 'ought'-operator should be explicable on the basis of the consistency constraints that apply to the relevant sorts of *planning* or *practical reasoning*. One possible form that such an explanation could take is the following. First, we would need the notion of a plan that is correct *conditionally on the assumption p_1*. Then, we would need to defend the principle that if a *maximally detailed* plan is correct conditionally on the assumption p_1, then the only way in which this plan can fail to be correct conditionally on the assumption '$p_1\,\&\,p_2$' is if adding p_2 to this maximally detailed plan results in some inconsistency within the plan. Given my account of the meaning of 'ought', this would then explain this logical feature of the dyadic 'ought'. However, it remains a task for further investigation to explain exactly why this principle holds.

way. Let us suppose that for every set of possible worlds, the relevant selection function will "favour" some subset of that set, in such a way that a statement of the form '$O\,(q/p)$' is true just in case q is true at all the worlds in the "favoured" subset of the p-worlds. Then to accommodate this logical feature of the dyadic 'ought', this selection function must meet the following condition: if p_2 implies p_1, and p_2 is true at some of the p_1-worlds that are "favoured" by the relevant selection function, then the p_2-worlds "favoured" by this selection function are the *intersection* of those at which p_2 is true and the p_1-worlds that are "favoured" by that selection function.

Now, I have also argued that the D principle holds for most kinds of 'ought', reflecting the idea that what ought to be the case is always at least logically possible. In our possible-worlds semantics, this is reflected in the constraint that the set of relevant worlds "favoured" by the relevant selection function is non-empty. Except where the proposition p is impossible in some way, the notion of what ought to be the case *given p* seems to be an 'ought' of the relevant kind; and if p_2 implies p_1, then p_1 will not be impossible unless p_2 is too. So, if p_2 implies p_1, and the set of p_2-worlds "favoured" by the relevant selection function is non-empty, then the set of p_1-worlds "favoured" by this selection function must also be non-empty.

Given these two conditions that we have just imposed on the selection function, it can be proved that this selection function—which maps sets of worlds onto "favoured" subsets of those sets of worlds—can be represented by means of a *partial ordering of worlds*.[13] For any proposition p, the "favoured" p-worlds will be those that are not ranked lower in the ordering than any other p-worlds; and for any propositions p_1 and p_2, if p_2 implies p_1, then the "favoured" p_2-worlds will either come equally high up in the ordering as the "favoured" p_1-worlds, or else they will come lower down in the ordering—the "favoured" p_2-worlds cannot come higher up than (or be unordered in relation to) the "favoured" p_1-worlds.

In effect, this dyadic deontic logic introduces a *ranking* of possible worlds— roughly, in terms of which worlds count as "more favoured" than others (according to whatever ranking of worlds is relevant to the specific sort of 'ought' that is in question). Formally speaking, the reason for introducing a ranking of possible worlds to make sense of the dyadic 'ought' is exactly the same as the reason for introducing an ordering of possible worlds (in terms of "closeness" or "similarity" to the actual world) in order to understand *counterfactuals*. Indeed, David Lewis's semantics for 'ought' is closely modelled on his semantics for counterfactuals, and explicitly appeals to the Leibnizian idea of the *best* possible worlds. According to Lewis, the counterfactual 'If it were the case that p, it would be the case that q' is true if and only if q is true at all the *closest* worlds where p is true; and the dyadic deontic statement 'Given that p is the case, it ought to be the case that q' is true if and only if q is true at all the *best* worlds where p is true; and a statement

13 For the details of the proof, see Lewis (1973: 58–9); compare Hansson (1968).

involving the monadic operator, of the form '*O (p)*', is true if and only if *p* is true at all the *best* possible worlds.[14]

This aspect of Lewis's dyadic deontic logic is often criticized. How can these technical logical considerations justify such a controversial move as postulating a fundamental connection between 'ought' and '*best*'? It might seem that postulating this connection between 'ought' and 'best' simply begs the question in favour of a consequentialist position such as that of G. E. Moore (1903: 146), who notoriously claimed that the term 'right' simply *means* "productive of most good".[15]

It is true that talking baldly about the "best possible world" may strongly suggest that one is considering the world as a whole, without giving any special privileged role to any particular time or agent in that world. (A natural way of voicing the central consequentialist thought is by saying that we ought always to do all we can to *make the world a better place*.) But this suggestion would be quite misleading in the present context.

The crucial point here is that 'best' is context-sensitive in at least as many ways as 'ought'.[16] Something can be best for the world as a whole; but something can also be best for me, or best for Oxford University; or it can be the best way to open a certain safe; or it can simply be the best thing for the agent *A* to do at a particular time *t*. With the practical 'ought', at least, the relevantly "best" possible worlds need not be the best possible worlds from an impersonal or agent-neutral point of view; they are simply the best possible worlds, *when evaluated with respect to how the relevant agent acts at the relevant time*. For example, it may be that a world in which *A* fails to prevent two murders at *t* counts as "better" in the relevant way than a world in which there are fewer murders overall but *A* himself commits a murder at *t*.[17] Thus, there is no reason at all to think that postulating this sort of connection between 'ought' and 'best' must lead to consequentialism (at least according to the standard understanding of what consequentialism involves).

According to a different and more subtle objection, this account of the semantics of 'ought' may not lead to a consequentialist account of 'ought', but it does at least lead to a *teleological* account of 'ought'. But even that is surely a highly controversial doctrine, which should not be built into the very semantics of the term itself.

John Rawls (1971: 24) defines a "teleological" theory as one in which "the good is defined independently from the right, and then the right is defined as

---

[14] See Lewis (1973 and 1974*b*). Strictly speaking, the statement of truth conditions that I have given assumes what Lewis calls the "Limit Assumption" — the assumption that there are always some best or closest *p*-worlds, under the relevant ordering of betterness or closeness. It is a straightforward matter to adjust the statement of truth conditions so that it does not rely on this assumption.

[15] For this objection to the standard semantics for deontic logic, see Horty (2001).

[16] The context-sensitivity of 'best' is rightly stressed in Thomson (2000).

[17] For the idea of an agent-relative betterness ordering, compare Sen (2000).

that which maximizes the good". There is no reason to expect that postulating a connection between 'ought' and 'best' in the way that I have done here will lead to a teleological theory of this kind.

The reason for this is simply that my approach does not require that the relevant notion of what is "better" need be intelligible independently of the relevant notion of what "ought" to be the case. Indeed, the picture that I have outlined goes more naturally with the view that the relevant ordering of worlds—according to which some worlds count as "better" than others—is actually constructed out of the truths about what ought to be the case. Very roughly, to say that one set of possible worlds is "better" than a second is just to say that there is some larger class of possible worlds, including both sets of worlds, such that it is the first set of worlds, and not the second, that ought to be the case when all members of the larger class of worlds are regarded as available. So it does not seem to me that postulating a connection between 'ought' and 'best', in the way that I have, leads to a theory that is "teleological" in the most controversial sense.

However, there are two more serious objections to my postulation of a fundamental conceptual connection between 'ought' and 'best' that need to be considered. The first objection is an argument that John Broome (2004: 34) gives against "teleological" theories (by which he means theories according to which what one ought to do is determined by the goodness of the available alternatives):

> The relation of betterness is transitive, which means that a normative theory must have a transitive structure if it is to be teleologized. Suppose a normative theory implies that, when the available alternatives are A and B, one ought to do A, and when the available alternatives are B and C, one ought to do B, and when the available alternatives are C and A, one ought to do C. This normative theory does not have a transitive structure. It cannot be the case that A is better than B, B better than C, and C better than A. So what one ought to do, according to this theory, cannot depend only on the goodness of the alternatives. The theory cannot be made teleological. It does not have what I call "teleological structure".

Now suppose that, as many philosophers believe, there are some plausible normative theories that do not have "teleological structure" (Broome gives the example of Frances Kamm's theory of when we ought to save someone's life). Then it seems that it is just implausible to claim, as I have done, that this connection between 'ought' and 'best' is actually a *logical* or *conceptual* truth.

However, Broome is making a rather specific assumption about what representing the normative theory in terms of the goodness of alternatives would involve. Specifically, Broome is assuming that the relevant notion of "betterness" will rank different alternatives *across different situations*. He is clearly assuming that this notion will be able to compare how good A is in the situation in which the only available alternatives are A and B with how good C is in the situation in which the only available alternatives are C and A. But these two situations must be different from each other (there is no agent x and time t such that at t, x is *both* in a situation in which the only available alternatives are A and B, *and* in a situation in which the only available alternatives are C and A).

My conception of how a betterness ranking can represent the normative theory is different from this. I am assuming that the sort of 'betterness' that corresponds to the practical 'ought', '$O_{<x,\ t>}$', is indexed to a particular agent x and time t in just the same way as this sort of 'ought' is. So this sort of betterness can only rank possible worlds that are available to x at t, and it ranks them only from the standpoint of x and t: it cannot rank other possible worlds, nor can it rank them from the standpoint of other agents or other times. This betterness ranking is constructed from 'ought'-propositions that are all indexed to the *same* agent and time. So it does not compare different alternatives across different situations. Instead, it compares possible worlds across different conditions that may be assumed to hold of the very same situation (such as the condition that the relevant agent does not stop taking heroin, or that he does not stop using dirty hypodermic needles, and so on). Broome has not produced an example of an intelligible normative theory that cannot be represented by means of a ranking of possible worlds in this way.

The last objection that I shall consider in this chapter is that any theory that postulates a fundamental connection between 'ought' and 'best' cannot make sense of *supererogation*: it implausibly equates 'right' and 'best', and so leaves no room for anything that falls short of the "best" to be "right".[18]

Here again we need to remember that 'ought' and 'best' are both context-sensitive. What is crucial to a supererogatory act is not that it is not true to say, in any context, that it is what the agent "ought" to do. (Indeed, we can imagine the saintly agent saying of herself that she has no doubt that she *ought* to perform the supererogatory act.) What is crucial to supererogatory acts is that even without any special excuse, one may be entirely *blameless* in refraining from a supererogatory act; it is not in any way blameworthy to refrain from such supererogatory acts.

Thus, one might express the fact that an act is supererogatory by saying, for example, 'Ideally, we ought to give more than this, but no one will be entitled to blame us if we don't.' In using the term 'ought' to indicate that it would be morally better to give more, one may be using it as a kind of moral 'ought', according to which what one ought to do is whatever is (a necessary component of) the morally best thing to do.

Alternatively, one might express the fact that an act is supererogatory by saying, for example, 'It would be better—more admirable and so on—for us to give more than this, but it's not true that we *ought* to do so.' Here, we are using the term 'ought' to indicate that there is nothing blameworthy in refraining from giving more. In so doing, we are using 'ought' to indicate what is necessary (absent any special excuse) for avoiding blameworthiness (so, on this

---

[18] For this objection, see Hansson (1997: 430–1).

interpretation, 'ought' is still connected to what is best—namely, what is best for avoiding blameworthiness).

An alternative understanding of supererogation would analyse the notion, not in terms of blameworthiness, but in terms of what (following Williams) I have called the "practical 'ought'". Perhaps what is essential to a supererogatory act is that it is *morally* better than some alternative act, but it is not true in the practical sense of the term that one *ought* to do it. Even if this is what supererogation is, the existence of supererogatory acts does not threaten the proposed connection between 'ought' and 'best'. What one ought in the practical sense to do is not necessarily whatever is a necessary component of what is *best morally speaking*—it is whatever is a necessary component of what is the *best thing to do, all things considered* (taking account not just of moral considerations, but also of non-moral considerations as well). It may be that giving more than we are currently giving is the morally best thing that we could do, but it is not the unique best thing for us to do, all things considered. We could indicate this fact by saying 'It would be better for us to give more than this, but it's not true that we *ought* to do so.' In short, once we recognize that the terms 'ought' and 'best' are both context-sensitive, it is clear that postulating a connection between 'ought' and 'best' in the way that I have leaves ample room for supererogation.

5.4 CONCLUSION

As I have argued, my conceptual role semantics for 'ought'—according to which the essential conceptual role of 'ought' is its regulative role in reasoning—can explain the central logical features of the term. It can explain the precise ways in which 'ought' is systematically context-sensitive; it can provide an explanation of why the principles of standard deontic logic are correct for each of the many concepts that can be expressed by 'ought'; and it enables us to answer the objections that have been raised against that standard deontic logic—even though this deontic logic commits us to something so controversial-sounding as postulating a conceptual connection between the concepts 'ought' and 'best'.

PART II

THE METAPHYSICS
OF NORMATIVE FACTS

6

The Metaphysical Issues

6.1 FROM SEMANTICS TO METAPHYSICS

In the first part of the book, I offered an account of the nature of normative concepts, and of the meaning of the normative terms that express those concepts. This account included an explanation of how the nature of each of these concepts determines the concept's semantic value—that is, how it determines which property or relation the concept refers to.

In giving this semantic account, I did not provide a full account of the nature of that property or relation itself: in particular, I did not resolve the metaphysical disputes between non-naturalists and naturalists, realists and anti-realists, and so on. In this second part of the book, I shall get to grips with some of these metaphysical issues.

In particular, I shall defend an account of these normative properties and relations according to which these normative properties and relations are both *irreducible* and *causally efficacious.* Since normative properties are irreducible, reductive forms of naturalism must be rejected. Nonetheless, I shall argue that this metaphysical conception of the normative is entirely consonant with a broader version of naturalism—specifically, with the idea that normative facts both supervene on, and are realized in, purely natural facts.[1]

First, however, before arguing for this metaphysical account of the nature of normative properties and relations, I shall explain how I conceive of these metaphysical issues.

---

[1] There are several other metaphysical questions that I shall not directly address here. The most notable of these are the following: whether normative truth is "epistemically constrained", or whether there can be unknowable normative truths; whether there is a distinctively "constructivist" interpretation of normative truth, and if so whether it is correct; and whether there is any reasonable interpretation on which Hamlet was right to say that "there is nothing either good or bad but thinking makes it so" (*Hamlet* II. ii. 247–8). I omit a discussion of these questions only to save space, not because I do not regard them as important. Even in a book as long as this one, not all pertinent issues can be discussed.

6.2 CONSTITUTIVE ACCOUNTS

The central task for the metaphysics of normative properties and relations is to give an account of the nature of these properties and relations. As we might also put it, the task is to give a *constitutive account* of these properties or relations. But what sort of "account" is this? What exactly is a "constitutive account"?

The idea of a "constitutive account" of some property or relation is expressed by many phrases that are commonly used by philosophers, though their meaning is rarely adequately explained. For instance, if we take as our example the property of value or being valuable, then one way to express this idea is to speak of an account of what *constitutes* a thing's value, or of what its being valuable *consists in*. As with almost all phrases that express this idea, this way of speaking can be transposed into the formal mode; we can speak of what the truth of the statement that a thing is valuable consists in, or of what constitutes the truth of that statement. Another phrase that seems to express the same idea is a special non-causal use of '*makes it the case that* ... '. Thus, we can speak of what makes it the case that a thing is valuable, or simply of what makes it valuable, or (in the formal mode) what makes it true that the thing is valuable. Other explanatory idioms can also express this idea. We can speak of that *in virtue of which* a thing is valuable, or of what the statement that it is valuable is *true in virtue of.* More simply, we can just ask *why* a thing is valuable, or why it counts as valuable, or what *explains* why it is valuable, so long as it is clear that 'why' and 'explanation' are not to be given a specifically causal interpretation. Finally, we may also speak of *what it is* for a thing to be valuable, or simply of what value fundamentally *is.* A statement of what value is, in this sense, may be called a *constitutive account* or *explanation* of value; in some sense of the terms, it could even be called an *analysis* or *definition* of value.

Though commonly used in philosophy, these phrases are hard to understand. Many philosophers assume that these "constitutive accounts" can be stated in the form of necessitated, universally quantified biconditionals. For instance, one example of such an account might be David Lewis's (1989) account of value:

Necessarily, for all x, x is a value if and only if under ideal conditions we would be disposed to value x.

Lewis's account is intended to be *non-circular*. Thus, the right-hand side of the biconditional is built up out of terms for properties and relations whose nature can be explained without making any reference to the property that is being accounted for—namely, the property of being a value.[2]

---

[2] I assume that if the nature of a property P_1 cannot be explained without mentioning a second property P_2, and the nature of P_2 cannot be explained without mentioning a third property P_3,

We should not assume that constitutive accounts of the nature of a property or relation have to be non-circular in this way. If a constitutive account of a property is non-circular in this way, then it seems to amount to a *reduction* of the property in question. Indeed, I shall argue later in this chapter that this is the best way to define the notion of a "reduction": if a necessary biconditional is to give a reduction of the property ascribed on its left-hand side, then it must not only be non-circular in this way, but the right-hand side must also give a constitutive account of what it is for the left-hand side to be true.[3]

In Part I of this book, I argued that the *semantics* of the concept expressed by 'ought' does not by itself imply any such reductive or non-circular account of the concept's semantic value; but we should not assume without further argument that this makes it impossible for any such reductive or non-circular account to be true. As I shall argue, a correct constitutive account of a property or relation does not have to be based on a semantic account of the meaning of any term (or of the nature of any concept) that stands for that property or relation.

Such biconditionals then do not have to be reductive or non-circular in order to be genuine constitutive accounts. But clearly not all necessary biconditionals are genuine constitutive accounts: otherwise, there would never be any reason to read such a biconditional as giving a constitutive account of the property ascribed by the left-hand side of the biconditional, rather than the property ascribed by the right-hand side. The biconditional would simply reveal its two sides to be necessarily equivalent: we would have no reason to regard it as a constitutive account of the property ascribed by one side rather than the other. In many cases of constitutive accounts, however, we do have a reason to treat the two sides of the biconditional in this asymmetric fashion.

Someone might propose that such a biconditional is a constitutive account of the property ascribed by its left-hand side just in case it is a *conceptual* truth, guaranteed to be true by the nature of the concept that is used on the left-hand side to ascribe the property in question. But this proposal can be shown to be inadequate by appeal to the following example. It is highly plausible that the following is a conceptual truth, guaranteed to be true by the nature of the concept *water*:[4]

---

then the nature of P_1 also cannot be fully explained without mentioning P_3. So, if the right-hand side of a constitutive account of P_1 is built out of terms for properties whose nature can be fully explained without mentioning P_1, it will also be possible to explain the nature of these properties without mentioning any *other* properties whose nature cannot be explained without mentioning P_1.

[3] This is the view of Michael Dummett (1993*b*: 57), who states that a reduction must give an account of what the reduced sentence is true in virtue of, if it is true. (An alternative understanding of reductions is simply as property identities, involving the identification of the property ascribed by a "suspect" concept, with the property ascribed by some "kosher" concept. But I have never encountered an adequate account of what this distinction between "suspect" and "kosher" concepts amounts to; so I am sceptical about whether this is a particularly useful conception of reductions.)

[4] This view of the concept *water* has been advocated by many philosophers, including Davies and Humberstone (1980: 18–21) and Wright (1992: 130), among others.

Necessarily: for all x, x is a sample of water if and only if x is a sample of the underlying natural kind that actually typically causes the sort of experience that we use as our primary means of recognizing water.

But intuitively this is not a constitutive account of the nature of water. This connection to human experience is not part of what water is; it is incidental to what makes something a sample of water.

Moreover, it seems that being a conceptual truth is not always even necessary to make a biconditional into a constitutive account. Consider the following biconditional:

For all x, x is a sample of water if and only if x is a sample of H_2O.

This is obviously not a conceptual truth. Still, it seems to me to give a constitutive account of water: it explains what it is about something that makes it a sample of water; it tells us what water fundamentally is. Admittedly, it may be that many constitutive accounts are conceptual truths. But the general point still holds: constitutive accounts are not always conceptual truths, and conceptually true biconditionals are not always constitutive accounts.

As the example of water makes clear, a constitutive account of a property tells us something about the *property itself*, and need not explain the meaning of any of the terms, or the nature of any of the concepts, that may be used to talk or think about that property. Of course, we could give a constitutive account of a concept too: we could grapple, not with the question 'What is water?', but with the question 'What is the concept *water*?' But that would be an account of something entirely different: it would not be an account of water, of a type of material stuff; it would be an account of a concept or type of thought.[5] Perhaps our concept *water*—that is, the way in which we typically *think* of water—depends on our perceptual experiences of water; it does not follow that water itself has any such dependence on our experiences. Part I of this book was devoted to giving an account of the nature of normative *concepts*—that is, an account of what it is to have *thoughts* about what ought to be the case. Part II of the book is devoted to giving an account of normative *properties* and *relations*—that is, an account of what it is for something to *be* something that ought to be the case.

Once it is clear that we are considering constitutive accounts of properties themselves, not just constitutive accounts of the concepts that we use to ascribe those properties, then we may well wonder how the biconditional linking water with H_2O can be a constitutive account of water. It is highly plausible that the property of being made of water is exactly the same property as the property of

---

[5] Thus, an account of the *concept water* will not be of the form: x is a sample of water if and only if $A(x)$. That is the form of an account of water itself, not an account of the concept *water*. An account of the concept *water* should take the form: For all concepts C, $C =$ the concept *water* if and only if $A(C)$.

being made of H_2O. Indeed, in general, all instances of the following schema are plausible: if there is a correct constitutive account of the property of being F, to the effect that necessarily, for all x, x is F if and only if x is G, then for something to be F just *is* for it to be G, and this makes it plausible that the property of being F is *identical* to the property of being G.[6] But then why should we take one side of the biconditional as giving an account or analysis of the other, rather than vice versa? We simply have the same property twice over, once on each side of the biconditional.

Part of the answer to this challenge must be that, even if the property ascribed on each side of the biconditional is the same, the analysing side speaks of certain other objects or properties that are not spoken of on the analysed side. Thus, if we analyse water as H_2O, we speak not only of the property being analysed—namely, water or H_2O—but also of hydrogen and oxygen, which are not spoken of on the analysed side of our biconditional. This is why the analysing side of these biconditionals is generally *more complex* than the analysed side.

This, however, is only part of the answer. Even if both sides of a biconditional ascribe the same property, but one side also speaks of certain further objects or properties that the other side does not speak of, the biconditional could still fail to give a constitutive account of that property. For example:

For all x, x has the property of being wrong iff x has the property that I am actually now thinking about.

The phrases 'the property of being wrong' and 'the property that I am actually now thinking about' both refer to the very same property; and the right-hand side of the biconditional is more complex than the left-hand side. Moreover, when the 'actually' operator is understood in the standard way, as was explained by Davies and Humberstone (1980), this biconditional is also necessary. But obviously this does not count as a proper constitutive account of what it is to be wrong. So what else must be true of a biconditional to make it into a constitutive account?

6.3 ESSENCE AND MODALITY

Aristotle clearly believed that when Socrates asked Euthyphro "What is piety?", he was seeking a *real definition* of piety.[7] A real definition of some object (whether a particular or a universal) is a formula that states the essence of that object. Perhaps then the feature that makes a necessary biconditional into a constitutive account is that it should be a real definition, or state the essence, of a particular

[6] This criterion of property identity is suggested by Yablo (1992*a*: 251).

[7] See Irwin (1995: 25–6, §15); Irwin refers there to Aristotle's *Metaphysics* (987b1–4 and 1078b23–30).

or universal that is spoken of on the left-hand side. This proposal seems the more plausible since Aristotle's favourite formula for essence—phrases of the form 'what it is for something to be a human being'—is also, as we have seen, one of the phrases that contemporary philosophers employ to indicate that they are giving a constitutive account.

As I claimed in the previous section, there is no reason to demand that all constitutive accounts should be non-circular. To impose this demand is to insist that these accounts should be reductive. But real definitions do not have to be reductive or non-circular. This, then, is the proposal that I shall try to develop here: that constitutive accounts are in fact nothing other than real definitions or statements of essence.

This proposal faces a serious obstacle, however. This obstacle is the widespread belief that the notions of real definition and of essence, if they are intelligible at all, are reducible to more simple modal terms. Most of the contemporary philosophers who are willing to tolerate the notion of essence at all simply define the essence of an object as those properties which it is impossible for the object to exist without. But then the distinction between a necessary biconditional, and one that states the essence or gives a real definition of something that is spoken of on the left-hand side, will simply collapse. It is impossible for water to exist without being the basic kind of stuff that is actually dominantly causally responsible for the experiences that we use as our primary means of recognizing water. So it would follow that this connection to our experience is an essential feature of water, according to this modal view of essence.

There are however strong reasons against this modal definition of essence. As Kit Fine has pointed out, it has several quite unacceptable consequences. It is impossible for Socrates to exist without being a member of the set that includes Socrates and all the natural numbers. So according to the modal definition of essence, it is part of the essence of Socrates that he is a member of this set. But intuitively, this is not part of Socrates' essence or nature. As Fine (1994: 5) puts it: "Strange as the literature on personal identity may be, it has never been suggested that in order to understand the nature of a person one must know which sets he belongs to."[8]

Rather than repeating Fine's attack on the modal conception of essence, I shall simply assume that we need a new conception of essence. But I shall not attempt any reductive definition of essentialist notions in other, non-essentialist

---

[8] Fine's two other main objections are as follows. (i) Where p is any necessary proposition, then, for any object x, it is necessary that if x exists then p is true; so the essence of anything involves all necessary truths (which is absurd). (ii) It seems possible for two philosophers to agree on all the modal facts while disagreeing about essence: e.g., two philosophers might agree that it is necessary that all persons have both minds and bodies; but one of these philosophers might think that persons can be defined as embodied minds, and so are ontologically dependent on minds, whereas the other thinks that minds are abstractions from persons, so that minds are ontologically dependent on persons.

terms. It seems plausible to me that Fine is right: these essentialist notions are fundamental metaphysical concepts, which are incapable of any non-circular definition. Still, these essentialist notions can be explicated by characterizing their logical properties, and their connections to other metaphysical concepts.

As I have said, we may think of the essence of an object (whether an individual or a universal) as given by the *real definition* of that object—that is, by the basic metaphysical principle that states the nature of that object. If the object is an individual, then this basic principle may be a principle about what it is for something to be that individual—that is, the principle that determines which individual (if any), in any possible world, is identical to the individual in question. In this way then, the essence of an individual may be what explains its identity—that is, its *principium individuationis*, what individuates it, or makes it different from all other things. On the other hand, if the object in question is not an individual but a property or relation, then the basic principle may be a principle about what it is for a sequence of objects to exemplify this property or relation. In this way, the essence of the property may reveal what "unifies" the property, or constitutes the "real similarity" shared by all its instances, both actual and merely possible.[9]

In addition, the essence of an object must somehow explain—either directly or indirectly—why certain propositions about the object are metaphysically necessary or metaphysically impossible. Indeed, it seems plausible to me that all truths about which propositions are metaphysically necessary and which are not should be explained—either directly or indirectly—on the basis of these fundamental principles about the essences of things.[10]

For example, suppose that the essence of what it is for something to be *red* is for it to have some intrinsic natural property that would typically cause objects to look red when seen in suitable conditions. Then this fundamental principle about the essence of redness would explain various further modal truths about redness, such as the impossibility of "fool's red", or the possibility of red objects that are never seen, or of red objects that are physically quite unlike the red things of the actual world. In this way, then, this approach allows us to insist that the truths about which propositions are metaphysically necessary, and which are not, do not amount to a formless chaotic jumble of metaphysical truths, of which no explanation is possible. On the contrary, these metaphysical modal truths form

---

[9] In the terminology of Fine (1995*b*), I am understanding the essence of an object as its *constitutive* essence—the proposition that defines what the object essentially is—rather than as its *consequential* essence, which is the closure of its essence under logical consequence.

[10] If truths, or true propositions, are just sets of possible worlds, then it would make little sense to try to explain modal truths—especially if (as in S5 modal logic) all modal truths are themselves necessary truths (on this point, see Stalnaker 1996*a*: 112–17). As I explained in Chapter 3, however, I am assuming a different conception of propositions: specifically, I am assuming that propositions are abstract entities, constructed out of individuals, properties, and relations, by means of operations analogous to predication, negation, conjunction, and so on, along the lines suggested by George Bealer (1982: chs. 1–4).

an explicable structure, since they can all be explained on the basis of the essences of some object or objects.

Indeed, this approach allows us to make a general suggestion about what it is for a proposition to be metaphysically necessary. Whenever a proposition is metaphysically necessary, its metaphysical necessity must be explained (either directly or indirectly) by the nature or essence of some object or objects.

Of course, the notion of metaphysical necessity has fundamental connections to certain other notions as well. In particular, the propositions that are metaphysically necessary impose an outer limit to certain other modalities: for example, it seems plausible that nothing that is metaphysically impossible can be either physically possible or deontically possible (that is, permissible). Moreover, metaphysical necessities interact in a certain way with counterfactual conditionals. David Lewis (1973: ch. 1) suggested that all counterfactuals with metaphysically impossible antecedents are simply vacuously true. That seems intuitively wrong. 'If I were a hippopotamus, I would fly through the air on feathered pinions' seems clearly false in a way in which 'If I were a hippopotamus, I would wallow in the muddy waters of the Nile' does not. But at least the following is true: metaphysical necessities form a set of truths such that all members of this set would still be true no matter what else (consistent with this set) were the case.[11] However, in addition to these more familiar features, I propose that it is a central feature of metaphysically necessary propositions that their necessity is explained by the essences of objects.

What exactly is meant by saying that the essences of objects *explain* why these propositions are necessary? It is intuitively plausible that the modal truths about an object can be explained in some way, since it would be puzzling if the modal truths about an object just formed a vast chaotic jumble, which could not be explained in any way. Still, it is not entirely clear what such "explanations" of a modal truth would amount to.

It is important to distinguish the task of explaining a modal truth from the task of explaining the *semantic* fact that a certain *statement* expresses a necessary truth. This semantic fact demands a semantic explanation, based on fundamental truths about the *meaning* of the terms that occur in the statement in question.[12] Intuitively, however, such questions as 'Why is it necessary that anything that has natural property B is morally wrong?' is not a semantic question about the meaning of the word 'wrong'. It is a question

---

[11] That is, metaphysical necessities form a "counterfactually stable" set of truths in the sense that is defined by Marc Lange (1999).

[12] These semantic questions sometimes play an important role in metaphysical discussions—especially the question of how it can be explained why an *a posteriori*, empirical statement expresses a necessary truth. For example, Chalmers (1996: 131–40) claims that it is inexplicable how an *a posteriori* statement could express a necessary proposition unless the "primary proposition" expressed by the statement is contingent. I shall give some reasons for thinking that Chalmers is wrong about this in Chapter 9, *n.* 16.

about a certain metaphysical connection, between a natural property and a moral property. An answer to this question would involve deriving this metaphysical connection from certain more fundamental truths. As I shall suggest, it would involve explaining this metaphysical connection at least in part on the basis of fundamental truths about the nature or essence of the relevant natural and moral properties.

I shall suppose that the fundamental principles that give the essence of some object or objects can themselves be stated using the notion of metaphysical necessity. In effect, then, the principles that give the essences of things are the most *fundamental* modal truths—the fundamental modal truths on the basis of which all other modal truths about metaphysical necessity can be explained. Specifically, all the other modal truths about which propositions are metaphysically necessary (and which are not) will be explained by these fundamental principles, because they will all be logical consequences of these principles, perhaps together with certain other, non-modal truths,[13] according to whatever is the appropriate logic for the notion of metaphysical necessity.[14]

I have put all these points about the connections between essence and metaphysical necessity entirely in terms of propositions, without making any use of the notion of "possible worlds". But we shall at several points find it helpful to make use of the apparatus of possible worlds in order to give a perspicuous formulation of various modal claims. So it is helpful to see how to couch this conception of metaphysical necessity and possibility in terms of possible worlds.

There are many different conceptions of possible worlds that I could use for this purpose. But to fix ideas, I shall suppose here that the correct conception of worlds is one according to which worlds are just sets of propositions. In effect, a world would be a *maximal logically consistent* set of propositions—that is, a logically consistent set of propositions that, for every proposition p, contains either p or its negation. (Since these sets are both logically consistent and maximal, they will also have the property of being closed under logical consequence.)

According to this conception, worlds will have the following features. First, one of these sets of propositions will contain only propositions that are actually true; this set corresponds to the *actual* world.

Secondly, it seems that some propositions are logically self-consistent but metaphysically impossible. (For example, the propositions that $2 + 2 = 5$, and

---

[13] If other non-modal truths are involved in the explanation, then the essences of things will provide an *indirect* explanation rather than a *direct* explanation for these modal truths. Fine (1995*b*) does not recognize the possibility of modal truths that are only indirectly explained by the essences of things in this way. I shall give some reasons in Chapter 9 for thinking that some modal truths, about which propositions are metaphysically necessary and which are not, are only indirectly explained by the essences of any object or objects.

[14] I shall discuss the appropriate logic for metaphysical necessity in Chapter 9. At all events, the appropriate logic will surely include *KT*. So, in particular, necessity entails truth; all logical truths are necessary; and if a set of propositions S logically implies q, then the necessitations of all the members of S will logically imply the necessitation of q.

that Tony Blair is a prime number, are not logically self-contradictory, but they certainly seem to be metaphysically impossible.) If worlds are just maximal logically consistent sets of propositions, then presumably some of these worlds will be "metaphysically impossible worlds": that is, they will be sets of propositions containing propositions that are actually metaphysically impossible.[15] (For example, one impossible world might contain the proposition that Blair is a prime number.) On the other hand, if a world contains no propositions that are metaphysically impossible in this way, then it is a metaphysically possible world.

Thirdly, if worlds are just maximal sets of propositions, then the propositions contained within each of these worlds will have to include *modal* propositions, including propositions about which propositions are possible and which are not. Some worlds will agree with the actual world about which propositions are possible and which are not; but some other worlds may not agree with the actual world about this. In general, we may say that one world w_1 "regards" a second world w_2 as a possible world just in case for every proposition p that is contained in w_2, w_1 contains the proposition *that p is possible*. In that case, as modal logicians put it, w_2 is "accessible" from w_1; as I prefer to put it, w_2 is possible "relative to" w_1. Now we can say that, for any proposition p, the proposition *that p is necessary* is true at a given world w just in case p is true at every world v that is possible relative to w, and the proposition *that p is possible* is true at w just in case p is true at some world u that is possible relative to w. (We shall return to the topic of such possible-worlds semantics for modal operators in Chapter 9.)

This then is the conception of "essence" that I shall be working with. A "constitutive account", as I understand it, is a real definition, or statement of the constitutive real essence of some object, property, or relation. These metaphysical ideas can be used to elucidate several crucial metaphysical notions, as I shall try to show in the rest of this chapter.

6.4 REDUCTIVE NATURALISM

First, we can use this conception of essence and modality to clarify the notion of what it is for a class of properties or relations to be *reducible*. In this book, we are particularly interested in *normative* properties and relations—that is, in the properties and relations that are referred to by normative terms and concepts.

---

[15] A metaphysically impossible world would not be a world that could not possibly *exist*. If a world is just a set of propositions, then all such sets of propositions exist—indeed, all such sets *actually* exist. An impossible world would be a world such that it was metaphysically impossible for all of its elements to be *true* (or to *be the case* or to *obtain*). For this conception of impossible worlds, compare Salmon (1986).

Roughly, for normative properties to be reducible is for it to be possible, at least in principle, to give a constitutive account of what it is for something to have each normative property in wholly non-normative, non-evaluative terms. Such an account would have to meet the following two conditions: first, it would have to be a universally quantified biconditional that gives necessary and sufficient conditions for exemplifying the relevant normative property in wholly non-normative terms; secondly, it would have to follow from the constitutive essence of the normative property itself.

What does it mean to say that the right-hand side of the biconditional is formulated in "wholly non-normative, non-evaluative terms"? Let us define a "natural property" in the following way. A property counts as a "natural property" if a constitutive account of the property need not refer to any normative or evaluative property or relation (or to any other entity a full account of which would in turn have to refer to some normative or evaluative property or relation); we may also define a "natural relation" in a precisely analogous way.[16] Then a reductive account of a normative property would be a constitutive account of the property that can be built up purely out of terms for natural properties and relations (together with topic-neutral terms, such as logical terms). This sort of account would be a reductive form of *naturalism* about the normative.

This conception of what a reduction amounts to involves the notion of a "constitutive account" that I tried to clarify in the previous two sections. I am assuming that any such reduction must give fully non-circular necessary and sufficient conditions for having the normative property; that is, it must construct a specification of these necessary and sufficient conditions purely out of terms for natural properties (together with topic-neutral terms like the logical constants). However, not every wholly naturalistic specification of necessary and sufficient conditions for a normative property will count as a reduction of that normative property. As we have already seen, under the standard interpretation of the term 'actually' as a rigidifying operator, *being morally wrong* is necessarily equivalent to *having the property that I am actually now thinking of*; but even if the concept 'having the property that I am actually now thinking of' is a wholly naturalistic concept, this necessary equivalence hardly gives us a genuine reduction of the property of being morally wrong. The reason seems to be that this equivalence does not follow from the *constitutive essence* of the property of being morally wrong.

The same example shows that we cannot define naturalistic reductions simply as identity statements in which we identify the property that is picked out by a

---

[16] Some philosophers might object to this definition, on the grounds that it makes it definitionally impossible for normative properties to *be* natural properties. But my terminology does not prevent us from expressing the idea that many philosophers would express as the idea that normative properties just are natural properties, since we can express this as the idea that normative properties are naturalistically reducible—that is, they are identical to properties whose nature can be explained using only naturalistic terms.

normative concept with the property that is picked out by a naturalistic concept. The following identity statement is undeniably true:

Being morally wrong = having the property that I am actually now thinking of.

Even if this identity statement does identify the property picked out by a normative concept ('being morally wrong') with the property that is picked out by a naturalistic concept ('having the property that I am actually now thinking of'), it obviously does not constitute a reduction of the property of being morally wrong.

In short, for a normative property to be naturalistically reducible, it must not only be necessarily equivalent to some naturalistically specifiable property, but this necessary equivalence must also follow from the constitutive essence of the normative property.

Similar issues, as we shall see, arise about whether *mental* properties are reducible. Here the debate typically focuses on whether mental properties are *physically* reducible. Let us understand the term 'physical property' broadly: physical properties include all *causally relevant* properties that are *non-mental*—in the sense that it is possible to give an account of the nature of these properties without referring to mental properties or relations—as well as all properties that can be constructed out of physical properties by means of operations like negation, conjunction, and so on.[17] For mental properties to be physically reducible would be for it to follow from the constitutive essence of each mental property that that mental property is necessarily equivalent to a property that can be specified using only terms for physical properties and relations (together with topic-neutral terms like logical terms).

For example, according to many forms of functionalism in the philosophy of mind, it is a fundamental truth about the nature or essence of each mental property that it is equivalent to the "functional property" of having some physical property that plays a certain causal role—where this causal role can be specified in completely physical or topic-neutral terms. So these sorts of functionalism count as physical reductions. A non-reductive conception of mental properties would deny that mental properties are physically reducible in this sense.

Many arguments have been offered in support of the claim that normative properties are irreducible. Most of these arguments are dubious. A great number of these arguments appeal, in effect, to a difference between the conceptual role that is played by normative concepts and the role that is played by the naturalistic concepts used in the purported reduction. Thus, for example, Mark Johnston (1989: 157–8) argues that, if you learn that something satisfies some naturalistic description (for example, if you learn that it is something that you would desire to desire if you were fully informed), you could quite rationally dismiss this

---

[17] This understanding of what "physical properties" are clearly seems to escape the objections of Crane and Mellor (1990).

information as irrelevant, with the feeling 'So what?'—whereas it could not be rational to respond in this way to the information that the thing in question is good or valuable.

Johnston's argument is a sound argument against putting forward any such naturalistic reduction as a *conceptual analysis* of normative concepts. But it is not a sound argument against the claim that such a naturalistic reduction is *true*. The fact that there is an important difference between two *concepts* does not show that there is a corresponding difference between the *properties* that the two concepts stand for. Otherwise, we could show that the property of being made of water is distinct from the property of being made of H_2O, since there are clearly pronounced differences between the conceptual role of the concept H_2O and that of the concept *water*. (One cannot possess the concept H_2O without having a grasp of a fair amount of modern chemistry, whereas ancient thinkers like Aristotle clearly possessed the concept *water* in spite of their radically false views about chemistry.)

So a philosophical argument for the irreducibility of normative properties and relations cannot just appeal to some important difference between normative concepts and naturalistic concepts. Importantly different concepts could still stand for the very same property or relation. To argue for the irreducibility of normative properties and relations, we would have to argue that the nature of these normative and naturalistic concepts *requires* that the properties and relations that the normative concepts stand for are distinct from those that any naturalistic concept stands for. I shall try to develop just such an argument in Chapter 8.

6.5 SUPERVENIENCE AND REALIZATION

Even if reductive naturalism turns out to be false, however, a weaker sort of metaphysical naturalism about the normative might nonetheless be true. In particular, it might still be true that normative properties and relations *supervene on*, and are *realized by*, natural properties.

It is widely held that normative properties supervene on natural properties. In fact, however, this question raises some delicate issues that I shall not address until Chapter 9. But a slightly weaker claim seems more plausible: normative properties supervene on what I shall call "non-normative properties", where a non-normative property is just a property that, as I shall put it, is "non-accidentally referred to" by some non-normative concept. The reason for adding the qualification 'non-accidentally' is to exclude concepts like *has the property that I am actually now thinking about*, which refer to a property purely by means of latching onto it by one of its accidental non-essential features.[18]

---

[18] This terminology is not entirely happy: if the property referred to by a normative concept is *identical* to a property that is non-accidentally referred to by a non-normative concept then

It certainly does seem plausible that normative properties supervene on non-normative properties. Consider, for example, an arbitrary possible situation, in which an action x has some normative property—say, *rightness*. In this situation, intuitively, it is *impossible* for there to be some action y that is indiscernible from x with respect to non-normative properties—that is, an action that has all and only the same non-normative properties as x—which does not also have the normative property in question—namely, rightness. For example, suppose that my action of writing a thank-you letter to a friend who sent me a birthday present was right. Then, surely, it is impossible for there to be an action that is indiscernible from my action of writing that thank-you letter in all non-normative respects, but is not also right. Note that what is intuitively compelling is not just the claim that there is no *actual* action y that is indiscernible from x with respect to non-normative properties but discernible with respect to normative properties, but the claim that it is *impossible* for there to be any such action y. That is, what is intuitively compelling is not mere weak supervenience, but strong supervenience.[19]

So I shall understand the doctrine that the normative supervenes on the non-normative as follows:

> For every normative property A, necessarily, for every object x and every set of non-normative properties S, if x has A, and x has all and only the non-normative properties belonging to S, then, necessarily, for every object y, if y has all and only the non-normative properties belonging to S, then y also has A.

If we allow ourselves to talk in terms of possible worlds, then we can formulate strong supervenience without quantifying over sets of properties:

> For every normative property A, every possible world w_1, and every object x, if x has A at w_1, then, for every world w_2 that is possible relative to w_1, and every object y, if y has all and only the same non-normative properties at w_2 as x has at w_1, then y also has A at w_2.

It will simplify matters considerably if we assume that families of properties (like the normative properties, or the non-normative properties) are closed under Boolean operations like conjunction, negation, and so on. With this assumption

this property would be, in my sense, both a normative property and a non-normative property. However, so long as we are clear about what these terms mean, no confusion should result from this.

[19] For the distinction between strong and weak supervenience, see Kim (1993: 80). Clearly, "non-normative properties" must include highly relational properties, such as the property of having certain consequences in the remote future, or the property of occurring in a certain social context. But is there no limit to how relational these non-normative properties may be? Can they include the property (which is in fact possessed by everything) of *being such that Plato taught Aristotle*, for example? In fact, it will not matter for my purposes exactly what the answer to this question is, and so I shall not try to answer this question here.

in place, we can also formulate strong supervenience as follows (compare Horgan 1993: 567, and Kim 1993: 80):

> For every normative property A, necessarily, for every object x, if x has A, then, for some non-normative property B, x has B, and, necessarily, for every object y, if y has B, then y also has A.

That is, it is necessary that, whenever something has a normative property, it also has some non-normative property that necessitates that normative property. I shall assume that both occurrences of 'necessarily' in these statements of strong supervenience express *metaphysical* necessity. Strong supervenience implies that it is a *metaphysically* necessary feature (not just a causally or physically necessary feature) of normative properties that they are *metaphysically* (not just causally) connected to non-normative properties.

Some philosophers may object to my claim that normative properties supervene on non-normative properties. For example, James Griffin has recently sought to cast doubt on the claim "that values do supervene on natural facts" (1996: 44). Offhand, it may seem that his objections also apply to my (different but related) claim that normative properties strongly supervene on non-normative properties.

First, Griffin suggests that we cannot really separate evaluative properties from non-evaluative properties at all; as he puts it, "supervenience ... assume[s] a sort of separation of fact and value that does not exist" (1996: 48).

But supervenience does *not* assume that the relevant normative and non-normative properties are "separable" in any strong sense. It presupposes only that we have some well-defined way of picking out the two kinds of properties. I have picked out these two kinds of properties in terms of the *concepts* that non-accidentally refer to them: normative properties are those that are non-accidentally referred to by normative concepts, non-normative properties those that are non-accidentally referred to by non-normative concepts. This will be an adequately well-defined way of picking out these properties if there is a coherent distinction to be drawn here between normative and non-normative concepts. But as I argued in Part I of the book, there is a coherent way of singling out the normative concepts and distinguishing them from all non-normative concepts. The two kinds of concept have different essential conceptual roles. The essential role of normative concepts is a certain regulative role that these concepts play in reasoning (such as practical reasoning); this is a distinctive feature of these concepts that sets them apart from concepts of other kinds. So, if we can indeed distinguish normative and non-normative concepts in this way, then we have all we need to formulate the claim that normative properties supervene on non-normative properties.

What might Griffin mean by claiming that normative and non-normative properties are "inseparable"? Suppose that the relevant non-normative properties include *mental* properties, and suppose that mental and normative properties are inseparable in the sense that it is impossible to give an adequate constitutive account of mental properties without mentioning normative properties. In that case, mental properties would not be "natural properties" (as I have defined them); and the claim that normative properties supervene on a collection of properties that includes mental properties would not amount to any sort of naturalism about the normative at all. But this would not provide any reason to think that the claim that normative properties supervene on non-normative properties is *false*. That claim may be true even if it does not amount to a kind of naturalism about the normative. The claim may capture an intuitively compelling and metaphysically important feature of normative properties, even if it does not by itself show how normative properties can be integrated into a naturalistic conception of the world.

Moreover, even if it turns out for this reason that the claim that normative properties supervene on a collection of properties that includes mental properties does not in itself amount to a form of naturalism, this claim might still *support* a form of naturalism. For example, it might be possible to argue that normative properties supervene on a collection of properties consisting of mental, biological, and social properties, and that these properties in turn all supervene on *physical* properties. Since supervenience is a transitive relation, it would follow that normative properties also supervene on physical properties. But physical properties are the paradigm case of natural properties. So the claim that the normative supervenes on the non-normative may still help to support a form of naturalism.

Griffin's second objection to the claim that values supervene on natural properties is that this claim implies not only that there must be some natural difference whenever there is an evaluative difference, but also that there must be some natural difference that is *relevant* to the evaluative difference (1996: 45); he then suggests that we have no reason to think that there is always a natural difference that is relevant in this way. As he puts it:

> If we could mention *any* natural properties to establish a difference, then we could always, though uninterestingly, come up with one. Smith's poetry is a genuine accomplishment; Jones's poetry, just as long, varied, innovative, and so on, is not. But Smith and Jones must at least have written in different-colour ink or in different places. But these differences will not do; we need properties that are "relevant" in the sense explained earlier. ... [But a] lot that is natural is not relevant, and a lot that is relevant is not natural. (Griffin 1996: 46–7)

For example, Griffin suggests, perhaps Smith's poetry is better than Jones's because it "is full of understanding of important matters". But, as he rightly points out, the notion of "importance" relevant here does not "fit comfortably within the class of the 'natural'". So this difference between Smith's poetry and Jones's cannot be the relevant *natural* difference.

Griffin's objection relies what he calls the "relevance requirement"—the idea that there must always be some natural difference that is *relevant* to each evaluative difference. But the statement of supervenience that I gave earlier does not involve any such relevance requirement. Griffin suggests that without the relevance requirement, supervenience becomes "a much less interesting relation" (1996: 47). But we should not accept this suggestion. The bare, unadorned supervenience principle that I gave earlier is certainly not trivial (in the strict sense of being obviously equivalent to some logical truth), and it seems intuitively highly compelling. (Moreover, even if this relevance requirement is correct—so that there must always be a relevant natural difference between things whenever there is a normative difference between them—the difficulty of specifying such a relevant natural difference does not show that there is no such difference. It might be that there must always be such a relevant natural difference, but it is hard to specify in strictly naturalistic terms.) So Griffin does not provide any compelling objections to the claim that normative properties supervene on non-normative properties. I shall proceed on the assumption that that claim is true.

In characterizing the notion of strong supervenience above, I have *not* required that the principle that a normative property A supervenes on non-normative properties must be any sort of essential truth about the nature of the normative property A. So, on this understanding of supervenience, there could be cases of supervenience that do not reveal anything essential about the supervening property. For example, to borrow an example from Timothy Williamson (2001), the mathematical facts all supervene on drunkenness facts—that is, facts about who is drunk and who is not. But this is just because the mathematical facts are necessary and so supervene, trivially, on anything whatsoever. So this point reveals nothing essential about mathematical facts over and above the point that they are metaphysically necessary. Or more simply still, everything supervenes, trivially, on itself. So every property A trivially supervenes on any set of properties that itself includes A. This point tells us nothing at all about the essence of A.

However, suppose that a property A strongly supervenes on a certain set of properties (call them the B-properties). According to this strong supervenience principle, if an object x has property A, then x has some B-property that necessitates having property A. Suppose, moreover, that this supervenience principle *is* an essential feature of the supervening property A. So it is part of the very nature or essence of having A that anything that has A must have some B-property that necessitates its having A.

Now, if there is any B-property—say, B_1—that necessitates having A, then any strengthening of B_1 (say by adding some irrelevant conjunct) will also necessitate A. (For example, if knowing p necessitates believing p, then the conjunctive property of knowing-p-and-wearing-a-white-shirt will also necessitate believing p.) Moreover, if there are *two* properties—say, B_1 and B_2—each of which necessitates A, then their *disjunction* will also necessitate A. (For example, knowing p necessitates believing p, and so too does being duped into believing p; so the disjunction of these two properties—either knowing p or being duped into believing p—will also necessitate believing p.)

Suppose that there is a property B_3 that counts as the *weakest* of all the *non-disjunctive* B-properties that x has that necessitate A. Then, as some philosophers would put it, B_3 would be x's "minimal supervenience basis" for having A. I shall say that in this case it is x's having B_3 that *realizes* its having A: in the case of x, A is realized in B_3 (the minimal supervenience basis for A that is present in x). In short, to say that in the case of x, A is "realized" in B_3 is to say that it is an essential feature of property A that it should supervene on properties of a certain kind, and B_3 is the minimal supervenience basis of this kind that x actually instantiates.

The strongest kind of metaphysical naturalism about the normative would be the reductive form of naturalism, according to which it is possible, at least in principle, to give a full constitutive account of normative properties in wholly naturalistic terms. A much weaker form of metaphysical naturalism about the normative would just claim that normative properties supervene on natural properties. An intermediate form would claim that normative properties are always at least realized in natural properties.

In Chapter 8, I shall argue against the reductive form of naturalism: normative properties and relations are irreducible. But as I shall also argue, in Chapter 9, my conception of normative properties is quite compatible with the claim that they are always realized in natural properties. Thus, although I shall reject the strongest form of metaphysical naturalism about the normative, my account will be quite compatible with the weaker and intermediate forms of naturalism.

7

The Normativity of the Intentional

7.1 THE ESSENCE OF CORRECTNESS

In this chapter I shall explicate and defend my central proposal about the nature or essence of normative properties. According to this proposal, the essence of normative properties consists above all in a certain fundamental role that these properties play in relation to *mental* properties. In explicating and defending this proposal, I shall be building on the account of the semantic value of normative concepts that I proposed in Part I of this book.

In Part I, I proposed and defended an account of the nature of normative concepts—that is, of the concepts that can be expressed by paradigmatic normative terms like 'ought'. This account involved an account of these concepts' *semantic value*, their contribution to the truth conditions of thoughts in which they appear. For example, one of these normative concepts was what I called the "practical or deliberative 'ought'", which is always at least implicitly indexed to an agent A and a time t. I expressed this sort of 'ought' by means of the symbol '$O_{<A,t>}$'. According to my account, a proposition of the form '$O_{<A,t>}(p)$' is true if and only if there are fully correct plans, for A to have about what to do at t, that logically imply p, and no such fully correct plans that logically imply the negation of p. In effect, the operator '$O_{<A,t>}$' stands for that property of a proposition p that makes it correct for A to incorporate p into his plans for what to do at t, and incorrect for A to incorporate the negation of p into his plans for what to do at t.

It seems plausible that this is an *essential* (and not a merely accidental) feature of this property—that it is the property that makes it correct for A to incorporate any proposition that has this property into his plans, and incorrect to incorporate the negation of any such proposition into his plans. If this is right, then it seems that the best way to investigate the nature or essence of this normative property will be by trying to understand what exactly is involved in a plan's being in the relevant sense *correct*.

In fact, a certain account of what it is for a mental state to count as "correct" was implicit in my arguments in Chapter 2, where I argued that we must interpret normative judgments as having a propositional content, such that a normative judgment counts as a "winning" judgment (or as I later suggested, a "correct" judgment) if and only if its propositional content is true. The account that was implicit in that argument is roughly as follows. Suppose that the following two claims are true: first, it is essential to the relevant type of mental state that mental states of this type tend to be regulated by certain standards of justification or rationality; and secondly, there is some ultimate purpose or goal or point in conforming to these standards. Then, for a mental state of this type to be "correct" is for it to achieve this ultimate purpose or goal or point. (For example, it seems plausible that (i) it is essential to *beliefs* that they are causally regulated by certain standards of rational or justified belief, and (ii) the ultimate purpose or point of conforming to these standards is not just to have rational or justified beliefs purely for their own sake, but to ensure that one believes the proposition in question if and only if that proposition is true. If so, then we may conclude that a belief counts as correct if and only if the proposition believed is true.)

However, this outline of an account of what it is for a mental state to be correct stands in need of further clarification. What exactly would it mean to claim that it is essential to a given type of mental state that it is causally regulated by such standards of justification or rationality? And what does it mean to claim that these standards have some ultimate "purpose" or "goal" or "point" to them? The first task for this chapter, then, is to clarify exactly what these claims mean.

Even once it has been clarified exactly what these claims mean, it would still not have been shown that these claims are *true*. That is, it would not yet have been shown that it *is* essential to mental states of the types in question that they are regulated by any such standards of justification or rationality, or that the relevant standards of justification or rationality have any such ultimate goal or purpose. If these claims are not true, then it will not be plausible that the normative properties and relations that normative terms like 'ought' stand for can be accounted for by using this notion of what it is for a mental state to be "correct". So the second task for this chapter is to argue that these claims are in fact true. This will enable us to give an account of the nature of the crucial normative property of being a correct mental state.

7.2 'CORRECT' AND 'RATIONAL'

As we have seen, this account of the property of being a *correct mental state* is based on two claims. The first of these claims is that it is essential to the relevant type of mental state that it tends to be regulated by certain standards of rationality or justification. The second claim is that these standards have some ultimate point or purpose; for example, the ultimate point or purpose of conforming to the standards of justified or rational belief is to ensure that one believes the proposition that one is considering if and only if that proposition is true.

This second claim is in effect a claim about the essential structure of the standards of rationality or justification. Thus, for example, the standards of rational belief must all in some sense be "geared" or "oriented" towards some goal (which, since it is essential to belief that it is regulated by these standards, is in effect the goal of having *correct* beliefs); and in the same way, the standards of rational choice are geared towards some goal (in effect, the goal of choosing correctly).

Unfortunately, it remains controversial in *what* sense exactly the standards of rational belief or rational choice are "oriented" towards some "goal" like believing or choosing correctly. In rest of this section, I shall give a very quick sketch of one interpretation of this second claim—the claim that it is an essential structural feature of the standards of rational belief or rational choice that they are oriented towards the goal of believing or choosing correctly; but I shall not be able to elaborate and defend this interpretation in detail (doing so would take us far away from the metaphysical issues concerning normative properties, and deep into issues in epistemology and the theory of rational choice).[1] Then, in the remaining sections of this chapter, I shall focus on elaborating and defending the first of these two claims—the claim that it is essential to each of the relevant types of mental state that it tends to be regulated by certain standards of rationality or justification.

It seems plausible to me that the concept of a "rational" mental state and the concept of a "correct" mental state are both essentially *normative* concepts. These concepts count as normative concepts because their essential conceptual role is very closely related to the conceptual role of the concepts that are expressed by 'ought' which I investigated in Chapters 4 and 5. Specifically, it is essential to or constitutive of these concepts that they play a *regulative* role in *reasoning*. Thus, it is a constitutive feature of the concept 'correct' that, if one judges that a certain mental state S_1 is correct and a certain alternative mental state S_2 is not correct, then one is thereby committed to having mental state S_1 rather than S_2, if one has either. For example, suppose that you judge that it is correct for you to believe p and not correct for you to have any alternative belief state with respect to p. Then it is a constitutive feature of the concept 'correct' that you are thereby committed to believing p rather than having any alternative belief state with respect to p. In effect, to say that a belief is not correct is to say that in a certain sense it is *wrong* to have that belief, whereas to say that a belief is correct is to say that in a certain sense it is *permissible* or *all right* to have that belief (that is, it is not the case that it is wrong to hold that belief).[2]

---

[1] For the idea that it is an essential structural feature of the standards of rational belief that they are geared or oriented towards the goal of believing the truth, see especially Goldman (1986: 98–101) and Wedgwood (2002c). For the stronger claim that in forming beliefs *we* are actually "aiming" at the truth, see Alston (1989: 84) and Peacocke (1986: 46). For some criticism of the idea that the standards of rational belief are oriented towards the goal of believing the truth, see especially Pollock and Cruz (1999: 175–6).

[2] We need to remember that the term 'wrong' is a much more general term than terms like 'blameworthy': there are many cases in which someone does something wrong (or forms the wrong

The concept 'rational' is a normative concept for broadly similar reasons. It is a constitutive feature of the concept 'rational' that, if you correctly judge that given your current information, it is rational for you to suspend judgment about *q* and not rational for you to believe *q*, then it must be true that your current information commits you to suspending judgment about *q* rather than believing *q*. The crucial difference between the concepts 'correct' and 'rational' is that 'irrational' corresponds to an information-relative 'ought', whereas 'incorrect' corresponds to a more objective 'ought'. Thus, a belief can be rational in relation to one body of information I_1, but not rational in relation to another body of information I_2 (whereas a belief is either correct or not correct *simpliciter*, without any relativization to bodies of information or the like). Sometimes, then, terms like 'rational' and 'irrational' can be used in a way that is overtly relativized to a body of information. It is also common, however, for these terms to be used in a way that not overtly relativized to any body of information. For example, one might say that it is rational for a certain thinker *x* to come to believe a certain proposition *p* at a certain time *t*. This statement seems to be equivalent to saying that it is rational, in relation to the total information that *x* possesses at *t*, for *x* to come to believe *p* at *t*.

It is not completely clear what might be meant by claiming that the standards of rational belief are "oriented" towards the goal of having correct beliefs. Very roughly, I propose that this claim means something like the following: in general, a belief counts as rational, in relation to a given body of information *I*, just in case that body of information *I* makes it *highly likely* that the belief in question is correct.[3]

A similar picture applies in the case of other mental states besides belief. It is a constitutive feature of the concepts of a "correct" choice and of a "rational" choice that they play an analogous regulative role in practical reasoning. Suppose that you judge, in a situation with "no relevant uncertainty" (as I put it in Chapter 1), that choosing to do *x* would be a correct choice for you to make, while choosing to do *y* would not be a correct choice for you to make. Then you are committed to choosing *x* rather than *y*, if you choose either—and at all events, to not choosing *y*. The standards of rational choice are "oriented" towards the goal of making correct choices because—roughly—a choice counts as rational, in relation to a body of information *I*, just in case given *I*, that choice maximizes one's expectation of coming as close as possible to making a correct choice.

---

conclusion about a question) but is not 'blameworthy' in any way. Similarly, 'wrong' is much more general than the concepts typically expressed by 'duty' and 'obligation'. There are many cases where a certain choice is the wrong choice to make, but you have no 'duty' or 'obligation' not to make it. Thus, my belief that the fundamental concepts of epistemic appraisal are normative concepts does not commit me to the view that Plantinga (1993: 11–29) stigmatizes as "epistemic deontologism".

[3] This is a very rough characterization of the sense in which the principles of rationality are "oriented" towards the "goal" of having mental states that are correct. I have attempted a more precise account elsewhere (Wedgwood 1999*a* and 2002*c*).

Some philosophers will dispute whether the concepts 'correct' and 'rational' really are normative concepts. According to these philosophers, the term 'correct' when applied to beliefs is just a synonym for 'true', which these philosophers regard as expressing a broadly speaking *logical* concept rather than a normative concept; and similarly, these philosophers will try to argue that the concept of 'rationality' is also really a logical concept rather than a normative concept.[4]

It is certainly true that some philosophers have tried to give a "definition" of rationality in broadly logical terms: for example, some philosophers influenced by decision theory have tried to define what it is for a set of preferences and credences to be rational in terms of various formal conditions of coherence, which could be regarded as broadly logical in character. But these "definitions" are both highly *controversial* and highly *complex*. This casts doubt on the idea that the very concept of a "rational attitude" just *is* the concept of an attitude that meets these conditions of logical coherence. It seems more plausible that these "definitions" are attempts at giving a *real* definition—that is, at giving a statement of the *essence* of rationality—where the correct account of the essence of rationality is not something that is necessarily known by everyone who possesses the concept of rationality (even if this account is ultimately accessible by means of a sort of *a priori* reflection to anyone who possesses this concept). Even while philosophers dispute about what is the correct account of rationality, they continue to treat 'rationality' as a normative concept. That is, they treat the judgment that an attitude is rational as permitting them to have that attitude, and treat the judgment that an attitude is irrational as committing them not to have that attitude.[5] So, it seems overwhelmingly plausible that 'rational' is indeed a normative concept.

As I have already noted, with respect to the concept 'correct', some philosophers may suggest that even though terms like 'right', 'correct', and so on, express normative concepts in some contexts (as when we speak of someone's making the right choice, or tying a bow-tie correctly), when we speak of correct beliefs or correct assertions, 'correct' is just a synonym for 'true'. But this cannot be quite right. It is *propositions* or *sentences* that count as "true" or "false", while it is *speech acts* (like assertions) or *propositional attitudes* (like beliefs) that count as "correct" or "incorrect": strictly speaking, it is a solecism to describe a sentence or a proposition as correct.

However, this objection might be reformulated as the suggestion that when applied to beliefs or assertions, 'is correct' is just a synonym for 'has a true proposition as its content'. But now this objection seems to amount to the suggestion that it is simply a chance ambiguity that the word 'correct' is used

---

[4] For this complaint, see especially Horwich (1998*b*) and Schroeder (2003).

[5] Indeed, I would be very surprised if it did not turn out that even the philosophers whose explicit theoretical stance is that 'rationality' is not a normative concept in fact treat it as one in their reasoning.

both in a normative sense and in this sense where it just means *has a true proposition as its content* (just as it is a chance ambiguity that 'bank' can mean both *money bank* and *river bank*); and that suggestion is surely implausible, to say the least. Moreover, if 'is correct' were simply a synonym for 'has a true proposition as its content', we should be able to describe other mental states as correct just in case their content was true.[6] We should be able to say such things as 'He imagined that he was Julius Caesar on the edge of the Rubicon, but his imagining was incorrect' (as we can say, 'He imagined that he was Julius Caesar, but what he imagined was not true'), or 'He hoped to be offered a Professorship at Harvard but his hope was incorrect' (as we can say, 'He hoped to be offered a position at Harvard, but what he hoped for did not come true'). But we do not in fact use the term 'correct' in this way. So it seems more plausible, for both of these reasons, to regard the term 'correct' as a normative term even when it is applied to beliefs and assertions.

I shall assume then that the account of the concepts 'correct' and 'rational' that I have sketched here is at least roughly along the right lines. As we have seen, if this account is correct, it will also explain what is meant by the metaphorical claim that the ultimate "goal" or "purpose" of the standards of rational or justified belief is to have correct beliefs rather than incorrect ones, or that the ultimate "goal" or "purpose" of the standards of rational choice or decision is to make correct choices or decisions rather than incorrect ones. For the rest of this chapter, however, I wish to concentrate on the second of the two claims that I identified in the first section of this chapter—the claim that it is essential to each of the relevant types of mental state that they tend to be regulated by the standards of rationality or justification that apply to mental states of those types. What does this claim mean? And what reason is there to think that it is true?

7.3 AN INTERPRETATION OF THE SLOGAN "THE INTENTIONAL IS NORMATIVE"

It seems to me that this claim—that it is essential to each of the relevant types of mental state that it tends to be causally regulated by certain standards of justification or rationality—is best interpreted as a version of the claim that *the intentional is normative*. In the next two sections, I shall explain the particular version of this claim that I have in mind. Then, in the last two sections of the chapter, I shall present some reasons for thinking that the claim is true.

Many philosophers have claimed that the intentional is normative. (This claim is the analogue, within the philosophy of mind, of the claim that is often made within the philosophy of language, that *meaning is normative*.) But it is not immediately clear what this claim amounts to.

---

[6] I owe this point to Gideon Rosen.

First, what is meant here by 'the intentional'? For present purposes, I shall take the "intentional" to be a subset of the mental. Many mental states—indeed, some philosophers would say, all mental states—are *about* something; they are "concerned with" or "directed towards" something. For example, some of my beliefs are *about Plato*; some of my intentions are *about buying a birthday present for my niece*; and some of my fears are *about snakes*. As many philosophers put it, these mental states all have *intentional content*, and so may be called "intentional states".[7]

I propose that we should interpret the claim that the intentional is normative as the claim that in giving an account of the nature or essence of intentional states, we must mention normative properties or relations. Equivalently, in giving an account of the nature of an intentional fact—in other words, an account of what the intentional fact consists in—we must state some normative fact. In that sense, intentional facts are partially constituted by normative facts.[8]

On this understanding, then, the claim that the intentional is normative is a metaphysical claim concerning the nature or essence of intentional states, or concerning the constitution of intentional facts. It is *not* a semantic thesis about the meaning of intentional *terms*, or a conceptual thesis about the nature of our *concepts* of intentional states. Such semantic or conceptual theses could be true even if the corresponding metaphysical thesis is false. It could be that, even if we ordinarily *think* of intentional states as states that we "ought" to be in under such-and-such circumstances, the *nature or essence* of those states can be explained in wholly non-normative terms.

According to the claim that the intentional is normative, then, normative properties must be mentioned in giving an account of the nature or essence of intentional mental properties. But what sort of account of the nature or essence of intentional mental properties is in question here?

One reason why it is not quite clear what sort of account is in question here is that there is an infinite number of such properties. (For example, for every natural number n, there is the state of believing that there are at least n things in existence.) For this reason, an account of these intentional mental properties could not possibly include a separate account for every single one of these properties. Instead, it need include only an account of the *basic constituents* of these properties—such as the various different types of *mental relation* or *attitude* (such as belief, desire, hope, fear, and so on) that one can have towards various different contents, and the various different *concepts* that can be combined to form such contents—and an account of how these basic constituents can be combined in order to form all the intentional mental properties that there are.

I have said that the claim that the intentional is normative is the claim that any adequate account of this kind must *mention normative properties*. I have not

---

[7] Compare Searle (1983: ch. 1).
[8] Compare the interpretation of this claim given by Gideon Rosen (2001).

said that it is the claim that any adequate account of this kind must actually *use* *normative terms*. It may be possible, at least in principle, to mention normative properties without using normative terms. For example, one way in which it might be possible to mention normative properties without using normative terms will be investigated in the next chapter: this is the way of mentioning normative properties that would be available if there were a simultaneous *reduction* of both the mental and the normative properties in purely physical and topic-neutral terms.

There is also another way in which it might be possible to mention normative properties without using normative terms. This is the way that would be available if it is possible, at least in principle, to articulate a principle that gives necessary and sufficient conditions for an attitude's being a *rational* attitude (for a thinker to have at a given time) in wholly non-normative, psychological terms. It is tempting to think that if there is a fundamental principle of this kind, it would articulate an *essential* feature of what it is for an attitude to be rational. So if there is such a principle, it would follow from the essential nature of rationality that rationality is equivalent to a relation that can be picked out by means of some complex psychological term.[9] As I suggested in the previous chapter (Section 6.2), it is plausible that all instances of the following schema are true: the property of being F is identical to the property of being G if a constitutive account of the nature or essence of this property entails that something is F if and only if it is G. Thus, if there is such a fundamental principle about the nature of rationality, the normative relation of rationality is *identical* to the relation that is picked out by this complex psychological term.

Articulating such a principle—in effect, a real definition, or statement of the essence, of rationality—will certainly be a difficult and challenging task, to say the least. Some philosophers, such as Child (1993), may even suspect that this task is impossible: in effect, these philosophers maintain that rationality is *uncodifiable*. But even if the task is possible, it seems virtually certain that these necessary and sufficient conditions will be highly *complex*. So even if the normative relation of rationality is identical to *some* relation that can be mentioned by means of some purely psychological term, it seems virtually certain that it will not be identical with any of the *basic constituents* of intentional mental properties.

For this reason, even if it is possible, in principle, to mention the normative relation of rationality using purely non-normative psychological terms, this possibility would not trivialize the claim that the intentional is normative. Since this relation is not identical with any of the basic constituents of intentional

---

[9] The existence of such essential necessary and sufficient conditions for a normative proper-ty—such as the property that the term 'ought' stands for, in a given context—need not conflict with the proposal that the essence of this property is given by the principle that the normative property is that property of a proposition that makes a certain attitude towards the proposition correct. The specification of these necessary and sufficient conditions could be regarded as teasing out the implications of what correctness in this case consists in.

mental properties, it will not be a trivial truth that any adequate account of these basic constituents of the intentional mental properties must mention this relation. Even if the relation can be picked out by means of some (highly complex) psychological term, it is still a highly informative point that any adequate account of the intentional mental properties will *have to* mention this relation.

7.4 A NORMATIVE THEORY OF INTENTIONAL MENTAL STATES

If it is true that any adequate account of intentional mental properties and relations must mention normative properties and relations, what form will such an account take? I shall continue to assume here that all intentional states or properties involve the following two elements: (i) a content, which is composed out of *concepts*, and (ii) a *mental relation* or *attitude* (such as belief, desire, hope, fear, and so on) towards that content. So any account of the nature of intentional mental properties would have two parts: first, a part that explains the nature of the various different concepts (and the nature of the ways in which those concepts can be combined to form more complex contents); and secondly, a part that explains the nature of the different types of attitude that can be taken towards such contents.

According to the particular version of the claim that the intentional is normative that I shall try to develop here, the nature of each concept is given *both* by the principle that defines when beliefs involving that concept are correct, and *also* by certain basic principles of rationality that apply to the use of that concept—that is, basic principles that specify certain ways of using that concept as either rational or irrational. Since a belief is correct if and only if the content of the belief is true, the conditions under which it is correct to form beliefs involving a concept would in effect determine the concept's *semantic value*—the contribution that the concept makes to the truth conditions of propositions in which it appears. On the other hand, the basic principles that specify certain ways of using the concept as *rational* (or specify certain other ways of using the concept as *irrational*) would determine the concept's *cognitive significance* (what Frege called its *Erkenntniswert*).[10]

---

[10] In this way, my account adopts a broadly *Fregean* view of intentional content, since it allows that these contents may be individuated so finely that (for example) the belief that Cicero is Cicero counts as a different intentional state from the belief that Cicero is Tully, and even from the belief that Tully is Tully. Other accounts adopt a more *Millian* view, according to which these contents must be individuated less finely, so that the content of the belief that Cicero is Cicero is just the same as that of the belief that Tully is Tully, and even of the belief that Cicero is Tully. The most prominent example of a neo-Fregean view is that of Gareth Evans (1982). For a more Millian view, see Nathan Salmon (1986). For a new approach to these issues, see the "relationalist" semantics that has recently been developed by Kit Fine (2003).

In effect, the account of the concepts that are expressed by 'ought' that I gave in Part I of this book was an account of this general form. For example, according to my account of the concept expressed by the practical 'ought', the nature of the concept essentially involves both the concept's semantic value, and the basic rule about how certain beliefs involving the concept *commit* the thinker to incorporating a certain proposition into his plans. This basic rule is in effect a principle of rationality: given how I am using the term 'commit', this rule in effect says that if it is rational for the thinker to believe the proposition '$O_{<me, t>}(p)$', then this makes it irrational for the thinker not to incorporate the proposition p into her ideal plans about what to do at t (at least if the question about how to relate p to her plans arises). This principle of rationality determines the concept's "cognitive significance"—which in the case of this concept consists principally in the fact that these beliefs involving this concept have this special connection to planning and practical reasoning.

Similar accounts might be given of other concepts. Thus, as I have already suggested in Chapter 4, the nature of logical concepts like 'or' and 'not' might be given both by their semantic values—their contribution to the truth conditions of thoughts in which they appear—and also by the basic principles that specify which inferences involving these concepts are rational. The nature of the concept '… is yellow' might be given both by the concept's semantic value—the property of yellowness that the concept stands for—and also by the principle that it is rational to make a judgment applying this concept to some perceptually presented object if one has a visual experience that represents that object in a certain distinctive way (and one has no special positive reason for regarding one's current experience as unreliable in the circumstances).

I shall assume that if an approach of this sort is plausible with respect to particular concepts, then a parallel approach is also plausible with respect to the various different types of attitude. Thus for example, the nature of the attitude of *belief* may be given both by the principle that a belief is correct if and only if the content of the belief is true, and by the principle that a belief is rational (in relation to a given body of information I) just in case I makes it sufficiently likely that the content of the belief is true.

Similarly, the nature of the attitude of *choice* or *decision* may be given by the following two principles. The first is the principle that the choices that one makes are correct if and only if one will realize those choices, and thereby act in a way that is genuinely choiceworthy; the second is the principle that a choice is rational (in relation to a body of information I) just in case—to put it roughly—given I, that choice maximizes one's rational expectation of coming as close as possible to choosing correctly. (Moreover, this approach could also be applied to other types of attitude, as I shall try to outline later, in Chapter 10.)

Different philosophers have given several different versions of such a normative theory of mental states, and different versions of such a conceptual role semantics for the concepts that figure in the contents of mental states. For example, some versions of conceptual role semantics explicitly aim to be non-normative, and to characterize a concept's essential role in wholly naturalistic terms.[11] My account is quite different from these, since my account characterizes the concept's essential conceptual role in overtly normative terms.

Even among the versions of conceptual role semantics that are overtly normative, however, there are some significant differences. For example, according to "inferentialist" accounts, such as the account of Robert Brandom (1994), the nature of each type of mental state is given by the role that the mental state plays in rational thinking, but the conditions under which the mental state in question is correct play no explanatory role at all. In my account, by contrast, both elements play a crucial explanatory role. Among the approaches that give an account of types of mental state in terms of their role in rational thinking, some may be *holistic*, claiming that all the rational ways of using the concept are equally involved in the concept's essential conceptual role, while others may reject such holism, and claim that only some of the rational ways of using the concept are involved in the concept's essential conceptual role.[12] My account of the concepts that are expressed by 'ought' is clearly non-holistic, since according to my account, only some, and not all, of the rational ways of using this concept formed part of the concept's essential conceptual role.

Finally, some normative theories of the intentional claim that the intentional is actually *reducible* to the normative—that is, that there is a correct reductive account of the nature of intentional states, and any such account must mention normative properties or relations.[13] My account makes no such claim: indeed, according to my view, the normative and the intentional must each be mentioned in giving any account of the other, so that the two domains of properties and relations are essentially interdependent, without either of the two being reducible to the other.

This then, roughly, is the core of this normative theory of intentional mental states—an account of the nature of the various concepts, and of the various attitudes or mental relations that we can have towards contents, in terms of the normative principles that apply to certain mental states involving these concepts or attitudes. But this core will need to be surrounded by a shell that explains what it is for a *thinker* to *possess* those concepts, or to *be capable of* those attitudes. If this is the correct account of the nature of the concepts that are expressed by 'ought' (or of the concept 'yellow', or of logical concepts like 'or' and 'not'), and of the nature of such attitudes as belief or choice, then what has to be true of a thinker if she is to possess these concepts, or if she is to be capable of having these attitudes?

---

[11] See for example Peacocke (1992: 139). This aspect of Peacocke's approach is criticized by Millar (1994).

[12] The most striking example of such a holistic conception is that of Brandom (1994). Brandom's holism is criticized by John McDowell (1997).

[13] For this view, see Morris (1992) and Brandom (1994)—at least, if Gideon Rosen's (1997) interpretation of Brandom is correct.

One plausible answer to this question is that the thinker must have some *disposition* to conform to the principle of rationality that figures in the account of the nature of the concept or type of attitude in question.[14] More specifically, the sort of disposition that a thinker must have, if she is to possess that concept or to be capable of that type of attitude, is a disposition to use the concept in ways that the principle in question specifies as rational. Such principles typically take the form of specifying some body of information or set of mental conditions such that—according to this principle—it is rational, in relation to that body of information, to have a certain further mental state. Then, the disposition that one must have, if one is to possess that concept or to be capable of that type of attitude, is a disposition to respond to one's actually being in that state of information by having that further mental state.

So, for example, the thinker must be disposed to form a judgment applying the concept '... is yellow' to a perceptually presented object whenever she has a visual experience that represents an object in the relevant way (at least so long as the question of the object's colour arises, and the thinker has no special evidence that her experience is unreliable). Similarly, she must be disposed to respond to its being rational for her to make a judgment of the form '$O_{<A_{me},\,t>}(p)$' by incorporating the proposition p into her ideal plans about what to do at t.[15] A similar point would apply to the principles of rationality that figure, not in an account of the nature of some concept, but in an account of the nature of some type of attitude. Suppose that the basic principle of rationality governing choices is the principle that I suggested earlier—the principle that it is rational, in relation to a body of information I, to choose a course of action if and only if given I, that choice maximizes one's expectation of coming as close as possible to choosing correctly on that occasion. Then, the disposition that one must have, if one is to be capable of making choices at all, is a disposition to respond to the information that one is in by making a choice that is rational in relation to that information.

As I explained in Chapter 1, the claim that a thinker has a disposition does not imply this disposition will be manifested in every possible case. A disposition can be defined by means of a function from stimulus conditions to corresponding response conditions. But to say that an object has the disposition is not to say that *whenever* the object is in one of the relevant stimulus conditions, it will *always* go into the response condition onto which the function in question maps that stimulus condition. It is to say that *ceteris paribus*, or in any *normal* case, when the object is in one of these stimulus conditions, it will also go into the

[14] Compare the "principle of charity" advocated by Davidson (2001: essay 9). A normative theory could avail itself of this idea without accepting Davidson's full-blown "interpretivism". As David Lewis (1974a) suggests, the reference to interpretation could just be taken as a way of dramatizing what is objectively constitutive of the intentional states in question.

[15] This is a somewhat rough characterization of the relevant dispositions. I shall give a more careful characterization in Chapter 10.

corresponding response condition. But the case can fail to be normal, and *cetera* can fail to be *paria*, in various ways. When this happens, there will presumably be some explanation of what the interfering factors were that caused things to go awry in this way. It is only when all such interfering factors are absent that the disposition is bound to be manifested.

Thus, this proposal—that everyone who is capable of having a certain type of mental state must have a disposition to a certain sort of rational thinking involving mental states of that type—does not imply the conclusion that we are always rational. Indeed, it does not even imply that irrational thinking is less common than rational thinking. The claim that we have these rational dispositions does not entail that we do not also have many irrational dispositions as well; and it also does not imply that these rational dispositions are always manifested. It implies only that when we do not conform to these very basic requirements of rationality, then the situation was in some way abnormal (*cetera* were not *paria*), and so there will presumably be some explanation of what went awry in this case. It seems possible, in especially unfortunate circumstances, for there to be an agent, or even an entire community of agents, for whom the situation is always abnormal, so that there are always interfering factors present that prevent these dispositions from being manifested.[16] Nonetheless, even though these dispositions can be masked in this way, according to the proposal that I am considering here, a thinker must *have* these dispositions in order to be capable of the types of mental state in question.

7.5 AN ARGUMENT FOR DISPOSITIONALISM

Why should we think that a view like the one that I outlined in the previous two sections is true? My argument for the correctness of this view, or at least of some view that is very much along these lines, has two main parts. First, I shall argue that it must be certain *dispositions* of the thinker—or perhaps certain dispositions of the thinker and the thinker's community as a whole—that determine precisely which concepts and attitude-types figure in the thinker's thoughts. Secondly, I shall argue that these dispositions must be essentially *rational* dispositions, of the kind that I described in the previous section.

The crucial point here is that it does not seem possible for the intentional states that we are in to float completely free of our dispositions. (When I refer to our "dispositions" here, I do not mean to focus exclusively on our behavioural dispositions; I mean to include our mental dispositions as well—such as our dispositions to revise our beliefs, intentions, and other attitudes, in response to various conditions.) For example, suppose that a community has a concept in

---

[16] I believe that by developing these points, my proposal can be made immune to the sorts of objections that are raised by Stein (1996).

their repertoire that they are all disposed to apply, quite systematically, to cats and only to cats; they base their judgments involving this concept on various sorts of evidence, but most often on precisely the sort of experiences that we would use to recognize something as a cat; and they also treat everything that falls under this concept as belonging to a single natural kind. Now consider the supposition that in this case, this concept is in fact the concept of a bicycle, and that almost all of these thinkers' beliefs involving this concept are incorrect and irrational. This supposition appears absurd.[17] In general, it seems that if there is a community the members of which possess a concept that they are disposed to use in all their reasoning in exactly the same way as we are disposed to use a certain concept in our repertoire, then their concept must be the same as ours. So it seems that it must be something about the thinker's dispositions, together perhaps with certain facts about his environment and the dispositions of other thinkers in his linguistic community, that determines which concepts figure in the thinker's thoughts.

Similarly, if there is a community that has a type of attitude that they are disposed to form and revise in just the same way as we are disposed to form and revise our beliefs, it would be absurd to suppose that this attitude is in fact the attitude of *disbelief*—so that almost all of their attitudes of this type are incorrect and irrational. Again, something about our dispositions with respect to an attitude-type must determine exactly which attitude-type it is that figures in our thoughts.

However, if it is true that facts about the thinker's dispositions determine which concepts and attitude-types figure in the thinker's thoughts in this way, then surely there must be some account of the precise way in which these dispositions determine this.[18] The bare claim that the thinker's dispositions determine which concepts and attitude-types figure in the thinker's thoughts is compatible with infinitely many different precise ways in which these dispositions might determine this. Surely there must be some general principle that captures the specific role that these dispositions play in determining this. Otherwise it will remain utterly mysterious why these dispositions determine this in the specific way in which they do, rather than in any of the infinitely many other possible ways.[19]

So it seems that there must, at least in principle, be some explanatory account of how the thinker's dispositions determine what intentional states he is in. There is no reason why this account should take the fully reductive form of giving an account of intentional states in terms of dispositions that are characterized in wholly non-intentional, non-normative terms. On the contrary, there is no

---

[17] On this point, compare Fricker (1991).   [18] Compare Boghossian (1991).

[19] I shall give a more careful statement of this argument, that strong supervenience creates a demand for an "explanatory account" of the vast plethora of modal facts whose existence it entails, in Chapter 9 (see also Wedgwood 1999*b* and 2000).

objection to characterizing these dispositions in *general* intentional terms—that is, precisely as *mental* dispositions, dispositions to form certain attitudes involving certain concepts in certain circumstances—so long as our characterization of these dispositions does not presuppose the identity of the particular concepts and attitude-types that they involve. It may well be a completely irreducible feature of you that you have attitudes and use concepts, or a completely irreducible feature of some state that you are in that it is a state of having some mental attitude to some conceptual content. However, it surely cannot be an irreducible feature of you that you are using a concept that refers to *cats* (as opposed to referring to *dogs* or to *cows*, for example); that must be explained in terms of the dispositions that you have with respect to this concept. That is, there should be an account, of how these dispositions determine which concepts and attitude-types figure in those dispositions, that meets the *non-circularity constraint* that I explained in Chapter 1 (Section 1.2) above.

Thus, we seem to need an account of the following form. This account may start out by unabashedly presupposing that we are dealing with a thinker who has attitudes towards contents that are composed of concepts. But it would start by treating these attitudes and concepts as initially *uninterpreted*.[20] The theory would start with a "neutral" characterization of the thinker's intentional dispositions—that is, a characterization of the thinker's dispositions with respect to these attitudes and concepts that does not in any way presuppose the exact identity of these attitudes and concepts. Then the theory could articulate certain principles concerning the nature of various attitudes and concepts, which would enable us to identify the thinker's attitudes and concepts—say, as the attitude of *belief*, or as the concept of *water*—on the basis of this neutral characterization of the thinker's intentional dispositions (along with further facts about the thinker's natural and social environment).

7.6 NORMATIVE DISPOSITIONALISM

I have argued that some sort of dispositionalism must be true. Now some philosophers—whom we may call "radical holists"—might claim that *all* of a thinker's dispositions with respect to a concept are *equally* involved in determining which concept it is that figures in those dispositions. As I shall argue in this section, this radical holistic view is implausible. Some of our dispositions with respect to any given concept are dispositions to make *mistakes* or to engage in *fallacious* reasoning. For example, many people have dispositions to accept certain fallacious inferences such as affirming the consequent or denying the antecedent.

---

[20] It may also be necessary to start out with presuppositions about the syntactic category that the various concepts belong to—whether they are general or predicative concepts or singular concepts or propositional operators, and so on.

But as I shall now argue, the fact that a concept features in a thinker's dispositions for these fallacious forms of reasoning is irrelevant to what makes it the case that the concept that figures in the thinker's thoughts is the concept 'if'; what makes it the concept 'if' is that it features in certain more rational dispositions (such as dispositions to accept inferences that have the form of *modus ponens* or conditional proof).

On the one hand, it seems very hard to see how any thinker could possess a concept without having *any* disposition to use the concept in any rational way: even extremely irrational thinkers, who are constantly committing such fallacies as affirming the consequent or denying the antecedent, are generally disposed also to accept certain basic rational inferences, such as inferences that have the form of *modus ponens*. On the other hand, it seems quite easy to see how this concept could be possessed by a thinker who had *no* disposition to use the concept in any irrational way. After all, it seems that any concepts that you have could be shared by a perfectly rational being who had no irrational dispositions at all. (For example, the perfectly rational being would need to possess these concepts in order to ascribe attitudes to you accurately, and to diagnose the various confusions and irrationalities that mar your thinking.) So that perfectly rational being would have to possess those concepts in virtue of some of her rational dispositions (since she has no irrational dispositions). This makes it plausible that we also possess those concepts in virtue of some of our rational dispositions, and not in virtue of our irrational dispositions.

Suppose that some of my dispositions with respect to the use of a concept F are dispositions to use the concept in irrational ways, such as dispositions to engage in fallacious forms of reasoning. According to the radical holistic view, then, it is partly in virtue of this irrational disposition that I possess the concept F. This disposition is part of what it is about me that makes it the case that I possess the concept F. In effect, to use the terms that I introduced in the previous chapter (Section 6.5), this disposition is an essential part of what *realizes* my possession of F. (That is, according to the holist, it is *essential* to possessing the concept F that one's possession of the concept F supervenes on one's total set of dispositions for using the concepts in one's repertoire; and the minimal supervenience base for possessing F that I actually instantiate is one that includes my having this irrational disposition.)

However, it seems most doubtful to me whether anyone's possession of a concept can rest on an irrational disposition in this way. If this really could be the case, then there could be a thinker who possesses a concept at least partly in virtue of an irrational disposition of this sort. But then the thinker's possession of the concept would be at least partly founded in irrationality, and any use that the thinker makes of this concept would depend on this irrationality; this irrationality would in a way underlie every single use that the thinker made of this concept. It seems most doubtful whether this could be the case. The possession of a concept is a cognitive *power* or *ability*—not a cognitive defect or liability.[21]

Thus, it seems to me that if one possesses a concept, the dispositions in virtue of which one possesses it must be essentially rational dispositions. Since almost all of us have irrational dispositions with respect to some of our concepts or attitudes, it follows that radical holism cannot be correct: it is not true that all of our dispositions are equally involved in determining the identity of the concepts that feature in our thoughts; it is only our *rational dispositions* that can be involved in determining this.

Thus, this is one of the crucial features that marks out the dispositions that determine the identity of the concepts (and of the types of attitude) that figure in one's thoughts: these dispositions must be essentially rational dispositions. More specifically, it may be that the dispositions that determine the identity of a concept that figures in one's thoughts are whatever are causally the most *basic* of one's rational dispositions with respect to the concept. According to this suggestion, if we are told that there is a concept C that figures in a thinker's thoughts, and we are also told (in terms that do not presuppose the identity of C) what are the most basic of the rational dispositions that the thinker has with respect to C, then this information will be enough to determine which concept C is.

This makes it plausible, it seems to me, that for each concept there is some *specific* rational disposition that is essential to possessing the concept. For example, in the case of the concept 'if' it seems plausible that it is the disposition for rationally accepting instances of inferences like *modus ponens* that is essential to possessing the concept. If this is so, then any adequate account of a concept (or of an attitude-type) must mention this specific rational disposition, which is essential to possessing that concept or being capable of that attitude-type.

This does not yet imply that every adequate account of the nature of a concept or an attitude-type must actually mention normative properties or relations (like the properties or relations that are referred to by the term 'rational'). It could be that such an account will single out the relevant rational dispositions by some feature *other* than their being rational dispositions—where this other feature *guarantees* that the dispositions in question are rational dispositions, but is not *equivalent* to their being rational disposition.

However, there is a reason for thinking that these dispositions cannot in fact be specified without mentioning normative properties or relations.[22] As I explained above, a disposition is specified by means of a function from stimulus

---

[21] Compare Gareth Evans's (1982: 331) insistence that understanding a linguistic expression is a species of knowledge, and so cannot be based on false belief: "Truth is seamless: there can be no truth which it requires acceptance of a falsehood to appreciate".

[22] When I speak of "specifying" a disposition, I do not mean an exhaustive complete account of how this disposition works. I simply mean "picking out" the disposition, by one of its essential or non-accidental features.

conditions to response conditions. As I shall now argue, a disposition cannot be an essentially rational disposition unless the stimulus conditions to which it responds are conditions that essentially involve those normative properties and relations.

We can illustrate this point by means of examples. Presumably, the relevant rational dispositions are all dispositions to form or revise one's mental states in some rational way. In a broad sense of the term, they are dispositions to engage in certain forms of *rational reasoning*. For example, one sort of rational reasoning might lead one from having a visual experience that presents an object in a certain distinctive way (in the absence of any special reason to believe one's experiences to be unreliable), to one's forming a belief that predicates the concept '... is yellow' of the object in question. A disposition for this sort of reasoning might be essential to mastering the basic rule of rationality that applies to the concept '... is yellow', and so also to possessing that concept.

Other sorts of rational disposition might be dispositions to accept rational deductive or inductive inferences, or to engage in rational sorts of practical reasoning. For example, one simple sort of rational practical reasoning might be the kind that leads from its being rational to believe a proposition involving the practical or deliberative 'ought', of the form 'I ought to φ', to forming an intention to φ. As I proposed in Chapter 4 (Section 4.1), a disposition for this sort of reasoning may be part of what is involved in mastering the basic rule of rationality that applies to the practical 'ought'—the rule that at least in the absence of relevant uncertainty a judgment of the form 'I ought to φ' rationally commits one to forming a corresponding intention to act. This disposition might be essential to possessing the concept that is expressed by this sort of 'ought'.

As these examples suggest, there seems not to be any way to specify the relevant sorts of rational reasoning without mentioning normative properties or relations. The specification that I gave of the sort of reasoning that leads from visual experiences to beliefs of the form 'x is yellow' included a proviso "in the absence of any *special reason* to believe one's experiences to be unreliable". But in specifying this sort of reasoning in this way, I mentioned the normative relation of being a *reason* to believe something. Similarly, my specification of the sort of reasoning that leads to an intention to φ is restricted to cases in which it is *rational* for one to believe that one ought to φ; and in specifying this type of reasoning in this way, I have mentioned the normative relation of its being *rational* for one to believe something.

The reason for specifying these sorts of reasoning in this normative way is clear. These sorts of reasoning are *defeasible*. That is, even if the input conditions of this sort of reasoning are present, certain defeating conditions must be absent if it is to be possible to form a rational belief or intention by means of this form of reasoning. But the nature of defeating conditions is precisely that they are those conditions that make it *irrational* for one to form the belief or intention in question in response to the relevant input conditions. There seems to be no way of specifying these defeating conditions without mentioning normative properties or relations.

For the dispositions for these sorts of reasoning to be essentially rational, then, it seems that these dispositions must be sensitive to the presence or absence of defeating conditions *as such*. That is, these dispositions must be dispositions whose manifestation tends to be *blocked* or *inhibited* by the presence of defeaters. This is not to say that this disposition will *never* be manifested in the presence of *any* defeaters—only that there is a wide enough range of defeaters in the presence of which these dispositions will not be manifested. In saying that possessing the concept requires having a disposition to use the concept in a certain basically rational way, I need not claim that this disposition must be *perfectly* rational; I need only claim that this disposition must to a greater or lesser degree *approximate* to such perfect rationality.

For this reason, it seems that the stimulus conditions to which the relevant rational dispositions respond cannot be specified without mentioning the absence of defeating conditions—which in effect involves mentioning certain normative properties and relations. So these rational dispositions cannot be specified without mentioning normative properties and relations. But the dispositions that are essential to possessing concepts, and to being capable of the various types of attitude, must be rational dispositions of this kind. So it seems that the dispositions that are essential to possessing concepts (and to being capable of attitude-types) cannot be specified without mentioning normative properties or relations. Hence the very nature of these concepts and attitude types cannot be explained without mentioning normative properties and relations.

There are various objections that philosophers might raise against this argument for the normativity of the intentional. Some philosophers might suggest that one could still be disposed to reason in accordance with these essentially rational forms of reasoning, even if normative properties or relations do not have to be mentioned in specifying these dispositions themselves. One might have a host of *separate* dispositions, such that the net effect of all these separate dispositions is that one forms and revises one's beliefs and other attitudes in just the same way as one would if one had the disposition that actually responds to such normative facts themselves. However, if this proposal is to be a genuine alternative to my proposal, this proposal must allow that it could just be a *fluke* that one has all these separate dispositions. But in that case, it actually seems to me quite doubtful whether the manifestation of these dispositions can really count as rational thinking at all. Indeed, this seems to be the case that was originally described by Ned Block (1978: 294–6), and has since come to be known as the "Blockhead", which arguably does not have any genuine intelligence at all.[23] So it seems most plausible that if there are any dispositions that are essential to

---

[23] Block's original example was of a machine that passes a "Turing Test" simply by means of a huge "look-up table".

possessing concepts (and to being capable of attitude-types), these dispositions must respond precisely to normative facts; hence these dispositions cannot be specified without mentioning such normative properties or relations.

Some other philosophers might insist that it is bound to be possible in principle, by using some highly complex psychological predicates, to specify these rational forms of reasoning in wholly non-normative terms. But I do not have to deny this. I have said that we cannot specify these rational dispositions *without mentioning normative properties or relations*; I have *not* said that we cannot specify these rational dispositions *without using normative terms*. It may well be possible, in principle, to mention these normative properties or relations without using normative terms. I do not have to deny this. As I explained in an earlier section of this chapter (Section 7.3), all that I need, in order to avoid trivialization of the claim that "the intentional is normative", is the assumption that these normative properties or relations cannot be specified by means of the relatively simple psychological terms that refer to the *basic constituents* of intentional mental properties. If it is only by means of highly *complex* psychological predicates that we can refer to the relevant normative properties or relations, then this threat of trivialization is avoided. And it certainly seems that if there are any purely psychological predicates that refer to the absence of defeating conditions, they will be immensely complex. Defeating conditions, after all, can come from *anywhere*—from experience, from memory, from the testimony of others, or even from elaborate deductive reasoning or scientific theorizing. The only *simple* way of specifying what these conditions all have in common is in normative terms—as conditions that make it irrational to reason in certain ways. Even if there is also some more complex way of specifying these defeating conditions in non-normative terms, my argument would not be undermined. The dispositions that are essential to possessing certain concepts, or to being capable of certain attitude-types, cannot be specified without mentioning normative properties or relations.

Yet another objection would take issue with my claim that the possession of a concept is always a rational power or ability, and never a defect or liability. Some philosophers have toyed with the idea that some concepts—perhaps especially the concepts that are routinely found problematic by philosophers—might be essentially incoherent concepts; that is, they might be concepts that essentially rest on irrational dispositions of some kind.[24] For example, Georges Rey (2007) has suggested that the concepts of "free will" and the traditional concept of the "soul" might all be intrinsically irrational concepts in this way.

In fact, however, it does not seem plausible to postulate incoherent concepts of this sort. The reason for this is similar to the reason against postulating concepts that essentially depend on mistaken beliefs. When I reject the existence of witches or unicorns, I am using the very same concepts that were used by the medieval

---

[24] A subtle version of this idea has been defended recently by Matti Eklund (2002).

thinkers who believed in witches and unicorns. If I were not using the very same concepts, I would not really be *disagreeing* with these medieval thinkers, in the sense of denying the very thought that they affirmed. But of course I do not make the mistakes that characterized medieval thinking about witches and unicorns. So making these mistakes does not seem to be necessary in order to possess these concepts.

It seems to me that an essentially similar point applies to the concepts that Rey mentions, such as the concepts of "free will" or of the "soul". Again, suppose that there were a perfectly rational being, who had no irrational dispositions of any kind. This perfectly rational being would have to possess these concepts in order to ascribe beliefs involving these concepts (for example, when thinking to herself 'Many human beings believe that they have an immortal soul'), and also in order to reject the mistaken beliefs that many human beings have involving these concepts (for example, when thinking to herself 'Human beings do not have immortal souls'). In general, it seems that any of the "problematic concepts" that appear to be deeply entwined in confused or irrational thoughts could be shared by a perfectly rational being, who was capable of diagnosing and rejecting our mistaken and irrational thoughts. So it does not seem that it is *essential* to possessing these concepts that one should have any irrational dispositions. In fact, then, these problematic concepts seem not to be essentially irrational concepts. The concepts themselves are perfectly innocent: it is our *use* of those concepts that is defective.[25]

So it seems to me that my argument stands. There must be some account that explains how the thinker's dispositions determine which concepts and attitude-types figure in his thoughts. That is, some sort of dispositionalism must be true. But as I have argued, the prospects for a purely non-normative dispositionalism are dim. Moreover, it appears that a normative sort of dispositionalism could avoid the problems that all the alternative theories face. So it seems that we have a good reason to accept the claim that I have been considering here—the claim that the intentional is normative.

This concludes my defence of the thesis of the normativity of the intentional. As we shall see, this thesis has highly important metaphysical implications for the nature of both normative properties and intentional mental properties. What exactly these metaphysical implications are will be the topic of the next chapter.

[25] For further discussion of the normativity of the intentional, see the debate between me (Wedgwood 2007) and Rey (2007).

8

Irreducibility and Causal Efficacy

8.1 WHAT FOLLOWS FROM THE NORMATIVITY OF THE INTENTIONAL?

In the previous chapter, I presented an argument for the claim that the intentional is normative. In this chapter, I shall explore the metaphysical implications of this argument.

The first metaphysical implication that I wish to highlight is that intentional properties—that is, content-involving mental properties—are not "natural properties" in the sense that I defined in Chapter 6 (Section 6.4). According to that definition, a property counts as a "natural property" just in case a full constitutive account of the property need not refer to any normative or evaluative property or relation. But according to the claim that the intentional is normative, a full account of intentional mental properties must refer to normative properties and relations. So according to this claim, intentional mental properties are not natural properties. If this is correct, then it follows that the intentional does not lie at a metaphysically more fundamental level than the normative; on the contrary, according to this claim, the normative is at least as metaphysically fundamental as the intentional.

It also follows that there cannot be any *reduction* of the normative to the mental.[1] Suppose that there is a true universally quantified biconditional according to which something has a normative property if and only if it has some property P that can be non-accidentally referred to without using any normative terms. If on the right-hand side of this biconditional, the property P is referred to by using intentional mental terms, this biconditional will not give a reduction of the normative—not even if the truth of this biconditional follows from the essence of the normative property in question. This is because an account of the intentional mental properties that are mentioned on the right-hand side of this biconditional would itself have to mention normative properties, of the kind that are mentioned on the biconditional's left-hand side. Such a biconditional could only count as reduction of normative properties if it uses neither normative *nor* intentional terms on its right-hand side.

---

[1] For this point, see especially Hurley (1989).

This last point is compatible with the view that the intentional is actually reducible to the normative—that is, that there is a correct reductive account of the nature of intentional states, and any such account must mention normative properties or relations.[2] But as I explained in the previous chapter, it seems to me that my account of the properties that are the semantic values of normative concepts supports the thesis that what is essential to these normative properties is precisely their relation to intentional mental properties and relations. For example, it is an essential and constitutive feature of the property referred to by the practical 'ought', when it is indexed to an agent A and time t, that it is the property of a proposition p that makes it correct for A to incorporate p into her ideal plans about what to do at t, and incorrect for A to incorporate the negation of p into any such plans. But *planning* is an intentional mental relation that holds between thinkers and propositions. So any adequate account of these normative properties will refer to intentional properties and relations.

Thus, according to the picture that is supported by the arguments of the previous chapters, the normative and the intentional must each be mentioned in giving any account of the other, so that the two domains of properties and relations are essentially interdependent, without either of the two being reducible to the other. In fact, it is the very same account that gives the essences of both the intentional properties and relations, and of the normative properties and relations as well. What is essential to these two classes of properties is precisely certain ways in which they are interconnected.

At the same time, it is important not to overstate the anti-reductionist implications of what was argued in the previous chapter. Some philosophers appear to think that if the intentional is normative in this way, then all forms of reductive naturalism about the intentional are ruled out immediately. That is, according to these philosophers, if the intentional is normative, then it follows immediately that there is no way of giving an account of the intentional in wholly non-normative, non-intentional terms—that is, presumably, in broadly speaking naturalistic terms.[3] In fact, however, at least as I have formulated it, this conclusion does *not* immediately follow from the claim that the intentional is normative; much further argument is needed to get from this claim to the conclusion that no form of reductive naturalism is correct.

What really follows immediately from the claim that the intentional is normative is that if there is any reduction of either the normative or the intentional, it would have to take the form of a *simultaneous* reduction of *both* the normative *and* the intentional in wholly naturalistic (non-intentional and non-normative) terms. But the existence of such a simultaneous reduction of both families of properties seems to be at least logically consistent with the claim

[2] For defences of this view, see e.g. Morris (1992), and also Brandom (1994) (at least, according to Rosen's (1997) interpretation of Brandom).
[3] See e.g. Lance and Hawthorne (1997).

that the intentional is normative. The claim that the intentional is normative, at least as I formulated it, is the claim that it is impossible to give an account of the essence or nature of intentional states without *mentioning normative properties or relations*. This claim is quite compatible with its being possible, in principle, to pick out those normative properties or relations *without using normative terms*.

Suppose that there is in fact a simultaneous reduction of the intentional and normative properties in wholly naturalistic terms (say, in broadly functionalist or behaviourist terms). A naturalistic reduction of a normative property P, as I explained in Chapter 6 (Section 6.4), is an account that gives us a purely naturalistic specification of some property that is necessarily equivalent to normative property P—where this equivalence follows from the constitutive essence of property P itself. But if it follows from the essence of property P that P is equivalent to property Q, it becomes plausible to say that for something to have property P just *is* for it to have property Q, and indeed that P is *identical* to Q. Thus, a reductive account of a property supports an identity statement concerning that property (just as the reduction of thermodynamics to molecular mechanics supports the identity statement 'Heat = molecular motion'). So, a naturalistic reduction of normative and intentional properties will in effect provide some non-normative naturalistic terms that pick out those normative properties. Since this reductive account of the nature of the intentional and normative properties *does* mention normative properties (albeit by means of these non-normative naturalistic terms), it does not amount to a counterexample to the claim that any correct account of intentional properties must mention normative properties.

In this way, then, the claim that the intentional is normative does not immediately rule out all forms of reductive naturalism about the intentional; nor does it immediately rule out all forms of reductive naturalism about the normative. It entails only that if there is a correct naturalistic reduction either of the intentional or of the normative, it must take the form of a simultaneous reduction of both the intentional and the normative.

8.2 REDUCTIONISM AND FUNCTIONALISM

In the previous section, I argued that the claim that the intentional is normative does not by itself rule out all forms of reductive naturalism. As I shall now argue, however, there are *other* considerations that tell against the possibility of any form of reductive naturalism. These considerations take the form of arguments that have been given within the philosophy of mind, to the effect that mental properties are irreducible. Assuming that the intentional mental properties are essentially normative, in the way that I have argued at the end of the previous chapter, the fate of normative properties is tied to the fate of mental properties. These two families of properties either both succumb to naturalistic reduction, or else both resist all such attempts at naturalistic reduction. Thus, if there are convincing arguments for the irreducibility of the mental, these arguments will also support the irreducibility of the normative.

Before giving these arguments for the irreducibility of the mental, I shall need slightly to refine my account of what a reduction amounts to. According to the account that I gave in Chapter 6, a reduction of a mental property M would be a constitutive account of M that is built up out of terms that refer to properties whose nature can be explained without any reference to mental properties. To be fully reductive, however, it seems to me, a constitutive account of M would not only have to be built out of terms that refer to properties whose nature can be explained without *referring* to mental properties; it would also have to avoid *quantifying* over mental properties. The easiest way to see this is by reflecting on the question of which forms of *functionalism* are reductive and which are not.

The core idea of functionalism is that there is some *theory* concerning the mental properties that in effect amounts in some way to an *implicit definition* of those mental properties. Different forms of functionalism would focus on different theories here. For example, the theory in question might be equivalent to a "Turing machine table"; or it might be a version of common-sense psychology (or "folk psychology" as it is often called); or it might be some kind of scientific psychology, such as a version of cognitive science, or a version of evolutionary psychology incorporating an account of the evolution of the relevant mental capacities through a process of natural selection. It might be a theory that solely concerns the mental economy of a particular individual at a particular time; or it might be a theory that concerns the role that mental properties play in the universe as a whole. It does not matter for our purposes exactly what sort of theory is employed here. The important point is just to appreciate how many possible forms of functionalism there are.

Different forms of functionalism also differ with respect to the precise way in which this theory is taken to give a definition of the mental properties that the theory refers to. First, we need the notion of a sequence of properties "satisfying" the theory. This notion can be explained by means of F. P. Ramsey's (1929) technique of replacing the psychological terms of the theory with *variables*. For simplicity, suppose that all the psychological terms of the theory are terms that refer to mental properties. Then following Ramsey's technique would involve uniformly replacing each of these terms in each of its occurrences in the theory by a variable. Thus, if the psychological terms of the theory are $\tau_1, \ldots, \tau_n$, and the content of the theory is equivalent to the sentence '$T(\tau_1, \ldots, \tau_n)$', the result of applying Ramsey's technique to the theory is the complex predicate or open sentence '$T(x_1, \ldots, x_n)$'. Then we can say a sequence of n properties "satisfies" the theory just in case this open sentence '$T(x_1, \ldots, x_n)$' is true of that sequence of properties (that is, the result of uniformly replacing each of these variables by a name of the corresponding property in this sequence is a true sentence).

Now, so long as the theory is true, then the properties that the theory refers to will form a sequence of properties that satisfies the theory. The simplest way in which the theory might be regarded as giving an "implicit definition" of these properties is if this sequence is not just *one* of the sequences of properties that satisfy the theory, but is in fact the *only* sequence of properties that satisfies the theory. Of course, the claim that there is only one sequence of properties that satisfies the theory is a highly non-trivial claim, about which many doubts can be raised.[4] But one way of taking the suggestion that this theory provides an implicit definition of the mental properties is to take it as equivalent to this claim.[5] In effect, this sort of functionalist definition uses the theory to construct an *identity statement* for each mental property. Suppose that the name of the mental property in question is τ_i; that is, this property is the ith mental property to be mentioned in the theory. Then this sort of functional definition identifies this property with the unique property x_i such that there are $n - 1$ other properties that, along with this property in the ith place, form the only sequence of properties that satisfies the theory. (This is sometimes referred to as the "Australian" version of functionalism.)

If a functionalist definition of this sort is correct, it would certainly provide a way of referring to each of the mental properties without using any psychological terms. Moreover, if the theory states an essential truth about the mental properties that are being defined, this non-psychological term would pick out the mental property by means of an essential feature of the property (not just by means of an accidental feature that it merely happens to have). As it stands, however, this sort of functionalism seems not to be reductive. One way of seeing this is by reflecting that it seems quite possible for there to be a functionalist definition of this sort of the most fundamental properties of physics, even if those properties are not in any way reducible to anything more basic.

Moreover, even if mental properties have a functionalist definition of this sort, this would still be quite compatible with the most radical sort of Cartesian dualism about mental properties. According to this radical form of Cartesian dualism, there could be thinking things that are not spatially extended at all, including utterly disembodied thinkers who had no spatially extended bodies or brains of any sort—not even brains that are made of some special "ghostly stuff", such as the "bundles of ectoplasm" that were once mentioned by Hilary Putnam (1967: 416). According to this Cartesian view then, mental properties do not need to be in any way implemented or grounded or realized in the states of the thinker's body or brain. However, this Cartesian view is quite compatible with this sort of functional definition: it could still be true that the only sequence of properties that satisfies the relevant psychological theory is a sequence consisting of these purely mental properties of Cartesian souls. But this Cartesian view is surely the paradigm case of a non-reductive conception of mental properties.

---

[4] See especially Bealer (1984 and 1997).
[5] For this form of functionalism, see especially Lewis (1983a: essays 6, 7, and 9).

Thus, the only way in which this sort of functionalist definition will be reductive is if it is revised so that it claims, not only that the mental properties are the only properties that satisfy the relevant psychological theory, but also that the mental properties are in fact *physical* properties—namely, those physical properties that uniquely satisfy the relevant psychological theory. (As I explained in Section 6.4, I am understanding "physical properties" broadly: physical properties include all causally relevant properties that are *non-mental*—in the sense that it is possible to give an account of the nature of these properties without referring to mental properties—as well as all properties that can be constructed out of physical properties by means of operations like negation, conjunction, and so on.) That is, to make this theory reductive we would have to insist that the variables in the Ramsey sentence that is constructed out of the theory range only over *physical* properties.

This reductive version of this first form of functionalism is in effect a version of the *identity* theory, according to which the mental property is actually identical to a physical property. But many functionalists wish to deny the identity theory, and hold instead that mental properties are capable of being "multiply realized" in many different physical properties.[6] For example, perhaps pain is realized in C-fibre firing in human beings, whereas in Martians, pain is realized in some completely different physical process. Some of these "Australian" functionalists—such as David Lewis (1980) and Frank Jackson (1996)—respond to this point by suggesting that the functionalist definition should be taken as a definition of such properties as *pain-in-normal-human-beings* and the like. But it is reasonable to complain that this is simply changing the subject. What we want is an account of the nature of mental properties like *pain*, which *ex hypothesi* is a property that human beings and Martians can share. Given the intuitively compelling possibility of multiple realization, no such identity theory of the mental properties seems acceptable.

For this reason, many functionalists offer a slightly different form of functionalist definition instead. Unlike the first form of functionalism, this other form of functionalism does not claim that the mental properties are the only properties that satisfy the relevant theory. On the contrary, this rival form of functionalism is compatible with the claim that there are *other* sequences of properties that also satisfy the theory. Still, according to this form of functionalism, there is a sense in which the theory provides an implicit definition of the mental properties. This is because (according to this second form of functionalism) it is true quite generally that something has the mental property in question if and only if it has the property that occupies the appropriate position in *some sequence of properties or other* that satisfies the theory. (While the first form is sometimes called "Australian" functionalism, this second form is sometimes called "American" functionalism.)

---

[6] For this second sort of functionalism, see especially Shoemaker (1981).

This second form of functionalism will also not be any sort of reduction of the mental unless the variables in the Ramsey sentence that is constructed out of the theory range only over physical properties. For suppose that these variables can range over a larger class of properties (including irreducible mental properties if there are any); and suppose that the theory out of which the definition is constructed is true. Since this theory is true, the mental properties must satisfy the theory. So whenever a thinker satisfies the left-hand side of this definition, she will also satisfy the right-hand side of the definition, because the mental properties themselves satisfy the theory and *ex hypothesi* the thinker has the mental property in question. So there is nothing reductive about the left-to-right direction of this definition. But there also need be nothing reductive about the right-to-left direction either. This is because one reason why the right-to-left direction could hold is because the mental properties are the only properties that satisfy the theory (even though this "American" version of functionalism does not *claim* that the mental properties are the only properties that satisfy the theory, it is still *compatible* with that claim). Since it could be that this is the reason why the definition is correct, then, just like the first "Australian" form of functionalism, this second "American" form of functionalism is quite compatible with the most radical form of non-reductive Cartesianism about the mental. So to ensure that this second form of functionalism expresses a reductive conception of the mental, we must again require that the variables that appear in the functionalist definition should range only over physical properties.

In a way, this point should not be surprising. Intuitively, the idea behind reductionism is that the reduced property can be analysed into, or constructed out of, the reducing properties and relations; the reduced property does not have to be viewed as something extra, over and above the reducing properties or relations. If the domain of the quantifiers is unrestricted, and may actually include irreducible mental properties (if such properties exist), then the fact that we can construct a quantified expression that refers to a mental property without using any overtly psychological terms only shows that the property has a unique role in this domain of properties. It does not show that this property can be *constructed* out of the reducing properties and relations. In an obvious sense, it may still be something over and above the reducing properties and relations: it may only be because our use of the quantifiers already recognizes the existence of these properties, by having a domain that already contains these properties, that we can construct an expression that refers to them.

On the other hand, if the domain of these quantifiers is restricted so that they range only over physical properties, then even this second form of functionalism will be a reductive account. According to this reductive form of functionalism, for a thinker x to have a given mental property is just for there to be a sequence of physical properties that are related to each other in a way that can be characterized in purely physical and topic-neutral terms, and for *x* to have an appropriate one of these physical properties. (As explained in Chapter 6, I am using constructions of the form 'For *x* to have the property *F* is for it to be the case that *A(x)*' to ascribe an *essential* feature of the property *F*.) This seems to be a reductive account of the property in question.

To conclude, then, there are two main sorts of functionalism. The first "Australian" sort claims that the mental properties are the only properties that satisfy the relevant theory. The second "American" sort claims that necessarily, a thinker has the mental property in question if and only if there is some sequence of properties that satisfies the relevant theory and the thinker has the property that occupies the appropriate position in this sequence. Each of these two sorts of functionalism has both a reductive and a non-reductive form: in both cases, the key difference between the reductive and non-reductive forms lies in whether the variables deployed in the functionalist definition are restricted so that they range only over physical properties, or are not so restricted—so that their domain would include even irreducible mental properties (if such there be).

8.3 THE FAILURE OF REDUCTIVE FORMS OF FUNCTIONALISM

I have belaboured the question of the conditions under which functionalism would count as a reductive theory for the following reason. It seems that the best hope for a reductive account of the mental and normative properties would be a form of functionalism. I have insisted that a reductive account of a property must articulate an essential feature of that property: the reduction cannot be a purely accidental feature of a property. But as I have argued in the previous chapter, the essential features of mental properties are their normative and dispositional features; and the essential features of normative properties are their relations to mental properties. There seems to be no way for a reductive account to capture any of these essential features of these properties unless the account is a form of functionalism. Moreover, the functionalist approach looks *prima facie* promising, because as I have already pointed out, the range of theories that could be co-opted by a functionalist account is enormous.

So the best hope for a reductive account of the mental and normative properties would be a big functionalist definition, which would give a simultaneous account of both families of properties. But if there are principled reasons for thinking that there is no reductive functionalist definition of the mental properties, then *a fortiori* there are reasons for thinking that there is no reductive functionalist definition that can define both the mental and the normative properties.

Now it seems to me that there are such principled reasons for thinking that all reductive functionalist definitions of mental properties will fail. Many philosophers have developed objections to reductive forms of functionalism over the years.[7] But the most convincing of these objections seems to me the objection of George Bealer (1997). This objection is as follows.

First, we must remember that a psychological theory has no chance of giving a definition of the nature of mental properties unless it is a fairly rich and detailed theory, which captures all the essential features of the mental properties. After all, if the theory is not detailed enough, then the mental properties will certainly not be the only properties that satisfy the theory; and the fact that there is a sequence of properties that satisfies the theory, and that a given object has a property that occupies an appropriate position in that sequence, will not be enough to guarantee that the object in question has the mental property that has that position in the theory. Anyway, the fundamental definition of the nature of mental properties must surely capture all of these properties' essential features; and only a sufficiently detailed theory can do that.

Now it seems to be an essential feature of pain that the following principle holds: if one is in pain, and is introspectively considering one's own mental state, then one will believe that one is in pain.[8] Let us call this principle P. (In fact, the precise details of principle P do not matter; all that matters is that it contains a psychological term embedded inside a propositional attitude ascription.) So it seems that the theory on which any adequate functionalist definition is based must include principle P (or at least some principle that resembles P in that it contains a psychological term embedded inside a propositional attitude ascription).[9]

Now to form a Ramsey sentence out of P, we would have to replace the psychological terms in P with variables, such as 'R_1', 'R_2', and so on:

If x has properties R_1 and R_2, then x will be related by relation R_3 to the proposition that he has property R_1.

This is the result of replacing the two occurrences of 'in pain' in P with 'has property R_1', 'introspectively considering one's mental state' with 'has property R_2', and 'believes' with 'is related by relation R_3 to'. This Ramsey sentence will form a conjunct in the larger Ramsey sentence that is formed out of the relevant theory.

Now suppose that reductive functionalism is correct, and that the Ramsey sentence is satisfied by a sequence of *physical* properties and relations; and

---

[7] For some other well-known objections to functionalism, see especially Block (1978).

[8] Actually, I would prefer to formulate the principle so that it states only that if one is *definitely* in pain and is introspectively considering one's mental state, then *ceteris paribus* one will believe that one is in pain. The reason for inserting 'definitely' into the antecedent but not into the consequent is to avoid the objections of Williamson (2000: ch. 4). The reason for inserting the qualification '*ceteris paribus*' into the consequent is that I believe that it is possible for a thinker under the influence of a false philosophical theory to be in pain but refuse to believe that he is in pain. However, none of these amendments would make any difference to the soundness of Bealer's argument.

[9] Bealer (2000) provides something close to a proof of the point that a functionalist theory that does not include anything like principle P will not be strong enough to provide a definition of the mental properties.

suppose that a particular person—say, Hecuba—is in pain, and is introspectively considering her mental state. Then we can infer that there is a sequence of physical properties and relations $(P_1, P_2, P_3, \ldots)$ that satisfies this theory, and Hecuba has P_1 and P_2, the first two properties in this sequence. Moreover, since the theory includes principle P, we can infer that Hecuba is related by P_3, the third property or relation in this sequence, to the proposition that she has physical property P_1. If the functional definition is correct, then being related to a proposition by the third property or relation in a sequence of properties that satisfies the theory guarantees that one *believes* that proposition. So we can infer that Hecuba believes that she has physical property P_1.

However, unless physical property P_1 is actually *identical* to the property of pain, Hecuba does *not* believe that she has physical property P_1; she believes that she is *in pain*! As we have seen, most contemporary philosophers of mind reject the identity theory; and as I argued in the previous section, they seem to have strong intuitive reasons for doing so.[10] So it seems that this reductive theory, together with the innocuous assumption that Hecuba is in pain, has consequences that we seem to have strong reasons to reject. As Bealer convincingly argues, none of the ways of amending the functionalist definition that are suggested by any known form of functionalism will succeed in avoiding this problem.[11] So it seems that all forms of reductive functionalism must be rejected.

On reflection, it should not seem surprising that reductive functionalism fails in this way. To count as a reduction, functionalism must start with a theory that captures the *essential* features of the mental properties, and it must also claim that a sequence of *physical* properties satisfies this theory. But to avoid being forced into the identity theory, it must also insist that these physical properties are *distinct* from the mental properties that the original theory is about. Thus, any form of reductive functionalism that rejects the identity theory must start with a theory that captures the special and distinctive features of mental properties, and then it must claim that if any of the mental properties are actually instantiated, then this theory is also true of some *other* properties (specifically, certain physical properties) as well.[12] But if the theory is true of these non-mental physical properties as well, that seems to conflict with the original claim that the theory captured what was distinctive and special about the mental properties in the first place. In this way, reductive functionalism seems doomed to undermine itself.

For these reasons, it seems to me that Bealer is right that all reductive forms of functionalism must be rejected. Moreover, Bealer's argument would surely also apply to a functionalist definition that sought to provide, not just a definition of

---

[10] See Bealer (1994) for a careful restatement of the arguments against the identity theory. (I should note that I do not accept all of the arguments that Bealer puts forward in that paper. I accept the argument against the identity theory (185–204); but I do not accept the argument for the possibility of disembodied minds (204–8).)

[11] Besides Bealer (1997), see also Bealer's responses to various critics (2000 and 2001).

[12] I owe this way of putting the point to Boris Kment.

the mental properties, but a simultaneous definition of both the mental and the normative properties. But I have also argued that the slogan that "the intentional is normative" is correct, and that the best hope for a reductive account of either mental properties or normative properties would be a reductive form of functionalism that sought to give a simultaneous definition of both the mental and the normative properties. So it seems that the best hope for a reductive account of either the mental or the normative has failed. It would seem then that there is no prospect of reducing mental properties and normative properties to any more basic family of properties. Mental and normative properties are metaphysically irreducible.

8.4 THE CAUSAL EFFICACY OF THE NORMATIVE

As I shall argue in this section, the argument that I gave in the previous chapter for the normativity of the intentional has a further implication about the metaphysical character of normative facts and normative properties. Specifically, it implies that normative facts and properties are *causally efficacious*. In order to bring out this implication of the argument, I shall try to restate the argument more carefully, and answer a number of objections that might be made against it.

My argument for the normativity of the intentional was based on the following two premises. First, the dispositions in virtue of which we possess concepts, or are capable of the various types of attitudes, must be *essentially rational* dispositions. Secondly, as I put it, an essentially rational disposition must be sensitive to the presence or absence of defeating conditions as such. A "defeating condition" is by definition a condition such that certain other conditions, which would normally make it rational for one to revise one's beliefs or other attitudes in a certain way, do not make it rational for one to revise one's attitudes in that way in the presence of this defeating condition. As I also argued in the previous chapter, the notion of a "rational" belief or other attitude is itself a normative notion. In this way, then, the absence of defeating conditions is an essentially normative fact. Thus, the facts to which an essentially rational disposition responds are themselves essentially normative facts.

Now the crucial point that we need to take note of here is that the notion of a disposition is a *causal* notion. Suppose that something manifests a disposition, and the disposition is a disposition to respond in a certain way to a stimulus condition of a certain type. Then the thing's responding in the relevant way on that occasion seems to be *caused* by its being in the relevant stimulus condition on that occasion. Thus, the argument that I gave in the previous chapter for the normativity of the intentional seems to imply that whenever we manifest one of these rational dispositions, there is a normative fact—namely, the fact that we are in certain mental states that (thanks to the absence of defeating conditions) make it rational to revise our attitudes in a certain way—which actually causes us to revise our attitudes in that way. The argument requires that normative facts should be causally efficacious.

Once we see that the argument implies something so controversial as the thesis that normative facts can be causally efficacious, we may start to have second thoughts about the argument. In this section and the next, I shall try to dispel those doubts: first, in the rest of this section, I shall offer some further considerations in support of the controversial thesis that normative facts can be causally efficacious; then, in the next section, I shall argue against the best-known objections that have been raised against this controversial thesis.

The further considerations that I shall offer in the rest of this section have to do with what is essentially involved in a thinker's *reasoning in a rational manner*. To simplify the discussion, I shall restrict my attention to cases in which the output of one's reasoning is the formation of a new belief or intention (as opposed to the revision or abandonment of an old belief or intention, or perhaps even the formation or revision of some quite different sort of mental state). Then I can say that part of what is involved in such rational reasoning is that one forms a new belief or intention in response to being in a set of antecedent mental states that makes it rational for one to form that belief or intention.

Whenever one's having certain antecedent mental states makes it rational for one to form a certain belief or intention, let us say that those antecedent mental states "rationalize" that belief or intention. Then it seems intuitively clear on reflection that for one to be reasoning in a rational manner, it is not enough that (i) one is in antecedent mental states that rationalize that belief or intention, and (ii) one's being in those mental states causes one to form that belief or intention.

The trouble is that it could be a pure *fluke* that these antecedent mental states both rationalize and cause the formation of this new belief or intention. The disposition that one manifests in forming this belief or intention in response to those antecedent mental states might be some bizarre compulsion (perhaps induced into one's mind by a whimsically manipulative neuroscientist), which in most cases produces the most weird transitions between one's mental states, but in this one case just happens to take one from antecedent mental states to the formation of a new belief or intention that is rationalized by those antecedent states.[13] Intuitively, this would not be a case of rational reasoning. For rational reasoning, one must manifest a disposition of the right kind.

Somehow we must rule out these cases in which it is simply a fluke that these antecedent mental states both rationalize and cause the formation of the new belief or intention. To rule out cases of this sort, the causal relation and the rationalizing relation cannot be independent of each other in this way. Instead,

[13] As I explain elsewhere (Wedgwood 2006*b*), this is a sort of "deviant causal chain" in reasoning (comparable to the more famous sorts of "deviant causal chains" that have been discussed in the philosophy of action and of perception). As I suggest in *n.* 15 below, I am optimistic that there is an important similarity between the answers to all these forms of the deviant causal chain problem; but I cannot undertake to study this question in detail here.

these antecedent states must cause one to form that belief or intention precisely *in virtue of* their rationalizing one's forming that belief or intention.[14]

What does it mean to say that these antecedent mental states cause one to form this belief or intention "in virtue of" their rationalizing one's formation of that belief or intention? It seems to be the common use of the phrase 'in virtue of' in causal explanations—such as in the claim that the impact of the aeroplanes caused the towers to collapse in virtue of the temperature of the ensuing fuel explosion, and not in virtue of the force of the impact. Of course, there are many frameworks that philosophers have developed for thinking about causation. But almost all these frameworks allow us to make sense of the idea that one event e_1 causes another event e_2 "in virtue of" a particular property that e_1 has (rather than in virtue of some other property that e_1 has). For example, if we are thinking of facts (rather than events) as causes, then we can articulate this claim about the causes of the towers' collapse by saying that it is the fact that the towers were hit by a fuel explosion of at least such-and-such a temperature—not the fact that they were hit by an impact of a certain force—that was the cause of the fact that the towers collapsed. If we think of causal relations as consisting in the manifestation of dispositions, then we can articulate this claim about the causes of the towers' collapse by saying that this causal process was the manifestation of a disposition that the towers had, to collapse in response to their being hit by explosions of a certain temperature—not the manifestation of any disposition that they had to collapse in response to their being hit by an impact of a certain force.

So, I propose, whenever one is reasoning rationally, one's antecedent mental states cause one to form a new belief or intention precisely *in virtue of* their rationalizing that new belief or intention; that is, one is caused to form a new belief or intention precisely *by the fact* that one is in antecedent mental states that rationalize forming that new belief or intention; one's formation of the new belief or intention is the manifestation of a *disposition* that responds to antecedent mental states that rationalize forming a belief in p by forming that very belief. In effect, this disposition must respond to *rationalizers as such*. It is this that makes the disposition an *essentially rational disposition*. Such a disposition would not be a mere liability (like my disposition to sneeze or to trip over my shoelaces); it would deserve to be called a "competence" or "ability", and to manifest such a disposition would be to "exercise" such a competence or ability. Thus, this proposal can capture the intuitively appealing idea that rational reasoning involves exercising a rational ability or competence.

As I suggested in Chapter 1, a disposition can be specified by means of a function from stimulus conditions to response conditions: for you to have the

---

[14] This formulation—'causation in virtue of rationalization'—has been used by other philosophers in discussing the problem of deviant causal chains; see Antony (1989: 168), and Brewer (1995: 238 and 247). However, these philosophers assume that the phrase 'in virtue of' must have a different sense here from the sense that it has in ordinary causal explanations. My proposal is that this phrase has *exactly* the same sense here as in those ordinary causal explanations.

disposition is for you to have some intrinsic feature in virtue of which, in any normal case in which you are in one of these stimulus conditions, you also go into the response condition onto which that function maps that stimulus condition. So, the disposition that you must manifest, if the relevant antecedent mental states are to cause you to form the belief in *p* precisely in virtue of their rationalizing your forming that belief, must be one that can be specified by means of a function that maps the stimulus condition *coming to be in some mental states or other that rationalize forming a belief in p* onto the response condition *forming a belief in p*.

Strictly speaking, it seems plausible that this disposition should not just be restricted to this one proposition *p*. As we might put it, in reasoning, we exercise some *general* kind of reasoning competence—not a special reasoning competence that is restricted to this single proposition *p*. At the same time, we need not require that in reasoning, one is exercising a *universal* competence that extends to all propositions whatsoever; it need only be a competence that extends across a range of related propositions. (Plausibly, this range of propositions will include all propositions that are sufficiently similar to *p* with respect to the sorts of mental states that rationalize forming a belief in those propositions.) So, the disposition that one must manifest in forming a belief in *p* by means of rational reasoning must be one that can be specified by means of a function that, for *any* proposition *q* within the relevant range, maps the stimulus condition *coming to be in some mental states or other that rationalize forming a belief in q* onto the response condition *forming a belief in q*.[15] A parallel account, I propose, will also apply to intention as well as to belief.[16]

This then is my account of rational reasoning. When one forms a belief or an intention by means of rational reasoning, one's formation of that belief or intention is the manifestation of a disposition that one has, to respond directly to the fact that one has come to be in some antecedent mental states that rationalize forming a belief or an intention within the relevant range, by forming that very belief or intention. In the remainder of this section, I shall defend this account of rational reasoning against various objections.

The first objection that I shall consider is the following. It might seem implausible to claim that everyone who forms the belief in *p* through rational

---

[15] This proposal is closely akin to David Lewis's (1986: 281–3) solution to the version of the deviant causal chains problem that arises in the case of *perception*. There are two main differences between my account and his. First, my account appeals to dispositions instead of counterfactuals. Secondly, because I am dealing with reasoning instead of perception, the relevant relation between the effect and the cause is not that of *veridically representing* the cause, but that of being *rationalized* by it. A broadly similar solution is, I believe, possible with respect to the version of the problem that arises in the case of *action*, but I do not have the space to go into the details here.

[16] That is, if one forms the intention to φ through rational reasoning, there must be a range of ways of behaving, suitably related to φ-ing, such that one must be generally disposed to respond to being in mental states that, for certain ways of behaving within that range, rationalize one's forming an intention to behave in one of those ways, by forming an intention to behave in one of those ways; and one's forming the intention to φ on this occasion must be the manifestation of that disposition.

reasoning has a disposition to form the belief in p in response to *all* rationalizers for forming that belief. Why shouldn't it be the case that you are disposed to respond to *certain* rationalizers for forming the belief in p, but not to all?

It certainly is implausible to claim that it is necessary that every such reasoner would form the belief in p in every possible case in which they came to be in mental states that rationalized forming that belief. Most of us fail to respond to certain rationalizers for forming certain beliefs. But as I have already said several times, the mere fact that a disposition is not manifested in every case does not show that one does not have this disposition: in "abnormal" cases, interfering factors of many kinds can prevent the manifestation of the disposition.

Moreover, we must not overestimate the number of cases in which one's antecedent mental states rationalize forming a new belief or intention. Just because the contents of one's antecedent beliefs *entail* a certain proposition p, it does not follow that those antecedent beliefs *rationalize* one's forming the belief in p. There are several reasons for this. For example, these antecedent beliefs will not rationalize one's forming the belief in p unless one actually *considers* the proposition p. So the mere fact that one does not believe all the logical consequences of the contents of one's beliefs does not show that one lacks the disposition to respond to the fact that one has come to be in mental states that rationalize forming the belief in p (or in any other proposition in the relevant range) by forming that very belief.

However, these points by themselves are not enough to answer this objection. Suppose that I am consciously considering the axioms of arithmetic and at the same time consciously considering Fermat's Last Theorem. In this case, since there is a possible process of rational reasoning leading from my beliefs in those axioms to my forming a belief in the theorem, my beliefs in those axioms surely *do* rationalize my forming a belief in the theorem. But there are clearly "normal" cases (where I am not affected by any "interfering factors" of the relevant sort) in which my antecedent beliefs in the axioms become conscious at the same time as I consciously consider the theorem, but I still do not form any belief in the theorem. So, even if I am disposed to form this belief in response to *some* rationalizers (such as the belief that I have been told by a reliable informant that the theorem has been proved), I seem not to be disposed to form this belief in response to *all* rationalizers for doing so.

This objection shows that my proposal must be refined. It seems that any piece of reasoning consists of a sequence of what may be called *basic steps*. Basic steps in reasoning are pieces of reasoning that do not themselves consist of any simpler pieces of reasoning. An account of rational reasoning can just focus on such basic steps in reasoning. More complex pieces of rational reasoning will just consist of a number of such basic steps.

I propose then that the account of rational reasoning that I have sketched here should be taken just as an account of such basic steps in reasoning. But this suggests that we should also restrict the range of rationalizers to which the disposition manifested in making such a basic step in reasoning responds. Certain antecedent mental states may rationalize your forming a new belief or intention by means of a long and complicated process of reasoning, even if they do *not* rationalize your forming that belief or intention by means of a basic step in reasoning. That is, these antecedent mental states do not make it rational for you to form that new belief or intention by means of a basic step; they only make it rational for you to form that belief or intention by means of a long and complicated process of reasoning.

In general, the mental states that rationalize your forming a certain belief or intention by means of a basic step will include those mental states that *immediately* rationalize forming that belief or intention—in the way in which believing p immediately rationalizes forming a belief in 'p or q', or having an experience as of a red surface in front of you immediately rationalizes forming the belief that there is a red surface in front of you. However, these may not be the only cases in which antecedent mental states rationalize your forming a certain belief or intention by means of a basic step. Suppose that there is a short series of possible pieces of reasoning, such that the input of each item in the series (except the first) consists of the output of its predecessor (together with other background mental states), and the input of each item in the series immediately rationalizes its output. Then, if you are a suitably experienced reasoner, it may be rational for you to take a "short cut", directly from the input of the first item in this series to the output of the last, by means of a basic step. In this case, the input to the first item in this series will not only rationalize the output of the last item, but it will rationalize that output by means of a basic step. More precisely, then, the disposition that one must have, if one rationally forms a belief through reasoning, is a disposition, with respect to every proposition p in the relevant range, to form a belief in p in response to one's coming to be in mental states that rationalize forming a belief in p *by means of a basic step*.

However, even if it is not implausible to suppose that ordinary reasoners have dispositions of this kind, we may still ask why such dispositions should be essential to all rational reasoning. Why shouldn't the disposition that one manifests in rational reasoning be a disposition that responds to the fact that one has come to be in antecedent mental states that one *takes* to rationalize forming that belief—rather than, as I am proposing, to the fact that one has come to be in antecedent mental states that *really do* rationalize forming that belief?

To assess this rival proposal about the nature of rational reasoning, we need to know how to interpret the phrase 'mental states that one takes to rationalize forming the belief in p'. One interpretation is that it simply means: "mental states that one *believes* to rationalize forming the belief in p".[17] On this interpretation of this rival proposal, then, rational reasoning involves manifesting

---

[17] Compare for example Robert Audi's (1993: essay 8) analysis of the "basing relation" as involving a "linking belief".

a disposition to form certain beliefs or intentions, in response to one's coming to be in mental states that one *believes* to rationalize forming those beliefs or intentions.

When it is interpreted in this way, there are at least two serious problems with this proposal. First, most of us are engaged in simple reasoning for much of our waking lives; but we rarely spend much time thinking about our own mental states and forming higher-order beliefs about whether those mental states rationalize certain new beliefs or intentions. Indeed, it even seems possible for there to be simple thinkers who engage in rational reasoning but do not even possess the concepts that are necessary for forming higher-order beliefs of this kind. Secondly, forming such higher-order beliefs would itself appear to be irrational unless those beliefs are themselves formed through rational reasoning. But rational reasoning cannot essentially depend on irrational beliefs. So the account that this rival proposal gives of rational reasoning suffers from a vicious regress: to form any belief through rational reasoning, one would first have to do a further piece of rational reasoning, to form the higher-order belief that one is in mental states that rationalize forming that first belief; and so on *ad infinitum*. So any account that appeals to higher-order beliefs seems clearly inferior to the account that I am proposing.

A second interpretation would understand 'mental states that one takes to rationalize forming belief in *p*' to refer, not to mental states about which one *actually* holds the higher-order belief that they rationalize one's forming the belief in *p*, but rather to those mental states that *dispose* one to hold that higher-order belief, should the relevant question arise. But the fact that a disposition to form the belief in *p* responds to one's being in mental states that dispose one to hold this higher-order belief seems not to guarantee that this is a disposition of the right kind. It still seems at least metaphysically possible for the manipulative neuroscientist to give you a weird disposition to form beliefs in a certain range of propositions in response to certain antecedent mental states—where those antecedent states almost never rationalize those beliefs, but thanks to further interventions from the neuroscientist, are the only states that, for any proposition *q* in the relevant range, dispose you to form the higher-order belief that you are in mental states that rationalize your forming a belief in *q*. This weird disposition appears to respond to those mental states that dispose you to hold the relevant higher-order belief; but intuitively, manifesting this weird disposition surely does not count as rational reasoning. So this version of the rival proposal also seems inferior to my account.

There is one other rival proposal that might be considered at this point. In effect, I argued for my proposal in two stages. First, I argued that the disposition that one manifests in rational reasoning must be an essentially rational disposition: in effect, it must be a disposition that it is always rational to manifest. Then, at the second stage, I argued that such a disposition must actually respond to a normative fact as such—such as the fact that one has come to be in mental states that rationalize forming a belief in p by means of a basic step in reasoning. But a rival approach might question this second stage of my argument.

According to my proposal, when one forms a belief in p through rational reasoning, one manifests a disposition that responds to the normative fact that one has come to be in mental states that *rationalize* forming a belief in p (or more precisely, rationalize forming this belief by means of a basic step). But it seems plausible that there is a fact, which can be stated in purely psychological terms, without using any overtly normative terms, that is *sufficient* for this normative fact to obtain. For example, this fact might be a fact about exactly what mental states one is in, and what mental states one is not in, and what purely mental dispositions one has. It does not seem possible for there to be another case that is just like the actual case with respect to all the mental states that one is in, all the mental states that one is not in, and all the mental dispositions that one has, but unlike the actual case with respect to whether or not one's mental states rationalize forming a belief in p. So, if one is disposed to form a belief in p in response to this purely mental, non-normative fact, then this disposition will always lead to one's forming a rational belief. That is, this will be a disposition that it is always rational to manifest. So why not say that it is a disposition of this kind that one must manifest in forming a belief in p by means of a rational basic step in reasoning?

The problem with this rival proposal is that the disposition that it appeals to is extraordinarily *specific*. The fact that this disposition responds to will have to be a highly specific fact about the mental state of the thinker. This fact may be sufficient for being in mental states that rationalize forming a belief in p, but it will certainly not be necessary. So one could have this highly specific disposition even if one does not have the disposition to form a belief in p in response to any *other* mental fact that would also guarantee that one is in mental states that rationalize forming a belief in p. In effect, one would have a highly specialized disposition for this extremely specific form of rational reasoning; this disposition would be independent of any disposition that one had for other forms of rational reasoning.

I do not wish to deny that in rationally forming a belief in p, the reasoner may well be manifesting a highly specific disposition of this kind. However, manifesting such a highly specific disposition does not seem to be sufficient for rational reasoning. It seems intuitively possible that such a highly specific disposition could just be some non-rational compulsion (perhaps implanted into one's mind by a manipulative neuroscientist), unconnected with any more general ability for rational reasoning; and it seems doubtful whether manifesting a non-rational compulsion of this sort could really be a case of rational reasoning.[18] In short, rational reasoning must involve exercising some relatively *general* reasoning

---

[18] As I suggested in the previous chapter, this point may also explain what is wrong with Ned Block's (1978: 294–6) example (which later came to be known as the "Blockhead") of a machine that passes a "Turing Test" simply by means of a huge "look-up table".

ability. For this reason then, it seems to me that the account that I have proposed is preferable all the rivals that I have considered here.

8.5 NATURALISM AND THE CAUSAL EFFICACY OF THE NORMATIVE

According to my proposal, in rational reasoning, one's antecedent mental states cause one to form a new belief or intention precisely *in virtue of* their rationalizing that new belief or intention. In that sense, my proposal entails that the fact that one has come to be in mental states that *rationalize* forming that belief or intention is a *causally efficacious fact*:[19] it is precisely this fact that causes one to form the belief or intention in question. This fact is, broadly speaking, a *normative* fact about one's mental states. A set of mental states rationalizes a certain belief or intention just in case those mental states make it *rational* for the thinker to form that belief or intention; and as I argued in the previous chapter, 'rational' should be regarded as a normative concept.

So my proposal is committed to the causal efficacy of the normative. There was a well-known debate between Gilbert Harman (1977: ch. 1) and Nicholas Sturgeon (1985) about the claim that there are correct "moral explanations"—that is, causal explanations in which moral facts are cited to explain contingent non-moral facts. My proposal is committed to making an analogous claim about "normative explanations". But the moral is a species of the normative. So it seems, *prima facie*, that all the objections that philosophers have directed against the idea of moral explanations will apply equally to the normative explanations that my proposal is committed to.

One prominent argument against moral explanations proceeds roughly as follows. It seems intuitively clear that if there are any moral facts (facts of the kind that are stated by moral statements), then it is an essential feature of these facts that they *strongly supervene* on non-moral facts (facts of the kind that are stated by non-moral statements): if a moral fact holds in one case, it cannot fail to hold in a second case unless the second case differs from the first in non-moral facts as well. So, for every moral fact M, there is some non-moral fact N that is a *minimal non-disjunctive supervenience basis* for M. (For example, a minimal non-disjunctive supervenience basis for the fact that an act is wrong might be the fact that the act was a killing motivated primarily by racist hatred.) In the terms that I introduced in Chapter 6, a

---

[19] Steward (1997: 200) says: "I do not think we should speak of causally efficacious properties", on the grounds that this usage may "encourage us to misrepresent the role played by properties in causality". I do not think that speaking of "causally efficacious facts" need mislead us, so long as we recall that there need be no more to a fact's being causally efficacious than that the fact causes something—that is, the fact appears as an *explanans* in a correct causal explanation.

non-moral fact N that is such a minimal non-disjunctive supervenience basis for the moral fact M is a *"realization"* of M. Specifically, N is in effect what Sydney Shoemaker (2003: 265) has called a *total realization* of M; since N is a supervenience basis for M, it is metaphysically impossible for N to obtain without M's also obtaining. Even though this non-moral fact N is in this way sufficient for the moral fact M, it seems plausible that N is not *necessary* for M. This is because of the possibility of "multiple realization": the moral fact M would have obtained even if it had been realized in a different non-moral fact (such as the fact that the act was a killing motivated primarily by the desire to steal the victim's property), and the first non-moral fact N had never obtained at all. Thus, even if M is equivalent to a *disjunction* of non-moral facts of which N is one disjunct, it is not equivalent (let alone identical) to N itself.

Now, however, the question arises whether the alleged effects of a moral fact are really the effects of the moral fact or instead of some non-moral fact in which that moral fact is realized. The trouble is that, for every attempt to explain something by appealing to a moral fact, there is another explanation, which seems intuitively correct, that appeals not to the moral fact, but rather to some non-moral fact in which that moral fact is realized. So it is hard to see what causally explanatory role the moral fact might play.[20] It seems that a similar argument can be made against normative explanations of the sort that my proposal is committed to. So it may seem plausible that these normative explanations are undermined by the existence of correct explanations that appeal, not to any such normative facts, but solely to the non-normative facts in which those normative facts are realized.

Even though this argument against moral explanations has been widely discussed, it has not been widely noted how similar this argument is to what Jaegwon Kim (1998: 37–47) has called the "causal exclusion" argument against *mental* causation. According to this argument against moral explanations, moral and normative facts are not causally efficacious because their causal role is excluded by the non-moral, non-normative facts in which those moral facts are realized. According to Kim's "exclusion" argument, mental facts are not causally efficacious because their causal role is excluded by the non-mental (presumably, physical) facts in which those mental facts are realized; and again, the possibility of "multiple realization" seems to prevent us from identifying the mental fact with the non-mental fact in which the mental fact is realized.

[20] For arguments of this sort, see Warren Quinn (1994: essay 5), and Crispin Wright (1992: 195–6). Another sort of argument against moral explanations that is sometimes offered claims that if the moral fact did not obtain, but the non-moral facts in which that moral fact is realized did obtain, the effect in question would still have occurred. But as Sturgeon in effect points out (1985: 245–8), if the relevant non-moral fact is what Shoemaker calls the "total realization" of the moral fact, it is simply impossible for the non-moral fact to obtain without the moral fact's also obtaining. So this argument seems to have no force at all.

I shall not try to determine exactly which response to these arguments is correct. The main point that I shall argue for here is that whatever the correct response to Kim's exclusion argument turns out to be, it can be adapted to provide an answer to these arguments against moral or normative explanations. I shall try to make this point plausible by considering the response that Stephen Yablo (1992*a*, 1992*b*, 1997) has given to Kim's exclusion argument. Then I shall argue that a similar response can be given in defence of the causal efficacy of the moral and the normative.

Yablo's answer to Kim goes roughly as follows. Suppose that you are in a certain mental state M_1, which is realized in your being in a certain physical state P_1, and you then form a certain new mental state M_2 (realized in another physical state P_2). Now, it could well be that if you had not been in mental state M_1, then you would not have formed the new mental state M_2; whereas if you had not been in physical state P_1 but had still been in mental state M_1 (because M_1 was realized in a slightly different physical state instead of P_1), you would still have gone on to form the new mental state M_2 (even if M_2 would then have been realized in a slightly different physical state instead of P_2).

In this case, we have a reason for thinking that the antecedent mental state M_1 is *better placed* than the antecedent physical state P_1 to count as the cause of your new mental state M_2. Since the physical state P_1 is the "total realization" of the mental state M_1, M_1 is entailed by and in a sense contained in P_1. But the physical state P_1 contains not only the mental state M_1 but numerous other elements as well that are quite unnecessary to causing the new mental state M_2. In this way, M_1 is more *proportional* to the effect M_2 than P_1: M_1 is no less causally sufficient (given the relevant background circumstances) to bring about the effect M_2, and compared to P_1, it contains fewer irrelevant elements that could be stripped away without making it any less sufficient to produce the effect M_2. So long as there are no other reasons for thinking that the physical state P_1 rather than the mental state M_1 is the cause of the new mental state M_2, we may conclude that if either P_1 or M_1 is the cause of M_2, it is M_1 and not P_1.

A similar point can be made about moral facts. Let us take an example from Judith Thomson (Harman and Thomson 1996: 81–3). Suppose that Donald behaves rudely, where the rudeness of his behaviour is realized in the fact that he shouted "Boo!", very loudly, in the middle of a visiting speaker's talk, whereupon the other members of the audience become annoyed with Donald. As with the case of mental causation that we have just considered, it could well be that in this case, if Donald had been rude without shouting "Boo!"—say, by shouting "Moron!", or by holding up a big placard bearing the words "You, Sir, are an utter disgrace to the philosophical profession!"—the other members of the audience would still have been annoyed with him, whereas if he had not behaved rudely they would not have got annoyed with him. To put it in picturesque terms, the audience's annoyance follows his rudeness around, across all the relevant nearby possible worlds.[21] This is a reason for thinking that the fact that he behaved rudely is better placed than the fact that he shouted "Boo!" to count as the cause of the audience's annoyance.

Nonetheless, this case differs in a significant way from the case of mental causation. In the case of mental causation, there is some plausibility in denying that the antecedent physical state P_1 is the cause of the new mental state M_2 at all (at best, P_1 is the cause of the physical state P_2 in which the mental state M_2 is realized). But there is next to no plausibility in denying that the fact that Donald shouted "Boo!" caused the audience's annoyance. Moreover, even though the fact that he behaved rudely has an advantage over the fact that he shouted "Boo!" in being in this way more "proportional" to the effect of the audience's annoyance, it also has a certain disadvantage. It is hard to see what the fact of his rudeness could cause, except a certain narrow range of mental reactions, such as annoyance, or the belief that he is being rude. On the other hand, the fact of his shouting "Boo!" can have a much wider range of causal effects, including, for example, the dog's pricking up its ears, or the presence of a "Boo!" sound on a tape recording of the talk.[22] His shouting "Boo!" has a firm position in the larger causal order, and by seeing the audience's annoyance as caused by it, we can see their annoyance as part of that order. So both Donald's rudeness and his shouting "Boo!" have good claims to count as the cause of the audience's annoyance.

A plausible conclusion to draw here is that both of these facts cause the audience's annoyance, in slightly different ways. At one point, Yablo (1992*b*: 424) distinguishes between what he calls "world-driven" and "effect-driven" causes. The "effect-driven" cause contains as little as possible that is not causally necessary in order to bring about the effect, while the "world-driven" cause contains more elements and so reveals more about how the effect came about in the actual world.[23] We could employ this distinction here, saying that Donald's rudeness is

[21] This is not to say that the rudeness causes the annoyance in *all* possible worlds in which either the rudeness or the annoyance occurs. The rudeness and the annoyance are clearly "distinct existences": each of them could occur without the other. So there is no need to worry that the rudeness is a pseudo-cause like *the fact that the cause of the audience's annoyance occurred*.

[22] Compare Wright (1992: 197–8). This may be related to the claim that Yablo makes in his later work (2003), that one fact counts as better placed to cause a certain effect than another if the first fact is more "natural"—in the sense of 'natural' that is explained by Lewis (1999: 13–14). I am not sure whether the moral fact is less "natural" than the non-moral fact in which the moral fact is realized, but perhaps we can just define the "naturalness" of a fact in terms of what Wright would call the "width" of its "cosmological role"—i.e., the range and miscellaneousness of the fact's causal effects.

[23] In his later work (2003), Yablo drops this idea. Instead, he claims that whenever one of two candidates for the role of being a cause of a certain effect is strictly entailed by (and so weaker than) the other, the one that is the more "natural" of the two is better placed to be a cause. It is only if the two candidates are equally natural that we should favour the weaker candidate if it is in his sense more "proportional" to the effect. But it is not clear why the criterion of "naturalness" should have lexical priority over the criterion of "proportionality" in this way. If the two criteria both have some weight, then there can be cases in which both of the two candidates are equally well placed to count

the effect-driven cause of the audience's annoyance, while his shouting "Boo!" is the world-driven cause.

The same approach can be used to defend the causal efficacy of the normative. Suppose that I have come to be in mental states that rationalize my forming an intention to go to London, where this normative fact about me is realized in a purely mental fact about the specific type and content of my mental states—say, the fact that I wish to go to a concert (along with other suitable background beliefs and desires). It could well be that in this case, if I had had somewhat different mental states that also rationalized my forming an intention to go to London—say, a wish to go to a party, instead of a wish to go to a concert—I would still have formed an intention to go to London, whereas if I had not been in any mental states that rationalized my forming an intention to go to London, I would not have formed any intention to go to London. So we can say that the normative fact is the effect-driven cause of my forming the intention to go to London, while the purely mental fact about the specific type and content of my mental states is the world-driven cause of my forming that intention.

This distinction between effect-driven and world-driven causes helps to answer some other objections that have been raised against the idea of moral explanations. Some philosophers, such as Brian Leiter (2001), object that there is no clear case in which a moral fact provides the best explanation of a contingent non-moral fact. But to defend the claim that moral and normative facts can be causally efficacious, we do not need to find any cases in which these facts provide the *unique best* causal explanation. We need only find some cases in which they provide a *correct* causal explanation; it does not matter if there is also another equally good causal explanation that appeals to the world-driven cause (the specific type and content of the reasoner's antecedent mental states) rather than to the effect-driven cause (the fact that the reasoner was in antecedent mental states that rationalized forming the relevant belief or intention). The false assumption that to defend the causal efficacy of the normative, we need to find cases in which normative facts provide the unique best explanation has made it seem that correct normative explanations would be rare and exotic phenomena. But according to my proposal, correct normative explanations are ubiquitous: there is a correct normative explanation whenever anyone engages in rational reasoning of any kind. So there is nothing strange or exotic about such normative explanations.

It may be that with many philosophers, however, there are deeper motivations for thinking that normative facts just cannot be the kind of facts that cause anything. One such deeper motivation for doubting whether normative facts can be causally efficacious is a conception of causation that often goes along with *naturalism* in philosophy.

---

as causes. In that case, we should surely allow that they are both causes, and Yablo's old terminology remains useful to explain the difference between the two causes.

Naturalism is a world-view that gives a fundamental role to the sorts of truths that are sought by the natural sciences. But one of the most important features of modern natural science is its rejection of *teleological* explanations of the sort that were regarded as central by many ancient and medieval thinkers. The interpretation of these pre-modern teleological explanations is controversial; but according to one interpretation, all these explanations seek to explain a contingent event by showing what is *good* about that event. If this interpretation is correct, then on this pre-modern view, it is a basic feature of the natural world that many contingent events occur precisely because it is *good* for them to occur. The goodness of some possible event can make that event actually occur. The plants put out leaves because it is good for them to do so; the rain falls because it is good for it to help the plants to grow; the stars move in a circular course around the earth because it is good for them to have such a perfect and beautiful motion.[24]

In explaining why someone forms a certain belief by pointing to the fact that it was rational for her to form that belief, it seems that we are explaining why a certain contingent event occurs (her forming that belief) by appeal to a certain sort of goodness—specifically, rationality—that is exemplified by that event. So, why aren't these explanations a reversion to a sort of pre-modern teleology?[25] Surely naturalism implies that the basic causal truths about the world are the hard truths of physics, among which such teleological explanations are now believed to have no place at all.

We should, I think, concede that the sort of normative explanations that my proposal is committed to are teleological explanations, at least according to this interpretation of what teleological explanation involves. But nonetheless, there is no conflict with a modern naturalistic world-view. My proposal is quite compatible with the following claims. Such normative explanations are restricted to the domain of the mental (they have no place in natural sciences such as physics or biology). Moreover, normative explanations are true in virtue of ordinary causal relations between normative and mental facts. The normative fact is an *antecedent* fact—the fact that one is in antecedent mental states that rationalize forming the new belief or intention; so there is no problem with regarding this sort of causation as ordinary "efficient" causation, rather than some special kind of "backwards causation". Finally, these causal relations between normative and mental facts are themselves *realized in* physical causal relations between the physical realizations of those facts.

In this sense then, the normative could be causally efficacious even if naturalism is true. There only seems to be a conflict if one assumes that according to naturalism, all real causal relations are of the metaphysically fundamental kind

---

[24] This interpretation of teleological explanations is due to Bedau (1992).

[25] According to Hampton (1998: 109–14), "reasons explanations" *are* committed to the sort of teleology that is anathema to modern natural science.

that is investigated by physics; but there is no obvious reason to believe this. A plausible form of naturalism need only claim that all causal relations whatsoever are *realized* in causal relations of this fundamental kind; naturalism need not claim that all real causal relations are *identical* to relations of this fundamental kind.

8.6 CONCLUSION

In this chapter and in its predecessor, I have outlined the core of my metaphysical conception of the nature or essence of normative properties and relations. The essence of these properties is given by certain fundamental interconnections between normative properties, on the one hand, and intentional mental proper-ties, on the other. As I have argued, the precise nature of these interconnections implies that normative properties are both irreducible and causally efficacious.

As I suggested in the Introduction, this metaphysical conception can be viewed as a kind of Platonism about the normative. First, my conception implies that normative properties and normative facts are indispensably involved in any adequate account of the mind and of its characteristic causal processes. So, if we understand "reality" as Kit Fine (2001) has proposed, as whatever provides the fundamental metaphysical account or explanation of what is the case, then normative properties and normative facts are partially constitutive of reality. There is no accounting for these mental aspects of the world without mentioning normative properties and relations. Moreover, since these normative properties are irreducible, this fundamental metaphysical account will have to mention them *as such*: there is no way of mentioning these properties by referring merely to some complex arrangement of metaphysically more basic properties.

Finally, as I also suggested in the Introduction, the thesis that the intentional is normative is a way of cashing out Plato's image of the sun (*Republic* 507a–509c). We only count as having intelligence because we are capable of rational reasoning, and in rational reasoning we are directly sensitive to certain normative facts themselves. Intelligence necessarily involves sensitivity to these normative facts, which have their source in the necessary and eternal nature of the normative and mental properties, just as vision involves sensitivity to light, which has its source in the sun.

As we have seen in Part I of the book, this metaphysical conception does not prevent us from giving a credible semantic account of how the terms in our language and the concepts in our thoughts succeed in referring to these irreducible normative facts and properties. On the contrary, this metaphysical conception underwrites the sort of conceptual role semantics that seems to provide the best available account of the meaning and logic of our normative thought and discourse. I shall argue in Part III that it also provides a credible epistemological account of how we can know these normative facts, or at least achieve rational or justified beliefs in normative propositions.

As I have also explained, we can jettison the most burdensome of the antiquated baggage that has traditionally been associated with Platonism about the normative—namely, the full-strength pre-modern teleology, according to which it is a fundamental explanatory feature of the whole natural world, and not just the mental part of the world, that it is somehow drawn towards the right and the good. However, one further metaphysical hurdle remains to be overcome if we are to reconcile this Platonist metaphysical picture with a plausible form of naturalism about the world. This problem will be the topic of the following chapter; unfortunately, the solution to this problem will lead us deep into some thorny questions about the meaning and even the logic of the concept of metaphysical necessity.

9

Non-reductive Naturalism

9.1 NATURALISM AND IRREDUCIBILITY

In the previous chapter, I argued that the claim that normative facts are causally efficacious is quite consistent with a conception of causation according to which all causal relations are realized in causal relations between physical facts. In giving that argument, I assumed that naturalism entails that all contingent normative and mental facts are themselves realized in physical facts. However, I also argued earlier in the previous chapter that mental and normative facts and properties are irreducible. This creates a problem: if these mental and normative facts are irreducible, how can it be a universal feature of all contingent mental and normative facts that they are realized in physical facts? In this way, it may seem that my claim that mental and normative properties are irreducible is hard to reconcile with naturalism.

In the first two sections of this chapter, I shall try to give this problem a sharper formulation. Then, in later sections of this chapter, I shall give a solution to this problem: that is, I shall try to show how the thesis that mental and normative properties are irreducible can be reconciled with naturalism. I shall not attempt to argue in favour of naturalism. A great many philosophers are attracted to one form or another of naturalism (although it remains controversial exactly what the best formulation of naturalism is). My goal in this chapter is just to show that the thesis that mental and normative properties are irreducible is not in tension with naturalism. I shall do this by assuming, purely for the sake of argument, that naturalism is true; and then I shall show how certain apparently highly puzzling facts whose existence is entailed by naturalism can still be satisfactorily explained even if no reductive account of mental and normative properties is true.

Indeed, I shall deliberately assume a relatively strong form of naturalism. If the claim that mental and normative facts are irreducible is compatible with this relatively strong form of naturalism, then *a fortiori* it is compatible with all weaker forms of naturalism. Specifically, I shall assume the relatively strong form of naturalism entails that it is *necessary* that all contingent mental and normative facts are *realized* in *physical facts*. As I explained in Chapter 6, I am interpreting the term 'physical' in a broad sense: physical properties include all causally efficacious properties that are *non-mental*—in the sense that it is possible to give an account of the nature of these properties without referring to mental properties or relations—as well as all properties that can be constructed out of physical properties by means of operations like negation, conjunction, and so on.

When it is understood in this way, "naturalism" must be distinguished from the thesis that is sometimes called "ethical naturalism", which was famously attacked by G. E. Moore (1903: ch. 1)—namely, the thesis that ethical facts and properties are all *reducible* to facts and properties of the kind that form the "subject matter of the natural sciences". Now, Moore seems to have assumed that if any such reduction is true it would have to be some sort of conceptual truth.[1] My account of the nature of normative concepts certainly supports the claim that no such reduction is a conceptual truth. But it seems clear that Moore was wrong to assume that any such reduction would have to be a conceptual truth: many of the paradigm cases of successful reductions—such as the reduction of heat to molecular kinetic energy—are clearly not conceptual truths of any kind. Nonetheless, I have argued in the previous chapter that no such reductive form of naturalism is true. For this reason, I shall restrict my attention in this chapter to non-reductive forms of naturalism.

There is a further difference between the form of naturalism that I shall consider here and the thesis, which Moore attacked, according to which ethical properties are reducible to the "subject matter of the natural sciences". Philosophers who have debated this thesis have generally followed Moore in supposing that the relevant "natural sciences" include psychology, so that the set of facts and properties to which ethical facts and properties would be reducible if this thesis is true is usually assumed to include *mental* facts and properties. But I have defended a version of the doctrine that the intentional is normative: it is impossible to give an account of the nature of intentional mental properties and relations without mentioning normative properties and relations. So if "natural" properties are properties whose nature can be explained without mentioning normative properties, then mental properties are not natural properties in that sense.

The whole point of naturalism with respect to normative properties, I shall suppose, is to be a doctrine about how normative properties are related to properties at some ontologically more basic level. As I have argued, mental properties are not ontologically more basic than normative properties; so the only properties that are ontologically more basic than the normative properties are *physical* properties (in the broad sense in which I am using the term 'physical properties'). Thus, if my arguments are correct, naturalism will have to take the form of a kind of physicalism (at least on my broad interpretation of 'physical properties'). This is why the version of non-reductive naturalism that I shall

---

[1] For an illuminating discussion of the weaknesses of Moore's argument, see Kalderon (2004).

focus on here will be the version according to which all contingent mental and normative facts are realized in physical facts.

As I shall argue, the problem for non-reductive naturalism arises because naturalism entails the existence of a vast number of modal truths; these modal truths seem to cry out for explanation, but at first glance it is hard to see how these truths could all be satisfactorily explained unless some reductive account is true. The solution to the problem, I propose, involves relying on the idea that the explanations of these troublesome modal truths may themselves involve *contingent* truths. As we shall see, this idea will require rejecting *S5* as the appropriate logic for metaphysical modality. Many philosophers will think that rejecting *S5* is too high a price to pay for non-reductive naturalism. But I shall argue that it is not: *S5* should probably be rejected anyway.

9.2 A PROBLEM FOR NON-REDUCTIVE NATURALISM

In Chapter 6, I gave an account of what it is for the fact that an object x has property A to be "realized" by the fact that x has property B. According to this account, to say that the fact that x has A is "realized" in the fact that x has B is to say that it is an essential feature of property A that it strongly supervenes on properties of a certain kind, and B is the minimal non-disjunctive supervenience basis of this kind that is actually instantiated by x.[2] As I explained in the previous section, I am assuming that naturalism is the thesis that all contingent facts are realized in physical facts; and I am understanding the term 'physical property' broadly, so that physical properties include all causally relevant properties that are non-mental (in the sense that it is possible to give an account of their nature without mentioning mental properties or relations), as well as all properties that can be constructed out of physical properties by means of operations like negation, conjunction, and so on.

Thus, naturalism entails that for every individual x and mental property A, if x has property A, then the fact that x has property A is realized in the fact that x has some physical property B. If this is true, then it must be part of the nature or essence of mental properties that they strongly supervene on physical properties. For example, since being in pain is a mental property, naturalism entails that it

---

[2] Strictly, this is just an account of what it is for the *atomic* fact that x has property A to be realized in a fact about some corresponding B-property. There are various ways in which this account could be extended to an account of what it is for *any* fact involving property A to be realized in some corresponding fact about B-properties. The simplest way would just be to insist that since the A-properties are closed under logical operations like negation and conjunction and the like, every fact involving A-properties is logically equivalent to an atomic fact of this form: for example, the fact that it is not the case that x has property A is logically equivalent to the atomic fact that x has the property of not having A. (Actually, since I am something of an enthusiast for "free logic", I would prefer a slightly more complicated approach; but the issue is orthogonal to our present concerns.)

is part of the nature or essence of pain that it strongly supervenes on physical properties. As I explained in Chapter 6, strong supervenience is equivalent to the claim that whenever anything has a mental property (like being in pain), it also has some physical property that necessitates that mental property.

Thus, if naturalism is true, whenever an individual x is in pain, x has some physical property that necessitates pain. Suppose that one such property is physical property B. Then:

(1) Necessarily, for all individuals y, if y has physical property B, then y is in pain.

Facts like this proposition (1) are what Terence Horgan and Mark Timmons (1992*a*: 226) call "*specific* supervenience facts"—that is, facts about *exactly which* physical properties necessitate a particular mental property, like being in pain.

It seems that these "specific supervenience facts" cannot be *fundamental* modal truths that need no further explanation. There may be some plausibility in claiming that the *general* principle of supervenience is a fundamental modal truth, built into the constitutive essence of mental properties, and so requiring no further explanation. But this seems much less plausible in the case of the *specific* supervenience facts. The fact that pain is necessitated by *C-fibre firing* in particular (rather than, say, by *D-fibre firing*) surely cries out for further explanation.

The problem is that, at least to some extent, we have an intuitive idea of what is involved in the essence of pain, and of what is involved in the essence of C-fibre firing; and it seems clear that the truth of (1) *cannot* form part of the fundamental constitutive essence of pain, or part of the constitutive essence of C-fibre firing. But as I explained in Chapter 6, I am assuming that if any proposition p is a *fundamental* truth about metaphysical modality—that is, a truth that neither requires nor admits of any further explanation—then p must form part of the constitutive essence of some object or objects. So each of these specific supervenience facts, like (1), demands explanation.

Moreover, given plausible assumptions, there is an *enormous number* of such specific supervenience facts. Assuming that pain is "multiply realizable", there is simply no end of logically independent physical properties that could realize pain. Since a property cannot realize pain without necessitating pain, there is no end of physical properties that could necessitate pain. At least assuming $S5$ modal logic, it follows that there is no end of physical properties that actually necessitate pain. Taken together, then, these specific supervenience facts, like (1), seem to form a vast—presumably infinite—array of logically independent modal facts, all clamouring to be explained.

These troublesome specific supervenience facts could certainly all be explained on the basis of a reductive account of the property of being in pain. For example, according to functionalism (in its reductive form), it is an essential feature of the property of being in pain that it is necessarily equivalent to the "functional property" of having some physical property or other that plays a certain causal role (where this causal role can be specified in physical or topic-neutral terms). So, if a physical property B necessitates pain, B must also necessitate this functional property. In the broad sense that I am using here, this functional property counts as a physical property. So the fact that B necessitates this functional property is just a fact about the modal connections between physical properties; and as such it can presumably be explained on the basis of fundamental truths about the essences of these physical properties, in some way that naturalists should find quite unproblematic. (For example, suppose that the essence of B is given by a "real definition" according to which B is defined as the property of having firing C-fibres, while being "wired up" in the way that is characteristic of human beings, and inhabiting a world in which such-and-such fundamental physical properties are instantiated and governed by such-and-such physical laws. Then it will presumably just follow from this definition of B that, necessarily, anything with B has a physical property that plays the relevant causal role.) But then the fact that B necessitates this functional property, together with the functionalist thesis, that pain is necessarily equivalent to this functional property, implies that B necessitates pain; and this functionalist thesis, if it is a genuine reduction, is itself an essential truth about the nature of the property of being in pain. In this way, a reductive account of pain, together with other facts that can themselves be explained in a way that naturalists should find quite unproblematic, can explain why B necessitates pain.

Thus, a reductive account of pain could explain all these troublesome specific supervenience facts. On the other hand, it can be argued that there are formidable difficulties in seeing how any non-reductive approach could explain all these specific supervenience facts.

This point is akin to a famous argument that is due to Jaegwon Kim (1993: 151–2): if being in pain strongly supervenes on physical properties, nothing can be in pain without having some physical property that necessitates pain; so, Kim concludes, the property of being in pain is necessarily equivalent to the *disjunction* of all the physical properties that necessitate pain.

However, given the definition of "reduction" that I am working with, Kim's argument does not show that pain is reducible. To show this, one would have to show, not only that pain is necessarily equivalent to some physical property, but also that this equivalence is an *essential* truth about the nature of the property of being in pain. Still, there is a train of thought that may make it seem overwhelmingly plausible that if there is a way of explaining all these specific supervenience facts, there must be some such reductive account of pain.

Let us assume then that every single case in which a physical property necessitates pain can be explained. Now it may seem that the only way in which such a modal truth can be explained is if that modal truth logically follows from certain fundamental truths about the essences of certain objects or properties. So let us assume (just for the sake of argument—we will question this supposition later) that all these specific supervenience facts can be explained in this way, by being logically derived from such fundamental truths about the essences of things.

How could such fundamental truths about the essences of things logically imply that a certain physical property necessitates pain? If these fundamental truths can provide this explanation, then they must surely include truths about the essential nature of pain, and perhaps also truths about the essential nature of the relevant physical properties. It is hard to see how an essential truth about the nature of pain can provide such an explanation unless the truth takes the form of a principle to the effect that every physical property that meets a certain physical condition must necessitate pain. Call any such condition a "pain-necessitating condition". Many of these explanations would also have to involve some essential truths about the nature of the relevant physical properties, in order to explain why the physical property in question meets the relevant pain-necessitating condition. But the important point is this: if every single case in which a physical property necessitates pain can be explained in this way, then no physical property can necessitate pain unless it meets one of the pain-necessitating conditions that are specified in these essential truths about the nature of pain.[3]

According to strong supervenience, nothing can be in pain unless it has some physical property that necessitates pain. So, assuming that every case in which a physical property necessitates pain can be explained in this way, nothing can be in pain unless it has some physical property that meets one of these pain-necessitating conditions. And it is obviously necessary that everything that has a physical property that meets one of these pain-necessitating conditions is in pain. So having a physical property that meets one of these pain-necessitating conditions is necessary and sufficient for being in pain. Moreover, this conclusion is entailed by the following premises: the fundamental truths that specify these pain-necessitating conditions, strong supervenience, and the assumption that every case in which a physical property necessitates pain can be explained in this way. It seems plausible that if these assumptions are true at all, then they must be essential truths about the nature of pain.

Thus, the essential truths about the nature of pain imply a list of physical pain-necessitating conditions, and they also imply that something is in pain if, and only if, it has the complex physical property of having some physical property that meets one of these physical conditions. In effect, these fundamental essential

---

[3] Why must each of these pain-necessitating conditions be a *physical* condition? Well, suppose that it were a mental condition instead. If (as we are currently assuming, for the sake of argument) all the truths involved in these explanations are essential truths about the nature of things, then these truths are presumably necessary rather than contingent. So it must be *necessary* that the physical property in question meets this mental condition. That is, it is necessary that anything having this physical property has a property that meets this mental condition. But this is precisely the sort of specific physical-to-mental modal connection that we are trying to explain. So the original problem is solved only if the relevant condition is a physical condition.

truths about pain imply that pain is necessarily equivalent to this complex physical property. That is, these fundamental essential truths provide a physical reduction of pain. So, if every case in which a physical property necessitates pain can be explained purely on the basis of fundamental truths about the essences of things, it seems extraordinarily hard to see how pain could fail to be reducible.

Now, the argument that I have just given relies only on the assumption that the mental properties strongly supervene on physical properties, along with the assumption (which I will soon call into question) that modal truths of the form 'It is metaphysically necessary that p' must all be capable of being explained by being derived from fundamental truths concerning the essences of things. This suggests that this argument should be capable of being generalized to all other cases of strong supervenience.

In particular, I argued in Chapter 6 that normative properties supervene on non-normative properties. So one might think that an analogous argument will support the conclusion that it follows from fundamental truths about the essence of normative properties that normative properties are equivalent to non-normative properties. For example, such a necessary equivalence might take the form: 'For all agents x, times t, and propositions p, it is rational for x to believe p at t if and only if $A(x, t, p)$'—where the right-hand side of this biconditional does not contain any normative terms.

However, there is no reason to think that this necessary equivalence will constitute a *reduction* of the normative property in question. The cases that make it intuitively plausible that normative properties supervene on non-normative properties are cases in which the non-normative properties in question explicitly include *mental* properties. For example, it is indeed plausible that if it is rational for x to believe p at t, then it is impossible for there to be any other thinker y such that x and y do not differ in their mental properties in any way, but it is not rational for y to believe p at t. So this argument will at most support the conclusion that the fundamental essential truths about the relevant normative property entail that the normative property is necessarily equivalent to a non-normative property that can be defined in partly psychological terms.

However, given that the intentional mental properties are essentially normative in the way that I have argued in Chapter 7, no principle according to which a normative property is necessarily equivalent to a property that is defined in partly *psychological* terms can count as a *reduction* of the normative property. A reduction would have to give an account of what it is for something to have the normative property in terms of ontologically more basic properties. But mental properties are not ontologically more basic than normative properties. So this argument does not put any pressure on the idea that normative properties are irreducible.[4] On the other hand, if it is true that mental and normative facts strongly supervene on *physical* facts, then, given that physical facts are

---

[4] For a slightly fuller treatment of this point, see my earlier paper (Wedgwood 1999*b*).

by definition facts whose nature can be explained in non-mental terms, the physicalist argument given earlier in this section does seem to put pressure on my earlier conclusion that mental and normative facts are irreducible. For this reason, I shall focus on this physicalist argument for the remainder of this chapter.

9.3 A SOLUTION TO THE PROBLEM

This argument for the conclusion that these specific supervenience facts can only be explained on the basis of a reductive account of the nature of pain depends crucially on the assumption that every one of these troublesome specific supervenience facts can be explained by being logically derived from fundamental truths about the essences of things. This suggests that the best way to avoid this conclusion is by rejecting that assumption—that is, to insist that there is some alternative way of explaining these troublesome specific supervenience facts that does not involve logically deriving them from fundamental truths about the essences of things.

However, as I explained in Chapter 6, I am assuming that all modal truths of the form 'It is metaphysically necessary that *p*' must be explained, either directly or indirectly, by these fundamental truths about the essences of things. So if the fact that this physical property necessitates pain cannot be explained solely on the basis of such fundamental essential truths, it must be *indirectly* explained by such fundamental essential truths. That is, it must be explained by some such fundamental essential truths, *together with* some other wholly non-modal truths.

What might these other non-modal truths be? Might they themselves be necessary truths? Non-modal truths can certainly be necessary truths. Modal truths (such as 'It is necessary that $2 + 2 = 4$') themselves involve modal operators, whereas some necessary truths (such as '$2 + 2 = 4$') may be non-modal truths that do not involve any modal operators at all. But if the non-modal truth that features in the explanation of a modal truth is itself a necessary truth, it would seem immediately to raise the further question of *why* this non-modal truth is necessary. If the reason why this non-modal truth is necessary is that it follows directly from fundamental truths about the essences of things, then it would also seem that these fundamental truths about the essences of things explain this non-modal truth itself (as well as why that truth is necessary). In that case, then, we would not have hit upon a case where there is a modal truth that cannot be explained solely on the basis of these fundamental truths about the essences of things.

So, I shall assume that if we want to find a case where a modal truth is explained not solely by fundamental truths about the essences of things, but also in part by some purely non-modal truths, it will be more promising to suppose that the non-modal truths in question are metaphysically *contingent* rather than metaphysically necessary.[5] In the rest of this section, I shall attempt to outline an explanation of this kind.

The problem is to explain modal facts of the following form:

(1) Necessarily, for all individuals y, if y has physical property B, then y is in pain.

I shall consider the prospect of explaining such facts on the basis of contingent facts about which physical properties are, as I shall put it, "regularly co-instantiated" with pain. As I shall use this term, to say that a physical property B is "regularly co-instantiated" with pain is to say that (i) there are cases in which a creature simultaneously has both physical property B and the property of being in pain, and (ii) it is a non-accidental regularity that whenever a creature has physical property B it simultaneously has the property of being in pain.[6] So, for example, one contingent fact of this sort, which might form part of the explanation of some specific supervenience fact such as (1), is the following:

(2) The property of having firing C-fibres, while being "wired up" in the way that is typical of human beings, is regularly co-instantiated with pain.

If a physical property B is regularly co-instantiated with pain, then it must be a non-accidental regularity that whenever a creature has physical property B it simultaneously has the property of being in pain. The idea of such non-accidental regularities linking physical properties with pain is controversial. Such regularities may seem to be what have been called "psycho-physical laws". Some philosophers suppose that it is only because there are no psycho-physical laws that we have reason to deny that mental properties are physically reducible.[7] However, as I shall argue here, even if we assume that these psycho-physical regularities are "laws" in the strict sense of the term, the existence of these regularities does *not* commit us to the physical reducibility of mental properties: it is compatible with

---

[5] If this non-modal truth is contingent, why isn't there a problem about *why* it is *contingent* (just as there is a problem about why it is necessary, if it is necessary)? But contingency is in a way the default status for propositions. A proposition is contingent so long as no fundamental truth about the essences of things (in conjunction with other non-modal truths) implies that there is anything impossible about either the proposition or its negation.

[6] In my first attempt (Wedgwood 2000) at developing this approach to explaining truths like (1), I appealed to a slightly different sort of fact, instead of the fact that physical property B is "regularly co-instantiated" with pain. I am indebted to Kit Fine for pointing out some serious grounds for doubt about whether facts of the sort that I originally appealed to really are contingent (as opposed to necessary).

[7] Donald Davidson (1970) is often interpreted as holding this view. Other philosophers, such as Crane (1993), have argued that physicalism is incompatible with the existence of contingent psycho-physical laws. This is not true when 'physicalism' is understood as I am understanding it, since it could be that even these psycho-physical laws are *realized* in some physical facts. However, the point is essentially otiose here, since I am not committed to saying that these psycho-physical laws are contingent. Indeed, I am inclined to regard it as plausible that all laws of nature are in fact necessary rather than contingent. (For a defence of such necessitarianism about laws, see Bird 2005.)

the existence of these regularities that there is *no* physical property to which any mental property is necessarily equivalent. So I see nothing wrong with basing an explanation of a specific supervenience fact, like (1), on some contingent fact such as (2).[8]

Suppose that there is a fundamental essential truth about the nature of pain that requires that (i) every instance of pain must also have some physical property that is regularly co-instantiated with pain, and (ii) if a physical property is regularly co-instantiated with pain, then in all possible worlds in which the same fundamental physical properties are instantiated as in the actual world, anything that has that physical property is also in pain. If we say that any world in which the same fundamental physical properties are instantiated as in w is a world that is "physically similar to w", then we can state this fundamental essential truth about pain as follows:

(3) For all possible worlds v, and all individuals x, if x is in pain in v, then for some physical property B_1, x has B_1 in v, and B_1 is regularly co-instantiated with pain in v, and, for all physical properties B_2, if B_2 is regularly co-instantiated with pain in v, then for all worlds w that are possible relative to v, and physically similar to v, and for all individuals y, if y has B_2 in w, y is also in pain in w.

(3) guarantees that in every possible world, every instance of pain falls under some non-accidental regularity that links some physical property with pain, such that in all worlds that are physically similar to that world, anything that has that physical property is in pain. In this way, (3) provides an explanation for the general supervenience fact that the property of being in pain supervenes on physical properties.

Moreover, together with contingent facts like (2), (3) can explain why certain specific physical properties necessitate pain. Suppose that an individual x is in pain in the actual world. By (3), x has some physical property B_1 that is regularly co-instantiated with pain in the actual world, and for all physical properties B_2, if B_2 is regularly co-instantiated with pain in the actual world, then in any world that is physically similar to the actual world, anything that has B_2 is also in pain. Now, suppose that (2) is true in the actual world: that is, the property of having firing C-fibres while being "wired up" in the relevant way is regularly co-instantiated with pain. Then it must also hold in all actually possible worlds that are physically similar to the actual world that anything that has the property of having firing C-fibres while being "wired up" in this way is in pain. So, the complex physical property of having firing C-fibres, while being wired

---

[8] Some physicalists (for example Horgan 1993: 578–9) insist that all modal facts like (1) must be explained on the basis of *purely physical facts*. But it is hard to see what (except a reductionist form of physicalism) could justify this demand. So even though (2) is not a purely physical fact, it seems to me perfectly acceptable as part of the explanation of the troublesome modal fact (1).

up in this way *and* inhabiting a world that is physically similar to the actual world, necessitates pain. In this way, we can explain why this complex physical property, and all other properties that necessitate this complex physical property, necessitate pain.

According to this approach, we explain why this physical property necessitates pain by appealing to (2), the fact that a certain physical property is regularly co-instantiated with pain in the actual world, and to (3), which implies that if any physical property is regularly co-instantiated with pain in the actual world, then in all actually possible worlds that are physically similar to the actual world, anything that has that physical property is also in pain. This approach provides no explanation whatsoever of (2), the fact that this physical property is regularly co-instantiated with pain in the actual world. On the contrary, this fact is taken as basic. This approach aims only to explain *modal* facts, such as the fact that the complex property of having this physical property while inhabiting a world that is physically similar to the actual world *necessitates* being in pain.

Clearly, we can generalize this approach for every physical property that is regularly co-instantiated with pain in the actual world. Thus, (3) will allow us to turn every claim about how a physical property B is regularly co-instantiated with pain into a corresponding claim to the effect that the property of having B while inhabiting a world that is physically similar to the actual world necessitates pain. Moreover, (3) guarantees that every actual instance of pain has a physical property that is regularly co-instantiated with pain. Thus, for every actual instance of pain, this approach allows us, in principle, (i) to identify a physical property of that instance of pain, such that that physical property necessitates pain, and (ii) to explain why that physical property necessitates pain. This makes it plausible that this approach will be able to explain every single case in which a physical property of some actual instance of pain necessitates pain.

9.4 AN OBJECTION TO THIS SOLUTION

According to this approach, these troublesome specific supervenience facts, like (1), are explained on the basis of (3), along with contingent truths about the actual world, like (2). For this reason, this approach is strictly limited to what can be explained on the basis of such *contingent* truths about *the actual world*.

Presumably, there could be pain in some possible world w_1 that is not in any way "physically similar" to the actual world—that is, a world in which radically different fundamental physical properties are instantiated from those of the actual world. (3) implies that in all worlds w_2 that are physically similar to w_1, anything that has the same physical properties as one of w_1's instances of pain will also be in pain in w_2. But neither (3) nor any of the contingent facts about the actual world tells us anything about which physical properties are regularly co-instantiated with pain in w_1. So this approach gives us no way, even in principle, to tell which physical properties necessitate pain in w_1.

This might seem a fatal problem with this approach. I am assuming that a naturalist conception of the world entails that mental and normative facts are realized in and so strongly supervene on physical facts. As I explained in Chapter 6 above, we may formulate strong supervenience as follows:

> (SS) For all A-properties A^*, all possible worlds w, and all individuals x, if x has A^* in w, then for some B-property B^*, x has B^* in w, and, for all worlds v that are possible relative to w, and all individuals y, if y has B^* in v, y also has A^* in v.

Most philosophers believe that strong supervenience entails *global* supervenience, which we may formulate as follows:[9]

> (GS$_1$) For any two possible worlds w_1 and w_2, if w_1 and w_2 are indiscernible with respect to B-properties then they are indiscernible with respect to A-properties as well.

Suppose—just for the sake of argument—that strong supervenience does indeed entail global supervenience. Now, imagine a maximally specific physical proposition p^*, such that any two worlds at which p^* is true are physically indiscernible. Global supervenience implies that there cannot be two possible worlds w_1 and w_2 at which p^* is true, such that in w_1 something is in pain, while in w_2 nothing is in pain. Either all possible worlds in which p^* is true are worlds in which something is in pain, or they are all worlds in which nothing is in pain. That is, one of the following two propositions is true, either

> (4) Necessarily, if p^* is true, then something is in pain

or

> (5) Necessarily, if p^* is true, then nothing is in pain.

If there is a possible world at which p^* is true, it is impossible for *both* these propositions to be true. So, which of these two propositions is true?

If all worlds at which p^* is true are physically quite dissimilar from the actual world, then neither (3) nor any of the contingent facts about the actual world can tell us anything about which of these two propositions, (4) or (5), is true. If the only way to explain specific supervenience facts like (1) is on the basis of (3) and contingent facts about the actual world like (2), then it seems that either (4) or (5) is a fact of this kind that defies explanation altogether. But as I have argued, facts of this kind cry out to be explained.[10]

---

[9] For a prominent example of a philosopher who argues that global supervenience follows from strong supervenience, see Kim (1993: 69 and 82).

[10] This objection cannot be answered by pointing out that (3) does at least guarantee that, if p^* were true and something were in pain, then there *would* be an explanation of why (4) was true. The

A parallel argument can be given for *every* maximally specific physical proposition that is true only at worlds that are physically dissimilar from the actual world. So it seems that there is a vast—indeed infinite—number of specific supervenience facts, like (4) or (5), that this approach cannot explain. In the end, it may seem, the approach that I have proposed still leaves us with a vast chaotic jumble of modal facts, all clamouring to be explained.

9.5 A POSSIBLE REBUTTAL: REJECTING $S5$

In fact, this objection is invalid in all relevant modal logics weaker than $S5$.[11] Most philosophers believe that $S5$ is the appropriate logic for metaphysical modality; but some philosophers (for example, Quinn 1982, Salmon 1984 and 1989, and Peacocke 1997: 567–8) suspect quite seriously that this may not be case.

This objection depends on global supervenience—or, more precisely, on the specific formulation of global supervenience that I gave above. Strong supervenience does indeed entail this version of global supervenience in $S5$. But in all relevant modal logics weaker than $S5$ this entailment does not hold. The argument from strong supervenience to this version of global supervenience crucially involves the following step, from 'In possible world w, it would be necessary that anything that has B^* must also have A', to 'It is *actually* necessary that anything that has B^* must also have A'. This step is invalid in all relevant modal logics weaker than $S5$. The fact that a proposition *would* be necessary, in some non-actual possible world, does not imply that it *is* necessary in the actual world. Except in $S5$, 'Possibly necessarily p' does not imply 'Necessarily p'. In general, so long as we do not assume that the relation of "accessibility" or relative possibility between worlds is an equivalence relation (that is, reflexive, symmetric, and transitive), it is quite straightforward to construct models in which strong supervenience is true but global supervenience is false.[12]

---

fact that there *would be* an explanation for (4) in some non-actual possible world does not imply that there *is* an explanation in the actual world. This version of global supervenience implies that either (4) or (5) must be true *simpliciter*—that is, *actually* true; and any explanation of an actual truth must itself consist of actual truths. The explanations outlined in Section 9.3 above appeal only to (3) and to *actual* contingent facts like (2); and if worlds in which p^* is true are physically quite dissimilar from the actual world, such truths could not possibly explain either (4) or (5).

[11] By a "relevant modal logic", I mean a KT logic—a logic in which necessity implies truth, every tautology is necessary, and the logical consequences of any set of necessary truths are themselves necessary.

[12] Here is such a model. (For a slightly fuller description of this model, see the appendix to an earlier paper of mine (Wedgwood 2000).) To keep things simple, suppose that there is just one primitive A-property, A^*, and just one primitive B-property, B^*. Assuming that the A-properties and the B-properties are both closed under Boolean operations, there will be other A-properties and B-properties as well. However, the only others we need consider are the *negations* of these

Consider again the maximally specific physical proposition p^*; any two worlds at which p^* is true are physically indiscernible. Strong supervenience does indeed imply that, if there is a possible world w_1 in which p^* is true and something is in pain, it is necessary *in w_1* that if p^* is true then something is in pain; and it also implies that, if there is a possible world w_2 in which p^* is true and nothing is in pain, it is necessary *in w_2* that if p^* is true then nothing is in pain. But unless S5 logic is sound in all cases, it does not imply that it is necessary *in the actual world* either that if p^* is true then something is in pain, or that if p^* is true then nothing is in pain. It may be then that it is *not* actually necessary either that if p^* is true then something is in pain, or that if p^* is true then nothing is in pain.

Let us return to our troublesome pair:

(4) Necessarily, if p^* is true, then something is in pain

and

(5) Necessarily, if p^* is true, then nothing is in pain.

As I have just argued, if S5 fails, it is compatible with strong supervenience that both (4) and (5) are actually false. Strong supervenience entails that (4) would be true if p^* were true and something were in pain, and it also entails that (5) would be true if p^* were true and nothing were in pain. But it does not entail that either (4) or (5) is *actually* true. So it is hardly an objection to this approach that it does not explain which of the two is true!

More generally, our problem has been to explain truths of the following form:

(1) Necessarily, for all individuals y, if y has physical property B, y is in pain.

If the appropriate logic is weaker than S5, then we need not accept that there are *any* truths of this form that cannot be explained on the basis of (3), together with contingent facts about the actual world like (2). Instead of forming an infinite jumble of unexplained logically independent modal truths, all such truths can be explained, on the basis of one fundamental modal truth (3), together with these contingent facts about which physical properties are regularly co-instantiated with pain in the actual world.

properties—the property of not having A^* and the property of not having B^*. (Since there is only one primitive A-property, the only A-properties not equivalent either to A^* or to its negation are either trivial or contradictory.)

For simplicity again, let the domain of the model consist of exactly three worlds—the actual world, w^*, and two other worlds, w_1 and w_2. Let the domain of each world consist of exactly one individual—in each case, the very same individual x. Suppose that, in the actual world w^*, x has the property of not having A^*, and also has the property of not having B^*. In w_1, x has both A^* and B^*. In w_2, on the other hand, x has B^* but not A^*. Now suppose that w_1 and w_2 are both actually possible (that is, they are both "accessible" from the actual world w^*); but w_1 is not possible at w_2, and w_2 is not possible at w_1 (that is, w_1 and w_2 are "mutually inaccessible"). It does not matter what we suppose about whether or not w^* is accessible from w_1 and from w_2. In this model, (SS) is true, but (GS_1) is false. Moreover, the conclusion of Kim's argument is also false: the strongly supervenient property A^* is *not* equivalent to the disjunction of the B-properties that necessitate it.

Of course, there will be many modal truths of other forms, which cannot be explained in this way: for example,

(6) Possibly: necessarily, if physical proposition p^* is true, then something is in pain.

But except in S5, truths of *this* form do not entail anything of the form of (1). Given what I said in Chapter 6, it is natural to assume that truths in which 'Possibly' has largest scope can be explained simply on the basis of the principle that *every* proposition is possible unless some fundamental truth about the essences of things (perhaps along with other true premises) entails that it is impossible.[13] If nothing in the essences of pain and of the various physical properties and relations mentioned in p^*, even in conjunction with any of the contingent truths about the actual world, entails that (4) is impossible, then that would explain why (6) is true. Moreover, we could give a precisely analogous explanation for the following as well:

(7) Possibly: necessarily, if physical proposition p^* is true, then nothing is in pain.

So, if this approach is correct, then we have no reason to recognize the existence of any modal truths that this approach cannot explain.

If there are no truths like (1) that cannot be explained on the basis of (3) and contingent facts about the actual world like (2), then (since the worlds at which p^* is true are radically physically dissimilar from the actual world) both (4) and (5) are indeed actually false. It is not actually necessary *either* that if p^* is true then something is in pain, *or* that if p^* is true then nothing is in pain. Some possible worlds in which p^* is true contain pain, and other such worlds do not. So (since *ex hypothesi* all worlds at which p^* is true are physically indiscernible), there are physically indiscernible worlds that are mentally discernible. That is, the formulation of global supervenience given above (GS_1) is false. But how can one reject global supervenience and still be a naturalist?

There are two reasons why the approach that I have proposed is still naturalist even though it rejects (this formulation of) global supervenience. First, given that there is pain in the actual world, (3) implies that only possible worlds that are physically quite dissimilar from the actual world can be physically indiscernible from each other but discernible with respect to pain: among all possible worlds that are physically similar to the actual world, physical indiscernibility implies indiscernibility with respect to pain. Secondly, (3) implies that each of these two worlds—the world in which p^* is true and nothing is in pain, and the world in which p^* is true and something is in pain—is *impossible relative to the other*. This

---

[13] In the modal logic B, 'Possibly necessarily p' implies p. So in B, (4) implies 'If physical proposition p^* is true, then something is in pain'. But that is true—vacuously true—since *ex hypothesi* its antecedent 'p^* is true' is not true (that is, not true at the actual world).

shows that there is a slightly different formulation of global supervenience that *is* entailed by strong supervenience. This different formulation is as follows:

(GS$_2$) For any possible world w_1, there is no world w_2 *possible relative to* w_1 such that w_2 is mentally discernible from w_1 but not physically discernible from w_1.

So this objection to the non-reductive approach that we are considering fails if the appropriate modal logic is weaker than *S5*. But wouldn't rejecting *S5* just be totally *ad hoc*?

Intuitively, the *S5* axiom says that the modal status of a proposition is never a merely contingent matter: if a proposition is possible, it is necessarily possible; and if a proposition is impossible, it is necessarily impossible. Contingent facts cannot make any difference to which propositions are possible and which are not.

According to the non-reductive approach that I have been considering, contingent facts form an indispensable part of the explanation of these troublesome specific supervenience facts. If there are modal facts that can only be explained on the basis of contingent facts in this way, then it seems plausible that these modal facts *depend* on contingent facts, in the sense that different modal facts would have obtained, if the contingent facts had been different. But then contingent facts *could* make a difference to which propositions are possible and which are not; there may be some propositions that are actually possible, but would not have been possible if different contingent facts had obtained. Clearly it is not simply *ad hoc* for a proponent of this sort of explanation to reject *S5*. The rejection of *S5* is directly supported by the central idea of this approach.

9.6 IS REJECTING *S5* TOO HIGH A PRICE TO PAY?

Even if it is not *ad hoc* for this approach to reject *S5*, however, rejecting *S5* may be too high a price to pay for non-reductive naturalism. It might just be intrinsically incredible to suppose that *S5* fails—that is, to suppose that some instances of the *S5* axiom could be false. Then my arguments would just be a *reductio ad absurdum* of non-reductive naturalism. So, is it intrinsically incredible to suppose that *S5* fails?

There is one approach to modal concepts that supports the view that the *S5* axiom is a *conceptual truth*.[14] According to this approach, the fundamental principles of modal logic are the following *non-circular definitions* of the modal concepts *possible* and *necessary*, in terms of quantification over worlds: (i) it is necessary that p is the case if and only if p is the case at all worlds, and (ii) it is possible that p is the case if and only if p is the case at some world. It does not

---

[14] For examples of this approach, see Lewis (1986) and Stalnaker (1984).

matter here how exactly worlds are understood: they may be concrete, as David Lewis believes, or they may be abstract entities of some kind. All that matters here is that, according to this approach, the concepts of a *world*, and of something's *being the case at a world*, are prior to — that is, intelligible independently of — the modal concepts *possible* and *necessary*.

According to this approach, modal claims are really only abbreviations of statements about what worlds there are, and about what is the case at those worlds. In principle, then, these statements about what worlds there are, and about what is the case at what worlds, could all be couched in entirely *non-modal* terms. Thus, a complete specification of what is the case at a given world need not include any modal terms, such as 'necessary' or 'possible'; and all the differences that there are between worlds can also be expressed in entirely non-modal terms. So, consider a proposition p that itself quantifies over worlds. According to this approach, it seems that if p is true at any world, it must be true at *all* worlds. According to this approach, as we have seen, there can be no differences between worlds that cannot be expressed in non-modal terms; and it seems that non-modal differences between worlds cannot make a difference to whether or not p is true at those worlds. For example, suppose that the proposition p is the proposition that there is some world at which q is the case. If p is true at any world, it is true at all worlds; and so in particular, if p is true at the actual world — that is, true *simpliciter* — it is true at all worlds. So, if there is a world at which q is the case, it must be true at all worlds that there is a world at which q is the case. But then the S5 axiom must be valid: 'Possibly p' implies 'Necessarily possibly p'.

Although some philosophers take this approach to modal concepts, many philosophers (for example, Forbes 1985: 89–95, and Rosen 1990) reject this approach. In Chapter 6 (Section 6.3), I also proposed a quite different conception of metaphysical necessity and of possible worlds. Specifically, I proposed that the notion of metaphysical necessity is ultimately a primitive metaphysical notion, although it has tight conceptual connections with the notion of essence, with other modal notions, and with the logic of counterfactuals.

Even though I did not support the claim that the notion of metaphysical necessity can be *defined* in terms of the notion of possible worlds, I did not reject the idea of possible worlds altogether. On the contrary, I proposed that possible worlds could be identified with *maximal consistent sets of propositions*. As I pointed out in Chapter 6 (Section 6.3), there is no reason why these sets of propositions should not include *modal* propositions, including propositions about which propositions are possible and which are not.

In effect, then, there is nothing conceptually absurd in the idea that some possible worlds may differ from the actual world with respect to which propositions are possible at those worlds. For example, it may be the case that at the actual world w^* a proposition p is possible, but at some other possible world w_1, p is impossible. In this case, we may say that a world w_2 at which p is the case is *actually* possible—that is, such a world w_2 is possible relative to the actual world w^*—but from the standpoint of w_1 such a world is not possible—that is, such a world w_2 is not possible relative to w_1.

As I explained in Chapter 6, this alternative approach demands an alternative interpretation of the principle that a proposition is necessary if and only if it is the case at all possible worlds. According to this alternative interpretation, a proposition p is necessary *at a world w* if and only if p is the case at all worlds that are *possible relative to w*. As we have seen, there is nothing conceptually absurd in the idea that, if w_1 is a possible world distinct from the actual world w^*, it may be the case at w^* that there is a possible world w_2 at which p is the case, but not the case at w_1 that there is any such possible world. But then the proposition p would be actually possible, but not necessarily possible—which would be a counter-instance to the S5 axiom.[15]

Thus, so long as we do not believe that the modal notions of *possible* and *necessary* can be defined in terms of conceptually prior notions of a *world* and of something's *being the case at a world*, there is nothing conceptually absurd in the idea that some instances of the S5 axiom could be false.

Even if the idea that some instances of the S5 axiom are false is not obviously incompatible with obvious conceptual truths, one might still wonder whether we can really make sense of this idea. If the S5 axiom fails, then there is a distinction that can be drawn between (i) those propositions that are not merely possible but also *necessarily* possible, and (ii) those propositions that are possible but only *contingently* so. But do we really have any grasp of what this distinction comes to?

It seems to me that we do have a grasp of this distinction. As I explained in Chapter 6, metaphysical necessities form a set of truths such that all members of this set would still be true no matter what else (consistent with this set) were the case. That is, the set of metaphysical necessities is "counterfactually stable" with respect to all hypotheses that are consistent with the set. So suppose that p_1 is not only possible but also necessarily possible, whereas p_2 is possible but only contingently so. Then there is *no* metaphysically possible proposition q such that the counterfactual 'If q were the case, then p_1 would not have been possible' is true; but there *is* some metaphysically possible proposition q such that the counterfactual 'If q were the case, then p_2 would not have been possible' is true.

We can illustrate this point with the case that I considered in this chapter, concerning the maximally detailed physical proposition p^*, such that all worlds at which p^* is true are (i) physically indiscernible from each other, and (ii) physically quite dissimilar from the actual world. Then I claim the proposition 'p^* is true and something is in pain' is possible, but not necessarily possible. The

---

[15] These points can be easily adapted to show that there is nothing conceptually incoherent in the idea that some instances of the S4 axiom, or even the B axiom, could also be false. Rejecting S4 requires the idea of "impossible worlds"—worlds that are not actually possible, but are possible at some non-actual possible world; rejecting B requires the idea that there is some actually possible world at which the actual world is not possible (compare Salmon 1984 and 1989).

fact that this proposition is not necessarily possible is revealed by the fact that the following counterfactual is true: 'If p^* were true and nothing were in pain, then it would not even have been possible for p^* to have been true and something to have been in pain'. (By contrast, take some proposition that is not just possible but necessarily possible, such as 'Something exists'. Then for *every* metaphysically possible proposition q, the following counterfactual will be *false*: 'If q were true, then it would be impossible for anything to exist'.) Thus, the notion of what is possible and the notion of what is necessarily possible will behave quite differently in such counterfactual contexts. It is by latching onto this difference between the two notions that we can grasp the distinction between them.

Still, even if the *S*5 axiom is not a conceptual truth, it may seem a highly plausible metaphysical principle. It may just seem hard to see how it could be a *contingent* matter that a certain state of affairs is *metaphysically possible*. How could the *modal* truth, that a certain state of affairs is metaphysically possible, depend on any contingent facts? This problem may seem especially hard if we accept the suggestion that I made in Chapter 6, that such modal truths should all be explained, as Kit Fine has urged, on the basis of fundamental truths about the essences of things. How can these fundamental truths about the essences of things explain why something is necessary or possible, but only contingently so?

According to Fine's conception, these fundamental truths about the constitutive essences of things explain all the modal truths about what is metaphysically necessary and what is not, because according to Fine, the metaphysically necessary truths may simply be *defined* as those that follow logically from these fundamental truths about the constitutive essences of things. But I suggest that we should slightly amend Fine's conception. We should take the notion of metaphysical necessity as primitive. Then we can allow that the fundamental truths about the constitutive essences of things may themselves *contain* modal operators. These fundamental truths explain all the other modal truths about which propositions are metaphysically necessary and which are not, in one of the following two ways. They will *directly* explain these other modal truths if these other modal truths follow (in the relevant modal logic, whatever exactly it is) from these fundamental truths about the essences of things. They will *indirectly* explain these other modal truths if these other modal truths follow from the conjunction of these fundamental essential truths with certain other contingent truths.

It is when these fundamental essential truths only provide an indirect explanation of these modal truths that the explanation of these modal truths involves contingent truths. For example, the explanation that I proposed of our trouble-some modal truth (1) involved not only the fundamental essential truth (3) but also the contingent truth (2). It may be useful to examine the general form of this type of explanation. The key point is just that the fundamental truths about the essences of things, which either directly or indirectly explain all these other modal truths, may themselves contain *embedded* modal operators. For example, there could be a fundamental truth about the essences of things, of the following form:

(8) Necessarily, if *p*, then necessarily *q*.

If (8) is true, then, intuitively, whether or not *q* is necessary may depend on whether—as a purely contingent matter of fact—*p* is the case. Suppose that as it happens, *p* is *not* the case. Then (8) creates no metaphysical obstacle to its being possible for *q* not to be the case. If no other fundamental truths about the essences of things, in conjunction with any non-modal truths, imply that it is impossible for *q* not to be the case, then according to the conception of metaphysical modality that I proposed in Chapter 6, it *is* possible for *q* not to be the case. But (8) clearly implies that at any possible world at which *p is* true, it *would be* necessary that *q* is true, and so *not* possible for *q* not to be the case.[16] Thus, it might be possible for *q* not to be the case, but not necessarily possible for *q* not to be the case: *q* might have been necessary, in which case it would not have been possible for *q* not to be the case.

Moreover, there is a clear theoretical advantage to allowing that modal truths may be explained at least in part on the basis of purely contingent facts. I have been assuming here that the modal truths do not form a huge formless jumble, but can all be explained on the basis of certain explanatorily basic truths. Now suppose that contingent non-modal facts cannot enter into the explanation of modal truths. Then, whenever a modal truth is explained, it must follow from necessary truths alone. This immediately raises the question of *why* those necessary truths are necessary. If contingent facts cannot enter into the explanation of why these truths are necessary, then within the framework that I am assuming here, the only plausible explanation of why these truths are necessary is just that they follow logically from the fundamental truths about the essential nature of things (which are truths that neither require nor admit of any further explanation). So absolutely all modal truths must follow logically from these fundamental essential truths. However, it seems that if these fundamental essential truths are to explain absolutely all modal truths,

---

[16] In this case, the proposition *p* is presumably not only contingent but *empirical*. If so, then the fact that modal truths can be explained by appealing to principles like (8) refutes two central contentions of David Chalmers. First, Chalmers claims that there are no "*a posteriori* constraints on the space of possible worlds" (1996: 136). If there are fundamental modal principles like (8), then this claim is clearly false: whether or not there is a possible world in which *q* is not the case depends on whether—as a purely *a posteriori* matter of fact—*p* is the case. Secondly, since the proposition *p* is empirical, it seems that the proposition that *q* is necessary, and the proposition *q* itself, can only be known on the basis of *p*, and so must also be empirical. In that case, even if *q* is necessary, it is easy to explain why the proposition *q* itself, and the modal proposition that *q* is necessary, are empirical: they are empirical because they can only be known on the basis of the empirical proposition *p*. This explanation is entirely compatible with denying that the statement that expresses *q* expresses a contingent "primary proposition". Such a denial would not make this necessary *a posteriori* proposition mysterious or inexplicable as Chalmers claims (1996: 136–8).

then they must be either extremely strong and controversial principles, or else extremely numerous, since (if contingent facts cannot enter into the explanation of modal truths) such fundamental truths can only explain their logical consequences.

Suppose, on the other hand, that modal truths may have contingent explanations. Then our explanations of modal truths can rely on a much smaller number of fundamental modal truths, by relying on contingent truths instead. If we ask, '*Why* are these truths contingent?', there is a simple explanation: these truths are contingent because nothing in the essential nature of things makes their negations impossible. So if we allow that modal truths may have contingent explanations, we will not have to postulate nearly so many fundamental truths about the essential nature of things as we will if we refuse to countenance modal truths having such contingent explanations.

So far, I have only raised doubts about the *S5* axiom. But in fact the considerations outlined here also seem to cast doubt on the *S4* axiom as well. Assuming that the appropriate logic for metaphysical modality is a *KT* logic, if *S5* fails, then either *S4* or *B* or both must also fail. The general idea behind my proposal—that modal facts may have contingent explanations, so that contingent facts may make a difference to which modal facts obtain—in fact casts doubt on *S4* just as much as on *S5*. If contingent facts may make a difference to which modal facts obtain, then surely they can make a difference to which propositions are necessary (or not possible), as well as to which propositions are possible (or not necessary). But if contingent facts can make a difference to which propositions are necessary, then there could be propositions that are in fact necessary, but might not have been necessary, had the contingent facts been otherwise—which would be a counter-instance to the *S4* axiom. On the other hand, this idea casts no doubt at all on the *B* axiom—the principle that every actual truth is necessarily possible. (Indeed, the *B* principle allows the contingent facts about which propositions are actually true to constrain not just what is possible at the actual world, but also what is possible at all actually possible worlds.) So the considerations that I am advancing here seem to tell against *S4* just as much as against *S5*.

In conclusion: rejecting *S5* is not a high price to pay at all, unless we believe that the modal concepts *possible* and *necessary* can be defined in terms of a conceptually prior notion of something's *being the case at a world*. Unless we hold this view of modal concepts, the view that *S5* is obviously the correct logic for metaphysical modality seems to be a prejudice, lacking any persuasive justification. Moreover, adherence to *S5* has the disadvantage that it precludes the theoretical economy that is made possible by allowing that some modal truths have contingent explanations. The fact that non-reductive naturalists must reject *S5* does not in any way undermine the plausibility of non-reductive naturalism.

9.7 CONCLUSION

I have argued in this chapter that it is possible after all to reconcile the thesis that normative and mental properties are irreducible with the strong naturalistic thesis that all contingent facts are necessarily realized in physical facts. The crucial point is that even if it is necessary that contingent mental and normative facts are realized in some physical facts or other, nothing in the constitutive essence of these mental and normative facts need determine exactly *which* physical facts they are realized in. That is something that is determined for each possible world by how things happen to be in that world.

Thus, even though there is no *actually* possible world that is just like the actual world in all physical respects but unlike the actual world in mental or normative respects, no actual truth determines what realizes these mental or normative facts in possible worlds that are radically unlike the actual world in physical respects. This is what allows it to remain completely open, from the standpoint of the actual world, exactly which physical properties necessitate mental and normative properties in those remote worlds. Indeed, there are many incompatible ways in which physical properties might necessitate mental and normative properties in those remote worlds, and all these ways count as perfectly possible from the standpoint of the actual world. Of course, from the standpoint of one of those remote worlds, that world does not count as remote at all; and from that standpoint, there is only one possible way in which physical properties can necessitate mental and normative properties in that world. In general, from the standpoint of each world, there is only one way in which physical properties can necessitate mental and normative properties in that world, even though from the standpoint of that world, there are many incompatible ways in which physical properties might necessitate mental and normative properties in remote worlds.

According to this picture, then, naturalism is true: at every world, the mental and normative properties are tied down to specific physical properties at that world and at all physically similar worlds. But reductionism fails: at no world is any mental normative property necessarily equivalent to any physical property. Since this picture seems to be quite consistent, we should conclude that it is in fact quite possible to reconcile naturalism and irreducibility.

PART III

THE EPISTEMOLOGY
OF NORMATIVE BELIEF

10

The Status of Normative Intuitions

10.1 THE EPISTEMOLOGY OF NORMATIVE BELIEF

How we can know, or even have rational or justified beliefs in, normative propositions (such as propositions about what ought to be the case, about what people ought to do or choose, or about what they ought to believe, or ought to feel)? Answering this question is the central task for the *epistemology of normative belief*. In Part III of this book, I shall outline a new answer to this epistemological question.

In the earlier chapters of the book, I advocated a robustly *realist* conception of the normative. According to this realist conception, normative statements express perfectly straightforward beliefs or "cognitive states", just like paradigmatic examples of "factual statements"; when these statements are true, there is a corresponding normative fact; and there is no way of reducing such normative facts to facts that could be stated, even in principle, by using terms that do not themselves refer to normative properties or relations.

Anti-realists often argue that realist conceptions of the normative cannot give any satisfactory epistemology for normative beliefs. Many realists say little more than that we have some cognitive faculty—sometimes called "intuition" or "reason" or "conscience"—which enables us to come to know and have justified beliefs in normative propositions; but they rarely give any account of how exactly this alleged faculty operates, or how it could serve as a reliable source of knowledge, or what could justify us in relying on it.[1] For this reason, anti-realists often accuse realists of failing to meet certain crucial demands for explanation. In the absence of any substantive explanation of how we can come to know or have justified beliefs in normative propositions, realism seems a sitting target for an objection that was famously pressed by J. L. Mackie (1977: 38): "if we were aware of [objective values], it would have to be by some special faculty of moral perception

---

[1] One notable recent exception is Peacocke (2004: ch. 7). According to Peacocke, our possession of moral concepts involves an "implicit conception" of the moral properties and relations that those concepts stand for (and so under favourable circumstances, our moral intuitions are causally explained by this implicit conception, in which case they may count as "entitling" us to the corresponding moral beliefs). In my view, however, Peacocke's account of moral concepts should be rejected, for basically the same reasons as the attempts at "conceptual analysis" that I criticized in Chapter 3; see my critical notice of Peacocke's book (Wedgwood forthcoming *b*).

or intuition, utterly different from our ordinary ways of knowing everything else". The account that I shall outline in this third part of the book will show how realists *can* provide a satisfactory explanation of the epistemology of normative beliefs. If this explanation is correct, then realism is not vulnerable to Mackie's objection.

The account that I shall give here will be based on the version of the idea that I defended earlier, in Chapter 7, that the intentional is normative—that is, that there is no way to give an account of the nature or essence of the types of mental states that have intentional content without mentioning normative properties and relations. It is this idea that makes it possible to give a plausible explanation of how we can know, or have justified or rational beliefs in, normative propositions. So, I shall argue, the claim that the intentional is essentially normative helps to provide an illuminating epistemology of normative beliefs. In a way, this is not surprising. According to this claim, normative truths are part of what makes mental states what they are: in effect, normative truths are already built into our minds, simply because they are minds at all; so it is not surprising that there is less of a problem about our "access" to such objective normative truths than there might at first seem to be.

In this third part of the book, I shall focus on giving an account of the epistemology of normative propositions of a certain specific sort—namely, propositions about which mental states or attitudes are "correct" and which are "rational". In view of what I argued earlier in this book, however, an account of the epistemology of propositions about which mental states are "correct" or "rational" will also shed light on the epistemology of many other normative propositions as well.

As I argued in Chapter 4, the nature of the concept that is expressed by what I called the "practical or deliberative 'ought'" guarantees that the semantic value of this concept, when it is indexed to an agent A and a time t, is that property of a proposition p that makes it *correct* for A to incorporate p into her ideal plans about what to do at t, and *incorrect* for A to incorporate the negation of p into any such plans. A similar claim holds for all the other concepts that can be expressed by the term 'ought' that I discussed in Chapter 5: the nature of those concepts guarantees that their semantic value can be specified in terms of the notion of various mental states' being correct or rational (for a certain thinker to have at a certain time). In this way then, there are conceptual truths that link the normative propositions that can be stated by means of the concepts that can be expressed by 'ought' with propositions about which mental states are correct and which are incorrect (or about which mental states are rational and which are irrational). This makes it plausible that if one can know which mental states are correct and which are rational, then one can also know the corresponding normative propositions that can be stated by using the various concepts that can be expressed by 'ought'.

Indeed, it may be plausible that the nature of several other normative or evaluative concepts determines that their semantic values can be specified in terms of which mental states are correct or which are rational. For example, it may be that the nature of the concept *admirable* determines that something falls under this concept if and only if it is *correct to admire* the thing in question. If that is so, then an account of how we can know, or have rational or justified beliefs in, propositions about whether or not it is correct to admire something would also be able to explain how we can know what is admirable and what is not. Similarly, it may be that the concept *desirable* determines that something falls under this concept if and only if it is *correct to desire* that thing; and so on for many other such evaluative concepts. In what follows, I shall rely on the assumption that evaluative concepts, like *admirable* and *desirable*, are indeed linked to the notion of correctness in this way. However, I am afraid that I shall not say anything more to defend this assumption here. Anyone who is sceptical about this assumption should take the proposals that I will make here as purely concerned with the epistemology of beliefs about which mental states are correct, or about which are rational.

10.2 PRIMITIVELY RATIONAL WAYS OF FORMING BELIEFS

My main topic in this part of the book is how we can know, or even form rational or justified beliefs in, normative propositions (such as propositions about which mental states are correct or rational). In this section, however, I shall outline some more general proposals about rational belief, which will help to structure my more focused discussion of when it is rational to form normative beliefs.

First, it will be helpful to recall some of the claims that I have already made about the concept of rationality. As I explained in Chapter 7 (Section 7.1), I am interpreting the term 'rational' so that it corresponds to what in Chapter 5 (Section 5.2) I called an "information-relative 'ought'". Strictly speaking then, a belief can be rational in relation to one body of information I_1, but not rational in relation to another body of information I_2. For the most part, however, I shall use the term 'rational' in a way that is explicitly relativized, not to a body of information, but rather to a thinker and a time. So, for example, when I say that it is rational for a thinker x to come to believe a certain proposition p at a certain time t, this is equivalent to saying that it is rational, in relation to the total information that x possesses at t, for x to come to believe p at t.

Another assumption about rationality that I articulated earlier in the book is that the standards of rational belief are all "oriented" towards the goal of having a correct belief. So far, my formulation of this assumption has been rather vague and metaphorical.[2] In some sense, it must be the case that a belief counts as

---

[2] For an attempt at a clearer formulation of the thesis that the principles of rationality are all "oriented" towards the "goal" of having mental states that are correct, see some of my work in epistemology (especially Wedgwood 1999*a* and 2002*c*).

rational in relation to a given body of information I just in case that body of information I makes it *highly likely* that the belief in question is correct. But the term 'likely' has been interpreted in so many ways that this assumption is at best suggestive, rather than a definite constraint that my proposals will have to meet.

In this third part of the book, I shall also make yet another assumption about rationality. Specifically, I shall assume that the view that epistemologists call "internalism" is correct—that is, the view that whether or not it is rational for a thinker to come to believe p at t is always determined purely by the facts that are in some way "internal" to the thinker's mind at t. (It is important to bear in mind that this view is completely different from the view that *metaethicists* call "internalism", which I defended in Chapter 1.) Specifically, I shall assume that whether or not it is rational for a thinker to believe p at t is entirely determined by the facts about what mental states the thinker has, what mental states the thinker lacks, and what reasoning abilities and dispositions the thinker has.[3]

The most prominent rival to this internalist view of rationality or justification is the "reliabilist" view. According to the reliabilist view, whether or not a thinker's belief is rational or justified depends on whether the methods that the thinker followed in arriving at that belief really are reliable ways of arriving at the truth.[4] I am in fact inclined to believe that the view that epistemologists call "internalism" is correct, and that reliabilism is incorrect. But I shall not argue for this belief here. I shall simply assume for the sake of argument that the internalist view is correct. In the present context, this assumption is harmless, since by making this assumption, I am making my task harder for myself, not easier. The task of answering the metaethical anti-realists, who question whether metaethical realists can give any plausible epistemology for normative beliefs, will require doing the following two things. First, we must show that a realist conception of normative beliefs can explain why our ordinary methods for forming such beliefs can yield rational or justified belief. Secondly, we must show that this realist conception can explain how these ordinary methods can, at least under favourable circumstances, yield knowledge. Now, practically all epistemologists—including many who reject the reliabilist conception of justified belief—accept that *knowledge* requires reliability. So, in arguing that the ordinary methods of normative thinking can yield knowledge, I will have to argue that they can be reliable ways of reaching the truth. So in that sense, I am already committed to offering an answer to any reliabilist who doubts whether realists can provide a satisfactory normative epistemology. On the other hand, if an internalist conception of justified or rational belief is correct, and reliabilism about justified belief is wrong, then justified or

---

[3] This sort of epistemological "internalism" is attacked by Goldman (1999) and defended by Conee and Feldman (2001). I have offered my own defence of internalism in some of my earlier work (Wedgwood 2002*a*).

[4] For this reliabilist conception of justified belief, see especially Goldman (1979).

rational belief will require some *further* condition, distinct from reliability. Since I am assuming an internalist conception of rational belief, arguing that our ordinary methods for forming normative beliefs can yield rational belief will involve arguing that the beliefs that result from these methods can meet this further condition, in addition to reliability. In this way, internalist assumptions make the task of answering the anti-realist opponent of realism harder, not easier.

With these assumptions in place, I shall now make a more substantive proposal about what *makes* it rational for a thinker to form beliefs in a given way. This proposal is suggested by considering why it is rational to form beliefs by taking one's *sensory experience* at face value. As I shall use the phrase, "taking one's sensory experiences at face value" involves forming a belief in a proposition p directly on the basis of a sensory experience as of p's being the case (so long as one has no special reason to think that one is not perceiving properly in the circumstances).[5] Why exactly is it rational to form beliefs by taking one's sensory experiences at face value?

In some cases, it seems intuitively highly plausible that it is rational to form a belief in a certain way W_1 only because it is *independently* or *antecedently* rational for one to believe that forming that belief in that way W_1 is reliable. That is, W_1 is a rational way of forming beliefs only because there is some *other* rational way W_2 of forming beliefs such that this other way W_2 can lead from one's current overall state of mind to one's forming (or reaffirming) the belief that the former way W_1 is reliable. For example, this seems to be the case with ways of forming beliefs that base beliefs on the use of measuring instruments. It is rational for me to form a belief about the temperature of the air around me on the basis of reading of thermometer; but this is only because it is *already* rational—quite independently of any beliefs that I form on the basis of this particular thermometer—for me to believe that the thermometer is reliable.

However, it would lead to an obvious infinite regress if we supposed that it can never be rational for one to form a belief in any way unless it is *already* independently or antecedently rational for one to believe that it is reliable to form that belief in that way.[6] So there must be certain *basic* ways in which it is rational for one to form beliefs, even though the rationality of one's forming beliefs in these basic ways is *not* due to its being independently or antecedently rational for one to regard these ways of forming beliefs as reliable. I shall call

---

[5] We may also have to require that the sensory experience in question should "basically represent" the proposition p. In some sense, an experience can "represent" an object as *a cathode ray tube*. However, it may not be rational to form the belief that a particular object is a cathode ray tube directly on the basis of having an experience of this kind; it would only be rational to form such a belief on the basis of having *both* such an experience and various rational background beliefs (such as the background belief that in the conditions that one is normally in, objects that look like *that* are usually cathode ray tubes). For this point, see Peacocke (2004: 65–9).

[6] For this point, see Pryor (2000).

these basic ways of forming beliefs the "primitively rational" ways of forming beliefs. It is plausible that it is in this sense "primitively rational" for one to form beliefs by taking one's sensory experiences at face value.

What *makes* it rational for one to form beliefs in these primitively rational ways? Given that we are assuming what epistemologists call an "internalist" conception of rationality, the rationality of these primitively rational ways of forming beliefs cannot be due to the fact that other people might be able somehow to demonstrate the reliability of these ways of forming beliefs, nor even to the fact that the thinker herself might be able to demonstrate their reliability at some other time. It must be due purely to some fact that is internal to the thinker's mind at the time in question. So, a primitively rational way of forming beliefs is rational purely because of some internal fact about the thinker's mind at the time, but not because of its being independently rational for the thinker to regard it as a reliable way of reaching the truth. Why then *is* it rational?

By definition, a primitively rational way of forming beliefs is not rational because it is already independently or antecedently rational to regard that way of forming beliefs as reliable. This makes it plausible that the rationality of such a primitively rational way of forming beliefs is not due to *any* empirical evidence that one has in favour of that way of forming beliefs. Given my internalist assumptions, it is natural to conclude that this way of forming beliefs must simply be *necessarily* rational, purely in virtue of the intrinsic nature of this way of forming beliefs, and of the various concepts and mental states that it involves. But how can the intrinsic nature of these concepts and mental states explain why it is rational to form beliefs by taking one's sensory experience at face value?

Part of the story might be that a disposition towards forming beliefs in this way is *constitutive* of possessing some of the concepts, or of having the capacity for some of the types of mental state, that are involved in this way of forming beliefs. But it is hard to see how this can be the whole story. According to the normative theory of mental states that I defended in Chapter 7, the fact that the disposition is constitutive of such a basic mental capacity is itself explained by the fact that it is a disposition towards a basic form of rational thinking. So it is hard to see how the fact that this way of thinking is rational could itself be entirely explained by the fact that the disposition to engage in this sort of thinking is constitutive of some such basic mental capacity.[7]

Given our assumption that the principles of rational belief are all "oriented" towards the goal of believing the truth, it seems that for a way of forming beliefs to count as primitively rational, there must be *some* connection between that way of forming beliefs and the truth. But it cannot be required that it should *always* be the case that whenever one forms a belief in a primitively

---

[7] In this way, I must amend the story that I sketched in an earlier paper of mine (Wedgwood 1999*a*).

rational way, the proposition that one thereby comes to believe is true. It seems equally rational for one to form beliefs by taking one's sensory experiences at face value even if one is undetectably being deceived by an evil demon or a manipulative neuroscientist—in which case most of the propositions that one comes to believe by taking one's experiences at face value are not true at all. Indeed, there could even be a possible world in which the vast majority of sensory experiences are produced by such deceiving neuroscientists; so it may not even be necessary that the practice of taking one's experiences at face value is generally reliable.

Nonetheless, it seems to me that *some* such connection to the truth must be part of what makes it primitively rational to form beliefs by taking experience at face value. As I have suggested, any such primitively rational way of forming beliefs is necessarily rational, purely in virtue of the intrinsic nature of the concepts and mental states involved. Thus, if this connection to the truth is part of what makes taking sensory experiences at face value a primitively rational way of forming beliefs, this connection to the truth must hold necessarily, purely in virtue of the nature of the concepts and mental states involved.

What sort of connection to the truth could this be? I propose that the practice of forming beliefs by taking one's sensory experiences at face value has the following essential connection with the truth. It may be that it is essential to sensory experiences that any subject who has such experiences at all has some *disposition* to have experiences that veridically represent certain aspects of her environment. More precisely, perhaps, for every possible subject of experience, there is a range of propositions such that for every proposition p within that range, under normal conditions, the subject will respond to being in a situation in which p is the case by having a sensory experience as of p's being the case. Even if the manifestation of this disposition is blocked or inhibited by other factors (such as the machinations of an evil demon), the subject may still have some disposition to have veridical experiences of this sort. Indeed, the fact that a mental state is of the kind that would be involved in manifesting this disposition in response to being in a situation in which p is the case may be an essential part of what makes this mental state count as a sensory experience as of p's being the case in the first place.[8] Whenever one's experience *does* consist in the manifestation of this essential disposition, then the content of the experience will be true.

It may be that this connection to the truth is part of the explanation of why it is rational for one to form beliefs by taking one's sensory experiences at face value (so long as one has no special reason to think that one is not perceiving properly in the circumstances). The rest of the explanation might go roughly as follows. We could not function as agents at all unless we had some beliefs about

---

[8] Compare Peacocke's (2004: 69) idea that experiences are "*instance-individuated* with respect to certain of their contents".

our immediate environment. So it would be unreasonable to demand that we should not form any beliefs about our immediate environment at all. It would also be unreasonable to demand that we should not form beliefs of this kind in any way unless we had independent or antecedent reasons for regarding that way of forming beliefs as reliable; we could have no such independent reason to regard a way of forming such beliefs as reliable unless there were some way of forming such beliefs that we already treated as basic or primitively rational. In short, we need to treat some way of forming beliefs about our environment as primitively rational; and so it would be unreasonable to expect us to do otherwise.

Still, this broadly "pragmatic" point is not enough to recommend any *particular* way of forming beliefs about our environment. (It does not recommend taking our sensory experiences at face value over astrology or reading the tea leaves, for example.) So it still seems reasonable to demand that if we do not have any independent or antecedent reason to regard a way of forming beliefs as reliable, we should not form beliefs in that way unless that way of forming beliefs has some essential connection to the truth. But if my proposal about the nature of sensory experiences is correct, there *is* an essential connection between our sensory experiences and the truth: it is essential to one's capacity for sensory experiences that one should have a disposition to have certain experiences in certain circumstances, and when this essential disposition is manifested, then the content of one's sensory experience is true. It may be some account along these general lines that explains why it is primitively rational to form beliefs by taking one's sensory experiences at face value.

These considerations seem to make it plausible that every rational way of forming beliefs meets one or the other of the following two conditions. On the one hand, it might be a *primitively* rational way of forming beliefs, and so have some essential connection to the truth, of the sort that I have tried to illustrate with this example of the practice of forming beliefs by taking one's sensory experiences at face value. Or else, alternatively, it might be rational only because it is *antecedently* or *independently* rational to regard it as a reliable way of forming correct beliefs—that is, of getting to the truth.

If this is correct, then it raises a problem for explaining how it can be rational to form *normative* beliefs. The problem is that it is not obvious how any of our ways of forming normative beliefs have any essential connection to the truth; so it is not obvious how any of these ways of forming normative beliefs might be primitively rational. It also seems doubtful whether *all* of our ways of forming normative beliefs could be such that it is antecedently and independently rational for us to regard them as reliable. Unless we have some primitively rational way of forming normative beliefs, it seems doubtful whether we could ever acquire any antecedent or independent reason for regarding any way of forming normative beliefs to be reliable at all.

For example, some philosophers have proposed that all that is needed, in order to explain how we can know or have rational or justified beliefs in normative propositions, is to appeal to a *coherentist* epistemology.[9] According to this view, what makes us justified in forming a new normative belief is just that this new belief helps to optimize coherence among our total system of beliefs as a whole. But of course a perfectly coherent system of beliefs might be largely false. It also does not seem essential to this method—the method of revising one's beliefs in such a way as to optimize coherence—that anyone capable of this method must have some disposition such that when this disposition is manifested, this method is a reliable way of getting to the truth. Moreover, we do not seem to have any antecedent or independent reason for thinking that this method is a reliable way of getting to the truth. So, at least if I am right about what is needed to show that a method of forming beliefs is rational, it seems that this purely coherentist epistemology cannot explain how it can be rational to form normative beliefs.

This seems to show that any plausible account of the epistemology of normative beliefs must identify some element in the rational ways of forming normative beliefs that plays the same role in normative thinking as *experience* plays in our thinking about the external world. Many philosophers have claimed that this element consists in what they call our *intuitions* about which normative propositions are true. However, it is not enough for a theory just to claim that we have such intuitions. They must also either explain how it is that these intuitions have some essential connection to the truth, or else explain how it is antecedently or independently rational for us to regard these intuitions as reliable. It is far from clear that many of the most recent intuitionists have succeeded in providing any such explanation.

Thus, several recent intuitionists have claimed that certain basic normative propositions are *self-evident*—that is, one is justified in believing these propositions purely in virtue of one's "understanding" of them.[10] But this seems not to meet the explanatory demand: how exactly does one's "understanding" of a normative proposition justify one in believing it? How is it that these intuitions have any essential connection to the truth, or what exactly gives us any antecedent or independent reason to regard these intuitions as reliable? So far, the intuitionists have not given much in the way of an answer to these questions. So it is not clear that the central problem of the epistemology of normative beliefs has yet been satisfactorily solved.

In the remainder of this chapter, I shall offer an account of our normative intuitions that seems to be able to provide the necessary explanation. This account

[9] For such a coherentist approach to moral epistemology, see for example Brink (1989).
[10] For this view, see e.g. Shafer-Landau (2003: ch. 11), Crisp (2002: 57–9), and Stratton-Lake (2002b: 22).

of our normative intuitions is based on the normative theory of intentional mental states that I sketched in Chapter 7.

10.3 AN EXTENSION OF OUR NORMATIVE THEORY OF MENTAL STATES

In this section, I shall first briefly review the interpretation of the claim that "the intentional is normative" that I defended in Chapter 7. Then in the rest of this section, I shall try to make it plausible to extend this claim so that it also applies to a wider range of mental states than just to the limited range of mental states that I have focused on so far.

As I claimed in Chapter 7, the most plausible version of the idea that the intentional is normative applies to both of the two main aspects of intentional mental states. That is, it applies both to the *content* of these intentional mental states (which I am assuming to be composed of *concepts*), and also to the *mental relation* or *attitude* towards such a content (such as the attitude of *belief* or *hope* or *fear*) that is involved in that intentional mental state. According to this version of the idea that the intentional is normative, the nature of both the various concepts, and of the various types of attitude that thinkers can have towards contents, is given in terms of the normative principles that apply to mental states involving those concepts or attitude-types.

Specifically, according to my version of the idea that the intentional is normative, the nature of each concept or attitude-type is given *both* by a principle that defines when certain mental states involving that concept or attitude-type are *correct*, and *also* by certain basic principles of *rationality* that apply to that concept or attitude-type. In earlier chapters, I have illustrated the sort of account that this approach calls for by means of various examples. For instance, the nature of logical concepts, like 'or' and 'not', might be given both by the conditions under which beliefs involving those concepts are correct (in effect, by those concepts' contribution to the truth conditions of thoughts in which they appear) and also by the basic principle that it is rational to make inferences in accordance with certain fundamental rules of inference for these logical concepts. The account of the concepts expressed by the term 'ought' that I gave in Chapters 4 and 5 is also an example of this type of approach.

According to this sort of theory, a similar story is true of the various *attitude-types* as well. Thus, for example, perhaps the nature of the attitude of *belief* is given both by the principle that a belief is correct if and only if the content of the belief is true, and by the principle that a way of forming one's beliefs counts as rational just in case one's antecedent mental states make it sufficiently likely (at least in some sense of the term 'likely') that any beliefs that are formed in that way are correct. This pair of principles illustrates a general relationship that seems to hold between the notions of correctness and rationality. In general, it is rational to form a mental state in a certain way if and only if one's antecedent mental states make it sufficiently likely (in the relevant sense, whatever exactly that may be) that the mental state in question is correct.

In Chapter 7, I focused on a limited range of attitude-types—specifically, on beliefs and judgments, on the one hand, and on intentions and choices or decisions, on the other. But this approach could also be applied to other types of attitude as well. Thus, perhaps the nature of the attitude of *admiration* is given by the following two principles. First, it is correct to admire something if and only if the object of one's admiration really is admirable in some suitable way. Secondly, it is rational to admire something if and only if one's antecedent mental states make it sufficiently likely that the object of one's admiration really is admirable. A similar story may also be true of the *moral emotions*. For example, it may be that it is correct to have the moral emotion of disapproval towards an action if and only if the action in question really is morally wrong, and it is rational to disapprove of an action if and only if one's antecedent mental states make it sufficiently likely that the action is wrong. These principles, about when the attitude of disapproval is correct and when it is rational, may be an essential part of what makes disapproval the type of attitude that it is.

As I also argued in Chapter 7, a plausible normative theory of mental states must include more than just an account of the nature of these concepts and attitude-types; it must also include an explanation of what it is for a *thinker* to *possess* those concepts, or to *be capable of* those attitude-types. Specifically, I argued, for a thinker to possess these concepts, or to be capable of those attitude-types, the thinker must have *dispositions* that amount to an appropriate sort of sensitivity to these normative principles that give the nature of the mental states in question. In most cases, it will be more plausible to suppose that the thinker must have a disposition to conform to the principles of rationality that give the nature of the relevant concepts or types of attitude than that she must have a disposition to conform to the corresponding principles of correctness. As I pointed out earlier, whether or not a mental state is correct is typically determined by the relation between that mental state and the external world; and one's dispositions to have many sorts of mental states do not respond directly to the external world, but only to one's antecedent mental states. Nonetheless, as I noted earlier, there seems to be a general relationship between correctness and rationality: it is rational for one to form a mental state in a certain way if and only if one's antecedent mental states make it sufficiently likely that the mental state in question is correct. So, if one has a disposition to conform to a principle of rationality that applies to mental states of a certain type, this disposition can be regarded as an *indirect* way of being sensitive to the conditions under which mental states of that type are correct.

Specifically, then, the sort of disposition that a thinker must have, if she is to possess a given concept, is a disposition to think in ways that the principle of rationality that figures in the account of the nature of the concept specifies as rational. Such principles typically take the form of specifying some set of antecedent mental states such that—according to this principle—it is rational to respond to being in those antecedent mental states by forming a certain further mental state. Then, the disposition that one must have, in order to possess the concept, will be a disposition to respond to one's actually being in those antecedent mental states by forming that further mental state. So, for example, if my account of the concept 'or' is correct, then for any pair of propositions p and q that the thinker can entertain, the thinker must be disposed to respond to the state of consciously considering the inference from p to 'p or q' (or the inference from q to 'p or q') by accepting the inference (where by "accepting this inference", we mean *conditionally* accepting the conclusion 'p or q', on the assumption of the premise). Similarly, if my account of the practical 'ought' is correct, then the thinker must be disposed to respond to a rational judgment involving the practical 'ought', of the form '$O_{<me,\,t>}(p)$', by incorporating the embedded proposition p into her ideal plans about what to do at t.

A similar point would apply to the principles of rationality that figure, not in an account of the nature of a concept, but in an account of the nature of some type of attitude. Suppose for example that the basic principle of rationality that applies to the attitude of admiration is the principle that I suggested earlier—the principle that an attitude of admiration is rational if and only if one's antecedent mental states make it sufficiently likely that the object of one's admiration really is admirable. Now emotions of admiration, like many other emotions, are typically *reactions* to some antecedent beliefs or experiences concerning the object of the emotion.[11] (As it is sometimes said, such emotions have "cognitive bases".) I hear my friend Charles playing the piano, and I react to this experience with a feeling of admiration for his playing. The disposition that I manifest in reacting in this way might be a disposition to respond to antecedent beliefs or experiences that make it highly likely that a certain object really is admirable, by having an attitude of admiration for that object. Perhaps having this disposition is essential to the capacity for the attitude of admiration at all.

This is not to say that when I manifest this disposition, the concept 'admirable' actually features in the content of my experience of Charles's piano playing, or in the content of my emotion of admiration. I may have no thoughts explicitly involving the concept 'admirable' at all. After all, my attitude of admiration is focused on his playing itself; and my experience is just an experience as of his

---

[11] This is what Hume meant by claiming that the passions are "secondary impressions" rather than "original impressions" (1739: II.i.1)—or as he also put it, "impressions of reflection" rather than "impressions of sensation" (1739: I.i.2). It may be what Locke (1690: II.20.3) meant by identifying passions with "internal" rather than "bodily" sensations. We should add, however, that such an emotion is not merely *causally triggered* by the belief or experience to which it is a reaction; it is a *psychologically intelligible response* to that belief or experience; we might even say that the emotion is *motivated* by that belief or experience.

playing Bach's French Suites, say, in a certain way.[12] Nonetheless, it may be that as a matter of fact, together with all my other antecedent mental states, this experience makes it sufficiently likely that Charles's playing really is admirable; and it is because my experience has this feature that I manifest this disposition, and respond to this experience (directly and without further ado) by having a corresponding attitude of admiration. It may be that a disposition towards having one's attitudes of admiration in this basically rational way is partially constitutive of being capable of the attitude of admiration at all.

As I explained in Chapter 7 (Section 7.4), this claim that every thinker must have these rational dispositions does not imply that these dispositions need be manifested in every possible case. To say that an object has a disposition is to say that *ceteris paribus*, or *normally*, when the object is in one of these stimulus conditions, it will also go into the corresponding response condition. But the circumstances can fail to be normal, and *cetera* can fail to be *paria*, in many ways. So my proposal does not imply that irrationality is necessarily less common than rationality; it implies only that a *disposition* towards certain *basic* forms of rational thinking is a necessary condition of being capable of the types of mental state that are in question. Moreover, as I also explained in Chapter 7, in addition to the various ways in which one's dispositions towards the basic kinds of rational thinking can be blocked or inhibited by interfering mental factors, one may also have many *other* mental dispositions, which may be dispositions that it is sometimes irrational to manifest. This too is quite compatible with its being the case that in general, one *also* has a general disposition towards certain basic kinds of rational thinking. So my claims are compatible with the existence of pervasive and deeply entrenched dispositions towards various forms of irrationality.

At the same time, if we extend this claim about the normativity of the intentional to emotional attitudes like admiration in the way that I have suggested, then we can explain a phenomenon that has long caught philosophers' attention. As G. E. M. Anscombe (1963: 70–1) famously claimed, there would be something baffling—indeed, something *prima facie* unintelligible—about someone's having a *desire for a saucer of mud*, unless the person in question also accepted some "desirability characterization" of having a saucer of mud (that is, a characterization which represents having a saucer of mud as in some way desirable). Indeed, Anscombe (1963: 71) appeared to draw the conclusion that such baffling and *prima facie* unintelligible desires are in fact conceptually impossible: "To say 'I *merely* want this' without any [desirability] characterisation is to deprive the word of sense".

Philippa Foot (1978: 113–14) made a similar point about the attitude of *pride*:

Consider, for instance, the suggestion that someone might be proud of the sky or the sea ... This makes sense only if a special assumption is made about his beliefs, for instance

---

[12] Thus, Johnston (2001*b*: 228) is mistaken in his claim that "for Wedgwood, affective states can only be consequential upon basic evaluative beliefs".

that he is under some crazy delusion and believes that he has saved the sky from falling, or the sea from drying up. The characteristic object of pride is something seen (*a*) as in some way a man's own, and (*b*) as some sort of achievement or advantage ... To see that the second condition is necessary, one should try supposing that a man happens to feel proud because he has laid one of his hands on the other, three times in an hour. Here again the supposition that it is pride that he feels will make perfectly good sense if a special background is filled in. Perhaps he is ill, and it is an achievement even to do this; perhaps this gesture has some religious or political significance, and he is a brave man who will so defy the gods or the rulers. But with no special background there can be no pride, not because no one could psychologically speaking feel pride in such a case, but because whatever he did feel could not logically be pride.

It is easy to construct examples of such baffling and *prima facie* unintelligible cases for other types of attitudes as well. Consider the example of someone who has an attitude of intense *admiration* for anyone who has a tendency to sneeze between 3 per cent and 8 per cent more often than the average human being. This attitude seems utterly puzzling; it calls out for explanation; and we would typically feel quite doubtful whether we had correctly interpreted this person if we ascribed to him this attitude of admiration for those who sneeze just slightly more than average in this way.

Admittedly, the claim that Anscombe seems to make, that it is *impossible* for anyone to desire an object without accepting a "desirability characterization" of that object, seems a strong and rather doubtful claim.[13] Likewise, analogous claims about other attitude-types such as pride or admiration would also seem doubtful: in general, such claims seem to underestimate the extent to which brain damage and malign cultural influences can cause strange and perverse attitudes of many kinds. Nonetheless, a good theory of the nature of desire and of other attitudes-types should give some account of why such attitudes strike us as immediately puzzling and hard to explain.

It seems to me that the version that I have proposed of the idea that the intentional is normative can account for this phenomenon. Suppose that one has an attitude as a response to beliefs or experiences that make it highly likely that the attitude in question is correct. (For example, one has an attitude of *desire* as a response to beliefs or experiences that make it likely that the object of one's desire really is *desirable*; or one has an attitude of *admiration* as a response to beliefs or experiences that make it highly likely that the object of one's admiration really is *admirable*.) Then according to my proposal, this attitude is the manifestation of a disposition that is *essential* to the capacity for having attitudes of this type in the first place. Because this disposition is essential to the capacity for having attitudes of this type, everyone who is capable of those attitudes will have this disposition. Hence this disposition is not an idiosyncratic or unusual disposition. On the contrary, it is a disposition that everyone has; in most cases, it will

---

[13] For some forceful criticisms of this claim, see Velleman (2000: essay 5).

also be a disposition the manifestation of which has formed part of everyone's conscious mental life. Hence it is unsurprising that we find manifestations of this disposition particularly intelligible and easy to understand, especially in contrast to more unusual dispositions that may reflect more idiosyncratic features of particular individuals; and attitudes that cannot be explained by appealing to these universal dispositions will seem puzzling and harder to explain. This point seems to me to provide some support for my proposal to extend my version of the idea that the intentional is normative to emotional attitudes in the way that I have outlined.

10.4 THE SOURCE OF NORMATIVE INTUITIONS

The version of the claim that the intentional is normative that I have proposed here seems to imply that the dispositions that are *essential* to the capacity for a given sort of mental state are *reliable indicators* of the truth of certain normative propositions concerning that sort of mental states. The disposition that is essential to possessing the concept 'or', for example, is a disposition to use the concept in *rational* ways. In this way, these essential dispositions are reliable indicators of the truth about which ways of thinking are rational.

Moreover, in a more indirect way, these essential dispositions are also reliable indicators of the truth about which mental states are *correct*. For example, I suggested above that the disposition that is essential to the capacity for admiration is a disposition to respond to a set of antecedent mental states that makes it highly likely that it is correct to admire a certain object, by having an attitude of admiration for that object. Thus, this essential disposition is a reliable indicator of which sets of antecedent mental states make it likely that it is correct to admire various objects.

As I have already noted, there are many philosophical controversies surrounding the interpretation of terms like 'likely'. Unfortunately, I cannot enter into these disputes here; nor can I defend a complete theory about what the relevant sort of "likelihood" amounts to. To fix ideas, however, I shall make the following assumption about the sort of "likelihood" that I have just appealed to here. We may illustrate this assumption by means of the following example. Suppose that the manifestation of a certain disposition is a reliable indicator of the fact that a certain set of antecedent mental states makes it highly likely that it is correct to admire a certain object. Then according to this assumption, the manifestation of this disposition is also a reliable indicator of the fact that, at least *in normal conditions*, if *all of those antecedent mental states are correct*, it is also correct to admire the object in question. Thus, a manifestation of the disposition that is essential to the capacity for admiration is a reliable indicator of the fact that at least in normal conditions, if all the antecedent mental states that trigger this manifestation of the disposition are correct, then the attitude of admiration that results from this manifestation of the disposition is itself also correct. More generally, I shall assume that the disposition that is essential to having the capacity for any type of emotional attitude is a reliable indicator of what—at least in normal conditions, if the relevant antecedent mental states are correct—it is correct to have the relevant emotional attitude towards.

In these ways, then, these essential mental dispositions are reliable indicators of corresponding normative truths. Now it seems possible for one to be sensitive to these reliable indicators of normative truths in forming and revising one's normative beliefs. In effect, one can treat the manifestations of one's mental dispositions as *prima facie* evidence of the corresponding normative truths. One can treat facts about what one is disposed to believe as evidence for what it is rational for one to believe, facts about what one is disposed to admire as evidence for what it is correct to admire, and so on. To form one's normative beliefs in this way is not necessarily to base one's normative beliefs on any conscious *judgments* about one's mental dispositions; one's normative beliefs can be *directly sensitive* to the contours of these mental dispositions themselves.

There are at least two ways in which one's normative beliefs may be directly sensitive to the contours of these mental dispositions. First, one may actually be *in* the conditions that trigger a manifestation of the disposition, and one may form the belief directly in response to that manifestation of the disposition. For example, suppose that I feel an emotion of admiration on reading about someone's action in the newspaper. This emotion of admiration is triggered by various beliefs that I have about the person's action. As I proposed above, if the disposition manifested in this case is the disposition that is essential to the capacity for admiration, then this emotion of admiration is a reliable indicator that at least in normal conditions, if all of those beliefs about the person's action are correct, then the person's action really is admirable. Suppose that I assume that conditions are normal (in part because my emotion of admiration is wholehearted, and not clouded by any countervailing emotions, and nothing else seems relevantly unusual about this case); and suppose that I also assume that the beliefs on which this emotion of admiration is based are correct. Then I may respond directly to this emotion by forming the belief that the action in question really is admirable.

This way of forming normative beliefs, however, is limited to those cases in which one is actually *in* the conditions that trigger the manifestation of the disposition in question. It may be possible to be sensitive to the contours of our mental dispositions even if we are not in conditions that actually trigger the manifestation of those dispositions. As several philosophers have recently claimed, we seem to have the capacity for a sort of *"offline simulation"* of the operation of our mental dispositions. We can imaginatively simulate being in certain mental states—having certain beliefs or experiences, say—and then we can respond in a way that simulates the way in which we are disposed to respond to actually being in those mental states.[14]

For example, suppose that you imagine a certain act (say, you imagine a doctor who kills one healthy patient to use his organs to save five patients who would otherwise die). Imagining this act is a sort of "make-believe": it involves a simulation of the state of believing that someone has performed an act of this kind. Then you might respond to this imagining with a simulation of the moral emotion that you are disposed to have in response to actually believing that a doctor has acted in this way. In the case of imagining this act in particular, you will most likely respond with a simulation of the moral emotion of wholehearted disapproval, unclouded by any countervailing emotions or inclinations. Then it is possible for you to respond to this sort of simulation of the emotion of such wholehearted disapproval by forming the corresponding moral belief that at least in normal conditions, any action of this kind is wrong.

If that is true, then it may be plausible that this is what our so-called "moral intuitions" actually consist in—either actual moral emotions, or the offline simulation of our dispositions for moral emotions. In this way, we can give a clear account of where our "moral intuitions" come from; we do not have to postulate any inscrutable mechanism for becoming aware of moral truths.

This kind of simulation of the operations of one's emotional dispositions need not involve actually *thinking* about one's own emotions, or indeed representing emotions in any way. Indeed, strictly speaking, it need not be an imagining *of* an emotion—just as visualizing an uninhabited island involves simulating a visual experience of the island, but it does *not* involve imagining the occurrence of a visual experience of the island (after all, one is precisely imagining the island as uninhabited).[15] When one imagines an act, and responds with a simulation of an emotion of moral disapproval towards that act, one's attention is wholly focused on the imagined act (not on one's own reactions towards the act).

A similar account could be given of our intuitions of what it is rational to choose. Suppose that I am wondering about what it is rational to choose in a certain situation—say, in the choice situation of Newcomb's problem.[16] I imagine the situation in question by simulating the beliefs and desires that define that situation; and I may then respond with a simulation of the choice that I am disposed to make in response to actually having the beliefs and desires in question. This response, which in my case reflects my disposition to be a "two-boxer" in situations of this kind, also disposes me to judge that it is *rational* to make this

---

[14] This idea, of the "offline simulation of our mental dispositions" has been invoked by several philosophers to explain how we ascribe mental states to others. See in particular Goldman (1989) and Heal (2003). (My own views would be considerably closer to Heal's than to Goldman's, as is no doubt suggested by my acceptance of a normative theory of intentional states.)

[15] For this point, see Williams (1973).

[16] For a thorough discussion of Newcomb's problem, see Joyce (1999).

choice in this situation. So this may be what my intuition that it is rational to be a "two-boxer" consists in — the offline simulation of my dispositions for making choices. A similar account could be given of our intuitions of what it is rational to believe.[17]

In general, according to this account, it is precisely the same dispositions that underlie both one's intuitions of rationality and one's intuitions of correctness. When one manifests or simulates the operation of a mental disposition that responds to a certain set of antecedent mental states by forming a certain new mental state, this will incline one to form two different beliefs (if the relevant question arises). The first of these two beliefs is the belief that it is *rational* to form that new mental state in response to *being in* those antecedent mental states, while the second is the belief that at least in normal conditions, if all of those antecedent mental states are *correct*, then the new mental state in question is also correct. When the manifestation or simulation of the disposition inclines one to form the former belief, it is an intuition of rationality; when it inclines one to form the latter belief, it is an intuition of correctness.

This proposal, that we can base our normative beliefs on intuitions, where intuitions are interpreted as consisting in either the manifestation or the offline simulation of our mental dispositions, has some advantages over another proposal that some philosophers have made — namely, the proposal that we can base our normative and evaluative beliefs directly on our *emotions* or *affective states*.[18] First, my proposal allows for a uniform treatment of beliefs about what it is rational to believe (which are surely not based on any emotions or affective states), and of beliefs about what it is correct or appropriate to admire or disapprove of. Secondly, it can accommodate the fact that so much of our thinking about normative matters focuses on imaginary cases, which (since we do not believe these cases to be actual) rarely inspire any actual emotions or affective states on our part.

10.5 THE QUEST FOR REFLECTIVE EQUILIBRIUM

Even though my proposal differs from the proposal that we base our evaluative beliefs directly on our emotions, it faces some of the same objections. As I have

---

[17] The main way in which the dispositions that are essential to possessing various particular *concepts* serve as a source of our normative intuitions is as the source of our intuitions about what it is *rational to believe*. (It may be that our beliefs about what it is *correct* to believe arise in the following simple way: wholeheartedly believing a proposition p inclines one to believe that it is correct to believe p — just as wholeheartedly admiring an object x inclines one to believe that that it is correct to admire x — and so if one simulates believing a proposition p, one will respond with a simulation of believing that it is correct to believe p, thus leading one to accept the inference from p to 'It is correct to believe p'.)

[18] See especially Tappolet (2000) and Johnston (2001*a*).

already pointed out, even if it is true that these "essential" mental dispositions are reliable indicators of corresponding normative truths, these dispositions may in many cases be blocked or inhibited by interfering factors. Moreover, we may also have many other dispositions to use a given concept, or to have attitudes of a given type, that are not essential to the capacity for that concept or attitude-type; and many of these other dispositions may be entirely *unreliable*. Thus, for example, people's moral emotions are notoriously unreliable. Slave owners might have the most wholehearted attitudes of moral disapproval towards slaves who defy their masters.[19] In general, many of our mental dispositions are most definitely *not* reliable indicators of corresponding normative truths.

So if our "intuitions" consist in simulations of the operations of our mental dispositions, or in the manifestation of those dispositions, some of these intuitions will be unreliable. Moreover, we seem to have no way of responding directly to the difference between our essential and our non-essential mental dispositions—nor, more generally, to the difference between reliable and unreliable dispositions. So, we have no way of responding directly to the difference between reliable and unreliable intuitions.

However, it may still be possible to correct for the errors that our normative intuitions may lead us into, just as we can correct for the errors that we might otherwise be led into by perceptual illusions and hallucinations and the like. We correct for such sensory illusions and hallucinations because we can use the beliefs that we base on our sensory experiences to build up a *theory*, or a set of *background beliefs*, about the world; and then we can sometimes reject as misleading those sensory experiences whose content fails to cohere in a satisfactory way with this theory or set of background beliefs. In general, such a failure of coherence between a sensory experience and one's rational background beliefs will *defeat* the justification that the experience would otherwise give to the belief that one could form by taking that experience at face value; that is, when there is such a failure of coherence it is not rational, as it might otherwise be, to form a belief by taking one's sensory experience at face value. Moreover, the *greater* the degree of coherence between a sensory experience and one's rational background beliefs, the *higher* the degree of justification that is enjoyed by the belief that one would form by taking that experience at face value.

I propose that something similar holds with respect to normative beliefs. One way in which one might set about building a normative theory on the basis of one's normative intuitions is suggested by John Rawls's (1971: § 9) account of the method of moral theory as a quest for "reflective equilibrium". This method would involve the following steps. First, we would have to try to canvas as many intuitions as we can, and then try to fit all these intuitions together into a coherent systematic set of normative beliefs. Our intuitions themselves suggest that some of these normative propositions demand explanation; so a coherent overall set

---

[19] Compare for example Mill (1869: ch. 1, para. 6).

of normative beliefs will have to give at least some outline of an explanation of some of these propositions in terms of other such normative propositions. In this way, we may be led to reject some of our intuitions if doing so leads to a more coherent overall set of normative beliefs. When we reject some of our initial pre-theoretical intuitions in this way, we will also be led to views about which sorts of empirical psychological explanations of an intuition are most likely to cast doubt on its reliability. Then, we can carry out psychological investigations of our own intuitions, to see whether any of them are best explained in ways that should lead us to view them with suspicion.

This broadly Rawlsian account seems to describe an unusually self-conscious reasoning process, which is more likely to be followed by theorists, who are explicitly aiming to reach a justified theory, than by ordinary thinkers who typically consider normative questions in a more piecemeal way, without explicitly aiming to achieve this sort of coherence in their belief system as a whole. However, ordinary thought may also be sensitive to the presence or absence of this sort of coherence. An ordinary thinker might refrain from forming a belief on the basis of a normative intuition if there is a serious failure of this sort of coherence; and in general an ordinary thinker might proportion her degree of confidence in a normative intuition to the intuition's degree of coherence with her normative background beliefs.

I propose then that one rational way of forming normative beliefs is to form a normative belief directly on the basis of a normative intuition, subject to the condition that that intuition coheres with one's rational background beliefs in the way that I have described. However, unless one's background beliefs are entirely arbitrary, it is hard to see what they will themselves have been based on, if not on other normative intuitions. So in the end all that this sort of sensitivity to coherence can achieve is a way of playing one's normative intuitions off against one another. Thus, even if one only relies on one's normative intuitions when the coherence constraint that I have described is met, this way of forming normative beliefs may not succeed in correcting for all the errors in one's intuitions. In particular, it will not succeed if one's initial pre-theoretical intuitions are so unreliable that further reflection based on these intuitions will only lead one deeper into error. It will succeed only if one's initial intuitions are at least sufficiently reliable that a process of reflection based on these intuitions will eventually lead one closer to the truth.

However, I do not see how one can have any *a priori* guarantee that one's initial pre-theoretical normative intuitions are sufficiently reliable in this way—any more than one can have an *a priori* guarantee that one's sensory experiences are veridical perceptions rather than hallucinations that an evil demon is implanting in one's mind. But it is doubtful whether there is any available alternative method that does not ultimately depend on one's pre-theoretical normative intuitions in this way (just as it is doubtful whether there is any method for detecting hallucinations that does not ultimately rely on one's sensory experiences).

Nonetheless, it seems to me that it is perfectly rational for us to form normative beliefs by means of this method. We need to have some normative beliefs if we are to act as reflective agents at all. It would be quite unreasonable to demand that we should suspend judgment about all normative propositions unless we have some infallible method of reaching true normative beliefs. It would also be unreasonable to demand that we should only form normative beliefs by methods that we have some independent or antecedent reason for regarding as reliable, since unless there is some basic or primitively rational way of forming normative beliefs, we could never have any such independent or antecedent reason for regarding any way of forming normative beliefs as reliable in the first place.

The only reasonable demand to make here is that we should not form normative beliefs in a certain way in the absence of any independent or antecedent reason for regarding that way of forming normative beliefs as reliable, unless that way of forming beliefs has some essential connection to the truth. If my account is correct, there *is* a general essential connection between our normative intuitions and the truth: these normative intuitions arise from our underlying mental dispositions, and some of these dispositions are guaranteed, by the essential nature of the concepts and mental states involved, to be reliable indicators of corresponding normative truths. Since this connection to the truth is guaranteed by the essential nature of the concepts and mental states that are involved in this way of forming beliefs, it may well be that this way of forming normative beliefs is primitively rational.

Moreover, it also seems plausible that in certain favourable cases, the beliefs that are formed in this way may count as *knowledge*. Suppose that one arrives at a normative belief, and the normative intuitions on which one relies in arriving at this belief consist purely in simulations of the operations of these essential dispositions. In that case—according to my account—all these intuitions will be true. Since the intuitions that one bases this belief on are all true, and the dispositions that these intuitions arise from are reliable indicators of the corresponding normative truths, it seems quite possible that the belief should be reliable, in the sense that it could not easily happen that one should follow that method in those circumstances but fail to form a belief that is true. If this belief is also rational, then this normative belief will plausibly count as knowledge.[20]

Some philosophers will object to my proposal that there is a parallel between the explanation of why it is rational to form normative beliefs by relying on one's normative intuitions and the explanation of why it is rational to form beliefs by taking one's experiences at face value. According to these philosophers, this proposal is vitiated by certain disanalogies between sensory experiences and normative intuitions. For example, while cognitive scientists often explain our

---

[20] For more about this conception of knowledge, see Wedgwood (2002c).

sensory experiences on the basis of the very facts that make those experiences veridical, there is no serious research program of attempting to explain our normative intuitions on the basis of the corresponding normative facts.

In fact, however, even if there is a disanalogy here, it is not clear that it undermines the proposal that I am making. According to my proposal, what we need to explain the rationality of relying on normative intuitions is some account of how these intuitions have some sort of essential connection to the truth—not necessarily a scientific practice of explaining these intuitions on the basis of the corresponding normative facts.

Anyway, I have argued in Chapter 8 that there is in fact no disanalogy here. According to the arguments that I developed there, it is a crucial (though no doubt often merely implicit) assumption of many psychological explanations that we often form a belief or other attitude *precisely because* our antecedent mental states make it rational for us to do so. Of course, such explanations would presuppose the existence of normative facts (such as the fact that certain antecedent mental states make it rational for the thinker to form a certain new belief), and the existence of such normative facts is philosophically controversial; and according to my proposal, the only primitively rational way of coming to know such facts relies on the very intuitions that are in question. But there is no disanalogy here with sensory experiences. The cognitive scientists' explanations of our experiences presuppose the existence of a material world, which is philosophically controversial (it is denied by Berkeleyan idealists), and the only primitively rational way of coming to know facts about the material world is by relying on the very experiences that are in question. This surely does not cast doubt on the rationality of forming beliefs by taking experiences at face value. So the analogous fact also does not cast doubt on the rationality of forming beliefs by relying on our normative intuitions.

This is not to say that there are no important disanalogies between sensory experiences and normative intuitions. One important disanalogy comes out particularly clearly in the case of normative intuitions that concern purely imaginary examples, and consist in the offline simulation of our underlying mental dispositions. In these cases, the belief that the intuition inclines one to form is a *general* belief—such as the belief that in any normal case of such-and-such a kind, it is correct to admire an action of such-and-such a kind. In this way, our normative intuitions are crucially different from our sensory experiences, whose contents are brutely particular—that is, they concern how things are in a particular situation at a particular time. In my view, any plausible account of the epistemology of normative beliefs must capture this crucial difference between normative intuitions and sensory experiences. Nonetheless, this does not rule out the limited sort of analogy between the two ways of forming beliefs that I have invoked above.

Many further problems will have to be solved before this approach can give a fully satisfactory epistemology of normative beliefs. Out of these many further problems, two stand out as particularly pressing. First, we need to resolve the question of whether this method of forming normative beliefs is empirical or *a priori*. Secondly, we need to explain how this method could produce rational beliefs in spite of the widespread disagreement that surrounds normative questions. I shall attempt to address these further questions in the next chapter.

11

Disagreement and the *A Priori*

11.1 EMPIRICAL OR *A PRIORI?*

Suppose that the proposal that I outlined in the previous chapter is correct. Would this make our knowledge of normative propositions empirical or *a priori?*

This question corresponds to a fundamental dilemma in the epistemology of normative beliefs. On the one hand, there seem to be strong arguments in favour of the view that if we ever know (or even ever have rational or justified beliefs in) any normative propositions, then it must be possible to know some of those propositions *a priori* (or at least to have *a priori* justification for believing those propositions). On the other hand, there are also other arguments that seem to show that no such aprioristic epistemology could possibly be true of normative beliefs.

The most important of the arguments in favour of an aprioristic epistemology for normative beliefs are closely related to Kant's arguments for the claim that fundamental moral principles are *a priori*. As Kant says in the Preface to the *Groundwork for the Metaphysics of Morals* (1785: 389):[1]

Everyone must admit that if a law is to hold morally, that is, as a ground of an obligation, it must carry with it absolute necessity: it is not as if the commandment *Thou shalt not lie* holds only for human beings, while other rational beings did not have to take account of it; and the same goes for all other genuine moral laws. Consequently, the ground of the obligation must not be sought in the nature of the human being, or in the circumstances in the world in which he is placed, but *a priori* purely in concepts of pure reason.

Kant's point here is that fundamental moral laws apply to all possible rational beings—not just to human beings, but also to angels, Martians and other extraterrestrials, and so on.[2] How could empirical information, about how things actually happen to be with human beings, be even relevant to establishing a principle that concerns all possible rational beings, in absolutely all possible worlds? If moral laws cannot be established on the basis of such empirical

---

[1] For other passages where Kant insists that the fundamental moral principles must be *a priori*, see Kant (1785: 406–12, 425–7). More recent defenders of the *a priori* status of fundamental moral principles include Christopher Peacocke (2004).

[2] For a related argument, in favour of the claim that there must be fundamental normative principles that do not depend on any contingent non-normative facts, see G. A. Cohen (2003).

information, then it seems that if they can be known at all, it must be possible to know them *a priori*.[3]

As it stands, this argument is open to a number of objections—although as I shall argue, it is possible to amend the argument so that it can successfully surmount these objections. First, as we have already seen, in Chapter 9, there may be some necessary truths such that the explanation for their necessity itself involves contingent facts; such truths will be necessary, but not necessarily necessary, and they will typically be only empirically knowable. To defend Kant's argument then, we will need to exclude these cases, and focus only on cases of truths the necessity of which does not depend on contingent facts in this way. We may do this by focusing on necessary truths that are themselves *modal* truths, about what is the case in all possible worlds. So long as these modal truths are necessary, the explanation of these truths cannot involve contingent facts; and so we will not have that reason for thinking that these truths can only be known empirically.

However, it is quite familiar by now that there are some necessary modal truths, about what is the case in all possible worlds, which can only be known empirically. For example, the proposition that it is true in all possible worlds that water is H_2O can only be known empirically, even though this proposition is a necessary truth about what is the case in all possible worlds. But Kant's argument can be amended so that it is also immune to this objection. The necessary modal truths that can only be known empirically all seem to involve concepts like 'water', the reference of which does not just depend on the concept's conceptual role in thinking and reasoning, but also depends on further contingent facts about the world (such as the causal relations between the thinker's use of the concept and the various natural kinds that are actually instantiated in the thinker's environment). There are other concepts, however, such as logical, mathematical, and psychological concepts, the reference of which depends purely on the concepts' inner conceptual role, and not on any further contingent facts about the world. Necessary modal truths involving concepts of this second kind seem to be knowable *a priori*.[4] According to the account that I outlined in Chapter 4, normative concepts, the concepts that can be expressed by terms like 'ought', are also concepts of this second kind: their reference or semantic value depends purely on their inner conceptual role, not on any contingent facts about

---

[3] Clearly, Kant is relying here on the principle that he famously articulated in the Introduction to the *Critique of Pure Reason* (1787: 3): "Experience teaches us, to be sure, that something is thus and so, but not that it could not be otherwise".

[4] For an argument for this point, see Bealer (1987) on the limits to "scientific essentialism". It would take too long to offer an explanation here of exactly *why* necessary modal truths involving only concepts of this sort must be knowable *a priori*. Very roughly, I would suggest something along the following lines: if such a truth holds it does so as a result of the nature or essence of the objects, properties, or relations that are mentioned in that truth; if the inner conceptual role of a concept determines the concept's semantic value, then it must also determine the nature or essence of that semantic value; and if that is the case, then that nature or essence must be accessible to *a priori* investigation.

the relations between the thinker and his environment. So any necessary modal truths that involve normative, psychological, logical, and mathematical concepts will also be knowable *a priori*.

A further drawback in Kant's argument is that it appears that Kant is overlooking the possibility that something could be known both empirically *and a priori*. For example, a mathematical truth can be known both *a priori* (as when one knows it directly on the basis of a mathematical proof) and empirically (for example, on the basis of the testimony of a credible expert). But in these cases, when the truth that can be known *a priori* is known empirically, this seems to be the case only because the empirical basis on which the knowledge is based in some way reflects the existence of an (actual or possible) *a priori* basis. Thus, in many cases, one knows a mathematical proposition p on the basis of testimony only because the testimony information derives ultimately from someone who knew p, not on the basis of testimony, but on the basis of an *a priori* proof. In other cases, one might come to believe a proposition q because one has empirical knowledge that a computer has produced a proof of q. In this case, no one actually knows q on the basis of this proof; nonetheless, the computer proof is a possible *a priori* basis for knowing the proposition in question (if we endowed the computer with an artificial intelligence so that it was capable of having beliefs and thoughts, it might know q on the basis of this proof).

So if there are necessary modal truths involving only normative concepts and other concepts whose reference depends purely on the concepts' inner conceptual role, then it seems that these truths will be knowable *a priori*, and it will be possible to know those truths on an empirical basis only if that empirical basis reflects the existence of some (actual or possible) *a priori* basis. In fact, it seems plausible that there are indeed necessary normative truths of just this kind.

I argued in Chapter 6 that it is plausible that normative truths strongly supervene on non-normative truths. If one agent A_1 ought to act in a certain way W at a certain time t_1, for example, then it is impossible for there to be an agent A_2 and time t_2 such that A_2's situation at t_2 is exactly like A_1's situation at t_1 in every non-normative respect, without its being the case that A_2 also ought to act in the same way W at t_2. As I explained there, it follows under certain natural assumptions that there is some non-normative relation between an agent and a time such that it is *necessary* that when an agent is related to a time in that way, the agent ought to act in the way W in question.

It also seems plausible that normative truths strongly supervene on truths that can be stated using non-normative concepts the reference of which does not depend on contingent facts about the thinker's environment. It seems highly doubtful whether the fact that one's situation involves water, rather than some other substance whose mental effects are just like those of water, could make any difference to what one ought to do, unless it also made a difference that could be described in psychological or sociological terms—such as making a difference to what type of act will count in the situation as keeping a promise or speaking truthfully or the like.[5] More specifically, it may be that what an agent ought to do at a time *t* strongly supervenes on *mental* and *social* facts about the agent's situation at *t*. If so, then every normative relation between an agent and a time is necessitated by some (possibly highly complex) mental and social relation between that agent and that time. Moreover, it seems plausible that whether or not such a mental and social relation necessitates a normative relation is never a merely contingent matter: if a mental and social relation necessitates a normative relation, or fails to necessitate a normative relation, it does so necessarily. It is hard to see how contingent facts about the actual world could make any difference to whether or not a mental and social relation necessitates a normative relation. So there are necessary modal truths to the effect that in all possible worlds, whenever such-and-such a mental and social relation holds between an agent and a time, the agent ought to do something of such-and-such a kind. Furthermore, these necessary modal truths will form a set of principles such that every instance of the normative relation falls under one of these principles.

As I have already suggested, it also seems plausible that such mental and social facts can be specified using concepts (like psychological, logical, and mathematical concepts) the reference of which is determined purely by the concepts' inner conceptual role. As I have also pointed out, it seems that if necessary modal truths involving only concepts of this sort can be known at all, then they can be known *a priori*. So, if normative truths strongly supervene on facts that can be specified using concepts of this sort, then there will necessary truths involving normative concepts that are knowable *a priori*. This then gives us a reason to be sympathetic to the Kantian position that the fundamental normative truths are knowable *a priori*.

On the other hand, there are also other reasons to be profoundly sceptical of the possibility of *a priori* normative knowledge. The paradigmatic cases of *a priori* knowledge include our knowledge of logical and mathematical truths. But our normative beliefs seem profoundly different from these paradigmatic cases of *a priori* knowledge. First of all, our logical and mathematical knowledge is based, directly or indirectly, on *proofs*. But there does not seem to be anything in our normative thinking that deserves to be called a "proof" of the sort that one finds in logic or mathematics. One sign of this is that mathematicians and logicians seem to *agree* with each other a lot more than ethicists and other normative theorists. Ethicists and normative theorists are famous for disagreeing more than theorists in almost any other domain of rational inquiry, whereas mathematicians and logicians all seem to agree about the major discoveries and theorems of their field. Different normative theorists seem to have very different fundamental normative intuitions, while mathematicians all seem to have the same fundamental mathematical intuitions. Moreover, normative intuitions are fallible to a much greater degree than mathematical intuitions, so that ethical

---

[5] For a slightly fuller argument for this point see Wedgwood (1999*a*: 201–2).

and normative propositions seem altogether to lack the sort of certainty that is characteristic of the paradigmatic forms of *a priori* knowledge, such as logic and mathematics.

It is controversial among philosophers how exactly *a priori* knowledge is best explained. Many different accounts of *a priori* knowledge have been offered over the years. But according to many of these accounts, our *a priori* intuitions stem from our grasp of concepts. According to one reasonably clear version of this account, this is because our grasp of concepts essentially involves some implicit conception of the nature of the object, property, or relation that is the concept's reference or semantic value; and our *a priori* intuitions consist in mental states in which we become aware of some immediate implication of the content of one of these implicit conceptions. Moreover, according to this account, the content of this implicit conception is guaranteed to be true, because the concept's semantic value is determined as that semantic value which makes this implicit conception come out true.[6] In that sense, this approach makes all *a priori* truths *conceptual* truths.

As I have already argued in Chapter 3, however, no account of normative concepts along these lines is acceptable. Such accounts cannot explain the "internalist" character of normative judgments—their essential (or "internal") connection to practical reasoning and motivation.

Moreover, such accounts also have a hard time explaining the prevalence of fundamental disagreement about normative questions. We can illustrate this point by comparing normative concepts to other concepts for which an account along these general lines seems particularly plausible. For example, it is plausible that anyone who grasps the concept 'uncle' must have at least some implicit conception of what it is for something to be an uncle (namely, that to be an uncle is to be the brother of a parent), and this may well explain how we come to have our fundamental intuitions about uncles, such as our intuition that any brother of a parent is an uncle. Similarly, it may be that possessing the concept 'chair' involves having some implicit conception of what it is for something to be a chair. It is true that if we asked an ordinary thinker to give an explicit account of the conditions under which something counts as a chair, they might give an account that was unclear or erroneous in some respect; nonetheless this does not prevent it from being the case that the ordinary thinker really does have an implicit conception of this kind.

The trouble with taking this approach to normative concepts is that in all the cases where it is most plausible that our possession of a concept essentially involves such an implicit conception, there are hardly ever any fundamental disagreements about the nature of the concept's semantic value. There is fundamental disagreement about the conditions under which actions are right or wrong, or under which choices are rational or irrational, as we see from all

---

[6] See Peacocke (1993); a broadly similar account is offered in Bealer (1999).

the attention that is devoted to these questions by academic researchers and peer-reviewed journals and the like. But academics do not convene international conferences to address questions like 'Are all brothers of parents uncles?', and it seems doubtful whether anyone has ever been given a significant research grant for a research project on the question 'Must all genuine chairs have backs as well as seats?' For these reasons then, this account of the *a priori* as flowing from the implicit conceptions that are essential to possessing various concepts seems to be inapplicable to normative concepts.[7]

In this way, any philosopher who seeks to offer an account of the epistemology of normative beliefs faces a dilemma: on the one hand, it seems that if normative knowledge is possible at all, at least some of it must be *a priori*; on the other hand, it seems that normative thinking is so unlike the paradigmatic examples of *a priori* thinking that normative thinking cannot be *a priori* at all. In the following section, I shall try to solve this problem by arguing that the account developed in the previous chapter does indeed make some normative knowledge *a priori*, in a sense; but it also makes this knowledge a very special case of the *a priori*, which is importantly different from most other forms of *a priori* knowledge.

11.2 A KANTIAN CONCEPTION OF THE *A PRIORI*

It will be important here exactly how we define the distinction between the empirical and the *a priori*. In this section, I shall outline an account of the *a priori*, and then I shall argue on the basis of this account that the proposal outlined in the previous chapter implies that under favourable circumstances, our knowledge of fundamental normative truths is *a priori*. However, this sort of normative knowledge is a special case of the *a priori*; it differs from most other kinds of *a priori* knowledge in certain crucial ways.

The account of the *a priori* that I shall outline here is broadly Kantian in inspiration. In the Introduction to the second edition of the *Critique of Pure Reason* (1787: 1), Kant introduces one of the central questions of his critical philosophy in the following terms:

But even though all our cognition begins with experience, it does not follow that it all arises out of experience. For it may well be that even our empirical cognition is composed both out of what we receive through impressions and out of what our own cognitive faculty (sensory impressions serving merely as the occasion) supplies out of itself.

This suggests the following way of characterizing the *a priori*: the *a priori* is what our relevant cognitive capacities "supply out of themselves". In other words, the *a priori* is what is in a sense "built into" these cognitive capacities. *A priori*

---

[7] This objection is closely akin to G. E. Moore's (1903: ch. 1) attack on the idea that fundamental ethical principles are analytic or conceptual truths.

knowledge is knowledge that is accessible, at least in principle, to anyone who has the relevant capacities. Those who possess these capacities are in a position to acquire such knowledge, simply through exercising those capacities, without relying on any information that is not necessarily available to everyone who possesses those capacities.

Which capacities are the "relevant cognitive capacities"? Different accounts of the *a priori* could give different answers to this question. For example, some accounts would say that the *possession of a concept* is always one of the relevant capacities. The propositions that have often been taken to be analytic (such as the proposition that *all uncles are male*, for example) are arguably propositions that everyone who possesses the concepts that the proposition involves is in a position to know. Tentatively, I suggest the following account of the matter. Perhaps possessing these concepts necessarily involves mastery of certain rules of inference, including (i) the rule of universal generalization, (ii) conditional proof, and (iii) the rule that allows one to infer from any proposition of the form '*x* is an uncle' to the corresponding proposition of the form '*x* is male'. (Instances of these three rules are always valid because the reference or semantic value of the relevant concepts must be determined in such a way as to make all instances of these rules valid.) Then the proposition that all uncles are male can be validly inferred, by means of these three rules of inference, from the empty set of assumptions—which is a way of coming to know the proposition.

Other accounts of the *a priori* could focus on a different set of capacities, rather than on the capacities that consist in one's possession of concepts. For example, Kant (1787: 3) defined "*pure* knowledge" as knowledge that was accessible to us purely in virtue of the capacities that we must have simply in virtue of being finite rational beings whose intuition is sensible. Our possession of "empirical concepts"—concepts that we possess only because of the specific content (as opposed to the form) of our experience—did not in his view count as a "relevant capacity" for the purpose of defining "pure knowledge".

Another possibility would be to insist that the relevant capacities must all be *innate*. This would lead to a more Leibnizian conception of the *a priori*. On this conception, normative knowledge would only count as *a priori* if all the capacities that we exercise in forming the relevant normative beliefs are innate. According to the account that I sketched in the previous chapter, these capacities include our emotional dispositions. Most of these dispositions seem not to be innate, but rather to be the products of a complex learning process which involves extensive interaction between the individual and her environment (including her social environment). So on this more Leibnizian conception, our normative knowledge would not count as *a priori*.

I propose a conception of the *a priori* that takes as the "relevant capacities" a set that includes both our possession of the various *concepts* that we possess, and our capacities for the various *types of attitudes* that we are capable of, and also whatever other capacities and dispositions we must have in order to possess these concepts or to be capable of these attitudes. These attitude-types include such attitudes as belief, choice, intention, and the various sorts of emotion, including moral emotions. If the normative theory of intentional states that I outlined in Chapter 7 is correct, then to have the capacity for these types of attitude, one must also have the dispositions to conform to the normative principles that define the nature of those attitudes.

The concepts that are particularly crucial for our purposes are normative concepts, such as the concept of a mental state's being "correct" or "rational", or the various concepts that can be expressed by uses of terms like 'ought'. As I conceded at the end of Chapter 4 (Section 4.5), possession of these normative concepts requires having the capacity to form normative beliefs in some way that counts as a primitively rational way of forming such beliefs; as I argued in the previous chapter, the primitively rational way to form normative beliefs is to base these beliefs on one's normative intuitions (so long as doing so would not lead to significant failure of coherence in one's beliefs); and these normative intuitions arise either from the manifestation or the "offline simulation" of various underlying mental dispositions.

The relevant set of capacities and dispositions, then, includes the dispositions that are essential to being capable of all the relevant attitude-types, the capacity for the sort of offline simulation of the operation of those dispositions that I discussed in the previous chapter, and the capacity for rationally forming normative beliefs on the basis of the normative intuitions that arise from this sort of offline simulation of these dispositions.

In certain cases, then, one might arrive at a belief in a normative proposition purely by means of exercising these capacities and dispositions. In these cases, the normative intuitions that one relies on in arriving at this belief consist purely in simulations of the operations of these essential dispositions. As I argued above, since these essential dispositions are always intrinsically rational dispositions, the intuitions that stem purely from these essential dispositions will all be true. Suppose that the belief that one bases on these true intuitions by means of exercising these capacities is both rational and reliable, in the sense that it could not easily happen that one should follow that method in those circumstances but fail to form a belief in a true proposition. Then as I argued in the previous chapter, this normative belief will plausibly count as knowledge. Moreover, this knowledge arises purely from the exercise of these capacities and dispositions: no further mental states that are not necessarily available to everyone who has those capacities and dispositions are required in order to be able to exercise these capacities and acquire this knowledge. So, since these capacities and dispositions all belong to the relevant set of cognitive capacities, this knowledge counts as *a priori*.

Thus, the proposal outlined here can respect the Kantian point that the fundamental principles about what one ought to do must be knowable *a priori*. On the other hand, this normative knowledge is in several ways a special case of the *a priori*. The classic cases of the *a priori* are considerably simpler: the only relevant capacities are the abilities to follow certain rules of inference, and the propositions that are knowable *a priori* in this way are those that can be inferred, by following those rules of inference, from the empty set of assumptions. According to the account that I gave in the previous chapter, *a priori* normative knowledge is crucially different. First, the rational dispositions that are involved include not just our disposition to make certain inferences, but a much wider range of rational dispositions, including our dispositions to respond to being in certain mental conditions by having certain emotions or by making certain choices. Secondly, it involves not just manifesting some of those rational dispositions—as when one manifests a disposition to form beliefs in a rational way—but also a kind of higher-order sensitivity or responsiveness to certain other rational dispositions that one may not be manifesting on that occasion, such as the sort of sensitivity to one's own dispositions that one achieves through the "offline simulation" of the operation of those dispositions.

These features of my proposal help to provide an answer to the objections that I considered in the previous section to the claim that our knowledge of such basic normative principles is *a priori*. To answer these objections, we need to show how this account—even though it makes some normative beliefs *a priori*—allows sufficient room for the uncertainty and disagreement that seems to be characteristic of normative thought. I shall argue for this in two steps: first, I shall show how (even though my account makes some fundamental normative truths knowable *a priori*) it allows a great deal of room for false and mistaken beliefs to arise, even in highly rational thinkers; secondly, I shall show how my account allows for these normative truths sometimes to be very hard for us to get to, in spite of the fact that they are in principle accessible *a priori*.

First, then, we should note that my account does not make all normative intuitions *a priori*. According to my account, the normative intuitions that arise from the simulation of one's *essential* dispositions are *a priori*; but there are also other normative intuitions that arise from the simulation of other, non-essential dispositions, and the latter intuitions are *not a priori*. There is no way to know for certain whether a normative intuition arises from one's essential dispositions, or from other non-essential dispositions instead. So there is no way of knowing for certain whether a normative intuition is an *a priori* intuition or not. Moreover, as I have already pointed out, there is a very wide range of dispositions the simulation of which may result in a normative intuition: these intuitions do not all arise from a single disposition to accept inferences of a particular kind. So there is very wide scope for false and misleading normative intuitions, and no way to tell for certain whether one's intuitions are true or false.

Secondly, as I have already repeatedly emphasized, one may possess a disposition even if that disposition is not manifested, but is instead blocked or inhibited by some interfering factors. Even the dispositions that are manifested in the simpler kinds of *a priori* reasoning can sometimes be blocked and inhibited in this way. One might have the disposition to infer from propositions of the form 'x is an uncle' to corresponding propositions of the form 'x is male', even if the manifestation of this disposition is blocked or inhibited by some interfering factor, and even if one rejects the proposition that all uncles are male. But in the more complicated case of *a priori* normative knowledge, there are yet more ways in which interfering factors can inhibit the manifestation of the relevant dispositions (and as I shall note in the next section, self-interest and other conflicting impulses of various sorts provide numerous sources of such interfering factors, especially in the case of *moral* thinking). Such interfering factors might inhibit the underlying disposition (such as the disposition to make certain choices or to have certain emotions in response to certain sorts of information about one's situation); or they might block or inhibit one's capacity for simulating the operations of that disposition; or they might inhibit the disposition of such simulations of the operations of the underlying disposition to incline one to believe the corresponding normative proposition.[8] Moreover, even if one has the relevant intuition, one's further normative reflections, based on one's *other* normative beliefs, may lead one to reject the intuition as unreliable even if in fact it is perfectly reliable. So even though some fundamental normative truths can be known *a priori*, they are anything but self-intimating. Many factors can prevent one from coming to believe these normative truths.

Thus, even though these fundamental normative propositions are knowable *a priori*, there are many ways in which one may come to believe normative falsehoods, and many ways in which one may fail to come to believe normative truths. Thus, there is no reason to regard the prevalence of disagreement about these normative propositions as casting doubt on the claim that these propositions can, at least in principle, be known *a priori*.

11.3 MORAL EVIL DEMONS

The prevalence of disagreement about certain fundamental normative questions raises other problems as well. In the rest of this chapter, I shall try to address some of these problems.

In discussing normative disagreement, I shall follow the example of many other philosophers, and concentrate on the case of *moral* disagreement. I shall assume for the purposes of this discussion that the moral is a species of the normative, and that the epistemology of moral judgments does not differ fundamentally

---

[8] A famous fictional instance of this last possibility is Huckleberry Finn: Finn's emotional dispositions would have led him to believe the truth about the injustice of slavery and the permissibility of helping runaway slaves to escape; but his deference (in belief, if not in behaviour) to social authority prevents these dispositions from having this effect. For a suggestive discussion of this case, see Bennett (1974).

from the epistemology of normative judgments of other kinds. Given these assumptions, the issue of moral disagreement will shed light on the epistemology of the normative in general.

It is not hard to see why moral issues should be the focus of more extensive—or at least more conspicuous—disagreement than other normative questions. Moral judgments play a particularly important role in the collective deliberations in which people seek to coordinate their actions in spite of diverging or conflicting interests. Moral consensus is particularly valuable in securing peaceful resolution of disputes and mutually beneficial cooperation; but different individuals, different groups and social classes have sharply diverging interests in exactly what sort of moral consensus emerges from these collective deliberations. Hence there are pressures and influences of many different kinds at work on people's moral judgments, which surely help to explain the prevalence of many of the moral disagreements that exist.

The problem that such disagreement poses for a realist conception of moral thought arises from the following point. If a realist conception of moral thought is correct, then in every case of moral disagreement, at least one of the parties to the disagreement believes something *false*; their belief is *mistaken* or *incorrect*.

However, it seems possible that in at least some of these cases, both parties to the disagreement are forming and revising their beliefs in procedurally rational ways, and neither side holds their belief because of any error or ignorance about the purely non-moral facts. The disagreement between those who think it morally wrong for people like you and me to eat meat, and those who disagree with them, may be a disagreement of this sort.[9] Another such disagreement may be the disagreement over whether or not moral requirements always provide overriding reasons (so that if it is morally wrong for one to φ, then φ-ing is also something that, all things considered, one ought not to do—that is, something that there is conclusive reason for one not to do). In disagreements of this sort, the two parties hold their incompatible beliefs, not because of procedurally irrational reasoning or non-moral error or ignorance, but because the two sides have sufficiently different *pre-theoretical moral intuitions*, which lead them to believe different and incompatible fundamental moral principles. If the dispute is of this kind, then, given that at least one party to the dispute has a false or mistaken belief about the issue in dispute, at least one of the parties must have had *misleading* pre-theoretical intuitions, which led them to a false and mistaken belief about this issue.

Now in some cases of this sort, the pre-theoretical moral intuitions of one of the two parties may contain some sort of incoherence that is not present in the intuitions of the other party. In that case, even though each of the two parties will base their thinking about this issue on their pre-theoretical moral intuitions, it may be fairly easy for the party whose belief is in fact mistaken to discover his mistake by means of this kind of thinking. In some other cases, however, the

---

[9] For a longer and more careful argument for this point, see Miller (1992: ch. 1).

misleading pre-theoretical moral intuitions of this party to the disagreement may be relatively *systematic*: that is, although these intuitions are in fact misleading, they also form an overall set that is no less coherent than the intuitions of the other party. In a case of this sort, even though one of the two parties has an incorrect or mistaken belief, ordinary moral reasoning is powerless to lead the believer to discover this mistake. Since any further reflection on the part of this believer will be based on the same misleading pre-theoretical intuitions, and these intuitions contain no incoherence that would alert the believer to his mistake, further reflection may be unable to lead the believer to correct his mistake. Something has caused the thinker to have the misleading initial intuitions that he has—his upbringing, or his culture, or his character, or something like that. Whatever it was, I shall call it a "moral evil demon"—something that causes moral error in a way that makes that error undetectable by ordinary means to the one who is deceived.

There is a striking difference between these moral evil demons and their more famous cousins, the Cartesian evil demons, who deceive their victims by giving them systematically misleading sensory experiences. The Cartesian evil demons are creatures of philosophical fantasy; they are not to be found in the actual world. Of course, hallucinations and optical illusions do occur. But when they do occur, there is usually some sort of incoherence in the content of one's experiences so that it is relatively easy to avoid being led into any mistaken beliefs. In real life, sensory hallucinations are never so systematic that they cannot be detected by the ordinary methods of empirical thinking. The moral evil demons, on the other hand, are in all probability *actual*. No doubt many moral disagreements are explained by procedurally irrational thinking on one side or the other, or by error or ignorance about relevant non-moral facts. But there seem to be some disagreements that are more plausibly explained by people's pre-theoretical moral intuitions; and in some of these cases, there is no reason to suspect that the intuitions of one of these disagreeing parties contains any sort of internal incoherence that is absent from the other's. In these cases, then, people's pre-theoretical moral intuitions are leading them astray, in a way that resists correction by ordinary moral reflection: that is, a moral evil demon has been at work.

This leads to a different argument for scepticism from the argument that is based on the mere *possibility* of an evil demon. Suppose that one is in a prison where one has strong reason to suspect that prisoners are *actually* routinely anaesthetized in their sleep and then have their brains removed and placed in vats. Surely this should lead one to entertain very serious doubts about one's ordinary perceptual beliefs. So surely, once we become aware that we live in a world in which we have strong reason to suspect that moral evil demons are actually at work, we should entertain very serious doubts about our moral beliefs—indeed, perhaps we should even completely suspend judgment about the large parts of our moral thought that seem likely to be subject to disagreements of this sort.

Let us focus on a symmetrical case. Imagine two thinkers; initially, each of these two thinkers has experiences, memories, intuitions, and background beliefs that make it rational for him to hold certain beliefs about a certain topic. Then each of these thinkers acquires information about the other's mental states and processes. Each of them learns that the other has significantly different experiences, memories, intuitions, or background beliefs, which lead them to hold very different beliefs about the topic in question, and that the most plausible explanation of this difference is that at least one of them is being deceived by an evil demon. Does this new information weaken, or even totally defeat, the justification that each of them had for their beliefs about the disputed topic?

It surely does seem plausible that the new information should at least *raise* the level of credence that each of them should place in the proposition 'I am being deceived by an evil demon'. As Henry Sidgwick (2000: 168)[10] put it:

I suppose that the conflict in most cases [of philosophical controversy] concerns intuitions—what is self-evident to one mind is not so to another. It is obvious that in any such conflict there must be error on one side or the other, or on both. The natural man will often decide unhesitatingly that the error is on the other side. But it is manifest that a philosophic mind cannot do this, unless it can prove independently that the conflicting intuitor has an inferior faculty of envisaging truth in general or this kind of truth; one who cannot do this must reasonably submit to a loss of confidence in any intuition of his own that thus is found to conflict with another's.

However, Sidgwick here only says that given the information that one is in a disagreement of this kind, one "must reasonably submit to a loss of confidence" in the intuition in question. This may be interpreted as the claim that in cases of this kind, one should *lower* one's degree of confidence in the intuition—not as the claim that in such cases one should lose *all* confidence whatsoever.

Suppose that we claimed that in cases of this kind, rationality may require only that one should lower one's confidence in the disputed proposition, and does *not* require that one should lose all confidence whatsoever. We still need not deny the following principle, which is also articulated by Sidgwick (2000: 145):

[A] difference in judgment from another whom he has no reason to regard as less competent to judge than himself, naturally and properly reduces a thinker to a "kind of suspense".

According to this principle, if one comes to know that some other thinker disagrees with one about some proposition, and (even after learning this) one is rationally required to regard that other thinker as no less competent to judge than oneself, then one is rationally required to suspend judgment about the question. We can continue to accept this principle while saying that in the cases that we have been considering, the very fact that the other thinker disagrees may, all by

---

[10] Compare also Sidgwick (1907: 341–2).

itself, be a reason to regard that other thinker as less competent to judge about the proposition in question than one is oneself.

In effect, perhaps these "symmetrical" cases are only symmetrical from a third-personal point of view. From the point of view of each of the two disagreeing thinkers, each is still entitled to regard it as more credible that the *other* is the victim of the demon than that he is himself. Perhaps, quite generally, it is rational for one to place greater trust in one's own intuitions, simply because these intuitions are one's own, than in the intuitions of other people. In other words, perhaps it is rational for each of us to have an *egocentric epistemic bias* in favour of our own intuitions. If that is right, then even if the new information that these two thinkers acquire *weakens* their justification for their beliefs on the disputed topic, it need not totally *defeat* their justification.

Is it rational to have an egocentric epistemic bias of this sort? I shall give a tentative argument here that it is. As I argued in the previous chapter, it must be rational to have a default presumption in favour of certain normative intuitions. That is, a rational agent will be disposed to take these intuitions at face value, even if she has no antecedent or independent reason to regard these intuitions as reliable, at least so long as she does not have any special reason to regard those intuitions as unreliable. As we may put it, the rational agent is disposed to have a *primitive trust* in these intuitions. But *whose* intuitions should one have this sort of primitive trust in? Only one's own intuitions, or anyone's intuitions?

In having this sort of primitive trust in certain intuitions, one is exposing oneself to an epistemic risk, since as we have seen, such intuitions may be mistaken. (Indeed, they may be extraordinarily mistaken: consider a creature constructed by an evil demon precisely in order to be a moral monster—a creature whose moral intuitions are as horrendously false as it is possible for such intuitions to be.) So it seems that although one cannot avoid having a primitive trust in some intuitions, one should also *minimize* the sort of risk that one is exposing oneself to in this way.

In general, it seems to be a general requirement of rationality that one must in some non-arbitrary way minimize the number of sources of information that one has this sort of primitive trust in. (The non-arbitrariness condition is crucial here: it would, for example, be arbitrary to have a primitive trust in one's vision but not in one's hearing or one's sense of touch.) If I have a primitive trust only in my own intuitions, then clearly there is a smaller number of sources of information that I have such a primitive trust in than there would be if I had such a primitive trust in everyone's intuitions. Moreover, it seems to me that it would not be arbitrary for me to have this sort of primitive disposition to trust only my own intuitions: after all, my own intuitions by their very nature involve my having an inclination to believe the corresponding proposition, whereas other people's intuitions do not involve *my* having any such inclination.

In saying this, I am certainly not denying that rationality may sometimes require that one should be impressed by other people's intuitions. On the contrary, other people's intuitions are certainly relevant evidence, which may be highly useful in checking and correcting for the defects in one's own intuitions. I am saying that one should rely on other people's intuitions only to the extent that it is *antecedently* or *independently* rational for one to regard their intuitions as reliable. The fundamental asymmetry between one's own intuitions and those of other people is just that it is rational to trust one's own intuitions even if one has no antecedent or independent reason to regard them as reliable, whereas it is only rational for one to trust other people's intuitions if one has some such antecedent reason to regard their intuitions as reliable.

Indeed, I suggest that this quite generally should be the attitude of rational adults towards the mental states of others. One should trust the mental states of others only to the extent that one has independent or antecedent reason to regard those mental states as reliable.[11] Once one has a large enough stock of rational background beliefs, including beliefs about the world, and about other people and how their minds work, one will almost always be in a position to make a rational judgment about how reliable another person's mind is likely to be about a certain question. For example, my background beliefs tell me that people's sensory perceptions are usually fairly reliable, whereas unless they have a special expertise, their beliefs about abstruse theoretical matters (such as about the age of the universe, or the correctness of various philosophical interpretations of quantum mechanics) are likely to be much less reliable.

In effect, this claim, that one should always respond to information about other people's mental states in the light of what one's own rational antecedent beliefs tell one about those people's mental states' reliability, amounts to the claim that a rational thinker is to a significant degree *autonomous*. She is directly guided by her own mental states, and only indirectly by the mental states of others. Of course, we only ever achieved the position of being a rationally autonomous thinker because we went through a period in our childhood when we were much more credulous and less autonomous.[12] But according to the conception that I

---

[11] This claim puts me at variance with the view of such philosophers as C. A. J. Coady (1992) and Tyler Burge (1997), who defend the rival view that it is rational to have a primitive trust in the mental states of others.

[12] *Pace* Gibbard (1990: 176–81), I deny that this point undermines my claim that it must be rational for the *adult* to have some independent reason for regarding another person's mental states as reliable before it is rational to trust that person's mental states. As I argue elsewhere (Wedgwood 2002c), the principles of rationality that apply to background beliefs are different from the principles that apply to the formation of new beliefs. So the fact that I cannot now offer an independent defence of all the background beliefs that I absorbed from other people while I was growing up does not show that it is now rational for me to trust other people's mental states in the absence of any independent reason to regard those mental states as reliable. For a similar response to arguments of this kind, see Fricker (1995 and 2004).

am advocating here, it is part of achieving the status of a fully rational thinker that one also achieves a measure of autonomy of this kind.

Some philosophers might be tempted to object to my idea that it is rational to have an egocentric epistemic bias on the grounds that it seems absurd for anyone to think to themselves 'I'm me, and he's not; so I'm right and he's wrong'. But this is a travesty of the proposal that I am advocating here. As I have already explained, I am understanding the notion of an "intuition" in such a way that having an intuition with the content p essentially involves an inclination to believe p. Thus, when I have an intuition with the content p, my attention is not on the fact that I am having this intuition, but rather on p itself. I might express this intuition by saying something like '*Prima facie*, it appears that p'. So in trusting one's intuition, one's attention is on the facts, as they appear to be. When a rational thinker is confronted with another person who has an intuition with the content *not-p*, she will think in response, 'He has an intuition with the content that *not-p*, but at least *prima facie*, it appears that p; so at least *prima facie*, it appears that his intuitions are untrustworthy on this question.' Even if she takes note of the fact that she herself is only relying on her own intuition, it will be rational for her to think, 'I have an intuition with the content that p; at least *prima facie*, it appears that p; so at least *prima facie*, it appears that my intuition is correct.'

The position that I am advocating also does not have the implausible implication that another person's intuition should *never* lead one to abandon one's own intuition. It can certainly happen that it is antecedently or independently rational for one to regard the other person as *more* reliable about propositions of the relevant kind than one is oneself. For example, suppose that you know that you and the other person agree about almost all propositions of this kind, but that in the few cases in which you have initially disagreed, you have always in the end been persuaded that she was right and you were in fact wrong. Then it might be rational for you to give equal or even greater weight to her intuitions than to your own.[13]

The conclusion of this section, then, is this. As I have tried to argue, there is a sort of rational asymmetry between one's own intuitions and the intuitions of other people: it is rational to have a primitive trust in one's own intuitions, but not in the intuitions of others. In consequence, even though we know full well that there is widespread disagreement about fundamental moral issues, and that most probably this shows that moral evil demons have been at work, this knowledge may not require us to suspend judgment about these moral issues completely. It may indeed require us to weaken our degree of confidence in our beliefs about those moral issues; but at least sometimes, it may allow each of us to continue having more confidence in the propositions that we believe than in the incompatible propositions that are believed by those who disagree with us.

---

[13] Thus, I need not disagree with the central claims of the argument of Karen Jones (1999).

11.4 NORMATIVE KNOWLEDGE IN CONTEXT

Even if the proposal of the preceding section is correct, so that the probable existence of actual moral evil demons does not totally defeat the justification of our moral beliefs on disputed topics, I have conceded that it surely does *weaken* our justification. What follows from this?

Consider the example of my beliefs about the morality of abortion. Perhaps, given my intuitions about early human foetuses, I am slightly more justified in believing the proposition that early abortions are morally permissible than I am in believing its negation. But can I really say that I *know* this? Indeed, can I even say that it is rational for me simply to have an *outright belief* in this proposition, rather than just to have a more cautious attitude of giving more credence to this proposition than to its negation?

We should concede, I think, that such moral beliefs are not extraordinarily highly justified. I am clearly less justified in believing the proposition that early abortions are morally permissible than I am in believing that $2 + 2 = 4$, or even that I am currently sitting in a chair. But perhaps I am nonetheless justified *enough* so that it is true to say that it is "rational" for me to have an outright belief in this proposition?

If the proposition in question is true, then a similar question arises about whether my belief counts as knowledge. The process that leads to my belief in this proposition certainly seems less reliable than the process that leads to my belief that $2 + 2 = 4$, or the process that leads to my belief that I am now sitting in a chair. Is it reliable enough so that, given that the belief is correct and rational, it is true to say that the belief counts as "knowledge"?

It seems to me that it is plausible here to appeal to a version of *epistemological contextualism*.[14] According to this view, there is no context-independent answer to the question of *how much* justification one needs for a proposition in order for it to be true to say that one's belief in that proposition is "justified". Similarly, there is no context-independent answer to the question of *how reliable* the process that leads to one's belief needs to be in order for it to be true to say that that belief counts as "knowledge". In some contexts when we talk about "rational beliefs" or about "knowledge", strict and demanding standards apply. In these contexts, one needs a very high level of justification for a proposition for it to be true to say that it is "rational" for one to have an outright belief in that proposition; and the belief needs both to have a high level of justification, and to arise from a highly reliable process, if it is to be true to say, in those demanding contexts, that the belief counts as "knowledge". In these strict and demanding contexts,

---

[14] For a more detailed presentation of this version of epistemological contextualism, see Wedgwood (2002c). The most important statements of epistemological contextualism in the literature include those of Stewart Cohen (1999), Keith DeRose (1995), and David Lewis (1996a).

it is not true to describe many outright beliefs as "rational" or as counting as "knowledge". In other contexts, however, more relaxed and undemanding standards apply. In these contexts, it may be true to say that it is "rational" to have an outright belief in a proposition even if one only has a much lower level of justification for the proposition (indeed, perhaps in some contexts, all that one needs is to have more justification for the proposition than for its negation). Similarly, it may be true to say that one "knows" that proposition even if the belief has a relatively low level of justification, and the process that leads to one's holding that belief has a relatively low level of reliability (indeed, perhaps in some contexts, any process that happens to lead to the truth is reliable enough).

Specifically, it may be that in any context, the term 'rational belief' (and the term 'justified belief') has the same semantic value as the term 'belief that is *justified enough for present purposes*'; and the term 'knowledge' has the same semantic value as the term 'true belief that is *justified enough* and *reliable enough, for present purposes*'. If this is right, then it becomes plausible that there will be many contexts in which the relevant purposes only require our moral beliefs (and more generally our normative beliefs) to meet fairly relaxed and undemanding conditions of justification and reliability. In those contexts, so long as one's belief in the moral proposition in question is based at least in part on the fact that one has more justification for believing that proposition than one has for believing its negation, it may be quite true to say that one's belief in that proposition is "rational" or "justified". If in addition the moral proposition in question is true (so that the method that leads one to believe that proposition is at least minimally reliable), then it may also be quite true to say that the belief in question counts as "knowledge".

Nonetheless, it must be conceded that this is a modest defence of the possibility of moral knowledge (and more generally, of normative knowledge) against the threat of a more sweeping epistemological scepticism with respect to moral (and normative) propositions. Nothing that I have said lends any credence to the idea that any moral or normative propositions are self-evident or have anything like the kind of certainty that is characteristic of logical or mathematical propositions. The epistemology that I am proposing here is a thoroughgoing form of fallibilism. All methods of moral thinking are fallible; practically no moral proposition is absolutely certain. We can never have any guarantee that we will not be rationally required to revisit and reconsider our moral beliefs, and perhaps revise them, in the light of further evidence and further reflection. "Reflective equilibrium" is in this sense an ideal, which we will most likely never reach.

Sometimes, we can be, as it is often said, "morally certain" of a moral proposition. That is, we can have decisive moral reasons to *act* as though there is no doubt whatsoever about the truth of that proposition.[15] Sometimes, life calls on us to be bold and resolute. It is this, I think, that sometimes creates the

---

[15] For a fascinating exploration of these phenomena, see R. M. Adams (1995).

illusion that some moral propositions are self-evident in something like the same way as logical or mathematical propositions. But closer inspection reveals, or so it seems to me, that this is not so. It is one of the hard facts of life that we must act in spite of lacking the sort of certainty in the rightness of our conduct that we quite rationally wish to have.

12

Conclusion

One good way to achieve a better understanding of a philosophical view is to see what its implications are for other debates and issues. In this concluding chapter, I shall briefly survey some of the implications for other philosophical debates of the theory that I outlined in the earlier chapters of this book. Logically speaking, of course, every theory has infinitely many implications. I shall try here to focus on what seem to me the philosophically most interesting implications of my theory. I shall focus on its implications for the following four areas in philosophy: (i) the philosophy of mind and language—including that special branch of the philosophy of mind that is known as "moral psychology"; (ii) the theory of rational belief and rational choice; (iii) first-order normative ethical theory; and (iv) the philosophy of religion.

12.1 IMPLICATIONS FOR THE PHILOSOPHY OF MIND AND LANGUAGE

In Part I of this book, I argued in favour of an account of normative thought and normative discourse. The argument had to go back and forth a number of times between discourse and thought—that is, between words or language, on the one hand, and concepts or mental states, on the other hand. The reason for this was that while the fundamental explanation of the meaning of normative discourse has to appeal to normative thought, the primary evidence for claims about normative thoughts is the evidence of normative discourse and language.

My account of normative discourse explained the meaning of each occurrence of a normative word (like 'ought') in terms of the *concept* that that occurrence of the word expresses, and in terms of the property or relation that is the *semantic value* both of that concept and of that occurrence of the word. My account of the nature of this concept was given in terms of its *essential conceptual role* in thought. As I understand it, this sort of conceptual role semantics is an instance of the more general approach to the philosophy of mind that was defended in Chapter 7. According to this general approach, the nature of every concept or type of attitude is given both by a principle about when mental states involving that concept or attitude-type count as correct, and also by a principle about how certain ways of thinking with those mental states count either as rationally permitted or as rationally required.

I argued for this position by attacking the principal rival accounts of normative thought and discourse. First of all, in Chapter 1, I argued for a version of the view that is generally known as *normative judgment internalism*. In Chapter 2, I argued against expressivist accounts of normative language, on the grounds that they could not give an adequate account of the sort of "discipline" that normative statements are subject to. In Chapter 3, I argued against the project of explaining the meaning of normative statements either by invoking the "causal theory of reference" or by giving a "conceptual analysis" of those statements, in large part on the grounds that they cannot give an adequate account of why normative judgment internalism is true. Instead, in Chapters 4 and 5, I defended a version of conceptual role semantics for these normative terms and concepts—although developing this sort of semantics in detail involved recognizing that normative terms are systematically context-sensitive, so that they express different concepts in different contexts.

One important implication of all this for the philosophy of language is that the argument of Chapter 2 looks as if it will generalize. Many other sorts of discourse are "disciplined" in precisely the same way as normative discourse seems to me to be. For example, it seems that mathematical discourse, modal discourse, discourse about the chances of things, and discourse about the unobservable postulates of empirical science all seem to be disciplined in essentially the same way as I have claimed normative discourse to be. It seems then that the fundamental account of the meaning of the characteristic statements of these branches of discourse must also be *truth-conditional* in the same way as I have argued to be the case with normative statements. Given the other assumptions that I made in Part I of the book, it follows that the meanings of words of this sort are to be explained by reference both to the *concepts* that occurrences of those words express, and to the *semantic values* of those concepts and of those occurrences of those words. This would certainly imply that the expressivist and quasi-realist approaches of Simon Blackburn (1998) and Allan Gibbard (1990 and 2003) are mistaken. However, it seems to me that it would also imply that the *minimalist* approaches of such philosophers as Hartry Field (2001) are also mistaken; if my arguments are sound, then the notion of truth conditions must play a more robust role in explaining the meaning of these statements than these minimalists seem willing to allow.

The principal implications of my arguments for the philosophy of mind are more varied. The most striking implication that my arguments have for the branch of the philosophy of mind that is known as "moral psychology" is that many versions of the "Humean Theory of Motivation" are false. In particular, my arguments seem to imply that the Humean Theory is wrong to claim that no mere belief or purely cognitive state is sufficient to motivate anyone to act. As I claimed, it is metaphysically impossible for anyone to be capable of the sort of judgments that are expressed by normative statements (such as statements of the form 'I ought to φ now'), without having a disposition to comply with the basic requirements of rationality that apply to these judgments. As I argued, this will amount to a disposition to respond to one's rationally judging something of the form 'I ought to φ now' by forming a corresponding intention to φ (at least so long as φ-ing is a course of action that is, as I put it in Chapter 1, "manifestly dependent on intention", and there is "no relevant uncertainty" about what else one ought to do at the relevant time). Thus, all that you need in order to be motivated to φ is for you to have this disposition, and for this disposition to be activated by your forming a judgment of the form 'I ought to φ now'. In effect, then, all that we need to appeal to in order to explain why you were motivated to φ is just that you made this judgment; we do not need to add that you have this disposition, since as I have claimed, this disposition is necessarily present in everyone who makes a judgment of this form. In that sense, my arguments lead fairly quickly to an anti-Humean theory of motivation.[1] Of course, this leaves us with the task of explaining what is wrong with the many arguments that philosophers have given for the conclusion that no such anti-Humean theory of motivation can be correct.[2] I have not attempted to diagnose exactly where all these arguments go wrong in this book. Although I am confident that it is possible to explain what is wrong with all those arguments, unfortunately that task must await another occasion.

In addition to this implication for moral psychology, the arguments of this book have implications for some wider issues in the philosophy of mind as well. If the arguments of Chapter 3 are sound, then neither the causal theory of reference nor the attempt to give conceptual analyses of concepts can give a correct account of the nature of all concepts in general. If the arguments of Chapter 4 and 5 are sound, then the only approach that could give such a general account of concepts would be a version of the conceptual role semantics approach.[3] I have not attempted to develop a general theory of concepts here, but to the extent that it is plausible that some such unified general theory of concepts is true, my arguments support the conceptual role semantics approach over the various rival theories of concepts.

The arguments of Chapters 7 and 8 have further implications for the philosophy of mind. According to Chapter 7, the nature of every concept and every attitude-type is given by certain *normative* principles about when mental states involving that concept or attitude-type are correct, and about which ways of thinking involving these mental states are rational. According to

---

[1] For another way of understanding the central claim of the "Humean Theory of Motivation", according to which I may count as an adherent of the theory rather than as an opponent of it, see Wedgwood (2002*b*).

[2] For such opponents of the anti-Humean theory of motivation, see especially Smith (1994, ch. 4) and Lewis (1988 and 1996*b*).

[3] This puts me at variance with such philosophers as Jerry Fodor (1990) who are staunchly opposed to a conceptual role semantics approach such as the one that I have advocated here.

Chapter 8, mental states are in a certain sense irreducible: this entails that no reductive form of functionalism, and no form of the identity theory that actually identifies mental properties with neurophysiological properties, can be correct.

These arguments tell us that the search for a reductive theory of the nature of the mind is mistaken. But they do not tell us to abandon the attempt to give an account of the nature of the various types of mental states: on the contrary, they point us in the direction of a distinctively normative sort of account of these types of mental state. According to this approach, an account of the nature of each of these types of mental state should principally consist in an account of certain principles that define when mental states of that type are correct, and which ways of thinking with those mental states are rational or irrational. Since I have argued that all thinkers must have some disposition to conform to the basic principles of rationality that apply to the type of mental states that they are capable of, it would also be compatible with the approach that I have outlined here to give an account of each of these types of mental state in terms of the rational dispositions that a thinker must possess in order to be capable of that type of mental state.

According to the epistemological account that I defended in the previous chapter, if the fundamental normative principles that apply to each type of mental state can be known at all, they can be known *a priori*. It follows from this that the correct central account of the nature of each type of mental state can also be known *a priori* (if it can be known at all). This points to a striking difference between mental states and many of the other properties and relations that are the object of systematic rational investigation. The nature of physical, chemical, and biological properties and relations cannot be known *a priori*: the sciences that seek to investigate their nature are fundamentally empirical. By contrast, *a priori* investigation can take one much further in understanding mental states than it can in understanding physics, chemistry, or biology.

It does not follow, however, that my approach is inimical to the project of creating an empirical scientific psychology. On the contrary, my approach leaves extensive room for such empirical psychological investigations. In particular, it leaves room for an empirical science that investigates the *contingent* features of our mental states and capacities. For example, it leaves room for an empirical science that investigates the kinds of states that *realize* our mental states and capacities. Moreover, these investigations can focus on several different levels of realizations of our mental states and capacities. Thus, some investigations—like contemporary neuroscience—could focus on the specific biochemical and biophysical mechanisms that realize our mental states and capacities. Other investigations—like contemporary cognitive science—could take a more abstract approach, and seek to give a more general description of the subpersonal information-processing mechanisms that realize these mental states and capacities. There is no conflict between my approach and the labours of contemporary scientific psychologists.

12.2 IMPLICATIONS FOR THE THEORY OF RATIONAL BELIEF AND RATIONAL CHOICE

There are two fundamental normative notions that play a particularly crucial role in my theory. The first is the notion of a form of thinking that is *rational*; and the second is the notion of a mental state that is *correct*.

The notion of *rationality* played a crucial role in my characterization of the conceptual role of concepts: a concept's conceptual role consists in some fact about how certain forms of thinking involving that concept count as rationally permitted or as rationally required. It also played a crucial role in my characterization of the dispositions that are essential to possessing concepts or to being capable of the various types of attitude: these dispositions are generally dispositions to conform to certain basic requirements of rationality that apply to the concepts or types of attitude in question. The notion of *correctness* played a particularly crucial role in my account of the reference or semantic value of normative concepts. For example, as I argued, a proposition involving the practical 'ought', indexed to the situation of a particular agent A and time t, of the form 'It ought to be the case that p' is true if and only if it is correct for A to incorporate p into her ideal plans about what to do at t, and not correct for A to incorporate the negation of p into any such ideal plans about what to do at t.

I have assumed that these two normative concepts 'correct' and 'rational' differ in roughly the following way: whether or not a way of thinking is *rational* is determined by its relation to the thinker's internal mental states, whereas whether or not a mental state is correct is typically determined by its relation to how things are in the external world. To put it slightly less roughly, the difference is this. The attitude of believing a certain proposition p is either correct or incorrect *simpliciter*. Similarly, an agent's attitude of incorporating a certain proposition q into her ideal plans about what to do at a certain time t is either correct or incorrect *simpliciter*. On the other hand, these attitudes cannot be said to be rational or irrational *simpliciter*: they are only rational or irrational *in relation to this or that body of information*. When we say, without further qualification, that it is rational for a particular thinker to form a certain belief at a certain time, this will be true if and only if forming that belief is rational in relation to the body of information that corresponds to the set of internal mental states that that thinker has at that time; and when we say that a certain way of thinking is rational, this is true if and only if the way of thinking in question consists in forming a certain attitude in response to a certain body of information in relation to which it is rational to form that attitude.

At the same time, I have also assumed that there is a systematic relationship between the principles of rationality and the principles of correctness. I gave a rough characterization of that relationship in Chapter 7. As I put it—metaphorically—the "ultimate goal or purpose" in conforming to the standards of rationality that apply to a particular type of mental state is to have mental states of that type that are correct. Less metaphorically, I suggested that the standards of rational belief have correct belief as their "ultimate goal or purpose" because—to put it roughly—a belief counts as rational, in relation to a given body of information I, just in case I makes it highly likely that the belief in question is correct. As I proposed in Chapter 7, both the concept 'correct' and the concept 'rational' are normative concepts; to use the terminology that I introduced in Chapter 5, they are related to each other as an objective 'ought' and the corresponding information-relative 'ought'.

These claims about rationality point in the direction of a definite program for investigating the principles of rational belief and of rational choice. First, we would have to specify, as precisely as possible, exactly what it is for a belief or for a choice to be correct. Then, we would have to characterize the nature of the "systematic relationship" that holds between the principles that specify when a certain type of mental state is correct, and the principles that specify which ways of thinking with those mental states are rational or irrational. Then, relying on our accounts of correct belief and of correct choice, and on our account of this systematic relationship, we could derive an account of which ways of forming and revising beliefs are rational and which are irrational, and also an account of which ways of forming and revising choices are rational and which are irrational.

This program for investigating the principles of rational belief and rational choice raises a number of questions. First, how should we set about evaluating rival accounts of the conditions of correctness for beliefs or for choices? Secondly, why exactly should this sort of "systematic relationship" hold between the objective normative notion of "correctness" and the corresponding information-relative notion of "rationality"? Thirdly, how exactly should our account of this systematic relationship be formulated? In the rough formulation that I sketched above, I invoked a notion of "likelihood" (or "probability"). But it is a familiar point that there are many different notions that are expressed by terms like 'likely' and 'probable'. Which of these notions is in place here? Is it a notion that will allow us to give a non-circular definition of the concept of "rationality" using no normative terms other than terms for objective notions like 'correct', or will we have to recognize that concepts like 'rational' are just primitive information-relative normative notions? Finally, how exactly is the concept 'knowledge' related to the concepts of a belief that is "correct" and of a belief that is "rational"? A satisfactory investigation of the topics of rational belief and rational choice would have to supply some answers to these questions.[4]

---

[4] I have already started to work on some of these further questions. On epistemology, see Wedgwood (1999*a*, 2002*a*, and 2002*c*); and on the theory of rational choice, see Wedgwood (2002*b* and 2003).

In addition, of course, in Part III of this book, I relied on some further assumptions about epistemology in particular. I relied on a particular account of the conditions that are necessary for a way of forming beliefs to be "primitively rational"—that is, rational despite the fact that the thinker has no independent or antecedent reason for believing that that way of forming beliefs is reliable. According to this account, the primitively rational ways of forming beliefs must have a certain weak but still essential connection to the truth. In addition, I also proposed an account of the *a priori*, according to which the *a priori* is, as Kant put it, what our relevant cognitive capacities "supply out of themselves"; I argued for the rationality of an "egocentric epistemic bias"; and I invoked a version of contextualism about certain key epistemological terms like 'knowledge' and 'justified belief'. These ideas would be undermined unless they have a more general application elsewhere in epistemology, and not just to the epistemology of normative beliefs. In this way, my account of the epistemology of normative beliefs has wider implications for the rest of epistemology.

12.3 IMPLICATIONS FOR FIRST-ORDER ETHICAL THEORY

The investigations that I have pursued in this book have been concerned with normative thought and discourse in general, not specifically with *moral* thought and discourse. Most of first-order ethical theory focuses on moral questions. This is not hard to explain. Moral thinking is the most *social* form of normative thinking: moral thinking plays the role of resolving social disputes in which the interests of different people do not completely coincide. Hence moral thinking is also the form of normative thinking in which controversies excite the greatest passions, so that moral questions naturally become the centre of discussion much more than other normative questions.

Nonetheless, the general normative notions that have been the focus of my investigations in this book also play an important role in moral theorizing. One crucial question in ethical theory is the question 'Why should I be moral?' As I pointed out in Chapter 1 (Section 1.3), in asking this question, one is not asking the inane question 'Why should I do what I should do?', nor the equally inane question 'Why am I morally required to do what I am morally required to do?' Thus, it seems that we must distinguish between the concept of what is "morally required" and the concept that is expressed by the general practical 'should' (or 'ought') that appears in this question.

Moreover, an adequate ethical theory must try to answer this question. Presumably, such a theory would have to articulate some relatively general thesis about what people "ought" to do (in this general practical sense of 'ought')—where this general thesis would help to explain under what circumstances one ought to do what one is morally required to do, and why this is the case. As I shall explain below, the broadly metaethical theory that I have defended above has a number of implications about what any complete theory of the nature of any normative property or relation would look like, and this includes both the properties and relations that are referred to by the various moral concepts (such as the concept of what is "morally required") and the property or relation that is referred to by the sort of 'ought' that features in the question 'Why ought I to be moral?'

First of all, in Part I of the book I gave an account of the nature of normative thoughts, such as the thoughts that one might express by means of statements involving the word 'ought'. This theory of the nature of normative thoughts may well be highly relevant to various branches of ethical theory. For example, it seems plausible that a good ethical theory will include a theory about what character traits count as virtues, and of what sorts of practical reasoning and decision making make the agent praiseworthy or blameworthy. It may be that virtuous character involves a disposition to engage in praiseworthy sorts of practical reasoning, and such praiseworthy sorts of reasoning may themselves involve normative thinking (such as thinking about what one ought to do). Clearly any such account of the virtues, or of these praiseworthy forms of practical reasoning and decision making, will have to be informed by a good account of the nature of normative judgments, such as the account that I have developed here.

After giving my broadly semantical account of the nature of normative thoughts and judgments in Part I of this book, I went on in Part II of the book to develop a broadly *metaphysical* account of the essential nature of normative properties and relations. This account built on my account in Chapter 4 of the reference or semantic value of normative concepts. As I explained there, that account was essentially a version of the "fitting attitude analysis": the properties and relations that our normative concepts stand for can all be defined in terms of the fundamental notion of a mental attitude's being *correct* (or in the case of some concepts, such as the information-relative 'ought', in terms of the notion of a mental attitude's being *rational* in relation to a certain body of information). As I argued in Chapter 7, this "fitting attitude analysis" is in effect an account of the essential nature of these normative properties and relations.

Now a large part of ethical theory consists in the attempt to articulate illuminating principles about the conditions under which a sequence of items exemplifies each of these normative properties and relations. Ultimately, it seems, all of these principles will be explained on the basis of some more fundamental principle about the essential nature of the normative properties or relations in question. Since my account includes some claims about the essential nature of these properties or relations, it seems that my account will have some implications about the form that such an ethical theory will take. Specifically, it implies that this fundamental principle about the essential nature of these normative properties and relations will take the form of a principle about the conditions under which certain crucial sorts of attitude are either correct or rational. According to the position that I argued for in Chapter 7, such a principle would be an account of the essential nature of *both* the relevant normative property or relation *and* the relevant sort of attitude. Thus, if I am right, the account that this sort of ethical theory is seeking would also give an account of the essential nature of this sort of attitude, by specifying in more illuminating detail exactly what it is for an attitude of this sort to be correct.

I shall illustrate this point about the form of ethical theories by explaining how a number of well-known ethical theories can be represented as grounded on a conception of the relevant sort of attitude, and of what it is for attitudes of that sort to be correct. I pick these theories not because I believe that they are true (in fact, I believe that they are all false), but because they are familiar and so will be useful examples to illustrate my point.

My first example is a well-known theory of *reasons for action*; a rough outline of this sort of theory seems to have been given by Bernard Williams (1980). Although this theory is usually put forward as a theory of what it is for one to have "conclusive (or overriding) reason" to do something, I believe that it can be taken as a theory of the general practical 'ought'. This theory is grounded on an essentially *procedural* conception of rational practical reasoning: according to this conception, rational practical reasoning can simply be defined as any reasoning that follows certain procedures, which can be specified in wholly non-normative terms. Then this theory claims that a choice is correct if and only if it can be arrived at by means of procedurally rational practical reasoning, on the basis of a set of non-normative background beliefs that includes no relevant falsehoods and includes all relevant truths. If these are the conditions under which a choice is correct, they are also conditions under which the proposition p that is the object of one's choice is choiceworthy. If, in addition, it is not correct for the negation of p to be the object of one's choice, then p is also a proposition that ought to be the case (from the standpoint of the relevant agent and time). This illustrates the more general point: the right account of the practical 'ought' (or of what one has overriding or conclusive reason to do) will go hand-in-hand with the right account of what it is for a choice or a plan to be correct.

A similar point will also hold of moral theory as well—including of the right account of what one has a *moral duty* to do. A plausible extension of the theory that I have proposed in this book might say something like the following: one has a moral duty to act in a way W in circumstances C if and only if acting in way W in circumstances C is called for by any system of rules towards which it is correct to have a certain attitude of *moral endorsement*. It may be plausible that this attitude of moral endorsement goes along with a certain sort of *collective practical agreement*: to give this sort of moral endorsement to a system of rules is to endorse those rules as rules for the whole community of intelligent agents to agree to live by. If that is right, then it seems that we can identify the correct moral rules with those rules that it is correct for the whole community of intelligent agents to agree to live by. This supports the idea that the correct moral theory will take the form of an account of which sets of rules it could be correct for the community of intelligent agents to agree to live by.

In fact, most of the best-known moral theories can be interpreted as offering an account of this form. Thus, for example, a Hobbesian theory such as that of David Gauthier (1986) can be represented as claiming that the correct agreement for a community to reach is the one which, after rational negotiation, each member of a set of fully informed, mutually unconcerned individuals would rationally choose sincerely to enter into, as the most effective means for pursuing her self-interest. An "average utilitarian" theory such as that of Harsanyi (1982) might hold that the correct agreement for such a community to enter into would be the one that, if sincerely acted upon by everyone, would maximize the expected welfare of each party to the agreement (under the assumption that it is equally probable that she could be *any one* of those whose interests are affected by the agreement). A Kantian theory such as that of Korsgaard (1996*a*) would maintain that the correct agreement for such a community to make is the one that can be rationally willed as a universal system of legislation uniting all rational beings into a Kingdom of Ends. One possible interpretation of this Kantian idea might be that of T. M. Scanlon (1999), according to which the correct agreement for the community of intelligent agents to make is the one that no member of that community could "reasonably object" to (given a certain conception of what it makes it "reasonable" to "object" to a set of rules that are proposed as rules for the community to agree to live by). My point here is not to endorse any of these ethical theories (as I have noted, I am in fact inclined to reject all of these ethical theories). My point is just to show how many moral theorists have assumed that the correct theory would have to take this sort of form. As I have tried to explain, my metaphysical account of the nature of normative properties and relations seem to help us to see why they are right to assume this: the correct ethical theory must indeed be capable of being cast into this sort of form.

Finally, in Part III, I developed an epistemological account of how we can know, or at least have justified or rational belief in, normative propositions. This part of the book is clearly relevant to the methodology of moral theorizing, which is simply a relatively systematic and abstract form of ordinary normative thinking. The methodological implications of the theory that I have proposed in Part III are hardly revolutionary. On the contrary, this theory supports what I take to be the ordinary methods of moral theorists. What is novel in this theory is not the method that it recommends, but rather its *explanation* of why this method is rational, and of how it may even, under favourable conditions, count as a reliable way of getting to the truth. Nonetheless, it may possibly help moral theorists to follow this method more faithfully, and to avoid some of the mistakes that they might otherwise fall into, if they are aware of the correct explanation of why this method is rational and, under favourable conditions, reliable.

12.4 IMPLICATIONS FOR THE PHILOSOPHY
OF RELIGION

As Kant understood, one of the deepest sources of religious belief in human beings is the fact that such religious belief can seem crucial to sustaining what we rightly feel to be the correct attitude towards the weightiest reasons that confront us in our lives. Kant of course identified these reasons with our duties. As he argued, we rightly feel that we should regard our duties as if they had an unconditional authority over us, even over our innermost thoughts; and, according to Kant (1788: 129, and 1794: 84 and 103), this is tantamount to regarding our duties as if they were commanded to us by a morally perfect and omniscient Creator, who knows our innermost hearts.

I believe that the theory that I have proposed in this book undercuts these Kantian arguments. My purely metaphysical theory is enough to sustain these attitudes towards the weightiest reasons that confront us, even if we decisively reject any sort of religious belief. According to the theory that I have proposed, the fundamental normative truths or facts are eternal and metaphysically necessary, and in no way dependent on us. No concealment or subterfuge on our parts will prevent us from falling within the scope of these normative truths. Indeed, there is a sense in which we are dependent on these normative truths, since according to my theory, they play the role that Plato assigned to the Form of the Good: just as we only count as sighted because we have the appropriate sort of sensitivity to light, the source of which is the sun, so too we only count as intelligent thinkers and agents at all because we have an appropriate sort of sensitivity to rational requirements, which have their source in these normative truths. In that sense, it is part of our essential nature—part of what makes us what we are—that we have some disposition to conform to the requirements of these normative truths. This conception of these normative truths is enough to warrant the attitude of regarding these truths as if they had a sort of "unconditional authority" over us.

However, these normative truths lack all the personal qualities that are thought to be typical of God. Unlike God, these normative truths do not know anything or intend anything; they do not perform actions; they do not have any attitudes such as love or compassion, nor will they punish us if we fail to conform to their demands. They are in a clear sense more abstract than any personal god is traditionally supposed to be. One possible hypothesis that atheists might investigate is that the central mistake of theism is not the idea that there are some aspects of the world that are appropriate objects of some of the religious emotions (like awe and wonder and the like), but rather the idea that these aspects of the world must in some sense be *persons*, rather than essentially more abstract items than any person could possibly be.

Famously, G. E. M. Anscombe (1958) argued that the sense that philosophers often give to certain central moral or normative terms, such as 'duty' or 'obligation', can have no coherent application except on the hypothesis that God exists. Her argument is obscure, but part of what is motivating her may be the sense that without the belief in God, duties and obligations have no really powerful motivations to call upon. Religious belief can summon up the psychic equivalents of nuclear weapons,[5] such as a feeling of love for a being who is conceived to be infinitely superior to oneself, and the fear of being rejected or cut off from that love. Without religious belief, it is not clear what motivations our normative judgments can call on.

It seems to me doubtful, however, that there is anything defective about an account of normative thought that does not give a central role to such motivational equivalents of nuclear weapons. It is only under exceptional and unfortunate circumstances that such motivations would be necessary to help us to conform to the requirements of normative truths; and as history has shown us all too often, these motivations can easily lead people to act in ways that are utterly pernicious and absurd. For normal circumstances, the motivations to which I have given a central role in my account seem far more reliable: these motivations are nothing more than the dispositions that are necessary if we are to possess the concepts involved, or to be capable of the relevant types of attitude—dispositions that are so basic that we are constantly manifesting these dispositions without even noticing that we are doing so.

As I have tried to explain, it is these dispositions that make us what we are—intelligent creatures, capable of the range of concepts and types of attitude that make up our mental lives. Moreover, according to my account, these dispositions constitute a direct and immediate sensitivity to rational requirements, and thereby to certain normative facts or truths. In this way, these normative truths are our constant and most intimate guides. Directly, they guide us to think and reason in rational ways. Indirectly—if we are not too unfortunate—they will lead us to think and live correctly, that is, to think and live as we really ought to do.

---

[5] This way of putting it was suggested to me in conversation by Mark Johnston.

Bibliography

Adams, R. M. (1995). "Moral Faith", *Journal of Philosophy*, 92: 75–95.

Alston, William (1989). *Epistemic Justification* (Ithaca, NY: Cornell University Press).

—— (1991). *Perceiving God: The Epistemology of Religious Experience* (Ithaca, NY: Cornell University Press).

—— (1993). *The Reliability of Sense Perception* (Ithaca, NY: Cornell University Press).

Anscombe, G. E. M. (1958). "Modern Moral Philosophy", *Philosophy*, 33 (January): 1–19. Reprinted in Anscombe (1981).

—— (1963). *Intention*, 2nd edn. (Oxford: Blackwell).

—— (1981). *The Collected Philosophical Papers of G. E. M. Anscombe, Vol. 3. Ethics, Religion and Politics* (Minneapolis: University of Minnesota Press).

Antony, Louise (1989). "Anomalous Monism and the Problem of Explanatory Force", *Philosophical Review*, 98: 153–87.

Åqvist, Lennart (1967). "Good Samaritans, Contrary-to-Duty Imperatives, and Epistemic Obligations", *Noûs*, 1: 361–79.

—— (1984). "Deontic Logic", in Dov Gabbay (ed.), *Handbook of Philosophical Logic* (Dordrecht: Reidel), 605–714.

Arpaly, Nomi (2000). "On Acting Rationally Against One's Best Judgment", *Ethics*, 110: 488–513.

Audi, Robert (1993). *The Structure of Justification* (Cambridge: Cambridge University Press).

Ayer, A. J. (1946). *Language, Truth and Logic*, 2nd edn. (London: Victor Gollancz).

Bealer, George (1982). *Quality and Concept* (Oxford: Clarendon Press).

—— (1984). "Mind and Anti-mind: Why Thinking Has No Functional Definition", *Midwest Studies in Philosophy*, 9: 283–328.

—— (1987). "The Philosophical Limits of Scientific Essentialism", *Philosophical Perspectives*, 1: 289–365.

—— (1994). "Mental Properties", *Journal of Philosophy*, 91/4 (April): 185–208

—— (1997). "Self-Consciousness", *Philosophical Review*, 106/1 (January): 69–117.

—— (1999). "A Theory of the A Priori", *Philosophical Perspectives*, 13: 29–55.

—— (2000). "Fregean Equivocation and Ramsification on Sparse Theories", *Mind and Language*, 15/5 (November): 500–10.

—— (2001). "The Self-Consciousness Argument: Why Tooley's Criticisms Fail", *Philosophical Studies*, 105/3 (September): 281–307.

Bedau, M. A. (1992). "Where's the Good in Teleology?", *Philosophy and Phenomenological Research*, 52: 781–806.

Belzer, Marvin (1998). "Deontic Logic", in Edward Craig (ed.), *Routledge Encyclopedia of Philosophy* (London: Routledge) <http://www.rep.routledge.com/article/Y043>.

Bennett, Jonathan (1974). "The Conscience of Huckleberry Finn", *Philosophy*, 49 (April): 123–34.

Bird, Alexander (1998). "Dispositions and Antidotes", *Philosophical Quarterly*, 48: 227–34.

Bird, Alexander (2005). "Laws and Essences", *Ratio*, 18/4 (December): 437–61.

Blackburn, Simon (1984). *Spreading the Word: Groundings in the Philosophy of Language* (Oxford: Clarendon Press).

—— (1992). "Gibbard on Normative Logic", *Philosophy and Phenomenological Research*, 52: 947–52.

—— (1993). *Essays on Quasi-Realism* (Oxford: Clarendon Press).

—— (1998). *Ruling Passions: A Theory of Practical Reason* (Oxford: Clarendon Press).

Block, Ned (1978). "Troubles with Functionalism", in C. Wade Savage (ed.), *Minnesota Studies in the Philosophy of Science* IX (Minneapolis: University of Minnesota Press).

—— (1987). "Functional Role and Truth Conditions", *Proceedings of the Aristotelian Society*, Suppl. Vol. 61: 157–81.

Boghossian, Paul (1991). "Naturalizing Content", in Barry Loewer and Georges Rey (eds.), *Meaning in Mind: Fodor and His Critics* (Oxford: Blackwell).

Bouwsma, O. K. (1986). *Wittgenstein: Conversations 1949–1951*, ed. J. L. Craft and Ronald E. Hustwit (Indianapolis: Hackett Publishing Company).

Boyd, Richard N. (1988). "How to Be a Moral Realist", in Geoffrey Sayre-McCord (ed.), *Essays on Moral Realism* (Ithaca, NY: Cornell University Press), 181–228.

Brandom, Robert (1994). *Making It Explicit* (Cambridge, MA: Harvard University Press).

—— (2000). *Articulating Reasons* (Cambridge, MA: Harvard University Press).

Brewer, Bill (1995). "Mental Causation", *Proceedings of the Aristotelian Society*, Suppl. Vol. 69: 237–53.

Brink, David (1986). "Externalist Moral Realism", *Southern Journal of Philosophy*, Suppl. Vol. 24: 23–42.

—— (1989). *Moral Realism and the Foundations of Ethics* (Cambridge: Cambridge University Press).

Broome, John (1997). "Reason and Motivation", *Proceedings of the Aristotelian Society*, Suppl. Vol. 71: 131–46.

—— (1999). "Normative Requirements", *Ratio*, 12: 398–419.

—— (2004). *Weighing Lives* (Oxford: Oxford University Press).

Burge, Tyler (1997). "Interlocution, Perception, and Memory", *Philosophical Studies*, 86/1 (April): 21–47.

Castañeda, Hector-Neri (1981). "The Paradoxes of Deontic Logic: The Simplest Solution to All of Them in One Fell Swoop", in Hilpinen (1981), 378–85.

Chalmers, David (1996). *The Conscious Mind* (Oxford: Clarendon Press).

Charles, David (1992). "Supervenience, Composition, and Physicalism", in David Charles and Kathleen Lennon (eds.), *Reduction, Explanation, and Realism* (New York: Oxford University Press), 265–96.

Child, T. W. (1993). "Anomalism, Uncodifiability, and Psychophysical Relations", *Philosophical Review*, 102: 215–45.

Chisholm, Roderick (1963). "Contrary-to-Duty Imperatives and Deontic Logic", *Analysis*, 24: 33–6.

Coady, C. A. J. (1992). *Testimony: A Philosophical Study* (Oxford : Clarendon Press).

Cohen, Stewart (1999). "Contextualism, Skepticism, and the Structure of Reasons", *Philosophical Perspectives*, 13: 57–88.

Conee, Earl, and Feldman, Richard (2001). "Internalism Defended", *American Philosophical Quarterly*, 38: 1–18

Crane, Tim (1993). "Reply to Pettit", *Analysis*, 53: 224–7.

_____ and Mellor, D. H. (1990). "There Is No Question of Physicalism", *Mind*, 99: 185–206. Reprinted in Mellor (1991), 82–103.

Crisp, Roger (2000). Review of Joel Kupperman, *Value ... and What Follows*, *Philosophy*, 75: 458–62.

_____ (2002). "Sidgwick and the Boundaries of Intuitionism", in Stratton-Lake (2002*a*), 56–75.

Cullity, Garrett, and Gaut, Berys (1997). "Introduction", in Cullity and Gaut (eds.), *Ethics and Practical Reason* (Oxford: Clarendon Press).

D'Arms, Justin, and Jacobson, Daniel (2000). "Sentiment and Value", *Ethics*, 110/4 (July): 722–48.

Darwall, Stephen (2002). "Ethical Intuitionism and the Motivation Problem", in Stratton-Lake (2002*a*) 248–70.

Davidson, Donald (1970). "Mental Events", in Laurence Foster and J. W. Swanson (eds.), *Experience and Theory* (Boston: University of Massachusetts Press). Reprinted in Davidson (1980), 207–25.

_____ (1980). *Essays on Actions and Events* (Oxford: Clarendon Press).

_____ (2001). *Inquiries into Truth and Interpretation*, 2nd edn. (Oxford: Clarendon Press).

Davies, Martin, and Humberstone, I. L. (1980). "Two Notions of Necessity", *Philosophical Studies*, 38: 1–30.

DeRose, Keith (1995). "Solving the Skeptical Puzzle", *Philosophical Review*, 104: 1–52.

Dretske, Fred (1981). *Knowledge and the Flow of Information* (Cambridge, MA: MIT Press).

Dummett, Michael (1978). *Truth and Other Enigmas* (London: Duckworth).

_____ (1981). *Frege: Philosophy of Language*, 2nd edn. (London: Duckworth).

_____ (1993*a*). *Origins of Analytical Philosophy* (London: Duckworth).

_____ (1993*b*). *The Seas of Language* (Oxford: Clarendon Press).

Dworkin, Ronald (1996). "Objectivity and Truth: You'd Better Believe It", *Philosophy and Public Affairs*, 25: 87–139.

Eklund, Matti (2002). "Inconsistent Languages", *Philosophy and Phenomenological Research*, 64: 251–75.

Evans, Gareth (1982). *The Varieties of Reference*, ed. J. H. McDowell (Oxford: Clarendon Press).

Fara, Michael (2005). "Dispositions and Habituals", *Noûs* 39/1 (January): 43–82.

Feldman, Fred (1986). *Doing the Best We Can* (Dordrecht: Reidel).

_____ (1990). "A Simpler Solution to the Paradoxes of Deontic Logic", *Philosophical Perspectives*, 4: 309–41.

Field, Hartry (1977). "Logic, Meaning and Conceptual Role", *Journal of Philosophy*, 69: 379–408.

_____ (1986). "The Deflationary Conception of Truth", in Graham McDonald and Crispin Wright (eds.), *Fact, Science and Value* (Oxford: Blackwell), 55–117.

_____ (1994). "Disquotational Truth and Factually Defective Discourse", *Philosophical Review*, 103: 405–52. Reprinted in Field (2001).

_____ (2001). *Truth and the Absence of Fact* (Oxford: Clarendon Press).

Fine, Kit (1994). "Essence and Modality", *Philosophical Perspectives*, 8: 1–16.

Fine, Kit (1995a). "Ontological Dependence", *Proceedings of the Aristotelian Society*, 95: 269–90.

_____ (1995b). "Senses of Essence", in Walter Sinnott–Armstrong (ed.), *Modality, Morality, and Belief* (New York: Cambridge University Press).

_____ (1995c). "The Logic of Essence", *Journal of Philosophical Logic*, 24: 241–73.

_____ (2001). "The Question of Realism", *Philosophers' Imprint*, 1/1 (January), <http://www.philosophersimprint.org/001001/>.

_____ (2003). *Reference, Relation and Meaning*, John Locke Lectures, <http://www.philosophy.ox.ac.uk/misc/johnlocke/index.shtml>.

Firth, Roderick (1952). "Ethical Absolutism and the Ideal Observer Theory", *Philosophy and Phenomenological Research*, 12: 317–45.

Fodor, Jerry (1987). *Psychosemantics* (Cambridge, MA: MIT Press).

_____ (1990). *A Theory of Content and Other Essays* (Cambridge, MA: MIT Press).

Forbes, Graeme (1985). *The Metaphysics of Modality* (Oxford: Clarendon Press).

Foot, Philippa (1978). *Virtues and Vices* (Oxford: Blackwell).

Frege, Gottlob (1964). *The Basic Laws of Arithmetic*, trans. Montgomery Furth (Berkeley: University of California Press).

_____ (1977). *Logical Investigations*, trans. P. T. Geach and R. H. Stoothoff (Oxford: Basil Blackwell).

_____ (1986a). "Über Sinn und Bedeutung", in *id.*, *Funktion, Begriff, Bedeutung*, ed. Günther Patzig (Göttingen: Vandenhoeck und Ruprecht).

_____ (1986b). "Der Gedanke", in *id.*, *Logische Untersuchungen*, ed. Günther Patzig (Göttingen: Vandenhoeck und Ruprecht).

Fricker, Elizabeth (1991). "Analyticity, Linguistic Practice and Philosophical Method", in Klaus Puhl (ed.), *Meaning Scepticism* (Berlin: De Gruyter), 218–50.

_____ (1995). "Telling and Trusting: Reductionism and Anti-Reductionism in the Epistemology of Testimony", *Mind*, 104/2 (April): 393–411.

_____ (2004). "Testimony: Knowing through Being Told", in Ilkka Niiniluoto (ed.), *Handbook of Epistemology* (Dordrecht: Kluwer Academic Publishers), 109–30.

Gauthier, David (1986). *Morals by Agreement* (Oxford: Clarendon Press).

Geach, P. T. (1972). *Logic Matters* (Oxford: Basil Blackwell).

_____ (1991). "Whatever Happened to Deontic Logic?", in *id.* (ed.), *Logic and Ethics* (Dordrecht: Kluwer), 33–48.

Gibbard, Allan (1990). *Wise Choices, Apt Feelings* (Cambridge, MA: Harvard University Press).

_____ (1992). "Reply to Blackburn, Carson, Hill and Railton", *Philosophy and Phenomenological Research*, 52: 969–80.

_____ (1996). "Thought, Norms, and Discursive Practice", *Philosophy and Phenomenological Research*, 56: 699–717.

_____ (2002). "Normative and Recognitional Concepts", *Philosophy and Phenomenological Research*, 64/1: 151–67.

_____ (2003). *Thinking How to Live* (Cambridge, MA: Harvard University Press).

Goldman, Alvin (1979). "What is Justified Belief?", in George Pappas (ed.), *Justification and Knowledge* (Dordrecht: Reidel), 1–24.

_____ (1986). *Epistemology and Cognition* (Cambridge, MA: Harvard University Press).

_____ (1989). "Interpretation Psychologized", *Mind and Language*, 4: 161–85.

_____ (1999). "Internalism Exposed", *Journal of Philosophy*, 96: 271–93.

Griffin, James (1996). *Value Judgement: Improving Our Ethical Beliefs* (Oxford: Clarendon Press).

Halbach, Volker (2001). "How Innocent is Deflationism?", *Synthese*, 126: 167–94.

Haldane, John, and Wright, Crispin (1993). *Reality, Representation, and Projection* (Oxford: Oxford University Press).

Hale, Bob (1993). "Can There Be a Logic of Attitudes?", in Haldane and Wright (1993), 337–63.

Hampton, Jean (1998). *The Authority of Reason*, ed. Richard Healey (Cambridge: Cambridge University Press).

Hansson, Bengt (1968). "Choice Structures and Preference Relations", *Synthese*, 18: 443–58.

Hansson, Sven Ove (1997). "Situationist Deontic Logic", *Journal of Philosophical Logic*, 26/4 (August): 423–48.

Hare, R. M. (1952). *The Language of Morals* (Oxford: Clarendon Press).

_____ (1963). *Freedom and Reason* (Oxford: Clarendon Press).

Harman, Gilbert (1973). Review of Roger Wertheimer, *The Significance of Sense*, *Philosophical Review*, 82: 235–39.

_____ (1977). *The Nature of Morality* (New York: Oxford University Press).

_____ (1986). "The Meaning of the Logical Constants", in Ernest Lepore (ed.), *Truth and Interpretation: Perspectives on the Philosophy of Donald Davidson* (Oxford: Blackwell), 125–34.

_____ (1999). "(Non-Solipsistic) Conceptual Role Semantics", in *id., Reasoning, Meaning and Mind* (Oxford: Clarendon Press), 206–31.

_____ and Thomson, Judith Jarvis (1996). *Moral Relativism and Moral Objectivity* (Oxford: Blackwell).

Harsanyi, J. C. (1982). "Morality and the Theory of Rational Behaviour", in Amartya Sen and Bernard Williams (eds.), *Utilitarianism and Beyond* (Cambridge: Cambridge University Press), 39–62.

Heal, Jane (2003). *Mind, Reason and Imagination* (Cambridge: Cambridge University Press).

Hilpinen, Risto (ed.) (1981). *New Studies in Deontic Logic: Norms, Actions, and the Foundations of Ethics* (Dordrecht: Reidel).

Horgan, Terence (1993). "From Supervenience to Superdupervenience: Meeting the Demands of the Natural World", *Mind*, 102: 555–86.

_____ and Timmons, Mark (1992a). "Troubles on Moral Twin Earth: Moral Queerness Revived", *Synthese*, 66: 223–60.

_____ (1992b). "Troubles for New Wave Moral Semantics: The 'Open Question Argument' Revived", *Philosophical Papers*, 21: 153–75.

_____ (2000a). "Nondescriptivist Cognitivism: Framework for a New Metaethic", *Philosophical Papers*, 29: 121–53.

_____ (2000b). "Copping Out on Moral Twin Earth", *Synthese*, 124: 139–52.

Horty, John F. (2001). *Agency and Deontic Logic* (Oxford: Oxford University Press).

Horwich, Paul (1998a). *Truth*, 2nd edn. (Oxford: Clarendon Press).

_____ (1998b). *Meaning* (Oxford: Clarendon Press).

Humberstone, I. L. (1983). "The Background of Circumstances", *Pacific Philosophical Quarterly*, 64: 19–34.

Hume, David (1739). *A Treatise of Human Nature*, Books I and II (London: John Noon).

____ (1740). *A Treatise of Human Nature*, Book III (London: Thomas Longman).

Hurley, S. L. (1989). *Natural Reasons* (Oxford: Oxford University Press).

Irwin, Terence (1995). *Plato's Ethics* (Oxford: Clarendon Press).

Jackson, Frank (1985). "On the Semantics and Logic of Obligation", *Mind*, 94: 177–95.

____ (1996). "Mental Causation: The State of the Art", *Mind*, 105/419 (July): 377–413.

____ (1998). *From Metaphysics to Ethics: A Defence of Conceptual Analysis* (Oxford: Clarendon Press).

____ and Pettit, Philip (1995). "Moral Functionalism and Moral Motivation", *Philosophical Quarterly*, 45: 20–40.

James, William, and Lange, Carl (1922). *The Emotions* (Baltimore: Williams & Wilkins).

Johnston, Mark (1989). "Dispositional Theories of Value", *Proceedings of the Aristotelian Society*, Suppl. Vol. 63: 139–74.

____ (1992). "How to Speak of the Colors", *Philosophical Studies*, 68: 221–63.

____ (1993). "Objectivity Refigured: Pragmatism without Verificationism", in Haldane and Wright (1993) 85–130.

____ (2001*a*). "The Authority of Affect", *Philosophy and Phenomenological Research*, 63: 181–214.

____ (2001*b*). "Is Affect Always Mere Effect?", *Philosophy and Phenomenological Research*, 63: 225–8.

Jones, Karen (1999). "Second-Hand Moral Knowledge", *Journal of Philosophy*, 96/2 (February): 55–78.

Joyce, J. M. (1999). *Foundations of Causal Decision Theory* (Cambridge: Cambridge University Press).

Kalderon, Mark E. (2004). "Open Questions and the Manifest Image", *Philosophy and Phenomenological Research*, 68/2 (March): 251–89.

____ (2005*a*). *Moral Fictionalism* (Oxford: Clarendon Press).

Kalderon, Mark E. (ed.) (2005*b*). *Fictionalist Approaches to Metaphysics* (Oxford: Clarendon Press).

Kant, Immanuel (1785). *Grundlegung zur Metaphysik der Sitten* (Riga: Hartknoch). Cited by the pagination of the edition of the Royal Prussian (later German) Academy (Berlin: 1900–), vol. 4.

____ (1787). *Kritik der reinen Vernunft*, 2nd (B) edn. (Riga: Hartknoch).

____ (1788). *Kritik der praktischen Vernunft* (Riga: Hartknoch). Cited by the pagination of the edition of the Royal Prussian (later German) Academy (Berlin: 1900–), vol. 5.

____ (1794). *Die Religion innerhalb der Grenzen der bloßen Vernunft*, 2nd edn. Cited by the pagination of the edition of the Royal Prussian Academy (later German) Academy (Berlin: 1900–), vol. 6.

Kavka, Gregory (1983). "The Toxin Puzzle", *Analysis*, 43: 33–6.

Kenny, Anthony (1963). *Action, Emotion and Will* (London: Routledge & Kegan Paul).

Kim, Jaegwon (1993). *Supervenience and Mind* (Cambridge: Cambridge University Press).

____ (1998). *Mind in a Physical World* (Cambridge, MA: MIT Press).

Kneale, William (1962). "Modality, De Dicto and De Re", in Nagel *et al.* (1962), 622–33.

Korsgaard, C. M. (1996*a*). *The Sources of Normativity* (Cambridge: Cambridge University Press).

_____ (1996*b*). "Skepticism about Practical Reason", in *id., Creating the Kingdom of Ends* (Cambridge: Cambridge University Press), 311–34.

_____ (2003). "Realism and Constructivism in Twentieth Century Moral Philosophy", in *Philosophy in America at the Turn of the Century*, APA Centennial Supplement, *Journal of Philosophical Research*: 99–122.

Kratzer, Angelika (2002). "The Notional Category of Modality", in Paul Portner and Barbara Partee (eds.), *Formal Semantics: The Essential Readings* (Oxford: Blackwell), 289–323.

Kripke, Saul (1980). *Naming and Necessity*, revised edn. (Oxford: Blackwell).

_____ (1982). *Wittgenstein on Rules and Private Language* (Cambridge, MA: Harvard University Press).

Lance, Mark, and Hawthorne, John (1997). *The Grammar of Meaning* (Cambridge: Cambridge University Press).

Lange, Marc (1999). "Laws, Counterfactuals, Stability, and Degrees of Lawhood", *Philosophy of Science*, 66: 243–67.

Leiter, Brian (2001). "Moral Facts and Best Explanations", *Social Philosophy and Policy*, 18: 79–101.

Lenman, James (2003). "Disciplined Syntacticism and Moral Expressivism", *Philosophy and Phenomenological Research*, 66: 32–57.

Lewis, D. K. (1970). "How to Define Theoretical Terms", *Journal of Philosophy*, 67: 427–46. Reprinted in Lewis (1983*a*).

_____ (1973). *Counterfactuals* (Oxford: Blackwell).

_____ (1974*a*). "Radical Interpretation", *Synthese*, 23: 331–44. Reprinted in Lewis (1983*a*).

_____ (1974*b*). "Semantic Analyses for Dyadic Deontic Logic", in Sören Stenlund (ed.), *Logical Theory and Semantic Analysis* (Dordrecht: Reidel), 1–14. Reprinted in Lewis (2000).

_____ (1980). "Mad Pain and Martian Pain", in Ned Block (ed.), *Readings in the Philosophy of Psychology*, Vol. 1 (Cambridge, MA: Harvard University Press), 216–22. Reprinted in Lewis (1983*a*).

_____ (1983*a*). *Philosophical Papers: Volume 1* (Oxford: Oxford University Press).

_____ (1983*b*). "New Work for a Theory of Universals", *Australasian Journal of Philosophy*, 61: 343–77. Reprinted in Lewis (1999), 8–55.

_____ (1986). *On the Plurality of Worlds* (Oxford: Blackwell).

_____ (1988). "Desire as Belief", *Mind*, 97/3 (July): 323–32. Reprinted in Lewis (2000).

_____ (1989). "Dispositional Theories of Value", *Proceedings of the Aristotelian Society*, Suppl. Vol. 63: 113–37. Reprinted in Lewis (2000).

_____ (1996*a*). "Elusive Knowledge", *Australasian Journal of Philosophy*, 74: 549–67. Reprinted in Lewis (1999).

_____ (1996*b*). "Desire as Belief II", *Mind*, 105/2 (April): 303–13. Reprinted in Lewis (2000).

_____ (1999). *Papers in Metaphysics and Epistemology* (Cambridge: Cambridge University Press).

_____ (2000). *Papers in Ethics and Social Philosophy* (Cambridge: Cambridge University Press).

Locke, John (1690). *Essay Concerning the Human Understanding* (London).

Loewer, Barry, and Belzer, Marvin (1983). "Dyadic Deontic Detachment", *Synthese*, 54: 295–319.

Mackie, J. L. (1977). *Ethics: Inventing Right and Wrong* (Harmondsworth: Penguin).

McDowell, John (1986). "Functionalism and Anomalous Monism", in Ernest LePore and Brian McLaughlin (eds.), *Actions and Events: Perspectives on the Philosophy of Donald Davidson* (Oxford: Blackwell), 387–98.

——— (1987). "In Defence of Modesty", in Taylor (ed.) (1987), 59–80.

——— (1997). "Brandom on Representation and Inference", *Philosophy and Phenomenological Research*, 58: 157–62.

——— (1998). "Virtue and Reason", reprinted in *id., Mind, Value, and Reality* (Cambridge, MA: Harvard University Press), 50–73.

Mellor, D. H. (1991). *Matters of Metaphysics* (Cambridge: Cambridge University Press).

Mill, J. S. (1869). *On Liberty* (London: Longmans, Green, Reader, and Dyer).

Millar, Alan (1994). Critical Notice of Christopher Peacocke, *A Study of Concepts, Mind*, 103: 73–82.

Miller, Richard W. (1992). *Moral Differences* (Princeton, NJ: Princeton University Press).

Moore, G. E. (1903). *Principia Ethica* (Cambridge: Cambridge University Press).

Morris, Michael (1992). *The Good and the True* (Oxford: Clarendon Press).

Nagel, Ernest, Suppes, Patrick, and Tarski, Alfred (1962). *Logic, Methodology and the Philosophy of Science: Proceedings of the 1960 International Congress* (Stanford, CA: Stanford University Press).

Parfit, Derek (1984). *Reasons and Persons* (Oxford: Oxford University Press).

——— (in preparation). *Rediscovering Reasons*.

Peacocke, Christopher (1986). *Thoughts: An Essay on Content* (Oxford: Blackwell).

——— (1987). "Understanding Logical Constants: A Realist's Account", *Proceedings of the British Academy*, 73: 153–99. Reprinted in Smiley (2004).

——— (1989*a*). "Possession Conditions: A Focal Point for Theories of Concepts", *Mind and Language*, 4: 50–6.

——— (1989*b*). "What are Concepts?", *Midwest Studies in Philosophy*, 14: 1–28.

——— (1992). *A Study of Concepts* (Cambridge, MA: MIT Press).

——— (1993). "How Are *A Priori* Truths Possible?", *European Journal of Philosophy*, 1/2 (August): 175–99.

——— (1997). "Metaphysical Necessity: Understanding, Truth and Epistemology", *Mind*, 106: 521–74.

——— (2004). *The Realm of Reason* (Oxford: Clarendon Press).

Perry, John (1993). *The Problem of the Essential Indexical and Other Essays* (Oxford: Clarendon Press).

Pettit, Philip (1991). "Realism and Response-Dependence", *Mind*, 100: 587–626.

——— (1993). *The Common Mind: An Essay on Psychology, Society and Politics* (New York: Oxford University Press).

Plantinga, Alvin (1993). *Warrant: The Current Debate* (New York: Oxford University Press).

Pollock, John, and Cruz, Joseph (1999). *Contemporary Theories of Knowledge*, 2nd edn. (Lanham, MD: Rowman & Littlefield).

Prawitz, Dag (1979). "Proofs and the Meaning and Completeness of the Logical Constants", in Jaako Hintikka, Ilkka Niiniluoto, and Esa Saarinen (eds.), *Essays on Mathematical and Philosophical Logic* (Dordrecht: Reidel), 25–40.

Price, Huw (1994). "Semantic Minimalism and the Frege Point", in Savas L. Tsohatzidis (ed.), *Foundations of Speech Act Theory* (London: Routledge), 132–55.

Prichard, H. A. (1949). *Moral Obligation* (Oxford: Clarendon Press).

_____ (2002). *Moral Writings*, ed. Jim MacAdam (Oxford: Clarendon Press).

Prior, Arthur (1958). "Escapism", in A. I. Melden (ed.), *Essays in Moral Philosophy* (Seattle: University of Washington Press), 135–46.

Pryor, James (2000). "The Skeptic and the Dogmatist", *Noûs*, 34: 517–49.

Putnam, Hilary (1967). "The Mental Life of Some Machines", in H. N. Castañeda (ed.), *Intentionality, Mind and Perception* (Detroit: Wayne State University Press). Reprinted in Putnam (1975), 408–28.

_____ (1975). *Mind, Language, and Reality: Philosophical Papers, Vol. 2* (Cambridge: Cambridge University Press).

Quinn, Philip (1982). "Metaphysical Necessity and Modal Logics", *The Monist*, 65: 444–55.

Quinn, Warren (1994). *Morality and Action*, ed. Philippa Foot (Cambridge: Cambridge University Press).

Rabinowicz, Wlodek, and Rønnow-Rasmussen, Toni (2004). "The Strike of the Demon: On Fitting Pro-attitudes and Values", *Ethics*, 114/3 (April): 391–423.

Ramsey, F. P. (1929). "Theories". Reprinted in Ramsey (1990), Essay 6.

_____ (1990). *Philosophical Papers*, ed. D. H. Mellor (Cambridge: Cambridge University Press).

Raphael, D. D. (ed.) (1969). *The British Moralists: 1650–1800* (Oxford: Clarendon Press).

Rawls, John (1971). *A Theory of Justice* (Cambridge, MA: Harvard University Press).

Rey, Georges (2007). "Psychology Isn't Normative", in Brian McLaughlin and Jonathan Cohen (eds.), *Contemporary Debates in Philosophy of Mind* (Oxford: Blackwell).

Richard, Mark (1990). *Propositional Attitudes* (Cambridge: Cambridge University Press).

Rosen, Gideon (1990) "Modal Fictionalism", *Mind*, 99: 327–54.

_____ (1994). "Objectivity and Modern Idealism: What is the Question?", in Michaelis Michael and John O'Leary-Hawthorne (eds.), *Philosophy in Mind* (Dordrecht: Kluwer Academic Publishers), 277–319.

_____ (1997). "Who Makes the Rules Around Here?", *Philosophy and Phenomenological Research*, 57: 163–71.

_____ (1998). "Blackburn's *Essays in Quasi-Realism*", *Noûs*, 32: 386–405.

_____ (2001). "Brandom on Modality, Normativity and Intentionality", *Philosophy and Phenomenological Research*, 63: 611–23.

Ross, Alf (1941). "Imperatives and Logic", *Theoria*, 7: 53–71.

Rumfitt, Ian (2000). " 'Yes' and 'No' ", *Mind*, 109: 781–823.

Salmon, Nathan (1984). "Impossible Worlds", *Analysis*, 44: 114–17.

_____ (1986). *Frege's Puzzle* (Cambridge, MA: MIT Press).

_____ (1989). "The Logic of What Might Have Been", *Philosophical Review*, 98: 3–34.

Sayre-McCord, Geoffrey (1988). *Essays on Moral Realism* (Ithaca, NY: Cornell University Press).

Scanlon, T. M. (1999). *What We Owe to Each Other* (Cambridge, MA: Harvard University Press).

Schroeder, Timothy (2003). "Davidson's Theory of Mind is Non-Normative", *Philosophers' Imprint*, 3/1 (May) <http://www.philosophersimprint.org/003001/>.

Schroeter, François, and Schroeter, Laura (2003). "A Slim Semantics for Thin Moral Terms?", *Australasian Journal of Philosophy*, 81: 191–207.

Schurz, Gerhard (1997). *The Is–Ought Problem: An Investigation in Philosophical Logic* (Dordrecht: Kluwer).

Searle, John (1983). *Intentionality* (Cambridge: Cambridge University Press).

Sen, Amartya (2000). "Consequential Evaluation and Practical Reason", *Journal of Philosophy*, 97/9 (September): 477–502.

Shafer-Landau, Russ (2003). *Moral Realism: A Defence* (Oxford: Oxford University Press).

Shoemaker, Sydney (1981). "Some Varieties of Functionalism", *Philosophical Topics*, 12: 93–119. Reprinted in Shoemaker (2003).

——— (2003). *Identity, Cause and Mind: Philosophical Essays*, 2nd edn. (Oxford: Clarendon Press).

Sidgwick, Henry (1907). *The Methods of Ethics*, 7th edn. (London: Macmillan).

——— (2000). *Essays on Ethics and Method*, ed. Marcus G. Singer (Oxford: Clarendon Press).

Sinnott-Armstrong, Walter (1993). "Some Problems For Gibbard's Norm-Expressivism", *Philosophical Studies*, 69: 297–313.

Smiley, Timothy (2004). *Logic and Knowledge* (Oxford: Oxford University Press).

Smith, Michael (1994). *The Moral Problem* (Oxford: Blackwell).

Stalnaker, Robert (1984). *Inquiry* (Cambridge, MA: Bradford Books, MIT Press).

——— (1996a). "On What Possible Worlds Could Not Be", in Adam Morton and S. P. Stich (eds.), *Benacerraf and his Critics* (Oxford: Blackwell), 104–18. Reprinted in Stalnaker (2003).

——— (1996b). "Varieties of Supervenience", *Philosophical Perspectives*, 10: 221–41. Reprinted in Stalnaker (2003).

——— (1999). *Context and Content* (Oxford: Clarendon Press).

——— (2003). *Ways A World Might Be: Metaphysical and Anti-metaphysical Essays* (Oxford: Clarendon Press).

Stampe, Dennis (1977). "Towards a Causal Theory of Linguistic Representation", in P. French, T. Uehling, and H. Wettstein (eds.), *Contemporary Perspectives in the Philosophy of Language* (Minneapolis: University of Minnesota Press), 81–102.

Stein, Edward (1996). *Without Good Reason: The Rationality Debate in Philosophy and Cognitive Science* (Oxford: Clarendon Press).

Steward, Helen (1997). *The Ontology of Mind* (Oxford: Clarendon Press).

Stocker, Michael (1979). "Desiring the Bad: An Essay in Moral Psychology", *Journal of Philosophy*, 76: 738–53.

Stratton-Lake, Philip (ed.) (2002a). *Ethical Intuitionism: Re-evaluations* (Oxford: Clarendon Press).

Stratton-Lake, Philip (2002b). "Introduction", in Stratton-Lake (2002a).

Strawson, P. F. (1992). *Analysis and Metaphysics: An Introduction to Philosophy* (Oxford: Oxford University Press).

Sturgeon, Nicholas (1985). "Moral Explanations", in David Copp and David Zimmerman (eds.), *Morality, Reason and Truth* (Totowa, NJ: Rowman and Allanheld), 49–78. Reprinted in Sayre-McCord (1988), 229–55.

Tappolet, Christine (2000). *Émotions et valeurs* (Paris: Presses Universitaires de France).

Taylor, Barry (ed.) (1987). *Michael Dummett: Contributions to Philosophy* (Dordrecht: M. Nijhoff).

Tennant, Neil (1987). *Anti-realism and Logic* (Oxford: Clarendon Press).

Thomson, Judith Jarvis (2000). *Goodness and Advice* (Princeton, NJ: Princeton University Press).

Velleman, J. David (2000). *The Possibility of Practical Reason* (Oxford: Clarendon Press).

Wedgwood, Ralph (1995). "Theories of Content and Theories of Motivation", *European Journal of Philosophy*, 3: 273–88.

_____(1997). "Non-cognitivism, Truth, and Logic", *Philosophical Studies*, 86: 73–91.

_____(1998). "The Essence of Response-Dependence", *European Review of Philosophy*, 3: 31–54.

_____(1999a). "The *A Priori* Rules of Rationality", *Philosophy and Phenomenological Research*, 59: 113–31.

_____(1999b). "The Price of Non-reductive Moral Realism", *Ethical Theory and Moral Practice*, 2: 199–215.

_____(2000). "The Price of Non-reductive Physicalism", *Noûs*, 34: 400–21.

_____(2001). "Conceptual Role Semantics for Moral Terms", *Philosophical Review*, 110: 1–30.

_____(2002a). "Internalism Explained", *Philosophy and Phenomenological Research*, 65: 349–69.

_____(2002b). "Practical Reason and Desire", *Australasian Journal of Philosophy*, 80: 345–58.

_____(2002c). "The Aim of Belief", *Philosophical Perspectives*, 16: 267–97.

_____(2003). "Choosing Rationally and Choosing Correctly", in Sarah Stroud and Christine Tappolet (eds.), *Weakness of Will and Varieties of Practical Irrationality* (Oxford: Clarendon Press), 201–29.

_____(2004). "The Metaethicists' Mistake", *Philosophical Perspectives*, 18: 405–26.

_____(2005). "How We Know What Ought to Be", *Proceedings of the Aristotelian Society*, 106/1 (September): 61–84.

_____(2006a). "The Meaning of 'Ought'", in Russ Shafer-Landau (ed.), *Oxford Studies in Metaethics*, vol. 1 (Oxford: Clarendon Press), 127–60.

_____(2006b). "The Normative Force of Reasoning", *Noûs*, 40/4 (December): 660–86.

_____(2007). "Normativism Defended", in Brian McLaughlin and Jonathan Cohen (eds.), *Contemporary Debates in Philosophy of Mind* (Oxford: Blackwell).

_____(forthcoming a). "The Normativity of the Intentional", in Brian McLaughlin (ed.), *Oxford Handbook of Philosophy of Mind* (Oxford: Oxford University Press).

_____(forthcoming b). Critical Notice of Christopher Peacocke, *The Realm of Reason*, *Philosophy and Phenomenological Research*.

Wiggins, David (1989). *Needs, Values, Truth*, 2nd edn. (Oxford: Basil Blackwell).

Williams, Bernard (1973). "Imagination and the Self", in *id.*, *Problems of the Self* (Cambridge: Cambridge University Press), 26–45.

_____(1980). "Internal and External Reasons", in Ross Harrison (ed.), *Rational Action* (Cambridge: Cambridge University Press, 1979), 17–28. Reprinted in Williams (1981b).

_____(1981a). "*Ought* and Moral Obligation", in Williams (1981b), 114–23.

_____(1981b). *Moral Luck* (Cambridge: Cambridge University Press).

_____(2002). "'Ought', 'Must', and the Needs of Morality" (unpublished).

Williamson, Timothy (2000). *Knowledge and its Limits* (Oxford: Clarendon Press).

_____(2001). "Ethics, Supervenience and Ramsey Sentences", *Philosophy and Phenomenological Research*, 62/3: 625–30.

Wright, Crispin (1988). "Moral Values, Projection and Secondary Qualities", *Proceedings of the Aristotelian Society*, Suppl. Vol.: 1–26.

_____ (1989). "Wittgenstein's Rule-Following Considerations and the Central Project of Theoretical Linguistics", in Alexander George (ed.), *Reflections on Chomsky* (Oxford: Oxford University Press), 233–64.

_____ (1992). *Truth and Objectivity* (Cambridge, MA: Harvard University Press).

Wright, G. H. von (1951). "Deontic Logic", *Mind*, 60: 1–15.

Yablo, Stephen (1992*a*). "Mental Causation", *Philosophical Review*, 101: 245–80.

_____ (1992*b*). "Cause and Essence", *Synthese*, 93: 403–49.

_____ (1997). "Wide Causation", *Philosophical Perspectives*, 11: 251–81.

_____ (2003). "Causal Relevance", *Philosophical Issues*, 13: 316–27.

Index